STATA LONGITUDINAL/PANEL DATA
REFERENCE MANUAL
RELEASE 9

A Stata Press Publication
StataCorp LP
College Station, Texas

Stata Press, 4905 Lakeway Drive, College Station, Texas 77845

The suggested citation for this software is

StataCorp. 2005. *Stata Statistical Software: Release 9*. College Station, TX: StataCorp LP.

Table of Contents

Cross-Referencing the Documentation

When reading this manual, you will find references to other Stata manuals. For example,

[U] **26 Overview of Stata estimation commands**

[R] **regress**

[D] **reshape**

The first is a reference to chapter 26, *Overview of Stata estimation commands* in the *Stata User's Guide*, the second is a reference to the `regress` entry in the *Base Reference Manual*, and the third is a reference to the `reshape` entry in the *Data Management Reference Manual*.

All the manuals in the Stata Documentation have a shorthand notation, such as [U] for the *User's Guide* and [R] for the *Base Reference Manual*.

The complete list of shorthand notations and manuals is as follows:

[GSM]	*Getting Started with Stata for Macintosh*
[GSU]	*Getting Started with Stata for Unix*
[GSW]	*Getting Started with Stata for Windows*
[U]	*Stata User's Guide*
[R]	*Stata Base Reference Manual*
[D]	*Stata Data Management Reference Manual*
[G]	*Stata Graphics Reference Manual*
[P]	*Stata Programming Reference Manual*
[XT]	*Stata Longitudinal/Panel Data Reference Manual*
[MV]	*Stata Multivariate Statistics Reference Manual*
[SVY]	*Stata Survey Data Reference Manual*
[ST]	*Stata Survival Analysis and Epidemiological Tables Reference Manual*
[TS]	*Stata Time-Series Reference Manual*
[I]	*Stata Quick Reference and Index*
[M]	*Mata Reference Manual*

Detailed information about each of these manuals may be found online at

http://www.stata-press.com/manuals/

Title

> **intro** — Introduction to longitudinal/panel data manual

Description

This entry describes this manual and what has changed since Stata 8.

Remarks

This manual documents the `xt` commands and is referred to as [XT] in cross-references.

Following this entry, [XT] **xt** provides an overview of the `xt` commands. The other parts of this manual are arranged alphabetically. If you are new to Stata's `xt` commands, we recommend that you read the following sections first:

[XT] **xt**   Introduction to xt commands
[XT] **xtreg**   Fixed-, between-, and random-effects, and population-averaged linear models

Stata is continually being updated, and Stata users are always writing new commands. To find out about the latest cross-sectional time-series features, type `search panel data` after installing the latest official updates; see [R] **update**.

What's new

This section is intended for previous Stata users. If you are new to Stata, you may as well skip it.

1. The big news is new command `xtmixed`—Stata now fits linear mixed models, also known as hierarchical models or multilevel models.

   Mixed models include what social scientists call random-effects models, including one-way, two-way, multi-way, and hierarchical models, and it includes random-coefficient models.

   Estimates are obtained using maximum likelihood (ML) or restricted maximum likelihood (REML). Covariances among random effects are estimated and may be identity (equal variance), independent (no covariance), exchangeable (common covariance and common pairwise covariance), or unstructured (unique covariance for each pair of effects).

   `xtmixed` estimates standard errors and confidence intervals for the fixed parameters, and it estimates the standard deviations (variances) and correlations (covariances) of the random effects and the full VCE matrix among them.

   For details, see [XT] **xtmixed**.

   After estimation with `xtmixed`,

   a. `estat recovariance` displays the estimated variance–covariance matrix of the random effects for each level.

   b. `estat group` summarizes the composition of the nested groups, providing minimum, average, and maximum group size for each level in the model.

1

`predict` after `xtmixed` can compute best linear unbiased predictions (BLUPs) for each random effect. It can also compute the linear predictor, the standard error of the linear predictor, the fitted values (linear predictor plus contributions of random effects), the residuals, and the standardized residuals.

2. Most [XT] estimation commands allow new option `vce()` for selecting how the variance–covariance estimates (VCE) of the estimated parameters are to be estimated. This new option provides direct support for panel- and cluster-based bootstrapping and for jackknifing the estimated parameters, and it provides an alternative way of specifying robust VCEs, where allowed.

   a. Option `vce(bootstrap)` specifies that standard errors, significance tests, and confidence intervals be normal-based bootstrap estimates, rather than the default analytic estimates based on the observed information matrix (OIM). After estimation, you can also obtain percentile-based or bias-corrected confidence intervals using new command `estat bootstrap`; see [R] **bootstrap postestimation**.

   b. Option `vce(jackknife)` specifies that standard errors, significance tests, and confidence intervals be jackknife estimates.

   c. Option `vce(robust)` is just a synonym for option `robust`.

   `vce(bootstrap)` and `vce(jackknife)` automatically perform cluster sampling if it is required by the estimator.

   Notably, both options compute bootstrap or jackknife estimates of the complete VCE matrix. This means that most of Stata's postestimation commands are available. You can form linear and nonlinear combinations or functions of the parameters and obtain jackknife or normal-based bootstrap standard errors and confidence intervals for the combinations using [R] **lincom** and [R] **nlcom**. Similarly, you can perform linear and nonlinear tests using [R] **test** and [R] **testnl**.

   [XT] estimation commands that support `vce(bootstrap)` and `vce(jackknife)` include `xtabond`, `xtfrontier`, `xtcloglog`, `xtgee`, `xthtaylor`, `xtintreg`, `xtivreg`, `xtlogit`, `xtprobit`, `xtrc`, `xtreg`, `xttobit`, all of which are documented in this manual.

3. New features have been added to the maximum likelihood estimators that do not have closed-form solutions and require numeric evaluation of the likelihood. These estimators include `xtlogit`, `xtprobit`, `xtpoisson`, `xtcloglog`, `xtintreg`, and `xttobit`.

   a. The likelihood may now be approximated using adaptive Gauss–Hermite quadrature (the new default) or nonadaptive quadrature (the previous default). Adaptive quadrature substantially improves the accuracy of the approximation, particularly on difficult problems such as data with large panel sizes or data with a large variance for the random effects.

   b. Linear constraints may now be imposed using the new option `constraints()`. Constraints are specified the standard way; see [R] **constraint**.

   c. New option `intpoints()` replaces old option `quad()`, although `quad()` continues to work. The new name is more meaningful, especially when used with estimators that integrate likelihoods using methods other than quadrature.

4. Existing command `xtreg` now allows options `robust` and `cluster()` when fitting fixed-effects (FE) and random-effects (RE) models; see [XT] **xtreg**.

5. Most [XT] commands that previously did not allow time-series operators now support them. These commands include `xtgls`, `xtreg`, `xtsum`, `xtcloglog`, `xtintreg`, `xtlogit`, `xtpoisson`, `xtprobit`, `xttobit`, and `xtgee`.

6. New command `xtrc` is old command `xtrchh`, renamed, and with new features. New option `beta` reports the best linear predictors (BLUPs) for the group-specific coefficients, along with their standard errors and confidence intervals. For details, see [XT] **xtrc**.

7. `predict` after `xtrc` has new option `group()` to compute the BLUPs of the dependent variable using the BLUPs of the coefficients.

8. New command `xtline` plots panel data and allows either overlaid or separate graphs for each panel; see [XT] **xtline**.

9. New section [XT] **glossary** of this manual defines commonly used terms and how they are used here.

For a complete list of all new features in Stata 9, see [U] **1.3 What's new**.

Also See

Complementary:	[U] **1.3 What's new**
Background:	[R] **intro**

Title

> **xt** — Introduction to xt commands

Syntax

$\texttt{xt}cmd \dots \left[\texttt{, i(}varname_i\texttt{) t(}varname_t\texttt{)} \dots \right]$

$\texttt{iis} \left[varname_i \right] \left[\texttt{, clear} \right]$

$\texttt{tis} \left[varname_t \right] \left[\texttt{, clear} \right]$

Description

The xt series of commands provide tools for analyzing panel data (also known as longitudinal data or in some disciplines as cross-sectional time-series when there is an explicit time component). Panel datasets have the form $\mathbf{x}_{it}$, where $\mathbf{x}_{it}$ is a vector of observations for unit i and time t. The particular commands (such as `xtdes`, `xtsum`, `xtreg`, etc.) are documented in the entries that follow this entry. This entry deals with concepts that are common across commands.

`iis` is related to the `i()` option on the other xt commands. Command `iis` or option `i()` sets the name of the variable corresponding to the unit index i. Specifying `iis` without an argument displays the current name of the unit variable.

`tis` is related to the `t()` option on the other xt commands. Command `tis` or option `t()` sets the name of the variable corresponding to the time index t. Specifying `tis` without an argument displays the current name of the time variable.

Some xt commands use time-series operators in their internal calculations, requiring that your data be `tsset`; see [TS] **tsset**. For instance, since `xtabond` uses time-series operators in its internal calculations, you must `tsset` your dataset before using it. As in [XT] **xtabond**, the manual entry for the command explicitly states that you must `tsset` your data before using the command. For these commands, `iis` and `tis` are neither sufficient nor recommended.

Note that specifying `iis` or `tis` clears any previous `tsset` settings. Also, specifying `tsset` overrides any settings specified by `iss` or `tis`.

If your interest is in general time-series analysis, see [U] **26.13 Models with time-series data** and the *Stata Time-Series Reference Manual*.

Options

$\texttt{i(}varname_i\texttt{)}$ specifies the variable name corresponding to index i in $\mathbf{x}_{it}$. This must be a single, numeric variable, although whether it takes on the values 1, 2, 3 or 1, 7, 9, or even -2, $\sqrt{2}$, π, is irrelevant. (If the identifying variable is a string, use `egen`'s `group()` function to make a numeric variable from it; see [D] **egen**.)

For instance, if the panel data are of persons in the years 1991–1994, each observation is a person in one of the years; there are four observations per person (assuming no missing data). $varname_i$ is the name of the variable that uniquely identifies the persons.

4

You can specify the i() option the first time you estimate, or you can use the iis command to set the i() beforehand. Note that it is not necessary to specify i() if the data have been previously tsset or if iis has been previously specified—in these cases, the group variable is taken from the previous setting.

t($varname_t$) specifies the variable name corresponding to index t in x_{it}. This must be a single, numeric variable, although whether it takes on the values 1, 2, 3 or 1, 7, 9, or even -2, $\sqrt{2}$, π, is irrelevant.

For instance, if the panel data are of persons in the years 1991–1994, each observation is a person in one of the years; there are four observations per person (assuming no missing data). $varname_t$ is the name of the variable recording the year.

You can specify the t() option the first time you estimate, or you can use the tis command to set the t() beforehand. Note that it is not necessary to specify t() if the data have been previously tsset or if tis has been previously specified—in these cases, the group variable is taken from the previous setting.

clear removes the definition of i() or t(). For instance, typing tis, clear makes Stata forget the identity of the t() variable.

Remarks

Consider having data on n units—individuals, firms, countries, or whatever—over T time periods. The data might be income and other characteristics of n persons surveyed each of T years, the output and costs of n firms collected over T months, or the health and behavioral characteristics of n patients collected over T years. In panel datasets, we write x_{it} for the value of x for unit i at time t. The xt commands assume that such datasets are stored as a sequence of observations on (i, t, x).

For a discussion of panel-data models, see Baltagi (2001), Greene (2003), Hsiao (2003), or Wooldridge (2002).

▷ Example 1

If we had data on pulmonary function (measured by forced expiratory volume or FEV) along with smoking behavior, age, sex, and height, a piece of the data might be

```
. list in 1/6, separator(0) divider
```

	pid	yr_visit	fev	age	sex	height	smokes
1.	1071	1991	1.21	25	1	69	0
2.	1071	1992	1.52	26	1	69	0
3.	1071	1993	1.32	28	1	68	0
4.	1072	1991	1.33	18	1	71	1
5.	1072	1992	1.18	20	1	71	1
6.	1072	1993	1.19	21	1	71	0

The other xt commands need to know the identities of the variables identifying patient and time. With these data, we would type

```
. iis pid
. tis yr_visit
```

Having made this declaration, we need not specify the i() and t() options on the other xt commands. If we resaved the data, we need not respecify iis and tis in future sessions.

◁

❑ Technical Note

Panel data stored as shown above are said to be in the long form. Perhaps the data are in the wide form with one observation per unit and multiple variables for the value in each year. For instance, a piece of the pulmonary function data might be

```
 pid   sex  fev91  fev92  fev93  age91  age92   age93
1071    1   1.21   1.52   1.32     25     26      28
1072    1   1.33   1.18   1.19     18     20      21
```

Data in this form can be converted to the long form by using reshape; see [D] **reshape**.

❑

▷ Example 2

Data for some of the time periods might be missing. That is, we have panel data on $i = 1, \ldots, n$ and $t = 1, \ldots, T$, but only T_i of those observations are defined. With such missing periods—called unbalanced data—a piece of our pulmonary function data might be

. list in 1/6, separator(0) divider

	pid	yr_visit	fev	age	sex	height	smokes
1.	1071	1991	1.21	25	1	69	0
2.	1071	1992	1.52	26	1	69	0
3.	1071	1993	1.32	28	1	68	0
4.	1072	1991	1.33	18	1	71	1
5.	1072	1993	1.19	21	1	71	0
6.	1073	1991	1.47	24	0	64	0

Note that patient ID 1072 is not observed in 1992. The xt commands are robust to this problem.

◁

❑ Technical Note

In many of the [XT] **xt** entries, we will use data from a subsample of the NLSY data (Center for Human Resource Research 1989) on young women aged 14–26 in 1968. Women were surveyed in each of the 21 years 1968 through 1988, except for the six years 1974, 1976, 1979, 1981, 1984, and 1986. We use two different subsets: nlswork.dta and union.dta.

For nlswork.dta, our subsample is of 4,711 women in years when employed, not enrolled in school and evidently having completed their education, and with wages in excess of $1/hour but less than $700/hour.

```
. use http://www.stata-press.com/data/r9/nlswork, clear
(National Longitudinal Survey.  Young Women 14-26 years of age in 1968)

. describe

Contains data from http://www.stata-press.com/data/r9/nlswork.dta
  obs:        28,534                          National Longitudinal Survey.
                                              Young Women 14-26 years of age
                                              in 1968
  vars:           21                          7 Dec 2004 17:02
  size:    1,055,758 (89.9% of memory free)
```

variable name	storage type	display format	value label	variable label
idcode	int	%8.0g		NLS id
year	byte	%8.0g		interview year
birth_yr	byte	%8.0g		birth year
age	byte	%8.0g		age in current year
race	byte	%8.0g		1=white, 2=black, 3=other
msp	byte	%8.0g		1 if married, spouse present
nev_mar	byte	%8.0g		1 if never yet married
grade	byte	%8.0g		current grade completed
collgrad	byte	%8.0g		1 if college graduate
not_smsa	byte	%8.0g		1 if not SMSA
c_city	byte	%8.0g		1 if central city
south	byte	%8.0g		1 if south
ind_code	byte	%8.0g		industry of employment
occ_code	byte	%8.0g		occupation
union	byte	%8.0g		1 if union
wks_ue	byte	%8.0g		weeks unemployed last year
ttl_exp	float	%9.0g		total work experience
tenure	float	%9.0g		job tenure, in years
hours	int	%8.0g		usual hours worked
wks_work	int	%8.0g		weeks worked last year
ln_wage	float	%9.0g		ln(wage/GNP deflator)

```
Sorted by:  idcode  year
```

(Continued on next page)

```
. summarize
```

Variable	Obs	Mean	Std. Dev.	Min	Max
idcode	28534	2601.284	1487.359	1	5159
year	28534	77.95865	6.383879	68	88
birth_yr	28534	48.08509	3.012837	41	54
age	28510	29.04511	6.700584	14	46
race	28534	1.303392	.4822773	1	3
msp	28518	.6029175	.4893019	0	1
nev_mar	28518	.2296795	.4206341	0	1
grade	28532	12.53259	2.323905	0	18
collgrad	28534	.1680451	.3739129	0	1
not_smsa	28526	.2824441	.4501961	0	1
c_city	28526	.357218	.4791882	0	1
south	28526	.4095562	.4917605	0	1
ind_code	28193	7.692973	2.994025	1	12
occ_code	28413	4.777672	3.065435	1	13
union	19238	.2344319	.4236542	0	1
wks_ue	22830	2.548095	7.294463	0	76
ttl_exp	28534	6.215316	4.652117	0	28.88461
tenure	28101	3.123836	3.751409	0	25.91667
hours	28467	36.55956	9.869623	1	168
wks_work	27831	53.98933	29.03232	0	104
ln_wage	28534	1.674907	.4780935	0	5.263916

For `union.dta`, our subset was sampled only from those with union membership information from 1970 to 1988. Our subsample is of 4,434 women. The important variables are `age` (16–46), `grade` (years of schooling completed, ranging from 0 to 18), `not_smsa` (28% of the person-time was spent living outside an SMSA—standard metropolitan statistical area), `south` (41% of the person-time was in the South), and `southXt` (`south` interacted with year, treating 1970 as year 0). The dataset also has variable `union`. Overall, 22% of the person-time is marked as time under union membership, and 44% of these women have belonged to a union.

```
. use http://www.stata-press.com/data/r9/union, clear
(NLS Women 14-24 in 1968)
. describe
Contains data from http://www.stata-press.com/data/r9/union.dta
  obs:        26,200                         NLS Women 14-24 in 1968
  vars:           10                         27 Oct 2004 13:51
  size:      393,000 (96.3% of memory free)
```

variable name	storage type	display format	value label	variable label
idcode	int	%8.0g		NLS id
year	byte	%8.0g		interview year
age	byte	%8.0g		age in current year
grade	byte	%8.0g		current grade completed
not_smsa	byte	%8.0g		1 if not SMSA
south	byte	%8.0g		1 if south
union	byte	%8.0g		1 if union
t0	byte	%9.0g		
southXt	byte	%9.0g		
black	byte	%8.0g		race black

```
Sorted by:
```

```
. summarize
```

Variable	Obs	Mean	Std. Dev.	Min	Max
idcode	26200	2611.582	1484.994	1	5159
year	26200	79.47137	5.965499	70	88
age	26200	30.43221	6.489056	16	46
grade	26200	12.76145	2.411715	0	18
not_smsa	26200	.2837023	.4508027	0	1
south	26200	.4130153	.4923849	0	1
union	26200	.2217939	.4154611	0	1
t0	26200	9.471374	5.965499	0	18
southXt	26200	3.96874	6.057208	0	18
black	26200	.274542	.4462917	0	1

With both datasets, we have typed

```
. iis idcode
. tis year
```

❏

❏ Technical Note

The `tis` and `iis` commands, as well as other `xt` commands that set the t and i index for `xt` data, do so by declaring them as characteristics of the data; see [P] **char**. In particular, `tis` sets the characteristic `_dta[tis]` to the name of the t index variable. `iis` sets the characteristic `_dta[iis]` to the name of the i index variable.

❏

❏ Technical Note

Note that `xtmixed` does not use the information pertaining to i and t that is stored by `iis`, `tis`, and `tsset`. Unlike the other xt commands, `xtmixed` can handle multiple nested levels of groups and thus uses its own syntax for specifying the group structure of the data.

❏

❏ Technical Note

Throughout the xt entries, when random-effects models are fitted, a likelihood-ratio test that the variance of the random effects is zero is included. These tests occur on the boundary of the parameter space, invalidating the usual theory associated with such tests. However, these likelihood-ratio tests have been modified to be valid on the boundary. In particular, the null distribution of the likelihood-ratio test statistic is not the usual χ_1^2, but is rather a 50:50 mixture of a χ_0^2 (point mass at zero) and a χ_1^2, denoted as $\overline{\chi}_{01}^2$. See Gutierrez, Carter, and Drukker (2001) for a full discussion, and see [XT] **xtmixed** for a generalization of the concept as applied to variance-component estimation in mixed models.

❏

(*Continued on next page*)

References

Baltagi, B. H. 2001. *Econometric Analysis of Panel Data*. 2nd ed. New York: Wiley.

Center for Human Resource Research. 1989. *National Longitudinal Survey of Labor Market Experience, Young Women 14–26 years of age in 1968*. Ohio State University.

Greene, W. H. 2003. *Econometric Analysis*. 5th ed. Upper Saddle River, NJ: Prentice Hall.

Gutierrez, R. G., S. L. Carter, and D. M. Drukker. 2001. sg160: On boundary-value likelihood-ratio tests. *Stata Technical Bulletin* 60: 15–18. Reprinted in *Stata Technical Bulletin Reprints*, vol. 10, pp. 269–273.

Hsiao, C. 2003. *Analysis of Panel Data*. 2nd ed. New York: Cambridge University Press.

Wooldridge, J. M. 2002. *Econometric Analysis of Cross Section and Panel Data*. Cambridge, MA: MIT Press.

Also See

Complementary:	[XT] **xtabond**, [XT] **xtcloglog**, [XT] **xtdata**, [XT] **xtdes**, [XT] **xtfrontier**, [XT] **xtgee**, [XT] **xtgls**, [XT] **xthtaylor**, [XT] **xtintreg**, [XT] **xtivreg**, [XT] **xtlogit**, [XT] **xtmixed**, [XT] **xtnbreg**, [XT] **xtpcse**, [XT] **xtpoisson**, [XT] **xtprobit**, [XT] **xtrc**, [XT] **xtreg**, [XT] **xtregar**, [XT] **xtsum**, [XT] **xttab**, [XT] **xttobit**, [TS] **tsset**

Title

estimation options — Estimation options

Description

This entry describes the options common to many xt estimation commands. Not all the options documented below work with all estimation commands; see the documentation for the particular estimation command. If an option is listed there, it is applicable.

Options

⌐ Model ⌐

i($varname_i$) specifies the variable name that contains the unit to which the observation belongs. You can specify the i() option the first time you estimate, or you can use the iis command to set i() beforehand. Note that you need not specify i() if the data have been previously tsset or if iis has been previously specified—in these cases, the group variable is taken from the previous setting. See [XT] **xt**.

t($varname_t$) specifies the variable name that contains the time period to which the observation belongs. You can specify the t() option the first time you estimate, or you can use the tis command to set t() beforehand. Note that you need not specify t() if the data have been previously tsset or if tis has been previously specified—in these cases, the group variable is taken from the previous setting. See [XT] **xt**.

noconstant suppresses the constant term (intercept) in the model.

offset(*varname*) specifies that *varname* be included in the model with the coefficient constrained to be 1.

exposure(*varname*) specifies a variable that reflects the amount of exposure over which the *depvar* events were observed for each observation; ln(*varname*) with coefficient constrained to be 1 is entered into the log-link function.

constraints(*numlist* | *matname*) specifies the linear constraints to be applied during estimation. The default is to perform unconstrained estimation. constraints(*numlist*) specifies the constraints by number after they have been defined using the constraint command; see [R] **constraint**. See [R] **reg3** for the use of constraints in multiple-equation contexts.

  constraints(*matname*) specifies a matrix containing the constraints; see [P] **makecns**.

  constraints(*clist*) is used by some estimation commands, such as mlogit, where *clist* has the form $\#\left[-\#\right]\left[,\ \#\left[-\#\right]\ \ldots\right]$.

force specifies that estimation is to be forced even though t() is not equally spaced. This is relevant only for correlation structures that require knowledge of t(). These correlation structures require that observations be equally spaced so that calculations based on lags correspond to a constant time change. If you specify a t() variable that indicates observations are not equally spaced, the (time-dependent) model will not be fitted. If you also specify force, the model will be fitted, and it will be assumed that the lags based on the data ordered by t() are appropriate.

_____⌐ Correlation ⌐_____

corr(*correlation*) specifies the within-group correlation structure; the default corresponds to the equal-correlation model, corr(exchangeable).

When you specify a correlation structure that requires a lag, you indicate the lag after the structure's name with or without a blank; e.g., corr(ar1) or corr(ar 1).

If you specify the fixed correlation structure, you specify the name of the matrix containing the assumed correlations following the word fixed, e.g., corr(fixed myr).

_____⌐ SE/Robust ⌐_____

robust specifies that the Huber/White/sandwich estimator of variance be used in place of the traditional calculation; see [U] **20.14 Obtaining robust variance estimates**. robust combined with cluster() allows observations that are not independent within cluster (although they must be independent between clusters).

If the command allows pweights and you specify them, robust is implied; see [U] **20.16 Weighted estimation**.

vce(robust) is a synonym for robust.

scale(x2 | dev | phi | #) overrides the default scale parameter. By default, scale(1) is assumed for the discrete distributions (binomial, negative binomial, and Poisson), and scale(x2) is assumed for the continuous distributions (gamma, Gaussian, and inverse Gaussian).

scale(x2) specifies that the scale parameter be set to the Pearson chi-squared (or generalized chi-squared) statistic divided by the residual degrees of freedom, which is recommended by McCullagh and Nelder (1989) as a good general choice for continuous distributions.

scale(dev) sets the scale parameter to the deviance divided by the residual degrees of freedom. This provides an alternative to scale(x2) for continuous distributions and for over- or underdispersed discrete distributions.

scale(phi) specifies that the scale parameter be estimated from the data. xtgee's default scaling makes results agree with other estimators and has been recommended by McCullagh and Nelder (1989) in the context of GLM. When comparing results with calculations made by other software, you may find that the other packages do not offer this feature. In such cases, specifying scale(phi) should match their results.

scale(#) sets the scale parameter to #. For example, using scale(1) in family(gamma) models results in exponential-errors regression (if you use assume independent correlation structure).

nmp specifies that the divisor $N - P$ be used instead of the default N, where N is the total number of observations and P is the number of coefficients estimated.

_____⌐ Reporting ⌐_____

level(#) specifies the confidence level, as a percentage, for confidence intervals. The default is level(95) or as set by set level; see [U] **20.6 Specifying the width of confidence intervals**.

noskip specifies that a full maximum-likelihood model with only a constant for the regression equation be fitted. This model is not displayed but is used as the base model to compute a likelihood-ratio test for the model test statistic displayed in the estimation header. By default, the overall model test statistic is an asymptotically equivalent Wald test of all the parameters in the regression equation being zero (except the constant). For many models, this option can substantially increase estimation time.

Also See

Background: [U] **20 Estimation and postestimation commands**,
[XT] **xt**

Title

quadchk — Check sensitivity of quadrature approximation

Syntax

quadchk [$\#_1$ $\#_2$] [, <u>noo</u>utput]

Description

quadchk checks the quadrature approximation used in the random-effects estimators of the following commands:

xtcloglog
xtintreg
xtlogit
xtpoisson with the normal option
xtprobit
xttobit

quadchk refits the model, starting from the converged answer, for different numbers of quadrature points and then compares the different solutions.

$\#_1$ and $\#_2$ specify the number of quadrature points to use in the comparison runs of the previous model. The default is to use $n_q - 4$ and $n_q + 4$ points, where n_q is the number of quadrature points used in the original estimation.

Option

nooutput suppresses the iteration log and output of the refitted models.

Remarks

Some random-effects estimators in Stata use adaptive or nonadaptive Gauss–Hermite quadrature to compute the log likelihood and its derivatives. As a rule, adaptive quadrature, which is the default integration method, is much more flexible. The quadchk command provides a means to look at the numerical soundness of either quadrature approximation.

Using the converged coefficients of the original model as starting values, the estimation is rerun using two different numbers of quadrature points. The log likelihood and coefficient estimates for the original model and the two refitted models are then compared. If the quadrature method is not valid, the number of quadrature points will affect the stability of the estimation results. The resulting instability will result in the refitted models' log likelihoods and coefficient estimates differing, sometimes dramatically, from the original model's results.

As a rule of thumb, if the coefficients do not change by more than a relative difference of 10^{-4} (0.01%), the choice of quadrature points does not significantly affect the outcome, and the results may be confidently interpreted. However, if the results do change appreciably—greater than a relative difference of 10^{-2} (1%)—then you should question whether the model can be reliably fitted using the chosen quadrature method.

Two aspects of random-effects models have the potential to make the quadrature approximation inaccurate: large group sizes and large correlations within groups. These factors can also work in tandem, decreasing or increasing the reliability of the quadrature.

It is easy to see why the quadrature breaks down when group sizes are large or when ρ is big. The likelihood for a group is an integral of a normal density (the distribution of the random effects) times a product of cumulative normals. There are T_i cumulative normals in the product, where T_i is the number of observations in the ith group. Any Gauss–Hermite quadrature procedure is based on the assumption that the product of normals can be approximated by a polynomial. When T_i is large or ρ is big, this assumption is no longer valid.

Adaptive Gauss–Hermite quadrature transforms the integrand so that it is sampled on a suitable range. Adaptive quadrature performs better than nonadaptive quadrature for large T_i and ρ.

Note that when an adaptive or nonadaptive quadrature method breaks down badly, increasing the number of quadrature points will not solve the problem. Increasing the number of quadrature points is equivalent to increasing the degree of the polynomial approximation. However, the points are positioned according to a set formula. When the number of points is increased, the range spanned by the points is also increased, and, on average, the points are only slightly closer together. If the true function is, for instance, very concentrated around zero, increasing the number of points is of little consequence because the additional points will mostly pick up the shape of the function far from zero.

When quadchk shows that the coefficient estimates change appreciably with different numbers of quadrature points, this indicates that the given polynomial approximation is poor, and increasing the number of quadrature points in that approximation will not help. You can convince yourself of this by continuing to increase the number of quadrature points. As you do this, the coefficient estimates will continue to change. In cases such as this, all coefficient estimates should be viewed with suspicion; you cannot claim that the results produced with larger numbers of quadrature points are more accurate than those produced with fewer points.

Simulations have shown that estimates of coefficients of independent variables that are constant within groups are especially prone to numerical instability. Hence, if your model involves independent variables of this sort, it is especially important to run quadchk.

If the quadchk command indicates that the estimation results are sensitive to the number of quadrature points and you are not using adaptive quadrature, switch to adaptive quadrature. Adaptive quadrature is the default. If that still shows sensitivity to the number of quadrature points, then you may want to consider an alternative such as a fixed-effects, pooled, or population-averaged model. Alternatively, a different random-effects model that is not fitted via quadrature (e.g., xtpoisson, re) may be a better choice.

(Continued on next page)

▷ Example 1

In this example, we synthesize data according to the model

$$y = 0.05\,x1 + 0.08\,x2 + 0.08\,x3 + 0.1\,x4 + 0.1\,x5 + 0.1\,x6 + 0.1$$

$$z = \begin{cases} 1 & \text{if } y \geq 0 \\ 0 & \text{if } y < 0 \end{cases}$$

where the intrapanel correlation is 0.5 and the x1 variable is constant within panels. We first fit a random-effects probit model, and then we check the stability of the quadrature calculation:

```
. use http://www.stata-press.com/data/r9/quad1

. xtprobit z x1-x6, i(id) nolog
```

Random-effects probit regression   Number of obs   =   6000
Group variable (i): id   Number of groups   =   300

Random effects u_i ~ Gaussian   Obs per group: min =   20
                                                          avg =   20.0
                                                          max =   20

                                           Wald chi2(6)   =   29.24
Log likelihood = -3347.1106   Prob > chi2   =   0.0001

z	Coef.	Std. Err.	z	P>|z|	[95% Conf. Interval]	
x1	.004306	.0607057	0.07	0.943	-.1146749	.123287
x2	.1000736	.0663309	1.51	0.131	-.0299326	.2300797
x3	.1503532	.0662501	2.27	0.023	.0205053	.280201
x4	.1230145	.0377088	3.26	0.001	.0491066	.1969224
x5	.1342981	.0657221	2.04	0.041	.0054852	.2631111
x6	.087993	.0455752	1.93	0.054	-.0013327	.1773187
_cons	.0757052	.060359	1.25	0.210	-.0425962	.1940067
/lnsig2u	-.0330735	.1026399			-.2342439	.168097
sigma_u	.9835992	.0504783			.8894767	1.087682
rho	.4917324	.025653			.4417053	.5419256

Likelihood-ratio test of rho=0: chibar2(01) = 1582.67 Prob >= chibar2 = 0.000

(*Continued on next page*)

```
. quadchk
```

Refitting model intpoints() = 8
  (*output omitted*)

Refitting model intpoints() = 16
  (*output omitted*)

	Quadrature check		
	Fitted quadrature 12 points	Comparison quadrature 8 points	Comparison quadrature 16 points
Log likelihood	-3347.1106	-3347.1245	-3347.1099
		-.01391602	.00073242	Difference
		4.158e-06	-2.188e-07	Relative difference
z: x1	.00430604	.00431541	.00430557
		9.367e-06	-4.666e-07	Difference
		.0021752	-.00010836	Relative difference
z: x2	.10007356	.10006361	.10007422
		-9.945e-06	6.629e-07	Difference
		-.00009938	6.624e-06	Relative difference
z: x3	.15035317	.15034198	.15035396
		-.00001119	7.839e-07	Difference
		-.00007444	5.214e-06	Relative difference
z: x4	.1230145	.12300694	.12301499
		-7.556e-06	4.977e-07	Difference
		-.00006142	4.046e-06	Relative difference
z: x5	.13429811	.13428746	.13429886
		-.00001066	7.417e-07	Difference
		-.00007935	5.523e-06	Relative difference
z: x6	.08799299	.08798684	.0879934
		-6.152e-06	4.074e-07	Difference
		-.00006991	4.630e-06	Relative difference
z: _cons	.07570524	.07572076	.07570445
		.00001551	-7.989e-07	Difference
		.00020492	-.00001055	Relative difference
lnsig2u: _cons	-.03307349	-.03416312	-.03299322
		-.00108964	.00008026	Difference
		.03294596	-.00242676	Relative difference

We see that the largest difference is in the lnsig2u variable with a relative difference of 0.2% between the model with 12 integration points and 16. The differences and relative differences are small, indicating that refitting the random-effects probit model with more integration points will likely yield a satisfactory result. Indeed, refitting the model using the intpoints(20) option yields satisfactory results when checked with quadchk.

Nonadaptive Gauss–Hermite quadrature does not yield such robust results.

```
. xtprobit z x1-x6, i(id) nolog intmethod(ghermite)
```

Random-effects probit regression	Number of obs	=	6000
Group variable (i): id	Number of groups	=	300

Random effects u_i ~ Gaussian	Obs per group: min =	20
	avg =	20.0
	max =	20

	Wald chi2(6)	=	36.15
Log likelihood = -3349.6926	Prob > chi2	=	0.0000

z	Coef.	Std. Err.	z	P>|z|	[95% Conf. Interval]	
x1	.1156763	.0554911	2.08	0.037	.0069157	.2244369
x2	.1005555	.066227	1.52	0.129	-.0292469	.230358
x3	.1542187	.0660852	2.33	0.020	.0246942	.2837432
x4	.1257616	.0375776	3.35	0.001	.0521109	.1994123
x5	.1366003	.0654695	2.09	0.037	.0082824	.2649182
x6	.0870325	.0453489	1.92	0.055	-.0018496	.1759147
_cons	.1098393	.0500502	2.19	0.028	.0117426	.2079359
/lnsig2u	-.0791821	.0971059			-.2695062	.1111419
sigma_u	.9611824	.0466682			.8739317	1.057144
rho	.4802148	.0242385			.4330283	.5277569

Likelihood-ratio test of rho=0: chibar2(01) = 1577.50 Prob >= chibar2 = 0.000

(Continued on next page)

```
. quadchk, nooutput
Refitting model intpoints() =  8
Refitting model intpoints() = 16
```

Quadrature check

	Fitted quadrature 12 points	Comparison quadrature 8 points	Comparison quadrature 16 points	
Log likelihood	-3349.6926	-3354.6372	-3348.3881	
		-4.9446636	1.3045064	Difference
		.00147615	-.00038944	Relative difference
z: x1	.11567632	.16153997	.07007833	
		.04586365	-.04559799	Difference
		.3964826	-.39418607	Relative difference
z: x2	.10055552	.10317831	.09937417	
		.00262279	-.00118135	Difference
		.02608296	-.01174825	Relative difference
z: x3	.1542187	.15465369	.15150516	
		.00043499	-.00271354	Difference
		.00282062	-.0175954	Relative difference
z: x4	.12576159	.12880254	.1243974	
		.00304096	-.00136418	Difference
		.02418032	-.01084739	Relative difference
z: x5	.13660028	.13475211	.13707075	
		-.00184817	.00047047	Difference
		-.01352977	.00344411	Relative difference
z: x6	.08703252	.08568342	.08738135	
		-.0013491	.00034883	Difference
		-.0155011	.00400808	Relative difference
z: _cons	.10983928	.11031299	.09654975	
		.00047371	-.01328953	Difference
		.00431278	-.12099065	Relative difference
lnsig2u: _cons	-.07918213	-.18133823	-.05815644	
		-.1021561	.02102569	Difference
		1.2901408	-.26553574	Relative difference

Here we see that the x1 variable (the one that was constant within panel) changed with a relative difference of nearly 40%! Hence we conclude that we cannot trust the nonadaptive quadrature approximation for this model, and all results are suspect. This is a clear demonstration of the benefit of adaptive quadrature methods.

◁

▷ Example 2

In this example, we synthesize data exactly the same way as in the previous example, but we make the intrapanel correlation equal to 0.1 instead of 0.5. We again fit a random-effects probit model and check the quadrature:

```
. use http://www.stata-press.com/data/r9/quad2

. xtprobit z x1-x6, i(id) nolog
```

```
Random-effects probit regression              Number of obs      =        6000
Group variable (i): id                        Number of groups   =         300

Random effects u_i ~ Gaussian                 Obs per group: min =          20
                                                             avg =        20.0
                                                             max =          20

                                              Wald chi2(6)       =       39.43
Log likelihood  = -4065.3145                  Prob > chi2        =      0.0000
```

z	Coef.	Std. Err.	z	P>|z|	[95% Conf. Interval]	
x1	.0246943	.025112	0.98	0.325	-.0245243	.0739129
x2	.1300123	.0587906	2.21	0.027	.0147847	.2452398
x3	.1190409	.0579539	2.05	0.040	.0054533	.2326284
x4	.139197	.0331817	4.19	0.000	.0741621	.2042319
x5	.077364	.0578454	1.34	0.181	-.036011	.1907389
x6	.0862028	.0401185	2.15	0.032	.007572	.1648336
_cons	.0922653	.0244392	3.78	0.000	.0443653	.1401652
/lnsig2u	-2.343939	.1575275			-2.652687	-2.035191
sigma_u	.3097563	.0243976			.2654461	.3614631
rho	.0875487	.0125839			.0658236	.1155574

```
Likelihood-ratio test of rho=0: chibar2(01) =   110.19 Prob >= chibar2 = 0.000
```

(*Continued on next page*)

```
. quadchk, nooutput

Refitting model intpoints() =  8
Refitting model intpoints() = 16
```

		Quadrature check			
	Fitted quadrature 12 points	Comparison quadrature 8 points	Comparison quadrature 16 points		
Log likelihood	-4065.3145	-4065.3145 0 0	-4065.3145 0 0	Difference Relative difference
z: x1	.02469427	.02469427 5.521e-11 2.236e-09	.02469427 -7.135e-12 -2.889e-10	Difference Relative difference
z: x2	.13001229	.13001229 -4.594e-10 -3.533e-09	.13001229 -6.234e-13 -4.795e-12	Difference Relative difference
z: x3	.11904089	.11904089 -1.886e-10 -1.584e-09	.11904089 -2.734e-13 -2.297e-12	Difference Relative difference
z: x4	.13919697	.13919697 2.726e-11 1.958e-10	.13919697 1.555e-13 1.117e-12	Difference Relative difference
z: x5	.07736398	.07736398 -1.631e-10 -2.108e-09	.07736398 -4.109e-13 -5.312e-12	Difference Relative difference
z: x6	.08620282	.08620282 1.583e-10 1.837e-09	.08620282 2.895e-13 3.358e-12	Difference Relative difference
z: _cons	.09226527	.09226527 1.649e-10 1.788e-09	.09226527 -1.635e-11 -1.772e-10	Difference Relative difference
lnsig2u: _cons	-2.3439389	-2.343939 -8.414e-08 3.590e-08	-2.3439389 -1.954e-10 8.335e-11	Difference Relative difference

Here we see that the quadrature approximation is stable. With this result, we can confidently interpret the results. Satisfactory results are also obtained in this case with nonadaptive quadrature.

Again note that the only difference between this example and the previous one is the value of ρ. Any quadrature approximation works wonderfully for small to moderate values of ρ, but it breaks down for large values of ρ. Indeed, for large values of ρ, we should do more than question the validity of the quadrature approximation; we should question the validity of the random-effects model itself.

◁

Methods and Formulas

quadchk is implemented as an ado-file.

Also See

Complementary: [XT] **xtcloglog**, [XT] **xtintreg**, [XT] **xtlogit**, [XT] **xtpoisson**, [XT] **xtprobit**, [XT] **xttobit**

Title

> **xtabond** — Arellano–Bond linear, dynamic panel-data estimation

Syntax

xtabond *depvar* [*indepvars*] [*if*] [*in*] [, *options*]

options	description
Model	
<u>noc</u>onstant	suppress constant term
<u>diff</u>vars(*varlist*)	already differenced exogenous variables
inst(*varlist*)	additional instrument variables
<u>l</u>ags(#)	use # lags of dependent variable; default is lags(1)
maxldep(#)	maximum lags of dependent variable for use as instruments
maxlags(#)	maximum lags of predetermined variables for use as instruments
<u>two</u>step	compute the two-step estimator instead of the one-step estimator
Predetermined, More predetermined	
pre(*varlist* [...])	predetermined variables; see *Options* for details
pre(*varlist* [...])	pre() can be specified more than once
SE/Robust	
<u>r</u>obust	compute standard errors using the robust/sandwich estimator
Reporting	
<u>l</u>evel(#)	set confidence level; default is level(95)
<u>sma</u>ll	report small-sample statistics
<u>art</u>ests(#)	use # as maximum order for AR tests; default is artests(2)

You must tsset your data before using xtabond; see [TS] **tsset**.

indepvars and all *varlists* may contain time-series operators; see [U] **11.4.3 Time-series varlists**. The specification of *depvar*, however, may not contain time-series operators

by, statsby, and xi may be used with xtabond; see [U] **11.1.10 Prefix commands**.

See [U] **20 Estimation and postestimation commands** for additional capabilities of estimation commands.

Description

Dynamic panel-data models allow past realizations of the dependent variable to affect its current level. xtabond fits a dynamic panel-data model using the Arellano–Bond estimator. Consider the model

$$y_{it} = \sum_{j=1}^{p} \alpha_j y_{i,t-j} + \mathbf{x}_{it}\boldsymbol{\beta}_1 + \mathbf{w}_{it}\boldsymbol{\beta}_2 + \nu_i + \epsilon_{it} \quad i = 1, \dots, N \quad t = 1, \dots, T_i \qquad (1)$$

where

the α_j are p parameters to be estimated

$\mathbf{x}_{it}$ is a $1 \times k_1$ vector of strictly exogenous covariates

$\boldsymbol{\beta}_1$ is a $k_1 \times 1$ vector of parameters to be estimated

$\mathbf{w}_{it}$ is a $1 \times k_2$ vector of predetermined covariates

$\boldsymbol{\beta}_2$ is a $k_2 \times 1$ vector of parameters to be estimated

ν_i are the random effects that are independent and identically distributed (i.i.d.) over the panels with variance σ_ν^2

and ϵ_{it} are i.i.d. over the whole sample with variance σ_ϵ^2.

The ν_i and the ϵ_{it} are assumed to be independent for each i over all t.

First-differencing (1) removes the ν_i and produces an equation that can be estimated using instrumental variables. Arellano and Bond (1991) derive a generalized method-of-moments estimator for α_j, $j \in (1, \ldots, p)$, $\boldsymbol{\beta}_1$, and $\boldsymbol{\beta}_2$ using lagged levels of the dependent variable and the predetermined variables and differences of the strictly exogenous variables. xtabond implements this estimator, known as the Arellano–Bond dynamic panel-data estimator. This method assumes that there is no second-order autocorrelation in the first-differenced idiosyncratic errors. xtabond includes the test for autocorrelation and the Sargan test of overidentifying restrictions for this model.

Options

noconstant; see [XT] **estimation options**.

diffvars(*varlist*) specifies a set of variables that already have been differenced to be included as strictly exogenous covariates.

inst(*varlist*) specifies a set of variables to be used as additional instruments. These instruments are not differenced by xtabond before including them into the instrument matrix.

lags(*#*) sets p, the number of lags of the dependent variable to be included in the model. The default is $p = 1$.

maxldep(*#*) sets the maximum number of lags of the dependent variable that can be used as instruments. The default is to use all $T_i - p - 2$ lags.

maxlags(*#*) sets the maximum number of lags of the predetermined variables that can be used as instruments. The default is to use all $T_i - p - 2$ lags of the dependent variable. If the predetermined variables are endogenous, the default is to use all $T_i - p - 2$ lags of these endogenous variables. If the predetermined variables are not endogenous, the default is to use all $T_i - p - 1$ lags of these variables.

twostep specifies that the two-step estimator be calculated.

pre(*varlist* [, lagstruct(*prelags*, *premaxlags*) endogenous]) specifies that a set of predetermined variables be included in the model. Optionally, you may specify that *prelags* lags of the specified variables also be included. The default for *prelags* is 0. Specifying *premaxlags* sets the maximum number of further lags of the predetermined variables that can be used as instruments. Additionally, if you specify endogenous, xtabond treats these variables as endogenous instead of predetermined. The default is to include $T_i - prelags - 1$ lagged levels as instruments for predetermined variables and $T_i - prelags - 2$ lagged levels as instruments for endogenous variables. You may specify as many sets of predetermined variables as you need within the standard Stata limits on matrix size. Each set of predetermined variables may have its own number of *prelags* and *premaxlags*.

SE/Robust

robust; see [XT] **estimation options**. robust may not be specified with twostep.

Reporting

level(#); see [XT] **estimation options**.

small specifies that t statistics be reported instead of Z statistics and that F statistics be reported instead of chi-squared statistics.

artests(#) specifies the maximum order of the autocorrelation test to be calculated and reported. The maximum order must be less than or equal to $p + 1$. The default is 2.

Remarks

Anderson and Hsiao (1981, 1982) propose using further lags of the level or the difference of the dependent variable to instrument the lagged dependent variables that are included in a dynamic panel-data model after the random effects have been removed by first-differencing. A version of this estimator can be obtained from xtivreg (see [XT] **xtivreg**). Arellano and Bond (1991) build upon this idea by noting that, in general, there are many more instruments available. Using the GMM framework developed by Hansen (1982), they identify how many lags of the dependent variable and the predetermined variables are valid instruments and how to combine these lagged levels with first differences of the strictly exogenous variables into a potentially very large instrument matrix. Using this instrument matrix, Arellano and Bond (1991) derive the corresponding one-step and two-step GMM estimators, as well as the robust VCE estimator for the one-step model. In addition, they derived a test of autocorrelation of order m and the Sargan test of overidentifying restrictions for this estimator.

▷ Example 1

In their article, Arellano and Bond (1991) apply their new estimators and test statistics to a model of dynamic labor demand that had previously been considered by Layard and Nickell (1986) using data from an unbalanced panel of firms from the United Kingdom. All variables are indexed over the firm i and time t. In this dataset, n_{it} is the log of employment in firm i inside the UK at time t, w_{it} is the natural log of the real product wage, k_{it} is the natural log of the gross capital stock, and ys_{it} is the natural log of industry output. The model also includes time dummies yr1980, yr1981, yr1982, yr1983, and yr1984. In table 4 of Arellano and Bond (1991), the authors present the results they obtained from several specifications.

In column (a1) of table 4, Arellano and Bond report the coefficients and their standard errors from the robust one-step estimators of a dynamic model of labor demand. To clarify some important issues, we will begin with the homoskedastic one-step version of this model and then consider the robust case. Here is the command using xtabond and the subsequent output for the homoskedastic case:

```
. use http://www.stata-press.com/data/r9/abdata

. xtabond n l(0/1).w l(0/2).(k ys) yr1980-yr1984, lags(2)
```

```
Arellano-Bond dynamic panel-data estimation      Number of obs    =        611
Group variable (i): id                           Number of groups =        140

                                                 Wald chi2(15)    =     575.84
Time variable (t): year                          Obs per group: min =         4
                                                                avg =   4.364286
                                                                max =         6
```

One-step results

D.n	Coef.	Std. Err.	z	P>|z|	[95% Conf. Interval]	
n						
LD.	.6862262	.1486163	4.62	0.000	.3949435	.9775088
L2D.	-.0853582	.0444365	-1.92	0.055	-.1724523	.0017358
w						
D1.	-.6078208	.0657694	-9.24	0.000	-.7367265	-.4789151
LD.	.3926237	.1092374	3.59	0.000	.1785222	.6067251
k						
D1.	.3568456	.0370314	9.64	0.000	.2842653	.4294259
LD.	-.0580012	.0583051	-0.99	0.320	-.172277	.0562747
L2D.	-.0199475	.0416274	-0.48	0.632	-.1015357	.0616408
ys						
D1.	.6085073	.1345412	4.52	0.000	.3448115	.8722031
LD.	-.7111651	.1844599	-3.86	0.000	-1.0727	-.3496304
L2D.	.1057969	.1428568	0.74	0.459	-.1741974	.3857912
yr1980						
D1.	.0029062	.0212705	0.14	0.891	-.0387832	.0445957
yr1981						
D1.	-.0404378	.0354707	-1.14	0.254	-.1099591	.0290836
yr1982						
D1.	-.0652767	.048209	-1.35	0.176	-.1597646	.0292111
yr1983						
D1.	-.0690928	.0627354	-1.10	0.271	-.1920521	.0538664
yr1984						
D1.	-.0650302	.0781322	-0.83	0.405	-.2181665	.0881061
_cons	.0095545	.0142073	0.67	0.501	-.0182912	.0374002

```
Sargan test of over-identifying restrictions:
       chi2(25) =      65.82       Prob > chi2 = 0.0000

Arellano-Bond test that average autocovariance in residuals of order 1 is 0:
       H0: no autocorrelation   z = -3.94   Pr > z = 0.0001
Arellano-Bond test that average autocovariance in residuals of order 2 is 0:
       H0: no autocorrelation   z = -0.54   Pr > z = 0.5876
```

The coefficients are identical to those reported in column (a1) of table 4, as they should be. Of course, the standard errors are different because we are considering the homoskedastic case. Only in the case of a homoskedastic error term does the Sargan test have an asymptotic chi-squared distribution. In fact, Arellano and Bond (1991) show that the one-step Sargan test over-rejects in the presence of heteroskedasticity. Since its asymptotic distribution is not known under the assumptions of the `robust` model, `xtabond` does not compute it when `robust` is specified. The Sargan test, reported by Arellano and Bond (1991, table 4, column a1), comes from the one-step homoskedastic estimator and is the same as the one reported here. By default, `xtabond` calculates and reports the Arellano–Bond test for first- and second-order autocorrelation in the first-differenced residuals. There are versions of this test for both the homoskedastic and the robust cases, although their values are different.

◁

▷ Example 2

Consider the output from the one-step robust estimator of the same model:

```
. xtabond n l(0/1).w l(0/2).(k ys) yr1980-yr1984, lags(2) robust
Arellano-Bond dynamic panel-data estimation    Number of obs     =       611
Group variable (i): id                          Number of groups  =       140

                                                Wald chi2(15)     =    618.58
Time variable (t): year                         Obs per group: min =        4
                                                               avg = 4.364286
                                                               max =        6

One-step results
```

D.n	Coef.	Robust Std. Err.	z	P>|z|	[95% Conf. Interval]	
n						
LD.	.6862262	.1445943	4.75	0.000	.4028266	.9696257
L2D.	-.0853582	.0560155	-1.52	0.128	-.1951467	.0244302
w						
D1.	-.6078208	.1782055	-3.41	0.001	-.9570972	-.2585445
LD.	.3926237	.1679931	2.34	0.019	.0633632	.7218842
k						
D1.	.3568456	.0590203	6.05	0.000	.241168	.4725233
LD.	-.0580012	.0731797	-0.79	0.428	-.2014308	.0854284
L2D.	-.0199475	.0327126	-0.61	0.542	-.0840631	.0441681
ys						
D1.	.6085073	.1725313	3.53	0.000	.2703522	.9466624
LD.	-.7111651	.2317163	-3.07	0.002	-1.165321	-.2570095
L2D.	.1057969	.1412021	0.75	0.454	-.1709542	.382548
yr1980						
D1.	.0029062	.0158028	0.18	0.854	-.0280667	.0338791
yr1981						
D1.	-.0404378	.0280582	-1.44	0.150	-.0954307	.0145552
yr1982						
D1.	-.0652767	.0365451	-1.79	0.074	-.1369038	.0063503
yr1983						
D1.	-.0690928	.047413	-1.46	0.145	-.1620205	.0238348
yr1984						
D1.	-.0650302	.0576305	-1.13	0.259	-.1779839	.0479235
_cons	.0095545	.0102896	0.93	0.353	-.0106127	.0297217

```
Arellano-Bond test that average autocovariance in residuals of order 1 is 0:
        H0: no autocorrelation   z =  -3.60   Pr > z = 0.0003
Arellano-Bond test that average autocovariance in residuals of order 2 is 0:
        H0: no autocorrelation   z =  -0.52   Pr > z = 0.6058
```

The coefficients are the same but not the standard errors, and the value of the test for second-order autocorrelation matches that reported in Arellano and Bond (1991, table 4, column a1). Most of the robust standard errors are higher than those that assume a homoskedastic error term. Note that xtabond does not report the Sargan statistic in this case.

Overall, the test results from the one-step model are mixed. The Sargan test from the one-step homoskedastic estimator rejects the null hypothesis that the overidentifying restrictions are valid, but this could be due to heteroskedasticity. In both the homoskedastic and the robust cases, we reject the null hypothesis of no first-order autocorrelation in the differenced residuals, but we cannot reject the null hypothesis of no second-order autocorrelation. First-order autocorrelation in the differenced residuals does not imply that the estimates are inconsistent, but second-order autocorrelation would imply that the estimates are inconsistent. (See Arellano and Bond [1991, 281–282] for a discussion on this point.) The output above indicates that we have included several statistically insignificant variables, which we will not remove since we want the results to change with the estimation procedure for a given model.

◁

▷ Example 3

xtabond reports the Wald statistic of the null hypothesis that all the coefficients except the constant are zero. In our previous example, the null hypothesis is soundly rejected. In column (a1) of table 4, Arellano and Bond report a chi-squared test of the null hypothesis that all the coefficients are zero, except the constant and the time dummies. Here is an example of this test in Stata:

```
. test ld.n l2d.n d.w ld.w d.k ld.k l2d.k d.ys ld.ys l2d.ys
 ( 1)   LD.n = 0
 ( 2)   L2D.n = 0
 ( 3)   D.w = 0
 ( 4)   LD.w = 0
 ( 5)   D.k = 0
 ( 6)   LD.k = 0
 ( 7)   L2D.k = 0
 ( 8)   D.ys = 0
 ( 9)   LD.ys = 0
 (10)   L2D.ys = 0
            chi2( 10) =   408.29
          Prob > chi2 =    0.0000
```

Since the rejection of the null hypothesis of the Sargan test may indicate the presence of heteroskedasticity, we might expect the two-step estimator to greatly improve efficiency. The two-step estimator of the same model produces the following output:

```
. xtabond n l(0/1).w l(0/2).(k ys) yr1980-yr1984, lags(2) twostep
```

Arellano-Bond dynamic panel-data estimation			Number of obs	=	611
Group variable (i): id			Number of groups	=	140
			Wald chi2(15)	=	1035.56
Time variable (t): year			Obs per group: min =		4
			avg =		4.364286
			max =		6

Two-step results

D.n	Coef.	Std. Err.	z	P>|z|	[95% Conf. Interval]	
n						
LD.	.6287089	.0904543	6.95	0.000	.4514216	.8059961
L2D.	-.0651882	.0265009	-2.46	0.014	-.117129	-.0132474
w						
D1.	-.5257597	.0537692	-9.78	0.000	-.6311453	-.420374
LD.	.3112899	.0940116	3.31	0.001	.1270305	.4955492
k						
D1.	.2783619	.0449083	6.20	0.000	.1903432	.3663807
LD.	.0140994	.0528046	0.27	0.789	-.0893957	.1175946
L2D.	-.0402484	.0258038	-1.56	0.119	-.0908229	.010326
ys						
D1.	.5919243	.1162114	5.09	0.000	.3641542	.8196943
LD.	-.5659863	.1396738	-4.05	0.000	-.8397419	-.2922306
L2D.	.1005433	.1126749	0.89	0.372	-.1202955	.321382
yr1980						
D1.	.0006378	.0127959	0.05	0.960	-.0244417	.0257172
yr1981						
D1.	-.0550044	.0235162	-2.34	0.019	-.1010953	-.0089135
yr1982						
D1.	-.075978	.0302659	-2.51	0.012	-.135298	-.0166579
yr1983						
D1.	-.0740708	.0370993	-2.00	0.046	-.146784	-.0013575
yr1984						
D1.	-.0906606	.0453924	-2.00	0.046	-.179628	-.0016933
_cons	.0112155	.0077507	1.45	0.148	-.0039756	.0264066

```
Warning: Arellano and Bond recommend using one-step results for
         inference on coefficients

Sargan test of over-identifying restrictions:
        chi2(25) =     31.38      Prob > chi2 = 0.1767

Arellano-Bond test that average autocovariance in residuals of order 1 is 0:
        H0: no autocorrelation   z =  -3.00   Pr > z = 0.0027
Arellano-Bond test that average autocovariance in residuals of order 2 is 0:
        H0: no autocorrelation   z =  -0.42   Pr > z = 0.6776
```

Arellano and Bond recommend using the one-step results for inference on the coefficients because the two-step standard errors tend to be biased downward in small samples. (See Arellano and Bond [1991] for details.) However, as this example illustrates, the two-step Sargan test may be better for performing inference on model specification.

When interpreting the output, the most important difference is that we can no longer reject the null hypothesis in the Sargan test. However, we can reject the null hypothesis of no first-order serial correlation in the differenced residuals. Note that the magnitudes of several of the coefficient estimates have changed and that one even switched its sign.

◁

▷ Example 4

In some cases, we cannot assume strict exogeneity. Recall that a variable x_{it} is said to be strictly exogenous if $E[x_{it}\epsilon_{is}] = 0$ for all t and s. If $E[x_{it}\epsilon_{is}] \neq 0$ for $s < t$ but $E[x_{it}\epsilon_{is}] = 0$ for all $s \geq t$, the variable is said to be predetermined. Intuitively, if the error term at time t has some feedback on the subsequent realizations of x_{it}, x_{it} is a predetermined variable. Since unforecastable errors today might affect future changes in the real wage and in the capital stock, we might suspect that the log of the real product wage and the log of the gross capital stock are not strictly exogenous but are predetermined. In this example, we treat w and k as predetermined and use levels lagged one or more periods as instruments.

```
. xtabond n l(0/1).ys yr1980-yr1984, lags(2) twostep pre(w, lag(1,.))
> pre(k,lag(2,.))
Arellano-Bond dynamic panel-data estimation      Number of obs      =       611
Group variable (i): id                           Number of groups   =       140

                                                 Wald chi2(14)      =   8256.24
Time variable (t): year                          Obs per group: min =         4
                                                                avg =  4.364286
                                                                max =         6

Two-step results
```

D.n	Coef.	Std. Err.	z	P>|z|	[95% Conf. Interval]	
n						
LD.	.8580958	.0377548	22.73	0.000	.7840977	.9320938
L2D.	-.081207	.02373	-3.42	0.001	-.1277169	-.0346972
w						
D1.	-.6910855	.0261903	-26.39	0.000	-.7424175	-.6397535
LD.	.5961712	.0446448	13.35	0.000	.508669	.6836734
k						
D1.	.4140654	.038103	10.87	0.000	.3393849	.4887459
LD.	-.1537048	.0364455	-4.22	0.000	-.2251366	-.082273
L2D.	-.1025833	.0274243	-3.74	0.000	-.156334	-.0488326
ys						
D1.	.6936392	.0713304	9.72	0.000	.5538341	.8334443
LD.	-.8773678	.0871927	-10.06	0.000	-1.048262	-.7064733
yr1980						
D1.	-.0072451	.0082134	-0.88	0.378	-.023343	.0088529
yr1981						
D1.	-.0609608	.0159285	-3.83	0.000	-.09218	-.0297415
yr1982						
D1.	-.1130369	.0235481	-4.80	0.000	-.1591903	-.0668835
yr1983						
D1.	-.1335249	.0305939	-4.36	0.000	-.1934878	-.0735619
yr1984						
D1.	-.1623177	.0337034	-4.82	0.000	-.2283751	-.0962602
_cons	.0264501	.0058596	4.51	0.000	.0149655	.0379346

```
Warning: Arellano and Bond recommend using one-step results for
         inference on coefficients

Sargan test of over-identifying restrictions:
         chi2(68) =     69.69      Prob > chi2 = 0.4204

Arellano-Bond test that average autocovariance in residuals of order 1 is 0:
         H0: no autocorrelation   z =   -4.95   Pr > z = 0.0000
Arellano-Bond test that average autocovariance in residuals of order 2 is 0:
         H0: no autocorrelation   z =   -1.18   Pr > z = 0.2370
```

The increase in the p-value of the Sargan test indicates that treating the w and k as predetermined makes it more difficult to reject the null hypothesis that the overidentifying restrictions are valid. This increase in the Sargan statistic suggests that w and k are better modeled as predetermined variables.

◁

▷ Example 5

Alternatively, we might suspect that w and k are endogenous in that $E[x_{it}\epsilon_{is}] \neq 0$ for $s \leq t$ but $E[x_{it}\epsilon_{is}] = 0$ for all $s > t$. By this definition, endogenous variables differ from predetermined variables only in that the former allow for correlation between the x_{it} and the ϵ_{it} at time t, while the latter do not. Endogenous variables are treated similarly to the lagged dependent variable. Levels of the endogenous variables lagged two or more periods can serve as instruments. In this example, we treat w and k as endogenous variables.

```
. xtabond n l(0/1).ys yr1980-yr1984, lags(2) twostep pre(w, lag(1,.) endog)
> pre(k,lag(2,.) endog)
```

```
Arellano-Bond dynamic panel-data estimation      Number of obs      =       611
Group variable (i): id                           Number of groups   =       140

                                                 Wald chi2(14)      =   4090.60

Time variable (t): year                          Obs per group: min =         4
                                                                avg =  4.364286
                                                                max =         6
```

Two-step results

D.n	Coef.	Std. Err.	z	P>|z|	[95% Conf. Interval]	
n						
LD.	.6640937	.0381357	17.41	0.000	.589349	.7388383
L2D.	-.041283	.0219202	-1.88	0.060	-.0842458	.0016799
w						
D1.	-.7143942	.0319557	-22.36	0.000	-.7770262	-.6517621
LD.	.3644198	.059816	6.09	0.000	.2471826	.481657
k						
D1.	.5028874	.0400827	12.55	0.000	.4243269	.581448
LD.	-.2160842	.0429556	-5.03	0.000	-.3002756	-.1318927
L2D.	-.0549654	.0258917	-2.12	0.034	-.1057121	-.0042187
ys						
D1.	.5989356	.0849071	7.05	0.000	.4325207	.7653505
LD.	-.6770367	.0928439	-7.29	0.000	-.8590074	-.4950659
yr1980						
D1.	-.0061122	.0103052	-0.59	0.553	-.0263099	.0140855
yr1981						
D1.	-.04715	.0186144	-2.53	0.011	-.0836337	-.0106664
yr1982						
D1.	-.0817646	.026651	-3.07	0.002	-.1339997	-.0295295
yr1983						
D1.	-.0939251	.0354398	-2.65	0.008	-.1633859	-.0244644
yr1984						
D1.	-.117228	.0397795	-2.95	0.003	-.1951944	-.0392615
_cons	.0208857	.0065937	3.17	0.002	.0079623	.0338092

```
Warning: Arellano and Bond recommend using one-step results for
         inference on coefficients

Sargan test of over-identifying restrictions:
      chi2(56)  =     51.93       Prob > chi2 = 0.6296

Arellano-Bond test that average autocovariance in residuals of order 1 is 0:
      H0: no autocorrelation    z =  -4.42   Pr > z = 0.0000
Arellano-Bond test that average autocovariance in residuals of order 2 is 0:
      H0: no autocorrelation    z =  -1.26   Pr > z = 0.2074
```

While some estimated coefficients changed in magnitude, none changed in sign, and these results are very similar to those obtained by treating w and k as predetermined.

◁

▷ Example 6

Treating variables as predetermined or endogenous increases the size of the instrument matrix very quickly. (See *Methods and Formulas* for a discussion of how this matrix is created and what determines its size.) There are two potential problems with a very large instrument matrix. First, GMM estimators with too many overidentifying restrictions may perform poorly in small samples. (See Kiviet [1995] for a discussion of the dynamic panel-data case.) Second, the problem may become too large to estimate because the instrument matrix cannot exceed the current limit on matsize. For instance, to fit the above model, matsize must be at least 101. Here is what would happen if we attempted the estimation with a smaller matsize:

```
. set matsize 50

. xtabond n l(0/1).ys yr1980-yr1984, lags(2) twostep pre(w, lag(1,.))
> pre(k,lag(2,.))
matsize too small
    You have attempted to create a matrix with more than 50 rows or columns or
    to fit a model with more than 50 variables plus ancillary parameters.
    You need to increase matsize using the set matsize command; see help
    matsize.
matsize must be at least 101
(you have 101 instruments)
```

To handle these problems, you can set a maximum number of lagged levels to be included as instruments for the predetermined variables. Here is an example in which a maximum of three lagged levels of the predetermined variables are included as instruments:

Manuel Arellano (1957–) was born in Elda in Alicante, Spain. He earned degrees in economics from the University of Barcelona and the London School of Economics. After various posts in Oxford and London, he returned to Spain as Professor of Econometrics at Madrid in 1991. He is a leading expert on panel-data econometrics.

Stephen Roy Bond (1963–) earned degrees in economics from Cambridge and Oxford. Following various posts at Oxford, he now works mainly at the Institute for Fiscal Studies in London. His research interests include company taxation, dividends, and the links between financial markets, corporate control, and investment.

```
. xtabond n l(0/1).ys yr1980-yr1984, lags(2) twostep pre(w,lag(1,3))
> pre(k,lag(2,3))
```

Arellano-Bond dynamic panel-data estimation	Number of obs	=	611
Group variable (i): id	Number of groups	=	140
	Wald chi2(14)	=	1497.84
Time variable (t): year	Obs per group: min =		4
	avg =		4.364286
	max =		6

Two-step results

D.n	Coef.	Std. Err.	z	P>|z|	[95% Conf. Interval]	
n						
LD.	.931121	.0552599	16.85	0.000	.8228135	1.039428
L2D.	-.0759918	.0325497	-2.33	0.020	-.1397881	-.0121956
w						
D1.	-.6475372	.0459787	-14.08	0.000	-.7376539	-.5574206
LD.	.6906238	.0670804	10.30	0.000	.5591487	.8220989
k						
D1.	.3788106	.0688291	5.50	0.000	.243908	.5137133
LD.	-.2158533	.059655	-3.62	0.000	-.332775	-.0989316
L2D.	-.0914584	.039393	-2.32	0.020	-.1686673	-.0142495
ys						
D1.	.7324964	.1032756	7.09	0.000	.5300798	.9349129
LD.	-.9428141	.1205785	-7.82	0.000	-1.179144	-.7064846
yr1980						
D1.	-.0102389	.0104698	-0.98	0.328	-.0307594	.0102815
yr1981						
D1.	-.0763495	.0183512	-4.16	0.000	-.1123173	-.0403818
yr1982						
D1.	-.1373829	.02646	-5.19	0.000	-.1892436	-.0855223
yr1983						
D1.	-.1825149	.0352377	-5.18	0.000	-.2515795	-.1134502
yr1984						
D1.	-.2314023	.0408105	-5.67	0.000	-.3113894	-.1514151
_cons	.0310012	.0067092	4.62	0.000	.0178515	.044151

```
Warning: Arellano and Bond recommend using one-step results for
         inforonco on coofficionto
Sargan test of over-identifying restrictions:
       chi2(52) =    51.76     Prob > chi2 = 0.4835
Arellano-Bond test that average autocovariance in residuals of order 1 is 0:
       H0: no autocorrelation   z =  -4.70   Pr > z = 0.0000
Arellano-Bond test that average autocovariance in residuals of order 2 is 0:
       H0: no autocorrelation   z =  -1.28   Pr > z = 0.1997
```

◁

▷ Example 7

xtabond handles data in which there are missing observations in the middle of the panels. In the following example, we deliberately set the dependent variable to missing in the year 1980:

(Continued on next page)

```
. replace n=. if year==1980
(140 real changes made, 140 to missing)

. xtabond n l(0/1).w l(0/2).(k ys) yr1980-yr1984, lags(2) robust
note: yr1981 dropped due to collinearity
note: yr1982 dropped due to collinearity
note: the residuals and the L(1) residuals have no obs in common
      The AR(1) is trivially zero
note: the residuals and the L(2) residuals have no obs in common
      The AR(2) is trivially zero
```

```
Arellano-Bond dynamic panel-data estimation     Number of obs      =        115
Group variable (i): id                          Number of groups   =        101

                                                Wald chi2(11)      =      42.19

Time variable (t): year                         Obs per group: min =          1
                                                               avg =   1.138614
                                                               max =          2
```

One-step results

D.n	Coef.	Robust Std. Err.	z	P>|z|	[95% Conf. Interval]	
n						
LD.	.1782912	.2213558	0.81	0.421	-.2555582	.6121406
L2D.	.0305248	.0524455	0.58	0.561	-.0722665	.133316
w						
D1.	-.265179	.1497362	-1.77	0.077	-.5586565	.0282986
LD.	.1861825	.1430316	1.30	0.193	-.0941542	.4665193
k						
D1.	.3971506	.0887184	4.48	0.000	.2232657	.5710354
LD.	-.0310769	.0908215	-0.34	0.732	-.2090837	.14693
L2D.	-.0374041	.0642649	-0.58	0.561	-.163361	.0885528
ys						
D1.	.3872922	.3840567	1.01	0.313	-.365445	1.14003
LD.	-.6809435	.4930012	-1.38	0.167	-1.647208	.2853211
L2D.	.5562209	.4333161	1.28	0.199	-.2930632	1.405505
yr1980						
D1.	(dropped)					
yr1983						
D1.	-.006329	.0257789	-0.25	0.806	-.0568547	.0441968
yr1984						
D1.	(dropped)					
_cons	.0015564	.0104385	0.15	0.881	-.0189027	.0220154

```
Arellano-Bond test that average autocovariance in residuals of order 1 is 0:
       H0: no autocorrelation   z =       .   Pr > z =       .
Arellano-Bond test that average autocovariance in residuals of order 2 is 0:
       H0: no autocorrelation   z =       .   Pr > z =       .
```

There are two important aspects to this example. First, note the warnings and the missing values for the AR tests. xtabond did not have sufficient data to compute the tests, so it issued warnings and set the test statistics to missing. Second, since xtabond uses time-series operators in its computations, if statements and missing values are not equivalent. An if statement causes the false observations to be excluded from the sample, but it computes the time-series operators wherever possible. In contrast, missing data prevent evaluation of the time-series operators that involve missing observations. Thus the example above is not equivalent to the following one:

```
. use http://www.stata-press.com/data/r9/abdata

. xtabond n l(0/1).w l(0/2).(k ys) yr1980-yr1984 if year!=1980, lags(2) robust
note: yr1980 dropped due to collinearity
```

```
Arellano-Bond dynamic panel-data estimation        Number of obs       =        473
Group variable (i): id                             Number of groups    =        140

                                                   Wald chi2(14)       =     463.79

Time variable (t): year                            Obs per group: min  =          3
                                                                  avg  =   3.378571
                                                                  max  =          5
```

One-step results

D.n	Coef.	Robust Std. Err.	z	P>|z|	[95% Conf. Interval]	
n						
LD.	.7187143	.1304986	5.51	0.000	.4629417	.9744868
L2D.	-.0938608	.0583746	-1.61	0.108	-.2082729	.0205512
w						
D1.	-.6599329	.1753661	-3.76	0.000	-1.003644	-.3162217
LD.	.4654663	.1657696	2.81	0.005	.1405638	.7903688
k						
D1.	.3894823	.0731561	5.32	0.000	.2460989	.5328657
LD.	-.1122138	.0892247	-1.26	0.209	-.287091	.0626634
L2D.	-.0228185	.037552	-0.61	0.543	-.0964191	.050782
ys						
D1.	.4683059	.1830265	2.56	0.011	.1095805	.8270313
LD.	-.8632798	.2205727	-3.91	0.000	-1.295594	-.4309653
L2D.	.0991026	.1436945	0.69	0.490	-.1825336	.3807387
yr1981						
D1.	-.0655563	.0207481	-3.16	0.002	-.1062219	-.0248907
yr1982						
D1.	-.1092257	.0329365	-3.32	0.001	-.1737801	-.0446714
yr1983						
D1.	-.1268257	.0445178	-2.85	0.004	-.2140791	-.0395724
yr1984						
D1.	-.1249563	.0531627	-2.35	0.019	-.2291533	-.0207593
_cons	.0146263	.0107159	1.36	0.172	-.0063766	.0356291

```
Arellano-Bond test that average autocovariance in residuals of order 1 is 0:
        H0: no autocorrelation   z =  -3.85   Pr > z = 0.0001
Arellano-Bond test that average autocovariance in residuals of order 2 is 0:
        H0: no autocorrelation   z =   1.37   Pr > z = 0.1707
```

In this case, the year 1980 is dropped from the sample, but when the value of a variable from 1980 is required because a lag or difference is required, the 1980 value is used.

◁

(Continued on next page)

Saved Results

xtabond saves in e():

Scalars

e(N)	number of observations	e(F)	model F statistic (small only)
e(N_g)	number of groups	e(F_p)	p-value from model F (small only)
e(df_m)	model degrees of freedom	e(F_df)	restrictions in model F (small only)
e(g_max)	largest group size	e(df_r)	denominator df in F (small only)
e(g_min)	smallest group size	e(chi2)	model χ^2 statistic
e(g_avg)	average group size	e(chi2_p)	p-value from model χ^2
e(t_max)	maximum time in sample	e(chi2_df)	restrictions in model χ^2
e(t_min)	minimum time in sample	e(arm#)	test for autocorrelation of order #
e(n_lags)	number of lags of e(depvar)	e(sig2)	estimate of σ_ϵ^2
e(sargan)	Sargan test statistic	e(artests)	number of AR tests performed
e(sar_df)	degrees of freedom for sargan	e(zcols)	number of columns in instrument matrix Z_i

Macros

e(cmd)	xtabond	e(ivar)	variable denoting groups
e(depvar)	name of dependent variable	e(tvar)	time variable
e(depvar_ud)	name of dependent variable in undifference form	e(vcetype)	title used to label Std. Err.
		e(chi2type)	Wald; type of model χ^2 test
e(bnames_ud)	name of right-hand-side variable in undifference form	e(robust)	robust, if specified
		e(properties)	b V
e(inst_l)	additional level instruments	e(predict)	program used to implement predict
e(twostep)	twostep, if specified		

Matrices

e(b)	coefficient vector	e(V)	variance–covariance matrix of the estimators

Functions

e(sample)	marks estimation sample

Methods and Formulas

xtabond is implemented as an ado-file.

Consider dynamic panel-data models of the form

$$y_{it} = \sum_{j=1}^{p} \alpha_j y_{i,t-j} + \mathbf{x}_{it}\boldsymbol{\beta}_1 + \mathbf{w}_{it}\boldsymbol{\beta}_2 + \nu_i + \epsilon_{it}$$

where the variables are as defined as in (1).

Note that $\mathbf{x}$ and $\mathbf{w}$ may contain lagged independent variables and time dummies.

Let $X_{it} = (y_{i,t-1}, y_{i,t-2}, \ldots, y_{i,t-p}, \mathbf{x}_{it}, \mathbf{w}_{it})$ be the $1 \times K$ vector of covariates for i at time t, where $K = p + k_1 + k_2$.

Now rewrite this relationship as a set of N equations for each individual:

$$y_i = X_i\boldsymbol{\delta} + \nu_i\iota_i + \epsilon_i$$

Simplifying the notation, assume that there are no more than p lags of any of the covariates. For each i, y_i, ι_i, and ϵ_i are all $(T_i - p) \times 1$ vectors; y_i is the stacked values of y_{it} for person i, ι_i is a vector of ones, and ϵ_i contains the stacked values of ϵ_{it} for person i. The matrix X_i contains the p lags of y_{it}, the values of $\mathbf{x}_{it}$, and the $\mathbf{w}_{it}$. $\boldsymbol{\delta}$ is the $K \times 1$ vector of coefficients.

Define the first-differenced versions as

$$
y_i^* = \begin{pmatrix}
y_{i,t_{i0}+1+p} - y_{i,t_{i0}+p} \\
y_{i,t_{i0}+2+p} - y_{i,t_{i0}+1+p} \\
\vdots \\
y_{iT_i} - y_{i,T_i-1}
\end{pmatrix}
$$

$$
X_i^* = \begin{pmatrix}
X_{i,t_{i0}+1+p} - X_{i,t_{i0}+p} \\
X_{i,t_{i0}+2+p} - X_{i,t_{i0}+1+p} \\
\vdots \\
X_{iT_i} - X_{i,T_i-1}
\end{pmatrix}
$$

$$
\epsilon_i^* = \begin{pmatrix}
\epsilon_{i,t_{i0}+1+p} - \epsilon_{i,t_{i0}+p} \\
\epsilon_{i,t_{i0}+2+p} - \epsilon_{i,t_{i0}+1+p} \\
\vdots \\
\epsilon_{iT_i} - \epsilon_{i,T_i-1}
\end{pmatrix}
$$

where t_{i0} is the time period of the first nonmissing observation for person i.

The most difficult part of using these estimators is defining and implementing the matrix of instruments for each i, Z_i. Begin by considering a simple balanced-panel example in which our model is

$$
y_{it} = y_{i,t-1}\alpha_1 + y_{i,t-2}\alpha_2 + \mathbf{x}_{it}\boldsymbol{\beta} + \nu_i + \epsilon_{it}
$$

Note that there are no predetermined variables. Assume that the data come from a balanced panel in which there are no missing values. After first-differencing the equation, we have

$$
\Delta y_{it} = \Delta y_{i,t-1}\alpha_1 + \Delta y_{i,t-2}\alpha_2 + \Delta \mathbf{x}_{it}\boldsymbol{\beta} + \Delta \epsilon_{it}
$$

The first three observations are lost to lags and differencing. Because $\mathbf{x}_{it}$ contains only strictly exogenous covariates, Δx_{it} serves as its own instrument in estimating the first-differenced equation. Assuming that ϵ_{it} are not autocorrelated, for each i at $t = 4$, y_{i1} and y_{i2} are valid for the lagged variables. Similarly, at $t = 5$, y_{i1}, y_{i2}, and y_{i3} are valid instruments. We thus obtain an instrument matrix with one row for each time period that we are instrumenting:

$$
Z_i = \begin{pmatrix}
y_{i1} & y_{i2} & 0 & 0 & 0 & \cdots & 0 & 0 & 0 & \Delta\mathbf{x}_{i4} \\
0 & 0 & y_{i1} & y_{i2} & y_{i3} & \cdots & 0 & 0 & 0 & \Delta\mathbf{x}_{i5} \\
\vdots & \vdots & \vdots & \vdots & \ddots & \vdots & \vdots & \vdots & \vdots & \vdots \\
0 & 0 & 0 & 0 & \cdots & 0 & y_{i1} & \cdots & y_{i,T-2} & \Delta\mathbf{x}_{iT}
\end{pmatrix}
$$

Since $p = 2$, note that Z_i has $T - p - 1$ rows and $\sum_{m=p}^{T-2} m + k_1$ columns, where k_1 is the number of variables in x.

This extends to other lag structures with complete data. Unbalanced data and missing observations are handled by dropping the rows for which there are no data and filling in zeros in columns where missing data are required. For instance, suppose that, for some i, the $t = 1$ observation was missing but was not missing for some other panels. Our instrument matrix would then be

$$
Z_i = \begin{pmatrix}
0 & 0 & 0 & y_{i2} & y_{i3} & 0 & 0 & 0 & 0 & \dots & 0 & 0 & 0 & \Delta\mathbf{x}_{i5} \\
0 & 0 & 0 & 0 & 0 & 0 & y_{i2} & y_{i3} & 0 & \dots & 0 & 0 & 0 & \Delta\mathbf{x}_{i6} \\
\vdots & \vdots & \vdots & \vdots & \vdots & \vdots & \vdots & \vdots & \ddots & \vdots & \vdots & \vdots & \vdots \\
0 & 0 & 0 & 0 & 0 & 0 & 0 & 0 & \dots & 0 & y_{i2} & \dots & y_{iT-2} & \Delta\mathbf{x}_{iT}
\end{pmatrix}
$$

Note that Z_i has $T_i - p - 1$ rows and $\sum_{m=p}^{\tau-2} m + k_1$ columns, where $\tau = \max_i \tau_i$ and τ_i is the number of nonmissing observations in panel i.

Endogenous variables are treated similarly to the lagged dependent variables, and levels lagged two or more periods are valid instruments. For predetermined variables, levels lagged one or more periods are valid instruments. See Arellano and Bond (1991, 290) for an example.

Note that the number of columns in Z_i can grow very quickly for moderately long panels or models with several predetermined variables.

Let H_i be the $(T_i - p - 1) \times (T_i - p - 1)$ covariance matrix of the differenced idiosyncratic errors; that is,

$$
H_i = E[\epsilon_i^* \epsilon_i^{*'}] = \begin{pmatrix}
2 & -1 & 0 & \dots & 0 & 0 \\
-1 & 2 & -1 & \dots & 0 & 0 \\
\vdots & \vdots & \vdots & \ddots & \vdots & \vdots \\
0 & 0 & 0 & \dots & 2 & -1 \\
0 & 0 & 0 & \dots & -1 & 2
\end{pmatrix}
$$

Then for some instrument matrix Z_i, the one-step Arellano–Bond estimator of $\boldsymbol{\delta}$, $\widehat{\boldsymbol{\delta}}_1$ is given by

$$
\widehat{\boldsymbol{\delta}}_1 = Q_1^{-1} \left(\sum_{i=1}^{N} X_i^{*'} Z_i \right) A_1 \left(\sum_{i=1}^{N} Z_i' y_i^* \right)
$$

where

$$
Q_1 = \left(\sum_{i=1}^{N} X_i^{*'} Z_i \right) A_1 \left(\sum_{i=1}^{N} Z_i' X_i^{*'} \right)
$$

and

$$
A_1 = \left(\sum_{i=1}^{N} Z_i' H_i Z_i \right)^{-1}
$$

Using $\widehat{\boldsymbol{\delta}}_1$, the one-step residuals for i are

$$
\widehat{\epsilon}_i^* = y_i^* - X_i^* \widehat{\boldsymbol{\delta}}_1
$$

Assuming homoskedasticity, the variance–covariance estimator of the parameter estimator $\widehat{\boldsymbol{\delta}}_1$ is

$$\widehat{V}_1 = \widehat{\sigma}_1^2 Q_1^{-1}$$

where

$$\widehat{\sigma}_1^2 = \frac{1}{NT - K} \sum_{i=1}^{N} (\widehat{\epsilon}_i^{*'} \widehat{\epsilon}_i)^*$$

and $NT = \sum_{i=1}^{N} T_i - p - 1$.

The robust estimator is given by

$$\widehat{V}_{1r} = Q_1^{-1} \left(\sum_{i=1}^{N} X_i^{*'} Z_i \right) A_1 A_2^{-1} A_1 \left(\sum_{i=1}^{N} Z_i' X_i^* \right) Q_1^{-1}$$

where

$$A_2 = \left(\sum_{i=1}^{N} Z_i' G_i Z_i \right)^{-1}$$

and

$$G_i = \widehat{\epsilon}_i^* \widehat{\epsilon}_i^{*'}$$

The two-step estimator of δ, $\widehat{\delta}_2$ is given by

$$\widehat{\delta}_2 = Q_2^{-1} \left(\sum_{i=1}^{N} X_i^{*'} Z_i \right) A_2 \left(\sum_{i=1}^{N} Z_i' y_i^* \right)$$

where

$$Q_2 = \left(\sum_{i=1}^{N} X_i^{*'} Z_i \right) A_2 \left(\sum_{i=1}^{N} Z_i' X_i^{*'} \right)$$

The two-step VCE is

$$\widehat{V}_2 = Q_2^{-1}$$

For the one-step, homoskedastic case, the test for autocorrelation of order m in the differenced residuals $\widehat{\epsilon}_i^*$ is given by

$$AR_m = \frac{\sum_{i=1}^{N} (\widehat{\epsilon}_{mi}^{*'} \widehat{\epsilon}_i^*)}{B_1^{1/2}}$$

where

$$\widehat{\epsilon}_{mi}^* = L_m(\widehat{\epsilon}_i^*)$$

and L_m is the m-order lag operator, and

$$B_1 = \sum_{i=1}^{N} \widehat{\epsilon}_{mi}^{*'} H_i \widehat{\epsilon}_{mi}^* - 2 \left(\sum_{i=1}^{N} \widehat{\epsilon}_{mi}^{*'} X_i^* \right) Q_1^{-1} \left(\sum_{i=1}^{N} X_i^{*'} Z_i \right) A_1 \left(\sum_{i=1}^{N} Z_i' H_i \widehat{\epsilon}_{mi}^* \right)$$
$$+ \left(\sum_{i=1}^{N} \widehat{\epsilon}_{mi}^{*'} X_i^* \right) \widehat{V}_1 \left(\sum_{i=1}^{N} X_i^{*'} \widehat{\epsilon}_{mi}^* \right)$$

For the one-step, robust case, the test becomes

$$AR_m = \frac{\sum_{i=1}^{N} (\widehat{\epsilon}_{mi}^{*'} \widehat{\epsilon}_i^{*})}{B_{1r}^{1/2}}$$

where

$$B_{1r} = \sum_{i=1}^{N} \widehat{\epsilon}_{mi}^{*'} G_i \widehat{\epsilon}_{mi}^{*} - 2 \left(\sum_{i=1}^{N} \widehat{\epsilon}_{mi}^{*'} X_i^{*} \right) Q_1^{-1} \left(\sum_{i=1}^{N} X_i^{*'} Z_i \right) A_2 \left(\sum_{i=1}^{N} Z_i' G_i \widehat{\epsilon}_{mi}^{*} \right)$$

$$+ \left(\sum_{i=1}^{N} \widehat{\epsilon}_{mi}^{*'} X_i^{*} \right) \widehat{V}_{1r} \left(\sum_{i=1}^{N} X_i^{*'} \widehat{\epsilon}_{mi}^{*} \right)$$

For the two-step case, the test is

$$AR_m = \frac{\sum_{i=1}^{N} (\widehat{\widehat{\epsilon}}_{mi}^{*'} \widehat{\widehat{\epsilon}}_i^{*})}{B_2^{1/2}}$$

where

$$B_2 = \sum_{i=1}^{N} \widehat{\widehat{\epsilon}}_{mi}^{*'} G_{2i} \widehat{\widehat{\epsilon}}_{mi}^{*} - 2 \left(\sum_{i=1}^{N} \widehat{\widehat{\epsilon}}_{mi}^{*'} X_i^{*} \right) Q_2^{-1} \left(\sum_{i=1}^{N} X_i^{*'} Z_i \right) A_2 \left(\sum_{i=1}^{N} Z_i' G_{2i} \widehat{\widehat{\epsilon}}_{mi}^{*} \right)$$

$$+ \left(\sum_{i=1}^{N} \widehat{\widehat{\epsilon}}_{mi}^{*'} X_i^{*} \right) \widehat{V}_2 \left(\sum_{i=1}^{N} X_i^{*'} \widehat{\widehat{\epsilon}}_{mi}^{*} \right)$$

where

$$\widehat{\widehat{\epsilon}}_i^{*} = y_i^{*} - X_i^{*} \widehat{\boldsymbol{\delta}}_2$$

and

$$\widehat{\widehat{\epsilon}}_{mi}^{*} = L_m (\widehat{\widehat{\epsilon}}_i^{*})$$

and

$$G_{2i} = \widehat{\widehat{\epsilon}}_i^{*} \widehat{\widehat{\epsilon}}_i^{*'}$$

The Sargan test statistic for the one-step model is

$$S_1 = \left(\sum_{i=1}^{N} \widehat{\epsilon}_i^{*'} Z_i \right) A_1 \left(\sum_{i=1}^{N} Z_i' \widehat{\epsilon}_i^{*} \right) \left(\frac{1}{\widehat{\sigma}_1^2} \right)$$

The Sargan test statistic for the two-step model is

$$S_2 = \left(\sum_{i=1}^{N} \widehat{\widehat{\epsilon}}_i^{*'} Z_i \right) A_2 \left(\sum_{i=1}^{N} Z_i' \widehat{\widehat{\epsilon}}_i^{*} \right)$$

References

Anderson, T. W. and C. Hsiao. 1981. Estimation of dynamic models with error components. *Journal of the American Statistical Association* 76: 598–606.

——. 1982. Formulation and estimation of dynamic models using panel data. *Journal of Econometrics* 18: 47–82.

Arellano, M. and S. Bond. 1991. Some tests of specification for panel data: Monte Carlo evidence and an application to employment equations. *The Review of Economic Studies* 58: 277–297.

Baltagi, B. H. 2001. *Econometric Analysis of Panel Data.* 2nd ed. New York: Wiley.

Hansen, L. P. 1982. Large sample properties of generalized method of moments estimators. *Econometrica* 50: 1029–1054.

Kiviet, J. 1995. On bias, inconsistency, and efficiency of various estimators in dynamic panel data models. *Journal of Econometrics* 68: 53–78.

Layard, R. and S. J. Nickell. 1986. Unemployment in Britain. *Economica* 53: 5121–5169.

Also See

Complementary:	[XT] **xtabond postestimation**; [XT] **xtdata**, [XT] **xtdes**, [XT] **xtsum**, [XT] **xttab**, [TS] **tsset**
Related:	[XT] **xtivreg**, [XT] **xtreg**, [XT] **xtregar**
Background:	[U] **11.1.10 Prefix commands**, [U] **20 Estimation and postestimation commands**, [XT] **estimation options**, [XT] **xt**

Title

xtabond postestimation — Postestimation tools for xtabond

Description

The following postestimation commands are available for xtabond:

command	description
estat	VCE and estimation sample summary
estimates	cataloging estimation results
hausman	Hausman's specification test
lincom	point estimates, standard errors, testing, and inference for linear combinations of coefficients
mfx	marginal effects or elasticities
nlcom	point estimates, standard errors, testing, and inference for nonlinear combinations of coefficients
predict	predictions, residuals, influence statistics, and other diagnostic measures
predictnl	point estimates, standard errors, testing, and inference for generalized predictions
test	Wald tests for simple and composite linear hypotheses
testnl	Wald tests of nonlinear hypotheses

See the corresponding entries in the *Stata Base Reference Manual* for details.

Syntax for predict

predict [*type*] *newvar* [*if*] [*in*] [, xb e]

Options for predict

xb, the default, calculates the linear prediction from the first-differenced equation.

e calculates the residual error of the differenced dependent variable from the linear prediction.

Methods and Formulas

All postestimation commands listed above are implemented as ado-files.

Also See

Complementary:	[XT] **xtabond**,
	[R] **estimates**, [R] **hausman**, [R] **lincom**, [R] **mfx**, [R] **nlcom**,
	[R] **predictnl**, [R] **test**, [R] **testnl**
Background:	[U] **13.5 Accessing coefficients and standard errors**,
	[U] **20 Estimation and postestimation commands**,
	[R] **estat**, [R] **predict**

Title

> **xtcloglog** — Random-effects and population-averaged cloglog models

Syntax

Random-effects (RE) model

> xtcloglog *depvar* [*indepvars*] [*if*] [*in*] [*weight*] [, re *RE_options*]

Population-averaged (PA) model

> xtcloglog *depvar* [*indepvars*] [*if*] [*in*] [*weight*], pa [*PA_options*]

RE_options	description
Model	
i(*varname_i*)	use *varname_i* as the panel ID variable
<u>nocon</u>stant	suppress constant term
re	use random-effects estimator; the default
<u>off</u>set(*varname*)	include *varname* in model with coefficient constrained to 1
constraints(*constraints*)	apply specified linear constraints
Int opts (RE)	
<u>intm</u>ethod(*intmethod*)	integration method; *intmethod* may be <u>agh</u>ermite or <u>gh</u>ermite
<u>intp</u>oints(#)	use # quadrature points; default is intpoints(12)
SE	
vce(*vcetype*)	*vcetype* may be <u>boot</u>strap or <u>jack</u>knife
Reporting	
<u>l</u>evel(#)	set confidence level; default is level(95)
noskip	perform overall model test as a likelihood-ratio test
Max options	
maximize_options	control the maximization process; seldom used

PA_options	description
Model	
i(*varname_i*)	use *varname_i* as the panel ID variable
<u>nocon</u>stant	suppress constant term
pa	use population-averaged estimator
<u>off</u>set(*varname*)	include *varname* in model with coefficient constrained to 1
Correlation	
corr(*correlation*)	within-group correlation structure; see table below
force	estimate even if observations unequally spaced in time

SE/Robust

vce(*vcetype*)	*vcetype* may be <u>r</u>obust, <u>boot</u>strap, or <u>jack</u>knife
<u>r</u>obust	synonym for vce(robust)
nmp	use divisor $N - P$ instead of the default N
<u>sc</u>ale(#)	set scale parameter to #; default is scale(1)
<u>sc</u>ale(x2)	set scale parameter to Pearson chi-squared statistic
<u>sc</u>ale(dev)	set scale parameter to deviance divided by degrees of freedom
<u>sc</u>ale(phi)	do not rescale the variance

Reporting

<u>l</u>evel(#)	set confidence level; default is level(95)

Opt options

optimize_options	control the optimization process; seldom used

correlation	description
<u>exch</u>angeable	exchangeable; the default
<u>ind</u>ependent	independent
<u>uns</u>tructured	unstructured
<u>f</u>ixed *matname*	user-specified
ar #	autoregressive of order #
<u>stat</u>ionary #	stationary of order #
<u>non</u>stationary #	nonstationary of order #

depvar and *indepvars* may contain time-series operators; see [U] **11.4.3 Time-series varlists**.
bootstrap, by, jackknife, statsby, and xi may be used with xtcloglog; see [U] **11.1.10 Prefix commands**.
iweights, fweights, and pweights are allowed for the population-averaged model, and iweights are allowed
for the random-effects model; see [U] **11.1.6 weight**. Weights must be constant within panels.
See [U] **20 Estimation and postestimation commands** for additional capabilities of estimation commands.

Description

xtcloglog fits population-averaged and random-effects complementary log-log (cloglog) models. There is no command for a conditional fixed-effects model, as there does not exist a sufficient statistic allowing the fixed effects to be conditioned out of the likelihood. Unconditional fixed-effects cloglog models may be fitted with cloglog with indicator variables for the panels. The appropriate indicator variables can be generated using tabulate or xi. However, unconditional fixed-effects estimates are biased.

By default, the population-averaged model is an equal-correlation model; that is, xtcloglog, pa assumes corr(exchangeable). See [XT] **xtgee** for details on fitting other population-averaged models.

Note: xtcloglog, re, the default, is slow since it is calculated by adaptive Gauss–Hermite quadrature; see *Methods and Formulas*. Computation time depends on the number of points used for the quadrature. The default is intpoints(12). Simulations indicate that increasing the number of points does not appreciably change the estimates for the coefficients or their standard errors. See [XT] **quadchk**.

See [R] **logistic** for a list of related estimation commands.

Options for RE model

i(*varname$_i$*), noconstant; see [XT] **estimation options**.

re requests the random-effects estimator, which is the default.

offset(*varname*), constraints(*constraints*); see [XT] **estimation options**.

intmethod(*intmethod*) specifies the integration method to be used for the random-effects model. It accepts one of two arguments: the first is aghermite, the default, which specifies adaptive Gauss–Hermite quadrature; the second is ghermite, which specifies nonadaptive Gauss–Hermite quadrature.

intpoints(#) specifies the number of points to use for Gauss–Hermite quadrature. The default is 12. Increasing this value slightly improves the accuracy but also increases computation time. Computation time is roughly proportional to its value.

vce(*vcetype*); see [R] **vce_option**.

level(#), noskip; see [XT] **estimation options**.

maximize_options: difficult, technique(*algorithm_spec*), iterate(#), [no]log, trace, gradient, showstep, hessian, shownrtolerance, tolerance(#), ltolerance(#), gtolerance(#), nrtolerance(#), nonrtolerance, from(*init_specs*); see [R] **maximize**. Some of these options are not available if intmethod(ghermite) is specified. These options are seldom used.

Options for PA model

i(*varname$_i$*), noconstant; see [XT] **estimation options**.

pa requests the population-averaged estimator.

offset(*varname*); see [XT] **estimation options**

corr(*correlation*), force; see [XT] **estimation options**.

vce(*vcetype*); see [R] **vce_option**.

robust, nmp; see [XT] **estimation options**.

scale(x2 | dev | phi | #) overrides the default scale parameter of scale(1); see [XT] **estimation options**.

level(#); see [XT] **estimation options**.

optimize_options control the iterative optimization process. These options are seldom used.

iterate(#) specifies the maximum number of iterations. When the number of iterations equals #, the optimization stops and presents the current results, even if convergence has not been reached. The default is iterate(100).

tolerance(#) specifies the tolerance for the coefficient vector. When the relative change in the coefficient vector from one iteration to the next is less than or equal to #, the optimization process is stopped. tolerance(1e-6) is the default.

nolog suppresses display of the iteration log.

trace specifies that the current estimates be printed at each iteration.

Remarks

xtcloglog, pa is a shortcut command for fitting the population-averaged model. Typing

. xtcloglog ..., pa ...

is equivalent to typing

. xtgee ..., ... family(binomial) link(cloglog) corr(exchangeable)

Also see [XT] **xtgee** for information about xtcloglog.

By default or when re is specified, xtcloglog fits, via maximum likelihood, the random-effects model

$$\Pr(y_{it} \neq 0 | \mathbf{x}_{it}) = P(\mathbf{x}_{it}\boldsymbol{\beta} + \nu_i)$$

for $i = 1, \ldots, n$ panels, where $t = 1, \ldots, n_i$, ν_i are i.i.d., $N(0, \sigma_\nu^2)$, and $P(z) = 1 - \exp\{-\exp(z)\}$.

Underlying this model is the variance-components model

$$y_{it} \neq 0 \iff \mathbf{x}_{it}\boldsymbol{\beta} + \nu_i + \epsilon_{it} > 0$$

where ϵ_{it} are i.i.d. extreme-value (Gumbel) distributed with the mean equal to Euler's constant and variance $\sigma_\epsilon^2 = \pi^2/6$, independently of ν_i. The nonsymmetric error distribution is an alternative to logit and probit analysis and is typically used when the positive (or negative) outcome is rare.

▷ Example 1

Suppose that we are studying unionization of women in the United States and are using the union dataset; see [XT] **xt**. We wish to fit a random-effects model of union membership:

```
. use http://www.stata-press.com/data/r9/union
(NLS Women 14-24 in 1968)

. xtcloglog union age grade not_smsa south southXt, i(id) nolog
Random-effects complementary log-log model        Number of obs      =       26200
Group variable (i): idcode                         Number of groups   =        4434

Random effects u_i ~ Gaussian                      Obs per group: min =           1
                                                                  avg =         5.9
                                                                  max =          12

                                                   Wald chi2(5)       =      254.25
Log likelihood  = -10543.406                       Prob > chi2        =      0.0000
```

union	Coef.	Std. Err.	z	P>|z|	[95% Conf. Interval]	
age	.012174	.0032431	3.75	0.000	.0058176	.0185303
grade	.0688053	.0134512	5.12	0.000	.0424415	.0951692
not_smsa	-.2005603	.0637538	-3.15	0.002	-.3255156	-.0756051
south	-.8916002	.0857774	-10.39	0.000	-1.059721	-.7234797
southXt	.0161412	.0059561	2.71	0.007	.0044675	.0278149
_cons	-3.253156	.1952145	-16.66	0.000	-3.63577	-2.870543
/lnsig2u	1.177798	.0404105			1.098595	1.257001
sigma_u	1.802003	.03641			1.732036	1.874798
rho	.6637605	.0090189			.645861	.681202

```
Likelihood-ratio test of rho=0: chibar2(01) =  6001.59 Prob >= chibar2 = 0.000
```

The output includes the additional panel-level variance component, which is parameterized as the log of the standard deviation, $\ln\sigma_\nu$ (labeled `lnsig2u` in the output). The standard deviation σ_ν is also included in the output, labeled `sigma_u`, together with ρ (labeled `rho`),

$$\rho = \frac{\sigma_\nu^2}{\sigma_\nu^2 + \sigma_\epsilon^2}$$

which is the proportion of the total variance contributed by the panel-level variance component.

When `rho` is zero, the panel-level variance component is not important, and the panel estimator is no different from the pooled estimator (`cloglog`). A likelihood-ratio test of this is included at the bottom of the output, which formally compares the pooled estimator with the panel estimator.

As an alternative to the random-effects specification, you might want to fit an equal-correlation population-averaged cloglog model by typing

(Continued on next page)

```
. xtcloglog union age grade not_smsa south southXt, i(id) pa

Iteration 1: tolerance = .06580809
Iteration 2: tolerance = .00606963
Iteration 3: tolerance = .00032265
Iteration 4: tolerance = .00001658
Iteration 5: tolerance = 8.864e-07
```

GEE population-averaged model				Number of obs	=	26200
Group variable:			idcode	Number of groups	=	4434
Link:			cloglog	Obs per group: min =		1
Family:			binomial	avg =		5.9
Correlation:			exchangeable	max =		12
				Wald chi2(5)	=	232.44
Scale parameter:			1	Prob > chi2	=	0.0000

union	Coef.	Std. Err.	z	P>|z|	[95% Conf. Interval]	
age	.0045777	.0021754	2.10	0.035	.0003139	.0088415
grade	.0544267	.0095097	5.72	0.000	.035788	.0730654
not_smsa	-.1051731	.0430512	-2.44	0.015	-.189552	-.0207943
south	-.6578891	.061857	-10.64	0.000	-.7791266	-.5366515
southXt	.0142329	.004133	3.44	0.001	.0061325	.0223334
_cons	-2.074687	.1358008	-15.28	0.000	-2.340851	-1.808522

◁

▷ Example 2

In [R] **cloglog**, we showed these results and compared them with `cloglog, robust cluster()`. `xtcloglog` with the `pa` option allows a `robust` option (the random-effects estimator does not allow the `robust` specification), so we can obtain the population-averaged cloglog estimator with the robust variance calculation by typing

```
. xtcloglog union age grade not_smsa south southXt, i(id) pa robust nolog
```

GEE population-averaged model				Number of obs	=	26200
Group variable:			idcode	Number of groups	=	4434
Link:			cloglog	Obs per group: min =		1
Family:			binomial	avg =		5.9
Correlation:			exchangeable	max =		12
				Wald chi2(5)	=	153.64
Scale parameter:			1	Prob > chi2	=	0.0000

(Std. Err. adjusted for clustering on idcode)

union	Coef.	Semi-robust Std. Err.	z	P>|z|	[95% Conf. Interval]	
age	.0045777	.003261	1.40	0.160	-.0018138	.0109692
grade	.0544267	.0117512	4.63	0.000	.0313948	.0774585
not_smsa	-.1051731	.0548342	-1.92	0.055	-.2126462	.0022999
south	-.6578891	.0793619	-8.29	0.000	-.8134355	-.5023427
southXt	.0142329	.005975	2.38	0.017	.0025221	.0259438
_cons	-2.074687	.1770236	-11.72	0.000	-2.421647	-1.727727

These standard errors are similar to those shown for `cloglog, robust cluster()` in [R] **cloglog**.

◁

Saved Results

xtcloglog, re saves in e():

Scalars

e(N)	# of observations	e(rho)	ρ
e(N_g)	# of groups	e(sigma_u)	panel-level standard deviation
e(N_cd)	# of completely determined obs.	e(n_quad)	# of quadrature points
e(df_m)	model degrees of freedom	e(k)	# of parameters
e(ll)	log likelihood	e(k_eq)	# of equations
e(ll_0)	log likelihood, constant-only model	e(k_dv)	# of dependent variables
e(ll_c)	log likelihood, comparison model	e(p)	significance
e(g_max)	largest group size	e(rank)	rank of e(V)
e(g_min)	smallest group size	e(rank0)	rank of e(V) for constant-only model
e(g_avg)	average group size	e(ic)	# of iterations
e(chi2)	χ^2	e(rc)	return code
e(chi2_c)	χ^2 for comparison test	e(converged)	1 if converged, 0 otherwise

Macros

e(cmd)	xtcloglog	e(distrib)	Gaussian; the distribution of the random effect
e(depvar)	name of dependent variable		
e(title)	title in estimation output	e(vce)	*vcetype* specified in vce()
e(ivar)	variable denoting groups	e(vcetype)	title used to label Std. Err.
e(wtype)	weight type	e(opt)	type of optimization
e(wexp)	weight expression	e(ml_method)	type of ml method
e(offset)	offset	e(user)	name of likelihood-evaluator program
e(chi2type)	Wald or LR; type of model χ^2 test	e(technique)	maximization technique
e(chi2_ct)	Wald or LR; type of model χ^2 test corresponding to e(chi2_c)	e(crittype)	optimization criterion
		e(properties)	b V
e(intmethod)	integration method	e(predict)	program used to implement predict

Matrices

e(b)	coefficient vector	e(ilog)	iteration log
e(V)	variance–covariance matrix of the estimators	e(gradient)	gradient vector

Functions

e(sample)	marks estimation sample

(Continued on next page)

`xtcloglog, pa` saves in `e()`:

Scalars

e(N)	number of observations	e(chi2_dev)	χ^2 test of deviance
e(N_g)	number of groups	e(chi2_dis)	χ^2 test of deviance dispersion
e(df_m)	model degrees of freedom	e(deviance)	deviance
e(df_pear)	degrees of freedom for Pearson χ^2	e(dispers)	deviance dispersion
e(g_max)	largest group size	e(tol)	target tolerance
e(g_min)	smallest group size	e(dif)	achieved tolerance
e(g_avg)	average group size	e(phi)	scale parameter
e(chi2)	χ^2	e(rc)	return code

Macros

e(cmd)	xtgee	e(ivar)	variable denoting groups
e(cmd2)	xtcloglog	e(vce)	*vcetype* specified in vce()
e(depvar)	name of dependent variable	e(vcetype)	title used to label Std. Err.
e(family)	binomial	e(chi2type)	Wald; type of model χ^2 test
e(link)	cloglog; link function	e(offset)	offset
e(corr)	correlation structure	e(properties)	b V
e(crittype)	optimization criterion	e(predict)	program used to implement predict
e(scale)	x2, dev, phi, or #; scale parameter		

Matrices

e(b)	coefficient vector	e(R)	estimated working correlation matrix
e(V)	variance–covariance matrix of the estimators		

Functions

e(sample)	marks estimation sample

Methods and Formulas

`xtcloglog` is implemented as an ado-file.

`xtcloglog, pa` reports the population-averaged results obtained by using `xtgee, family(binomial) link(cloglog)` to obtain estimates.

For the random-effects model, assume a normal distribution, $N(0, \sigma_\nu^2)$, for the random effects ν_i,

$$\Pr(y_{i1}, \ldots, y_{in_i} | \mathbf{x}_{i1}, \ldots, \mathbf{x}_{in_i}) = \int_{-\infty}^{\infty} \frac{e^{-\nu_i^2/2\sigma_\nu^2}}{\sqrt{2\pi}\sigma_\nu} \left\{ \prod_{t=1}^{n_i} F(y_{it}, \mathbf{x}_{it}\boldsymbol{\beta} + \nu_i) \right\} d\nu_i$$

where

$$F(y, z) = \begin{cases} 1 - \exp\left\{ - \exp(z) \right\} & \text{if } y \neq 0 \\ \exp\left\{ - \exp(z) \right\} & \text{otherwise} \end{cases}$$

The integral can be approximated with M-point Gauss–Hermite quadrature

$$\int_{-\infty}^{\infty} e^{-x^2} g(x)dx \approx \sum_{m=1}^{M} w_m^* g(a_m^*)$$

where the w_m^* denote the quadrature weights and the a_m^* the quadrature abscissas. The log likelihood, L, where $\rho = \sigma_\nu^2/(\sigma_\nu^2 + 1)$, is then calculated using the quadrature approximation

$$L = \sum_{i=1}^{n} w_i \log \left\{ \Pr(y_{i1}, \ldots, y_{in_i} | \mathbf{x}_{i1}, \ldots, \mathbf{x}_{in_i}) \right\}$$

$$\approx \sum_{i=1}^{n} w_i \log \left[\frac{1}{\sqrt{\pi}} \sum_{m=1}^{M} w_m^* \prod_{t=1}^{n_i} F \left\{ y_{it}, \mathbf{x}_{it}\boldsymbol{\beta} + a_m^* \left(\frac{2\rho}{1-\rho} \right)^{1/2} \right\} \right]$$

and where w_i is the user-specified weight for panel i; if no weights are specified, $w_i = 1$.

The above is the formula for nonadaptive Gauss–Hermite quadrature. The default is to calculate the log likelihood, L, using adaptive Gauss–Hermite quadrature, which transforms the integrand

$$g(y_{it}, x_{it}, \nu_i) = \frac{e^{-\nu_i^2/2\sigma_\nu^2}}{\sqrt{2\pi}\sigma_\nu} \left\{ \prod_{t=1}^{n_i} F(y_{it}, \mathbf{x}_{it}\boldsymbol{\beta} + \nu_i) \right\}$$

so that it is sampled on a suitable range; see Liu (1994).

Both quadrature formulas require that the integrated function be well approximated by a polynomial. The number of time periods (panel size) affects whether

$$\prod_{t=1}^{n_i} F(y_{it}, \mathbf{x}_{it}\boldsymbol{\beta} + \nu_i)$$

is well approximated by a polynomial. As panel size (or ρ) increases, the quadrature approximation becomes less accurate. Adaptive quadrature gives better results for correlated data and large panels than nonadaptive quadrature; however we recommend that you use the quadchk command to investigate the applicability of the numeric technique used in this command.

References

Liang, K.-Y. and S. L. Zeger. 1986. Longitudinal data analysis using generalized linear models. *Biometrika* 73: 13–22.

Liu, Qing and D. A. Pierce 1994. A note on Gauss–Hermite quadrature. *Biometrika* 81: 624–629.

Neuhaus, J. M. 1992. Statistical methods for longitudinal and clustered designs with binary responses. *Statistical Methods in Medical Research* 1: 249–273.

Neuhaus, J. M., J. D. Kalbfleisch, and W. W. Hauck. 1991. A comparison of cluster-specific and population-averaged approaches for analyzing correlated binary data. *International Statistical Review* 59: 25–35.

Pendergast, J. F., S. J. Gange, M. A. Newton, M. J. Lindstrom, M. Palta, and M. R. Fisher. 1996. A survey of methods for analyzing clustered binary response data. *International Statistical Review* 64: 89–118.

Also See

Complementary:	[XT] **xtcloglog postestimation**; [XT] **quadchk**, [XT] **xtdata**, [XT] **xtdes**, [XT] **xtsum**, [XT] **xttab**, [R] **constraint**
Related:	[XT] **xtgee**, [XT] **xtlogit**, [XT] **xtprobit**, [R] **cloglog**
Background:	[U] **11.1.10 Prefix commands**, [U] **20 Estimation and postestimation commands**, [XT] **estimation options**, [XT] **xt**, [R] **maximize**, [R] *vce_option*

Title

---
xtcloglog postestimation — Postestimation tools for xtcloglog
---

Description

The following postestimation commands are available for xtcloglog:

command	description
adjust[1]	adjusted predictions of $\mathbf{x}\beta$, probabilities, or $\exp(\mathbf{x}\beta)$
* estat	AIC, BIC, VCE, and estimation sample summary
estimates	cataloging estimation results
lincom	point estimates, standard errors, testing, and inference for linear combinations of coefficients
lrtest	likelihood-ratio test
mfx	marginal effects or elasticities
nlcom	point estimates, standard errors, testing, and inference for nonlinear combinations of coefficients
predict	predictions, residuals, influence statistics, and other diagnostic measures
predictnl	point estimates, standard errors, testing, and inference for generalized predictions
test	Wald tests for simple and composite linear hypotheses
testnl	Wald tests of nonlinear hypotheses

[1] adjust does not work with time-series operators.

* estat ic may not be used after xtcloglog, pa.

See the corresponding entries in the *Stata Base Reference Manual* for details.

Syntax for predict

Random-effects (RE) model

> predict [*type*] *newvar* [*if*] [*in*] [, *RE_statistics* <u>nooff</u>set]

Population-averaged (PA) model

> predict [*type*] *newvar* [*if*] [*in*] [, *PA_statistics* <u>nooff</u>set]

RE_statistics	description
xb	linear prediction; the default
pu0	probability of a positive outcome
stdp	standard error of the linear prediction

PA_statistics	description
mu	predicted probability of *depvar*; considers the offset(); the default
rate	predicted probability of *depvar*
xb	linear prediction
stdp	standard error of the linear prediction
score	first derivative of the log likelihood with respect to $x_j\beta$

These statistics are available both in and out of sample; type predict ... if e(sample) ... if wanted only for the estimation sample.

Options for predict

xb calculates the linear prediction. This is the default for the random-effects model.

pu0 calculates the probability of a positive outcome, assuming that the random effect for that observation's panel is zero ($\nu = 0$). Note that this may not be similar to the proportion of observed outcomes in the group.

stdp calculates the standard error of the linear prediction.

mu and rate both calculate the predicted probability of *depvar*. mu takes into account the offset(). rate ignores those adjustments. mu and rate are equivalent if you did not specify offset(). mu is the default for the population-averaged model.

score calculates the equation-level score, $u_j = \partial \ln L_j(\mathbf{x}_j\beta)/\partial(\mathbf{x}_j\beta)$.

nooffset is relevant only if you specified offset(*varname*) for xtcloglog. It modifies the calculations made by predict so that they ignore the offset variable; the linear prediction is treated as $\mathbf{x}_{it}\beta$ rather than $\mathbf{x}_{it}\beta + \text{offset}_{it}$.

Also See

Complementary:	[XT] **xtcloglog**,
	[R] **adjust**, [R] **estimates**, [R] **lincom**, [R] **lrtest**, [R] **mfx**,
	[R] **nlcom**, [R] **predictnl**, [R] **test**, [R] **testnl**
Background:	[U] **13.5 Accessing coefficients and standard errors**,
	[U] **20 Estimation and postestimation commands**,
	[R] **estat**, [R] **predict**

Title

xtdata — Faster specification searches with xt data

Syntax

xtdata [*varlist*] [*if*] [*in*] [, *options*]

options	description
Main	
i(*varname_i*)	use *varname_i* as the panel ID variable
re	convert data to a form suitable for random-effects estimation
ratio(#)	ratio of random effect to pure residual (standard deviations)
be	convert data to a form suitable for between estimation
fe	convert data to a form suitable for fixed-effects (within) estimation
nodouble	keep original variable type; default is to recast type as double
clear	overwrite current data in memory

Description

xtdata produces a transformed dataset of the variables specified in *varlist* or of all the variables in the data. Once the data are transformed, Stata's regress command may be used to perform specification searches more quickly than xtreg; see [R] **regress** and [XT] **xtreg**. Using xtdata, re also creates a variable named constant. When using regress after xtdata, re, specify noconstant and include constant in the regression. After xtdata, be and xtdata, fe, you need not include constant or specify regress's noconstant option.

Options

> Main

i(*varname_i*) specifies the variable name corresponding to i in $\mathbf{x}_{it}$. You can specify the i() option the first time you estimate, or you can use the iis command to set i() beforehand. Note that you need not specify i() if the data have been previously tsset or if iis has been previously specified—in these cases, the group variable is taken from the previous setting. See [XT] **xt**.

re specifies that the data are to be converted into a form suitable for random-effects estimation. re is the default if be, fe, or re is not specified. ratio() must also be specified.

ratio(#) (use with xtdata, re only) specifies the ratio $\sigma_\nu/\sigma_\epsilon$, which is the ratio of the random effect to the pure residual. Note that this is the ratio of the standard deviations, not the variances.

be specifies that the data are to be converted into a form suitable for between estimation.

fe specifies that the data are to be converted into a form suitable for fixed-effects (within) estimation.

nodouble specifies that transformed variables keep their original types, if possible. The default is to recast variables to double.

Remember that `xtdata` transforms variables to be differences from group means, pseudodifferences from group means, or group means. Specifying `nodouble` will decrease the size of the resulting dataset, but may introduce round-off errors in these calculations.

`clear` specifies that the data may be converted even though the dataset has changed since it was last saved on disk.

Remarks

If you have not read [XT] **xt** and [XT] **xtreg**, please do so.

The formal estimation commands of `xtreg`—see [XT] **xtreg**—do not produce results instantaneously, especially with large datasets. Equations (2), (3), and (4) of [XT] **xtreg** describe the data necessary to fit each of the models with OLS. The idea here is to transform the data once to the appropriate form and then use `regress` to fit such models more quickly.

▷ Example 1

We will use the example in [XT] **xtreg** demonstrating between-effects regression. An alternative way to estimate the between equation is to convert the data in memory to the between data:

```
. use http://www.stata-press.com/data/r9/nlswork, clear
(National Longitudinal Survey.  Young Women 14-26 years of age in 1968)
. generate age2=age^2
(24 missing values generated)
. generate ttl_exp2 = ttl_exp^2
. generate tenure2=tenure^2
(433 missing values generated)
. generate byte black = race==2
. xtdata ln_w grade age* ttl_exp* tenure* black not_smsa south, be clear i(id)
. regress ln_w grade age* ttl_exp* tenure* black not_smsa south
```

Source	SS	df	MS		
Model	415.021613	10	41.5021613		
Residual	431.954995	4686	.092179896		
Total	846.976608	4696	.180361288		

Number of obs = 4697
F(10, 4686) = 450.23
Prob > F = 0.0000
R-squared = 0.4900
Adj R-squared = 0.4889
Root MSE = .30361

ln_wage	Coef.	Std. Err.	t	P>|t|	[95% Conf. Interval]	
grade	.0607602	.0020006	30.37	0.000	.0568382	.0646822
age	.0323158	.0087251	3.70	0.000	.0152105	.0494211
age2	-.0005997	.0001429	-4.20	0.000	-.0008799	-.0003194
(output omitted)						
south	-.0993378	.010136	-9.80	0.000	-.1192091	-.0794665
_cons	.3339113	.1210434	2.76	0.006	.0966093	.5712133

The output is the same as that produced by `xtreg, be`; the reported R^2 is the R^2 between. Using `xtdata` followed by just one `regress` does not save time. Using `xtdata` is justified when you intend to explore the specification of the model by running many alternative regressions.

◁

❑ Technical Note

It is important that, when using `xtdata`, you eliminate any variables that you do not intend to use and that have missing values. `xtdata` follows a casewise-deletion rule, which means that an observation is excluded from the conversion if it is missing on any of the variables. In the example above, we specified that the variables be converted on the command line. Alternatively, we could drop the variables first, and it might even be useful to preserve our estimation sample:

```
. use http://www.stata-press.com/data/r9/nlswork, clear
(National Longitudinal Survey.  Young Women 14-26 years of age in 1968)
. generate age2 = age^2
(24 missing values generated)
. generate ttl_exp2 = ttl_exp^2
. generate tenure2 = tenure^2
(433 missing values generated)
. generate byte black = race==2
. keep id year ln_w grade age* ttl_exp* tenure* black not_smsa south
. tsset id year
        panel variable:  idcode, 1 to 5159
         time variable:  year, 68 to 88, but with gaps
. save xtdatasmpl
file xtdatasmpl.dta saved
```

❑

▷ Example 2

`xtdata` with the `fe` option converts the data so that results are equivalent to those from estimating by using `xtreg` with the `fe` option.

```
. use http://www.stata-press.com/data/r9/xtdatasmpl, clear
(National Longitudinal Survey.  Young Women 14-26 years of age in 1968)
. xtdata, fe
. regress ln_w grade age* ttl_exp* tenure* black not_smsa south
```

Source	SS	df	MS			Number of obs =	28091
						F(9, 28081) =	651.21
Model	412.443881	9	45.8270979			Prob > F =	0.0000
Residual	1976.12232	28081	.07037222			R-squared =	0.1727
						Adj R-squared =	0.1724
Total	2388.5662	28090	.085032617			Root MSE =	.26528

ln_wage	Coef.	Std. Err.	t	P>|t|	[95% Conf. Interval]	
grade	-.0147051	4.97e+08	-0.00	1.000	-9.75e+08	9.75e+08
age	.0359987	.0030904	11.65	0.000	.0299414	.0420559
age2	-.000723	.0000486	-14.88	0.000	-.0008183	-.0006277
(output omitted)						
south	-.0606309	.0099763	-6.08	0.000	-.0801849	-.0410769
_cons	1.221668	6.23e+09	0.00	1.000	-1.22e+10	1.22e+10

The coefficients reported by `regress` after `xtdata, fe` are the same as those reported by `xtreg, fe`, but the standard errors are slightly smaller. This is because no adjustment has been made to the estimated covariance matrix for the estimation of the person means. The difference is small, however, and results are adequate for a specification search.

◁

▷ Example 3

To use `xtdata, re`, you must specify the ratio $\sigma_\nu/\sigma_\epsilon$, which is the ratio of the standard deviations of the random effect and pure residual. Merely to show the relationship of `regress` after `xtdata, re` to `xtreg, re`, we will specify this ratio as $.25790313/.29069544 = .88719358$, which is the number `xtreg` reports when the model is fitted from the outset; see the random-effects example in [XT] **xtreg**. For specification searches, however, it is adequate to specify this number more crudely, and, when performing the specification search for this manual entry, we used `ratio(1)`.

```
. use http://www.stata-press.com/data/r9/xtdatasmpl, clear
(National Longitudinal Survey.  Young Women 14-26 years of age in 1968)
. xtdata, clear re ratio(.88719358)
```

		theta		
min	5%	median	95%	max
0.2520	0.2520	0.5499	0.7016	0.7206

`xtdata` reports the distribution of θ based on the specified ratio. If these were balanced data, θ would have been constant.

When running regressions with these data, you must specify the `noconstant` option and include the variable `constant`:

```
. regress ln_w grade age* ttl_exp* tenure* black not_smsa south constant,
> noconstant
```

Source	SS	df	MS		Number of obs =	28091
					F(11, 28080) =	14303.11
Model	13272.3241	11	1206.57492		Prob > F =	0.0000
Residual	2368.75918	28080	.084357521		R-squared =	0.8486
					Adj R-squared =	0.8485
Total	15641.0833	28091	.556800517		Root MSE =	.29044

ln_wage	Coef.	Std. Err.	t	P>|t|	[95% Conf. Interval]	
grade	.0646499	.0017811	36.30	0.000	.0611588	.068141
age	.0368059	.0031195	11.80	0.000	.0306915	.0429204
age2	-.0007133	.00005	-14.27	0.000	-.0008113	-.0006153
(output omitted)						
south	-.0868927	.0073031	-11.90	0.000	-.1012072	-.0725781
constant	.238721	.0494688	4.83	0.000	.1417598	.3356822

Results are the same coefficients and standard errors that `xtreg, re` previously estimated. The summaries at the top, however, should be ignored, as they are expressed in terms of (4) of [XT] **xtreg**, and, moreover, for a model without a constant.

◁

❑ Technical Note

Obviously, using `xtdata` requires some caution. The following guidelines may help:

1. `xtdata` is intended for use only during the specification search phase of analysis. Final results should be estimated with `xtreg` on unconverted data.

2. After converting the data, you may use `regress` to obtain estimates of the coefficients and their standard errors. In the case of `regress` after `xtdata, fe`, the standard errors are too small, but only slightly.

3. You may loosely interpret the coefficient's significance tests and confidence intervals. However, for results after `xtdata, fe` and `re`, an incorrect (but very close to correct) distribution is assumed.

4. You should ignore the summary statistics reported at the top of `regress`'s output.

5. After converting the data, you may form linear, but not nonlinear, combinations of regressors; that is, if your data contained age, it would not be correct to convert the data and then form age squared. All nonlinear transformations should be done before conversion. (For `xtdata, be`, you can get away with forming nonlinear combinations *ex post*, but the results will not be exact.) ❏

❏ Technical Note

The `xtdata` command can be used to help you examine data, especially with `scatter`.

```
. use http://www.stata-press.com/data/r9/xtdatasmpl, clear
(National Longitudinal Survey.  Young Women 14-26 years of age in 1968)
. xtdata, be
. scatter ln_wage age, title(Between data) msymbol(o) msize(tiny)
```

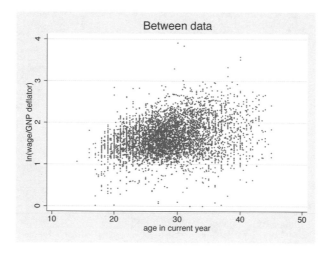

```
. use http://www.stata-press.com/data/r9/xtdatasmpl, clear
(National Longitudinal Survey. Young Women 14-26 years of age in 1968)
. xtdata, fe
. scatter ln_wage age, title(Within data) msymbol(o) msize(tiny)
```

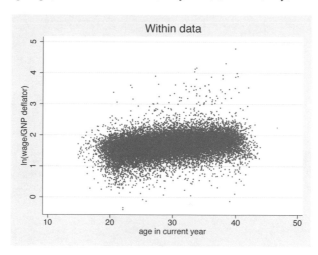

```
. use http://www.stata-press.com/data/r9/xtdatasmpl, clear
(National Longitudinal Survey. Young Women 14-26 years of age in 1968)
. scatter ln_wage age, title(Overall data) msymbol(o) msize(tiny)
```

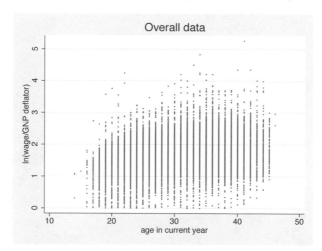

Methods and Formulas

xtdata is implemented as an ado-file.

(This section is a continuation of the *Methods and Formulas* of [XT] **xtreg**.)

xtdata, be, fe, and re transform the data according to (2), (3), and (4), respectively, of [XT] **xtreg**, except that xtdata, fe adds back in the overall mean, thus forming the transformation

$$\mathbf{x}_{it} - \overline{x}_i + \overline{\overline{x}}$$

xtdata, re requires the user to specify r as an estimate of $\sigma_\nu/\sigma_\epsilon$. θ_i is calculated from

$$\theta_i = 1 - \frac{1}{\sqrt{T_i r^2 + 1}}$$

Also See

Complementary: [XT] **xtreg**, [XT] **xtregar**,
                       [R] **regress**

Background: [XT] **xt**

Title

xtdes — Describe pattern of xt data

Syntax

xtdes $\big[$ *if* $\big]$ $\big[$ *in* $\big]$ $\big[$, *options* $\big]$

options	description
Main	
patterns(#)	maximum participation patterns; default is patterns(9)
i($varname_i$)	use $varname_i$ as the panel ID variable
t($varname_t$)	use $varname_t$ as the time variable
width(#)	display # width of participation patterns; default is width(100)

by may be used with xtdes; see [D] by.

Description

xtdes describes the participation pattern of cross-sectional time-series (xt) data.

Options

> Main

patterns(#) specifies the maximum number of participation patterns to be reported; patterns(9) is
the default. Specifying patterns(50) would list up to 50 patterns. Specifying patterns(1000)
is taken to mean patterns(∞); all the patterns will be listed.

i($varname_i$) specifies the variable name corresponding to i in x_{it}. You can specify the i() option
the first time you estimate, or you can use the iis command to set i() beforehand. Note that
you need not specify i() if the data have been previously tsset or if iis has been previously
specified—in these cases, the group variable is taken from the previous setting. See [XT] xt.

t($varname_t$) specifies the variable name corresponding to t in x_{it}. You can specify the t() option
the first time you estimate, or you can use the tis command to set t() beforehand. Note that
you need not specify t() if the data have been previously tsset or if tis has been previously
specified—in these cases, the group variable is taken from the previous setting. See [XT] xt.

width(#) specifies the maximum width of the participation patterns to be displayed; width(100) is
the default. The width of the display is determined by the range of the time variable and the minimum
time increment. The minimum time increment is displayed in the output as Delta(varname) =
d, where d is a real number. If the width of the display will exceed width() then d is computed
using the time range and width().

61

Remarks

If you have not read [XT] **xt**, please do so.

`xtdes` describes the cross-sectional and time-series aspects of the data in memory.

▷ Example 1

In [XT] **xt**, we introduced data based on a subsample of the NLSY data on young women aged 14–26 in 1968. Here is a description of the data used in many of the [XT] **xt** examples:

```
. use http://www.stata-press.com/data/r9/nlswork
(National Longitudinal Survey.  Young Women 14-26 years of age in 1968)

. xtdes, i(id) t(year)
   idcode:  1, 2, ..., 5159                              n =      4711
     year:  68, 69, ..., 88                              T =        15
            Delta(year) = 1; (88-68)+1 = 21
            (idcode*year uniquely identifies each observation)

Distribution of T_i:    min     5%    25%      50%    75%    95%     max
                          1      1      3        5      9     13      15

      Freq.  Percent    Cum. | Pattern
   ----------------------------------------------------
       136      2.89    2.89 | 1....................
       114      2.42    5.31 | ....................1
        89      1.89    7.20 | ................1.11
        87      1.85    9.04 | ..................11
        86      1.83   10.87 | 111111.1.11.1.11.1.11
        61      1.29   12.16 | ..............11.1.11
        56      1.19   13.35 | 11...................
        54      1.15   14.50 | .......1.11.1.11.1.11
        54      1.15   15.64 | ..............1.1.11
      3974     84.36  100.00 | (other patterns)
   ----------------------------------------------------
      4711    100.00         | XXXXXX.X.XX.X.XX.X.XX
```

`xtdes` tells us that we have 4,711 women in our data and that the `idcode` that identifies each ranges from 1 to 5,159. We are also told that the maximum number of individual years over which we observe any woman is 15. (The year variable, however, ranges over 21 years.) We are reassured that `idcode` and `year`, taken together, uniquely identify each observation in our data. We are also shown the distribution of T_i; 50% of our women are observed 5 years or less. Only 5% of our women are observed for 13 years or more.

Finally, we are shown the participation pattern. A 1 in the pattern means one observation that year; a dot means no observation. The largest fraction of our women (still only 2.89%) was observed in the single year 1968 and not thereafter; the next largest fraction was observed in 1988 but not before; and the next largest fraction was observed in 1985, 1987, and 1988.

At the bottom is the sum of the participation patterns, including the patterns that were not shown. We can see that none of the women were observed in six of the years (there are six dots). (The survey was not administered in those six years.)

We could see more of the patterns by specifying the `patterns()` option, or we could see all the patterns by specifying `patterns(1000)`.

◁

▷ Example 2

The strange participation patterns shown above have to do with our subsampling of the data, not with the administrators of the survey. Here are the data from which we drew the sample used in the [XT] **xt** examples:

```
. xtdes
    idcode:  1, 2, ..., 5159                                    n =        5159
      year:  68, 69, ..., 88                                    T =          15
             Delta(year) = 1; (88-68)+1 = 21
             (idcode*year does not uniquely identify observations)
 Distribution of T_i:     min      5%     25%     50%     75%     95%     max
                            1       2      11      15      16      19      30

      Freq.  Percent    Cum. |  Pattern
    -------------------------+---------------------------
       1034    20.04   20.04 |  111111.1.11.1.11.1.11
        153     2.97   23.01 |  1....................
        147     2.85   25.86 |  112111.1.11.1.11.1.11
        130     2.52   28.38 |  111112.1.11.1.11.1.11
        122     2.36   30.74 |  111211.1.11.1.11.1.11
        113     2.19   32.93 |  11...................
         84     1.63   34.56 |  111111.1.11.1.11.1.12
         79     1.53   36.09 |  111111.1.12.1.11.1.11
         67     1.30   37.39 |  111111.1.11.1.11.1.1.
       3230    62.61  100.00 |  (other patterns)
    -------------------------+---------------------------
       5159   100.00         |  XXXXXX.X.XX.X.XX.X.XX
```

Note that we have multiple observations per year. In the pattern, 2 indicates that a woman appears twice in the year, 3 indicates 3 times, and so on — **X** indicates 10 or more, should that be necessary.

In fact, this is a dataset that was itself extracted from the NLSY, in which t is not time but job number. In order to simplify exposition, we made a simpler dataset by selecting the last job in each year.

◁

Methods and Formulas

xtdes is implemented as an ado-file.

Also See

Related: [XT] **xtsum**, [XT] **xttab**

Background: [XT] **xt**

Title

> **xtfrontier** — Stochastic frontier models for panel data

Syntax

Time-invariant model

>   xtfrontier *depvar* [*indepvars*] [*if*] [*in*] [*weight*] , ti [*ti_options*]

Time-varying decay model

>   xtfrontier *depvar* [*indepvars*] [*if*] [*in*] [*weight*] , tvd [*tvd_options*]

ti_options	description
Model	
i(*varname_i*)	use *varname_i* as the panel ID variable
<u>nocon</u>stant	suppress constant term
ti	use time-invariant model; the default
cost	fit cost frontier model
<u>constr</u>aints(*constraints*)	apply specified linear constraints
SE	
vce(*vcetype*)	*vcetype* may be <u>boot</u>strap or jackknife
Reporting	
<u>l</u>evel(*#*)	set confidence level; default is level(95)
Max options	
maximize_options	control the maximization process; seldom used

tvd_options	description
Model	
i(*varname_i*)	use *varname_i* as the panel ID variable
t(*varname_t*)	use *varname_t* as the time variable
<u>nocon</u>stant	suppress constant term
tvd	use time-varying decay model
cost	fit cost frontier model
<u>constr</u>aints(*constraints*)	apply specified linear constraints
SE	
vce(*vcetype*)	*vcetype* may be <u>boot</u>strap or jackknife

Reporting

<u>level</u>(#)	set confidence level; default is level(95)

Max options

maximize_options	control the maximization process; seldom used

You must tsset your data before using xtfrontier; see [TS] **tsset**.

depvar and *indepvars* may contain time-series operators; see [U] **11.4.3 Time-series varlists**.

fweights and iweights are allowed; see [U] **11.1.6 weight**.

bootstrap, by, jackknife, statsby, xi may be used with xtfrontier; see [U] **11.1.10 Prefix commands**.

See [U] **20 Estimation and postestimation commands** for additional capabilities of estimation commands.

Description

xtfrontier fits stochastic production or cost frontier models for panel data. More precisely, xtfrontier estimates the parameters of a linear model with a disturbance generated by specific mixture distributions.

The disturbance term in a stochastic frontier model is assumed to have two components. One component is assumed to have a strictly non-negative distribution, and the other component is assumed to have a symmetric distribution. In the econometrics literature, the non-negative component is often referred to as the *inefficiency term*, and the component with the symmetric distribution as the *idiosyncratic error*. xtfrontier permits two different parameterizations of the inefficiency term: a time-invariant model and the Battese–Coelli (1992) parameterization of time effects. In the time-invariant model, the inefficiency term is assumed to have a truncated-normal distribution. In the Battese–Coelli (1992) parameterization of time effects, the inefficiency term is modeled as a truncated-normal random variable multiplied by a specific function of time. In both models, the idiosyncratic error term is assumed to have a normal distribution. The only panel-specific effect is the random inefficiency term.

See Kumbhakar and Lovell (2000) for a detailed introduction to frontier analysis.

Options for time-invariant model

    Model

i(*varname_i*); see [XT] **estimation options**.

ti specifies that the parameters of the time-invariant technical inefficiency model be estimated.

noconstant; see [XT] **estimation options**.

cost specifies that the frontier model be fitted in terms of a cost function instead of a production function. By default, xtfrontier fits a production frontier model.

constraints(*constraints*); see [XT] **estimation options**.

    SE

vce(*vcetype*); see [R] *vce_option*.

    Reporting

level(#); see [XT] **estimation options**.

⌐ Max options ⌐

maximize_options: <u>difficult</u>, <u>tech</u>nique(*algorithm_spec*), <u>iter</u>ate(*#*), [<u>no</u>]<u>log</u>, <u>tra</u>ce, <u>grad</u>ient, <u>showstep</u>, <u>hess</u>ian, <u>shownr</u>tolerance, <u>tol</u>erance(*#*), <u>ltol</u>erance(*#*), <u>gtol</u>erance(*#*), <u>nrtol</u>erance(*#*), <u>nonrtol</u>erance, <u>from</u>(*init_specs*); see [R] **maximize**. These options are seldom used.

Options for time-varying decay model

⌐ Model ⌐

i(*varname_i*), t(*varname*); see [XT] **estimation options**.

<u>noc</u>onstant; see [XT] **estimation options**.

tvd specifies that the parameters of the time-varying decay model be estimated.

cost specifies that the frontier model be fitted in terms of a cost function instead of a production function. By default, xtfrontier fits a production frontier model.

<u>constraints</u>(*constraints*); see [XT] **estimation options**.

⌐ SE ⌐

vce(*vcetype*); see [R] **vce_option**.

⌐ Reporting ⌐

<u>level</u>(*#*); see [XT] **estimation options**.

⌐ Max options ⌐

maximize_options: <u>difficult</u>, <u>tech</u>nique(*algorithm_spec*), <u>iter</u>ate(*#*), [<u>no</u>]<u>log</u>, <u>tra</u>ce, <u>hess</u>ian, <u>grad</u>ient, <u>showstep</u>, <u>shownr</u>tolerance, <u>tol</u>erance(*#*), <u>ltol</u>erance(*#*), <u>gtol</u>erance(*#*), <u>nrtol</u>erance(*#*), <u>nonrtol</u>erance, <u>from</u>(*init_specs*); see [R] **maximize**. These options are seldom used.

Remarks

Remarks are presented under the headings

>   *Introduction*
>   *Time-invariant model*
>   *Time-varying decay model*

Introduction

Stochastic production frontier models were introduced by Aigner, Lovell, and Schmidt (1977) and Meeusen and van den Broeck (1977). Since then, stochastic frontier models have become a popular subfield in econometrics; see Kumbhakar and Lovell (2000) for an introduction. xtfrontier fits two stochastic frontier models with distinct specifications of the inefficiency term and can fit both production- and cost-frontier models.

Let's review the nature of the stochastic frontier problem. Suppose that a producer has a production function $f(\mathbf{z}_{it}, \beta)$. In a world without error or inefficiency, in time t, the ith firm would produce

$$q_{it} = f(\mathbf{z}_{it}, \beta)$$

A fundamental element of stochastic frontier analysis is that each firm potentially produces less than it might due to a degree of inefficiency. Specifically,

$$q_{it} = f(\mathbf{z}_{it}, \beta)\xi_{it}$$

where ξ_{it} is the level of efficiency for firm i at time t; ξ_i must be in the interval $(0, 1]$. If $\xi_{it} = 1$, the firm is achieving the optimal output with the technology embodied in the production function $f(\mathbf{z}_{it}, \beta)$. When $\xi_{it} < 1$, the firm is not making the most of the inputs $\mathbf{z}_{it}$ given the technology embodied in the production function $f(\mathbf{z}_{it}, \beta)$. Since the output is assumed to be strictly positive (i.e., $q_{it} > 0$), the degree of technical efficiency is assumed to be strictly positive (i.e., $\xi_{it} > 0$).

Output is also assumed to be subject to random shocks, implying that

$$q_{it} = f(\mathbf{z}_{it}, \beta)\xi_{it}\exp(v_{it})$$

Taking the natural log of both sides yields

$$\ln(q_{it}) = \ln\{f(\mathbf{z}_{it}, \beta)\} + \ln(\xi_{it}) + v_{it}$$

Assuming that there are k inputs and that the production function is linear in logs, defining $u_{it} = -\ln(\xi_{it})$ yields

$$\ln(q_{it}) = \beta_0 + \sum_{j=1}^{k} \beta_j \ln(z_{jit}) + v_{it} - u_{it} \qquad (1)$$

Since u_{it} is subtracted from $\ln(q_{it})$, restricting $u_{it} \geq 0$ implies that $0 < \xi_{it} \leq 1$, as specified above.

Kumbhakar and Lovell (2000) provide a detailed version of this derivation, and they show that performing an analogous derivation in the dual cost function problem allows us to specify the problem as

$$\ln(c_{it}) = \beta_0 + \beta_q \ln(q_{it}) + \sum_{j=1}^{k} \beta_j \ln(p_{jit}) + v_{it} - su_{it} \qquad (2)$$

where q_{it} is output, the z_{jit} are input quantities , c_{it} is cost, the p_{jit} are input prices, and

$$s = \begin{cases} 1, & \text{for production functions} \\ -1, & \text{for cost functions} \end{cases}$$

Intuitively, the inefficiency effect is required to lower output or raise expenditure, depending on the specification.

❑ Technical Note

The model that `xtfrontier` actually fits has the form

$$y_{it} = \beta_0 + \sum_{j=1}^{k} \beta_j x_{jit} + v_{it} - su_{it}$$

so in the context of the discussion above, $y_{it} = \ln(q_{it})$ and $x_{jit} = \ln(z_{jit})$ for a production function; for a cost function, $y_{it} = \ln(c_{it})$, the x_{jit} are the $\ln(p_{jit})$, and $\ln(q_{it})$. You must perform the natural logarithm transformation of the data before estimation to interpret the estimation results correctly for a stochastic frontier production or cost model. xtfrontier does not perform any transformations on the data.

❏

Equation (2) is a variant of a panel-data model in which v_{it} is the idiosyncratic error and u_{it} is a time-varying panel-level effect. Much of the literature on this model has focused on deriving estimators for different specifications of the u_{it} term. Kumbhakar and Lovell (2000) provide a survey of this literature.

xtfrontier provides estimators for two different specifications of u_{it}. To facilitate the discussion, let $N^+(\mu, \sigma^2)$ denote the truncated-normal distribution, which is truncated at zero with mean μ and variance σ^2, and let $\overset{\text{iid}}{\sim}$ stand for independently and identically distributed.

Consider the simplest specification in which u_{it} is a time-invariant truncated-normal random variable. In the time-invariant model, $u_{it} = u_i$, $u_i \overset{\text{iid}}{\sim} N^+(\mu, \sigma_\mu^2)$, $v_{it} \overset{\text{iid}}{\sim} N(0, \sigma_v^2)$, and u_i and v_{it} are distributed independently of each other and the covariates in the model. Specifying option ti causes xtfrontier to estimate the parameters of this model.

In the time-varying decay specification,

$$u_{it} = \exp\{-\eta(t - T_i)\}u_i$$

where T_i is the last time period in the ith panel, η is the decay parameter, $u_i \overset{\text{iid}}{\sim} N^+(\mu, \sigma_\mu^2)$, $v_{it} \overset{\text{iid}}{\sim} N(0, \sigma_v^2)$, and u_i and v_{it} are distributed independently of each other and the covariates in the model. Specifying option tvd causes xtfrontier to estimate the parameters of this model.

Time-invariant model

▷ Example 1

xtfrontier, ti provides maximum likelihood estimates for the parameters of the time-invariant decay model. In this model, the inefficiency effects are modeled as $u_{it} = u_i$, $u_i \overset{\text{iid}}{\sim} N^+(\mu, \sigma_\mu^2)$, $v_{it} \overset{\text{iid}}{\sim} N(0, \sigma_v^2)$, and u_i and v_{it} are distributed independently of each other and the covariates in the model. In this example, firms produce a product called a widget, using a constant-returns-to-scale technology. We have 948 observations—91 firms, with 6–14 observations per firm. Our dataset contains variables representing the quantity of widgets produced, the number of machine hours used in production, the number of labor hours used in production, and three additional variables that are the natural logarithm transformations of the three aforementioned variables.

We fit a time-invariant model using the transformed variables:

```
. use http://www.stata-press.com/data/r9/xtfrontier1

. xtfrontier lnwidgets lnmachines lnworkers, ti
Iteration 0:   log likelihood = -1473.8703
Iteration 1:   log likelihood = -1473.0565
Iteration 2:   log likelihood = -1472.6155
Iteration 3:   log likelihood =  -1472.607
Iteration 4:   log likelihood = -1472.6069
```

```
Time-invariant inefficiency model          Number of obs      =        948
Group variable (i): id                     Number of groups   =         91
Time variable (t): t                       Obs per group: min =          6
                                                          avg =       10.4
                                                          max =         14
                                           Wald chi2(2)       =     661.76
Log likelihood   = -1472.6069              Prob > chi2        =     0.0000
```

lnwidgets	Coef.	Std. Err.	z	P>|z|	[95% Conf. Interval]	
lnmachines	.2904551	.0164219	17.69	0.000	.2582688	.3226415
lnworkers	.2943333	.0154352	19.07	0.000	.2640808	.3245858
_cons	3.030983	.1441022	21.03	0.000	2.748548	3.313418
/mu	1.125667	.6479217	1.74	0.082	-.144236	2.39557
/lnsigma2	1.421979	.2672745	5.32	0.000	.898131	1.945828
/ilgtgamma	1.138685	.3562642	3.20	0.001	.4404204	1.83695
sigma2	4.145318	1.107938			2.455011	6.999424
gamma	.7574382	.0654548			.6083592	.8625876
sigma_u2	3.139822	1.107235			.9696821	5.309962
sigma_v2	1.005496	.0484143			.9106055	1.100386

In addition to the coefficients, the output reports estimates for the parameters `sigma_v2`, `sigma_u2`, `gamma`, `sigma2`, `ilgtgamma`, `lnsigma2`, and `mu`. `sigma_v2` is the estimate of σ_v^2. `sigma_u2` is the estimate of σ_u^2. `gamma` is the estimate of $\gamma = \sigma_u^2/\sigma_S^2$. `sigma2` is the estimate of $\sigma_S^2 = \sigma_v^2 + \sigma_u^2$. Since γ must be between 0 and 1, the optimization is parameterized in terms of the inverse logit of γ, and this estimate is reported as `ilgtgamma`. Since σ_S^2 must be positive, the optimization is parameterized in terms of $\ln(\sigma_S^2)$, and this estimate is reported as `lnsigma2`. Finally, `mu` is the estimate of μ.

◁

❏ Technical Note

Our simulation results indicate that this estimator requires relatively large samples to achieve any reasonable degree of precision in the estimates of μ and $\sigma_\mu{}^2$.

❏

Time-varying decay model

`xtfrontier, tvd` provides maximum likelihood estimates for the parameters of the time-varying decay model. In this model, the inefficiency effects are modeled as

$$u_{it} = \exp\{-\eta(t - T_i)\}u_i$$

where $u_i \stackrel{iid}{\sim} N^+(\mu, \sigma_\mu^2)$.

When $\eta > 0$, the degree of inefficiency decreases over time; when $\eta < 0$, the degree of inefficiency increases over time. Since $t = T_i$ in the last period, the last period for firm i contains the base level of inefficiency for that firm. If $\eta > 0$, the level of inefficiency decays toward the base level. If $\eta < 0$, the level of inefficiency increases to the base level.

▷ Example 2

When $\eta = 0$, the time-varying decay model reduces to the time-invariant model. The following example illustrates this property and demonstrates how to specify constraints and starting values in these models.

Let's begin by fitting the time-varying decay model on the same data that were used in the previous example for the time-invariant model.

```
. xtfrontier lnwidgets lnmachines lnworkers, tvd
Iteration 0:    log likelihood = -1551.3798  (not concave)
Iteration 1:    log likelihood = -1502.2637
Iteration 2:    log likelihood = -1476.3093  (not concave)
Iteration 3:    log likelihood = -1472.9845
Iteration 4:    log likelihood = -1472.5365
Iteration 5:    log likelihood =  -1472.529
Iteration 6:    log likelihood = -1472.5289
```

Time-varying decay inefficiency model				Number of obs	=	948
Group variable (i): id				Number of groups	=	91
Time variable (t): t				Obs per group: min =		6
				avg =		10.4
				max =		14
				Wald chi2(2)	=	661.93
Log likelihood = -1472.5289				Prob > chi2	=	0.0000

lnwidgets	Coef.	Std. Err.	z	P>|z|	[95% Conf. Interval]	
lnmachines	.2907555	.0164376	17.69	0.000	.2585384	.3229725
lnworkers	.2942412	.0154373	19.06	0.000	.2639846	.3244978
_cons	3.028939	.1436046	21.09	0.000	2.74748	3.310399
/mu	1.110831	.6452809	1.72	0.085	-.1538967	2.375558
/eta	.0016764	.00425	0.39	0.693	-.0066535	.0100064
/lnsigma2	1.410723	.2679485	5.26	0.000	.885554	1.935893
/ilgtgamma	1.123982	.3584243	3.14	0.002	.4214828	1.82648
sigma2	4.098919	1.098299			2.424327	6.930228
gamma	.7547265	.0663495			.603838	.8613419
sigma_u2	3.093563	1.097606			.9422943	5.244832
sigma_v2	1.005356	.0484079			.9104785	1.100234

The estimate of η is very close to zero, and the other estimates are not too far from those of the time-invariant model.

We can use **constraint define** to constrain $\eta = 0$ and obtain the same results produced by the time-invariant model. Although there is only one statistical equation to be estimated in this model, the model fits five of Stata's [R] **ml** equations; see [R] **ml** or Gould, Pitblado, and Sribney (2003). The equation names can be seen by listing the matrix of estimated coefficients.

```
. matrix list e(b)

e(b)[1,7]
        lnwidgets:   lnwidgets:   lnwidgets:    lnsigma2:   ilgtgamma:          mu:
        lnmachines    lnworkers        _cons        _cons        _cons        _cons
y1     .29075546     .2942412    3.0289395    1.4107233    1.1239816    1.1108307

              eta:
            _cons
y1       .00167642
```

To constrain a parameter to a particular value in any equation, except the first equation, you must specify both the equation name and the parameter name using the syntax

constraint define # [*eqname*] _b[*varname*] = *value*   or

constraint define # [*eqname*] *coefficient* = *value*

where *eqname* is the equation name, *varname* is the name of variable in a linear equation, and *coefficient* refers to any parameter that has been estimated. More elaborate specifications with expressions are possible; see the example with constant returns to scale below, and see [R] **constraint** for general reference.

Suppose that we impose the constraint $\eta = 0$; we get the same results as those reported above for the time-invariant model, except for some minute differences attributable to an alternate convergence path in the optimization.

```
. constraint define 1 [eta]_cons = 0

. xtfrontier lnwidgets lnmachines lnworkers, tvd constraints(1)

Iteration 0:   log likelihood = -1540.7124  (not concave)
Iteration 1:   log likelihood = -1515.7726
Iteration 2:   log likelihood = -1473.0162
Iteration 3:   log likelihood = -1472.9223
Iteration 4:   log likelihood = -1472.6254
Iteration 5:   log likelihood =  -1472.607
Iteration 6:   log likelihood = -1472.6069
```

Time-varying decay inefficiency model		Number of obs	=	948
Group variable (i): id		Number of groups	=	91
Time variable (t): t		Obs per group: min =		6
		avg =		10.4
		max =		14
		Wald chi2(2)	=	661.76
Log likelihood = -1472.6069		Prob > chi2	=	0.0000

lnwidgets	Coef.	Std. Err.	z	P>|z|	[95% Conf. Interval]	
lnmachines	.2904551	.0164219	17.69	0.000	.2582688	.3226414
lnworkers	.2943332	.0154352	19.07	0.000	.2640807	.3245857
_cons	3.030963	.1440995	21.03	0.000	2.748534	3.313393
/mu	1.125507	.6480444	1.74	0.082	-.1446369	2.39565
/eta	0	.	.	.	.	.
/lnsigma2	1.422039	.2673128	5.32	0.000	.8981155	1.945962
/ilgtgamma	1.138764	.3563076	3.20	0.001	.4404135	1.837114
sigma2	4.145565	1.108162			2.454972	7.000366
gamma	.7574526	.0654602			.6083575	.862607
sigma_u2	3.140068	1.107459			.9694878	5.310649
sigma_v2	1.005496	.0484143			.9106057	1.100386

◁

Saved Results

xtfrontier saves in e():

Scalars

e(N)	number of observations	e(chi2)	χ^2
e(k)	number of estimated parameters	e(sigma_u)	standard deviation of
e(k_eq)	number of equations		technical inefficiency
e(k_dv)	number of dependent variables	e(sigma_v)	standard deviation of random error
e(df_m)	model degrees of freedom	e(rank)	rank of e(V)
e(ll)	log likelihood	e(p)	model significance
e(rc)	return code	e(ic)	number of iterations

Macros

e(cmd)	xtfrontier	e(chi2type)	Wald; type of model χ^2 test
e(depvar)	name of dependent variable	e(vce)	vcetype specified in vce()
e(title)	name of model	e(vcetype)	title used to label Std. Err.
e(function)	production or cost	e(opt)	type of optimization
e(model)	ti, after time-invariant model; tvd,	e(ml_method)	type of ml method
	after time-varying decay model	e(user)	name of likelihood-evaluator program
e(ivar)	variable denoting groups	(e(technique)	maximization technique
e(tvar)	variable denoting time periods	e(crittype)	optimization criterion
e(wtype)	weight type	e(properties)	b V
e(wexp)	weight expression	e(predict)	program used to implement predict

Matrices

e(b)	coefficient vector	e(V)	variance–covariance matrix
e(ilog)	iteration log (up to 20 iterations)		of the estimators

Functions

e(sample)	marks estimation sample

Methods and Formulas

xtfrontier is implemented as an ado-file.

xtfrontier fits stochastic frontier models for panel data that can be expressed as

$$y_{it} = \beta_0 + \sum_{j=1}^{k} \beta_j x_{jit} + v_{it} - su_{it}$$

where y_{it} is the natural logarithm of output, the x_{jit} are the natural logarithm of the input quantities for the production efficiency problem, y_{it} is the natural logarithm of costs, the x_{it} are the natural logarithm of input prices for the cost efficiency problem, and

$$s = \begin{cases} 1, & \text{for production functions} \\ -1, & \text{for cost functions} \end{cases}$$

For the time-varying decay model, the log-likelihood function is derived as

$$
\ln L = -\frac{1}{2}\left(\sum_{i=1}^{N} T_i\right)\{\ln(2\pi) + \ln(\sigma_S^2)\} - \frac{1}{2}\sum_{i=1}^{N}(T_i - 1)\ln(1-\gamma)
$$

$$
- \frac{1}{2}\sum_{i=1}^{N}\ln\left\{1 + \left(\sum_{t=1}^{T_i}\eta_{it}^2 - 1\right)\gamma\right\} - N\ln\{1 - \Phi(-\widetilde{z})\} - \frac{1}{2}N\widetilde{z}^2
$$

$$
+ \sum_{i=1}^{N}\ln\{1 - \Phi(-z_i^*)\} + \frac{1}{2}\sum_{i=1}^{N}z_i^{*2} - \frac{1}{2}\sum_{i=1}^{N}\sum_{t=1}^{T_i}\frac{\epsilon_{it}^2}{(1-\gamma)\sigma_S^2}
$$

where $\sigma_S = (\sigma_u^2 + \sigma_v^2)^{1/2}$, $\gamma = \sigma_u^2/\sigma_S^2$, $\epsilon_{it} = y_{it} - \mathbf{x}_{it}\boldsymbol{\beta}$, $\eta_{it} = \exp\{-\eta(t - T_i)\}$, $\widetilde{z} = \mu/\left(\gamma\sigma_S^2\right)^{1/2}$, $\Phi()$ is the cumulative distribution function of the standard normal distribution, and

$$
z_i^* = \frac{\mu(1-\gamma) - s\gamma\sum_{t=1}^{T_i}\eta_{it}\epsilon_{it}}{\left[\gamma(1-\gamma)\sigma_S^2\left\{1 + \left(\sum_{t=1}^{T_i}\eta_{it}^2 - 1\right)\gamma\right\}\right]^{1/2}}
$$

Maximizing the above log likelihood estimates the coefficients η, μ, σ_v, and σ_u.

References

Aigner, D. J., C. A. K. Lovell, and P. Schmidt. 1977. Formulation and estimation of stochastic frontier production function models. *Journal of Econometrics* 6: 21–37.

Battese, G. E. and T. J. Coelli. 1992. Frontier production functions, technical efficiency and panel data: with applications to paddy farmers in India. *Journal of Productivity Analysis* 3: 153–169.

———. 1995. A model for technical inefficiency effects in a stochastic frontier production for panel data. *Empirical Economics* 20: 325–332.

Caudill, S. B., J. M. Ford, and D. M. Gropper. 1995. Frontier estimation and firm-specific inefficiency measures in the presence of heteroskedasticity. *Journal of Business and Economic Statistics* 13(1): 105–111.

Coelli, T. J. 1995. Estimators and hypothesis tests for a stochastic frontier function: A Monte Carlo analysis. *Journal of Productivity Analysis* 6(4): 247–268.

Coelli, T. J., D. S. P. Rao, and G. E. Battese. 1998. *An Introduction to Efficiency and Productivity Analysis*. Boston: Kluwer.

Gould, W. W., J. S. Pitblado, and W. S. Sribney. 2003. *Maximum Likelihood Estimation with Stata*. 2nd ed. College Station, TX: Stata Press.

Kumbhakar, S. C. and C. A. K. Lovell. 2000. *Stochastic Frontier Analysis*. Cambridge: Cambridge University Press.

Meeusen, W. and J. van den Broeck. 1977. Efficiency estimation from Cobb–Douglas production functions with composed error. *International Economic Review* 18: 435–444.

Zellner, A. and N. Revankar. 1970. Generalized production functions. *Review of Economic Studies* 37: 241–250.

(Continued on next page)

Also See

Complementary:	[XT] **xtfrontier postestimation**, [R] **constraint**, [TS] **tsset**
Related:	[XT] **xtreg**, [R] **frontier**, [R] **regress**
Background:	[U] **11.1.10 Prefix commands**, [U] **20 Estimation and postestimation commands**, [XT] **estimation options**, [XT] **xt**, [R] **maximize**, [R] *vce_option*

Title

xtfrontier postestimation — Postestimation tools for xtfrontier

Description

The following postestimation commands are available for xtfrontier:

command	description
adjust[1]	adjusted predictions of $\mathbf{x}\beta$
estat	AIC, BIC, VCE, and estimation sample summary
estimates	cataloging estimation results
lincom	point estimates, standard errors, testing, and inference for linear combinations of coefficients
lrtest	likelihood-ratio test
mfx	marginal effects or elasticities
nlcom	point estimates, standard errors, testing, and inference for nonlinear combinations of coefficients
predict	predictions, residuals, influence statistics, and other diagnostic measures
predictnl	point estimates, standard errors, testing, and inference for generalized predictions
test	Wald tests for simple and composite linear hypotheses
testnl	Wald tests of nonlinear hypotheses

[1] adjust does not work with time-series operators.

See the corresponding entries in the *Stata Base Reference Manual* for details.

Syntax for predict

predict [*type*] *newvar* [*if*] [*in*] [, *statistic*]

statistic	description
xb	$\mathbf{x}_j\mathbf{b}$, fitted value; the default
stdp	standard error of the prediction
u	estimates of minus the natural log of the technical efficiency via $E\left(u_{it} \mid \epsilon_{it}\right)$
m	estimates of minus the natural log of the technical efficiency via $M\left(u_{it} \mid \epsilon_{it}\right)$
te	estimates of the technical efficiency via $E\left\{\exp(-su_{it}) \mid \epsilon_{it}\right\}$

where

$$s = \begin{cases} 1, & \text{for production functions} \\ -1, & \text{for cost functions} \end{cases}$$

Options for predict

xb, the default, calculates the linear prediction.

stdp requests prediction of the standard error of linear prediction.

u produces estimates of minus the natural log of the technical efficiency via $E\left(u_{it} \mid \epsilon_{it}\right)$.

m produces estimates of minus the natural log of the technical efficiency via the mode, $M\left(u_{it} \mid \epsilon_{it}\right)$.

te produces estimates of the technical efficiency via $E\left\{\exp(-su_{it}) \mid \epsilon_{it}\right\}$.

Methods and Formulas

All postestimation commands listed above are implemented as ado-files.

Continuing from the *Methods and Formulas* section of [XT] **xtfrontier**, estimates for u_{it} can be obtained from the mean or the mode of the conditional distribution $f(u|\epsilon)$.

$$E\left(u_{it} \mid \epsilon_{it}\right) = \widetilde{\mu}_i + \widetilde{\sigma}_i \left\{ \frac{\phi\left(-\widetilde{\mu}_i/\widetilde{\sigma}_i\right)}{1 - \Phi\left(-\widetilde{\mu}_i/\widetilde{\sigma}_i\right)} \right\}$$

$$M\left(u_{it} \mid \epsilon_{it}\right) = \begin{cases} -\widetilde{\mu}_i, & \text{if } \widetilde{\mu}_i >= 0 \\ 0, & \text{otherwise} \end{cases}$$

where

$$\widetilde{\mu}_i = \frac{\mu\sigma_v^2 - s\sum_{t=1}^{T_i} \eta_{it}\epsilon_{it}\sigma_u^2}{\sigma_v^2 + \sum_{t=1}^{T_i} \eta_{it}^2\sigma_u^2}$$

$$\widetilde{\sigma}_i^2 = \frac{\sigma_v^2\sigma_u^2}{\sigma_v^2 + \sum_{t=1}^{T_i} \eta_{it}^2\sigma_u^2}$$

These estimates can be obtained from predict *newvar*, u and predict *newvar*, m, respectively, and are calculated by plugging in the estimated parameters.

predict *newvar*, te produces estimates of the technical-efficiency term. These estimates are obtained from

$$E\left\{\exp(-su_{it}) \mid \epsilon_{it}\right\} = \left[\frac{1 - \Phi\left\{s\eta_{it}\widetilde{\sigma}_i - (\widetilde{\mu}_i/\ \widetilde{\sigma}_i)\right\}}{1 - \Phi\left(-\widetilde{\mu}_i/\ \widetilde{\sigma}_i\right)}\right] \exp\left(-s\eta_{it}\widetilde{\mu}_i + \frac{1}{2}\eta_{it}^2\widetilde{\sigma}_i^2\right)$$

Replacing $\eta_{it} = 1$ and $\eta = 0$ in these formulas produces the formulas for the time-invariant models.

Also See

Complementary:	[XT] **xtfrontier**,
	[R] **adjust**, [R] **estimates**, [R] **lincom**, [R] **lrtest**, [R] **mfx**,
	[R] **nlcom**, [R] **predictnl**, [R] **test**, [R] **testnl**
Background:	[U] **13.5 Accessing coefficients and standard errors**,
	[U] **20 Estimation and postestimation commands**,
	[R] **estat**, [R] **predict**

Title

xtgee — Fit population-averaged panel-data models using GEE

Syntax

xtgee *depvar* [*indepvars*] [*if*] [*in*] [*weight*] [, *options*]

options	description
Model	
i(*varname_i*)	use *varname_i* as the panel ID variable
t(*varname_t*)	use *varname_t* as the time variable
<u>f</u>amily(*family*)	distribution of *depvar*; see table below
<u>l</u>ink(*link*)	link function; see table below
Model 2	
<u>e</u>xposure(*varname*)	include ln(*varname*) in model with coefficient constrained to 1
<u>off</u>set(*varname*)	include *varname* in model with coefficient constrained to 1
<u>nocons</u>tant	suppress constant term
force	estimate even if observations unequally spaced in time
Correlation	
<u>c</u>orr(*correlation*)	within-group correlation structure; see table below
SE/Robust	
vce(*vcetype*)	*vcetype* may be <u>r</u>obust, <u>b</u>ootstrap, or <u>jack</u>knife
<u>r</u>obust	synonym for vce(robust)
nmp	use divisor $N - P$ instead of the default N
rgf	multiply the robust variance estimate by $(N - 1)/(N - P)$
<u>sca</u>le(x2)	set scale parameter to Pearson chi-squared statistic
<u>sca</u>le(dev)	set scale parameter to deviance divided by degrees of freedom
<u>sca</u>le(phi)	do not rescale the variance
<u>sca</u>le(#)	set scale parameter to #
Reporting	
<u>l</u>evel(#)	set confidence level; default is level(95)
<u>ef</u>orm	report exponentiated coefficients
Opt options	
optimize_options	control the optimization process; seldom used
†<u>nodi</u>splay	suppress display of header and coefficients

† nodisplay is not shown in the dialog box.

depvar and *indepvars* may contain time-series operators; see [U] **11.4 varlists**.

bootstrap, by, jackknife, statsby, and xi may be used with xtgee; see [U] **11.1.10 Prefix commands**.

iweights, fweights, and pweights are allowed; see [U] **11.1.6 weight**. Weights must be constant within panels.

See [U] **20 Estimation and postestimation commands** for additional capabilities of estimation commands.

family	description
<u>gau</u>ssian	Gaussian (normal); family(normal) is a synonym
<u>i</u>gaussian	inverse Gaussian
<u>b</u>inomial[#	*varname*]	Bernoulli/binomial
<u>po</u>isson	Poisson
<u>nb</u>inomial[#]	negative binomial
<u>gamma</u>	gamma

link	link function/definition
<u>i</u>dentity	identity; $y = y$
<u>log</u>	log; $\ln(y)$
<u>logit</u>	logit; $\ln\{y/(1-y)\}$, natural log of the odds
<u>p</u>robit	probit; $\Phi^{-1}(y)$, where $\Phi()$ is the normal cumulative distribution
<u>c</u>loglog	cloglog; $\ln\{-\ln(1-y)\}$
<u>pow</u>er[#]	power; y^k with $k = \#$; $\# = 1$ if not specified
<u>opo</u>wer[#]	odds power; $[\{y/(1-y)\}^k - 1]/k$ with $k = \#$; $\# = 1$ if not specified
<u>nb</u>inomial	negative binomial; $\ln\{y/(y+\alpha)\}$
<u>rec</u>iprocal	reciprocal; $1/y$

correlation	description
<u>exc</u>hangeable	exchangeable
<u>ind</u>ependent	independent
<u>uns</u>tructured	unstructured
<u>fix</u>ed *matname*	user-specified
ar #	autoregressive of order #
<u>stat</u>ionary #	stationary of order #
<u>non</u>stationary #	nonstationary of order #

For example,

```
. xtgee y x1 x2, family(gauss) link(ident) corr(exchangeable) i(id)
```

would estimate a random-effects linear regression—note that corr(exchangeable) does not provide random effects. It actually fits an equal-correlation population-averaged model equivalent to the random-effects model for linear regression.

Description

xtgee fits population-averaged panel-data models. In particular, xtgee fits general linear models and allows you to specify the within-group correlation structure for the panels.

See [R] **logistic** and [R] **regress** for lists of related estimation commands.

Options

    ⌐ Model ⌐

i(*varname$_i$*), t(*varname$_t$*); see [XT] **estimation options**.

    xtgee does not need to know t() for the corr(independent) and corr(exchangeable) correlation structures. Whether you specify t() makes no difference in these two cases.

family(*family*) specifies the distribution of *depvar*; family(gaussian) is the default.

link(*link*) specifies the link function; the default is the canonical link for the family() specified.

    ⌐ Model 2 ⌐

exposure(*varname*) and offset(*varname*) are different ways of specifying the same thing. exposure() specifies a variable that reflects the amount of exposure over which the *depvar* events were observed for each observation; ln(*varname*) with coefficient constrained to be 1 is entered into the regression equation. offset() specifies a variable that is to be entered directly into the log-link function with its coefficient constrained to be 1; thus, exposure is assumed to be $e^{varname}$. If you were fitting a Poisson regression model, family(poisson) link(log), for instance, you would account for exposure time by specifying offset() containing the log of exposure time.

noconstant specifies that the linear predictor has no intercept term, thus forcing it through the origin on the scale defined by the link function.

force specifies that estimation be forced even though t() is not equally spaced. This is relevant only for correlation structures that require knowledge of t() and that require observations to be equally spaced.

    ⌐ Correlation ⌐

corr(*correlation*); see [XT] **estimation options**.

    ⌐ SE/Robust ⌐

vce(*vcetype*); see [R] *vce_option*.

robust specifies that the Huber/White/sandwich estimator of variance is to be used in place of the default GLS variance estimator (see *Methods and Formulas* below). This produces valid standard errors even if the correlations within group are not as hypothesized by the specified correlation structure. It does, however, require that the model correctly specifies the mean. As such, the resulting standard errors are labeled "semi-robust" instead of "robust". Note that although there is no cluster() option, results are as if there were a cluster() option and you specified clustering on i().

    vce(robust) is a synonym for robust.

nmp; see [XT] **estimation options**.

rgf specifies that the robust variance estimate is multiplied by $(N-1)/(N-P)$, where N is the total number of observations and P is the number of coefficients estimated. This option can be used only with family(gaussian) when robust is either specified or implied by the use of pweights. Using this option implies that the robust variance estimate is not invariant to the scale of any weights used.

scale(x2|dev|phi|#) overrides the default scale parameter of scale(1); see [XT] **estimation options**.

┌ Reporting └

`level(#)`; see [XT] **estimation options**.

`eform` displays the exponentiated coefficients and corresponding standard errors and confidence
intervals as described in [R] **maximize**. For `family(binomial) link(logit)` (i.e., logistic
regression), exponentiation results in odds ratios; for `family(poisson) link(log)` (i.e., Poisson
regression), exponentiated coefficients are incidence-rate ratios.

┌ Opt options └

optimize_options control the iterative optimization process. These options are seldom used.

`iterate(#)` specifies the maximum number of iterations. When the number of iterations equals #,
the optimization stops and presents the current results, even if convergence has not been reached.
The default is `iterate(100)`.

`tolerance(#)` specifies the tolerance for the coefficient vector. When the relative change in the
coefficient vector from one iteration to the next is less than or equal to #, the optimization process
is stopped. `tolerance(1e-6)` is the default.

`nolog` suppresses display of the iteration log.

`trace` specifies that the current estimates be printed at each iteration.

The following option is available with `xtgee` but is not shown in the dialog box:

`nodisplay` is for programmers. It suppresses display of the header and coefficients.

Remarks

For a thorough introduction to GEE in the estimation of GLM, see Hardin and Hilbe (2003). Further
information on linear models is presented in Nelder and Wedderburn (1972). Finally, there have been
a number of illuminating articles on various applications of GEE in Zeger, Liang, and Albert (1988),
Zeger and Liang (1986), and Liang (1987). Pendergast et al. (1996) provide a survey of the current
methods for analyzing clustered data in regard to binary response data. Our implementation follows
that of Liang and Zeger (1986).

`xtgee` fits generalized linear models of y_{it} with covariates $\mathbf{x}_{it}$

$$g\{E(y_{it})\} = \mathbf{x}_{it}\boldsymbol{\beta}, \qquad y \sim F \text{ with parameters } \theta_{it}$$

for $i = 1,\ldots,m$ and $t = 1,\ldots,n_i$, where there are n_i observations for each group identifier i. $g(\ )$
is called the link function, and F is the distributional family. Substituting various definitions for $g(\ )$
and F results in a wide array of models. For instance, if y_{it} is distributed Gaussian (normal) and
$g(\ )$ is the identity function, we have

$$E(y_{it}) = \mathbf{x}_{it}\boldsymbol{\beta}, \qquad y \sim N(\ )$$

yielding linear regression, random-effects regression, or other regression-related models, depending
on what we assume for the correlation structure.

If $g(\ )$ is the logit function and y_{it} is distributed Bernoulli (binomial), we have

$$\text{logit}\{E(y_{it})\} = \mathbf{x}_{it}\boldsymbol{\beta}, \qquad y \sim \text{Bernoulli}$$

or logistic regression. If $g(\ )$ is the natural log function and y_{it} is distributed Poisson, we have

$$\ln\{E(y_{it})\} = \mathbf{x}_{it}\boldsymbol{\beta}, \qquad y \sim \text{Poisson}$$

or Poisson regression, also known as the log-linear model. Other combinations are possible.

You specify the link function using the `link()` option, the distributional family using `family()`, and the assumed within-group correlation structure using `corr()`.

The binomial distribution can be specified as (1) `family(binomial)`, (2) `family(binomial #)`, or (3) `family(binomial varname)`. In case 2, # is the value of the binomial denominator N, the number of trials. Specifying `family(binomial 1)` is the same as specifying `family(binomial)`; both mean that y has the Bernoulli distribution with values 0 and 1 only. In case 3, *varname* is the variable containing the binomial denominator, thus allowing the number of trials to vary across observations.

The negative binomial distribution must be specified as `family(nbinomial #)`, where # denotes the value of the parameter α in the negative binomial distribution. The results will be conditional on this value.

You do not have to specify both `family()` and `link()`; the default `link()` is the canonical link for the specified `family()`:

Family	Canonical link
family(binomial)	link(logit)
family(gamma)	link(reciprocal)
family(gaussian)	link(identity)
family(igaussian)	link(power -2)
family(nbinomial)	link(log)
family(poisson)	link(log)

If you specify both `family()` and `link()`, note that not all combinations make sense. You may choose among the following combinations:

	Gaussian	Inverse Gaussian	Binomial	Poisson	Negative Binomial	Gamma
Identity	x	x	x	x	x	x
Log	x	x	x	x	x	x
Logit			x			
Probit			x			
C. log-log			x			
Power	x	x	x	x	x	x
Odds Power			x			
Neg. binom.					x	
Reciprocal	x		x	x		x

You specify the assumed within-group correlation structure using the `corr()` option.

For example, call $\mathbf{R}$ the working correlation matrix for modeling the within-group correlation, a square $\max\{n_i\} \times \max\{n_i\}$ matrix. `corr()` specifies the structure of $\mathbf{R}$. Let $\mathbf{R}_{t,s}$ denote the t, s element.

The `independent` structure is defined as

$$\mathbf{R}_{t,s} = \begin{cases} 1 & \text{if } t = s \\ 0 & \text{otherwise} \end{cases}$$

The `corr(exchangeable)` structure (corresponding to equal-correlation models) is defined as

$$\mathbf{R}_{t,s} = \begin{cases} 1 & \text{if } t = s \\ \rho & \text{otherwise} \end{cases}$$

The corr(ar g) structure is defined as the usual correlation matrix for an AR(g) model. This is sometimes called multiplicative correlation. For example, an AR(1) model is given by

$$\mathbf{R}_{t,s} = \begin{cases} 1 & \text{if } t = s \\ \rho^{|t-s|} & \text{otherwise} \end{cases}$$

The corr(stationary g) structure is a stationary(g) model. For example, a stationary(1) model is given by

$$\mathbf{R}_{t,s} = \begin{cases} 1 & \text{if } t = s \\ \rho & \text{if } |t - s| = 1 \\ 0 & \text{otherwise} \end{cases}$$

The corr(nonstationary g) structure is a nonstationary(g) model that imposes only the constraints that the elements of the working correlation matrix along the diagonal be 1 and the elements outside of the gth band be zero,

$$\mathbf{R}_{t,s} = \begin{cases} 1 & \text{if } t = s \\ \rho_{ts} & \text{if } 0 < |t - s| \le g, \, \rho_{ts} = \rho_{st} \\ 0 & \text{otherwise} \end{cases}$$

corr(unstructured) imposes only the constraint that the diagonal elements of the working correlation matrix be 1.

$$\mathbf{R}_{t,s} = \begin{cases} 1 & \text{if } t = s \\ \rho_{ts} & \text{otherwise, } \rho_{ts} = \rho_{st} \end{cases}$$

The corr(fixed *matname*) specification is taken from the user-supplied matrix, such that

$$\mathbf{R} = matname$$

In this case, the correlations are not estimated from the data. The user-supplied matrix must be a valid correlation matrix with 1s on the diagonal.

Full formulas for all the correlation structures are provided in the *Methods and Formulas* below.

❑ Technical Note

Some family(), link(), and corr() combinations result in models already fitted by Stata:

family()	link()	corr()	Other Stata estimation command
gaussian	identity	independent	regress
gaussian	identity	exchangeable	xtreg, re (see note 1)
gaussian	identity	exchangeable	xtreg, pa
binomial	cloglog	independent	cloglog (see note 2)
binomial	cloglog	exchangeable	xtcloglog, pa
binomial	logit	independent	logit or logistic
binomial	logit	exchangeable	xtlogit, pa
binomial	probit	independent	probit (see note 3)
binomial	probit	exchangeable	xtprobit, pa
nbinomial	nbinomial	independent	nbreg (see note 4)
poisson	log	independent	poisson
poisson	log	exchangeable	xtpoisson, pa
gamma	log	independent	streg, dist(exp) nohr (see note 5)
family	*link*	independent	glm, irls (see note 6)

Notes:

1. These methods produce the same results only in the case of balanced panels; see [XT] **xt**.

2. For cloglog estimation, `xtgee` with `corr(independent)` and `cloglog` (see [R] **cloglog**) will produce the same coefficients, but the standard errors will be only asymptotically equivalent because cloglog is not the canonical link for the binomial family.

3. For probit estimation, `xtgee` with `corr(independent)` and `probit` will produce the same coefficients, but the standard errors will be only asymptotically equivalent because probit is not the canonical link for the binomial family. If the binomial denominator is not 1, the equivalent maximum-likelihood command is `bprobit`; see [R] **probit** and [R] **glogit**.

4. Fitting a negative binomial model using `xtgee` (or using `glm`) will yield results conditional on the specified value of α. The `nbreg` command, however, estimates that parameter and provides unconditional estimates; see [R] **nbreg**.

5. `xtgee` with `corr(independent)` can be used to fit exponential regressions, but this requires specifying `scale(1)`. As with probit, the `xtgee`-reported standard errors will be only asymptotically equivalent to those produced by `streg, dist(exp) nohr` (see [ST] **streg**) because log is not the canonical link for the gamma family. `xtgee` cannot be used to fit exponential regressions on censored data.

   Using the `independent` correlation structure, the `xtgee` command will fit the same model fitted with the `glm, irls` command if the family–link combination is the same.

6. If the `xtgee` command is equivalent to another command, using `corr(independent)` and the `robust` option with `xtgee` corresponds to using both the `robust` option and the `cluster(`*varname*`)` option in the equivalent command, where *varname* corresponds to the `i()` group variable. ❏

`xtgee` is a generalization of the `glm, irls` command and gives the same output when the same family and link are specified together with an independent correlation structure. What makes `xtgee` useful is

1. the number of statistical models that it generalizes for use with panel data, many of which are not otherwise available in Stata;

2. the richer correlation structure `xtgee` allows, even when models are available through other `xt` commands; and

3. the availability of robust standard errors (see [U] **20.14 Obtaining robust variance estimates**), even when the model and correlation structure are available through other `xt` commands.

In the following examples, we illustrate the relationships of `xtgee` with other Stata estimation commands. Remember that, although `xtgee` generalizes many other commands, the computational algorithm is different; therefore, the answers you obtain will not be identical. The dataset we are using is a subset of the `nlswork` data (see [XT] **xt**); we are looking at observations before 1980.

(Continued on next page)

▷ Example 1

We can use `xtgee` to perform ordinary least squares by `regress`:

```
. use http://www.stata-press.com/data/r9/nlswork2
(National Longitudinal Survey.  Young Women 14-26 years of age in 1968)

. generate age2 = age*age
(9 missing values generated)

. regress ln_w grade age age2
```

Source	SS	df	MS		
Model	597.54468	3	199.18156		
Residual	2265.74584	16081	.14089583		
Total	2863.29052	16084	.178021047		

	Number of obs =	16085
	F(3, 16081) =	1413.68
	Prob > F =	0.0000
	R-squared =	0.2087
	Adj R-squared =	0.2085
	Root MSE =	.37536

ln_wage	Coef.	Std. Err.	t	P>|t|	[95% Conf. Interval]	
grade	.0724483	.0014229	50.91	0.000	.0696592	.0752374
age	.1064874	.0083644	12.73	0.000	.0900922	.1228825
age2	-.0016931	.0001655	-10.23	0.000	-.0020174	-.0013688
_cons	-.8681487	.1024896	-8.47	0.000	-1.06904	-.6672577

```
. xtgee ln_w grade age age2, i(id) corr(indep) nmp

Iteration 1: tolerance = 1.310e-12
```

GEE population-averaged model			Number of obs	=	16085
Group variable:		idcode	Number of groups	=	3913
Link:		identity	Obs per group: min =		1
Family:		Gaussian	avg =		4.1
Correlation:		independent	max =		9
			Wald chi2(3)	=	4241.04
Scale parameter:		.1408958	Prob > chi2	=	0.0000
Pearson chi2(16081):		2265.75	Deviance	=	2265.75
Dispersion (Pearson):		.1408958	Dispersion	=	.1408958

ln_wage	Coef.	Std. Err.	z	P>|z|	[95% Conf. Interval]	
grade	.0724483	.0014229	50.91	0.000	.0696594	.0752372
age	.1064874	.0083644	12.73	0.000	.0900935	.1228812
age2	-.0016931	.0001655	-10.23	0.000	-.0020174	-.0013688
_cons	-.8681487	.1024896	-8.47	0.000	-1.069025	-.6672728

When `nmp` is specified, the coefficients and the standard errors produced by the estimators are exactly the same. Moreover, the scale parameter estimate from the `xtgee` command equals the MSE calculation from `regress`; both are estimates of the variance of the residuals.

◁

▷ Example 2

The identity link and Gaussian family produce regression-type models. With the independent correlation structure, we reproduce ordinary least squares. With the exchangeable correlation structure, we produce an equal-correlation linear regression estimator.

`xtgee, fam(gauss) link(ident) corr(exch)` is asymptotically equivalent to the weighted-GLS estimator provided by `xtreg, re` and to the full maximum-likelihood estimator provided by `xtreg, mle`. In balanced data, `xtgee, fam(gauss) link(ident) corr(exch)` and `xtreg, mle` produce exactly the same results. With unbalanced data, the results are close but differ because the two estimators handle unbalanced data differently. For both balanced and unbalanced data, the results produced by `xtgee, fam(gauss) link(ident) corr(exch)` and `xtreg, mle` differ from those produced by `xtreg, re`. Below we demonstrate the use of the three estimators with unbalanced data. We begin with `xtgee`; show the maximum likelihood estimator `xtreg, mle`; show the GLS estimator `xtreg, re`; and finally show `xtgee` with the `robust` option.

```
. xtgee ln_w grade age age2, i(id) nolog
```

```
GEE population-averaged model          Number of obs       =       16085
Group variable:                idcode  Number of groups    =        3913
Link:                        identity  Obs per group: min  =           1
Family:                      Gaussian                 avg  =         4.1
Correlation:             exchangeable                 max  =           9
                                       Wald chi2(3)        =     2918.26
Scale parameter:              .1416586 Prob > chi2         =      0.0000
```

ln_wage	Coef.	Std. Err.	z	P>|z|	[95% Conf. Interval]	
grade	.0717731	.00211	34.02	0.000	.0676377	.0759086
age	.1077645	.006885	15.65	0.000	.0942701	.1212589
age2	-.0016381	.0001362	-12.03	0.000	-.001905	-.0013712
_cons	-.9480449	.0869277	-10.91	0.000	-1.11842	-.7776698

```
. xtreg ln_w grade age age2, i(id) mle
```

```
Fitting constant-only model:
Iteration 0:   log likelihood = -6035.2751
Iteration 1:   log likelihood = -5870.6718
Iteration 2:   log likelihood = -5858.9478
Iteration 3:   log likelihood = -5858.8244

Fitting full model:
Iteration 0:   log likelihood = -4591.9241
Iteration 1:   log likelihood = -4562.4406
Iteration 2:   log likelihood = -4562.3526
```

```
Random-effects ML regression           Number of obs       =       16085
Group variable (i): idcode             Number of groups    =        3913

Random effects u_i ~ Gaussian          Obs per group: min  =           1
                                                      avg  =         4.1
                                                      max  =           9
                                       LR chi2(3)          =     2592.94
Log likelihood  = -4562.3526           Prob > chi2         =      0.0000
```

ln_wage	Coef.	Std. Err.	z	P>|z|	[95% Conf. Interval]	
grade	.0717747	.0021419	33.51	0.000	.0675766	.0759728
age	.1077899	.0068265	15.79	0.000	.0944102	.1211696
age2	-.0016364	.000135	-12.12	0.000	-.0019011	-.0013718
_cons	-.9500833	.0863831	-11.00	0.000	-1.119391	-.7807755
/sigma_u	.2689639	.004085			.2610754	.2770908
/sigma_e	.2669944	.0017113			.2636613	.2703695
rho	.5036748	.0086443			.486734	.5206089

```
Likelihood-ratio test of sigma_u=0: chibar2(01)= 4996.22 Prob>=chibar2 = 0.000
```

```
. xtreg ln_w grade age age2, i(id) re
```

Random-effects GLS regression   Number of obs   =   16085
Group variable (i): idcode   Number of groups   =   3913

R-sq: within = 0.0983   Obs per group: min =   1
        between = 0.2946   avg =   4.1
        overall = 0.2076   max =   9

Random effects u_i ~ Gaussian   Wald chi2(3)   =   2875.09
corr(u_i, X)   = 0 (assumed)   Prob > chi2   =   0.0000

ln_wage	Coef.	Std. Err.	z	P>|z|	[95% Conf. Interval]	
grade	.0717757	.0021665	33.13	0.000	.0675295	.076022
age	.1078042	.0068126	15.82	0.000	.0944518	.1211566
age2	-.0016355	.0001347	-12.14	0.000	-.0018996	-.0013714
_cons	-.9512088	.0863141	-11.02	0.000	-1.120381	-.7820363
sigma_u	.27383336					
sigma_e	.2662536					
rho	.51403157	(fraction of variance due to u_i)				

```
. xtgee ln_w grade age age2, i(id) nolog robust
```

GEE population-averaged model   Number of obs   =   16085
Group variable: idcode Number of groups   =   3913
Link: identity   Obs per group: min =   1
Family: Gaussian   avg =   4.1
Correlation: exchangeable   max =   9
                                                   Wald chi2(3)   =   2031.28
Scale parameter: .1416586   Prob > chi2   =   0.0000

                      (Std. Err. adjusted for clustering on idcode)

ln_wage	Coef.	Semi-robust Std. Err.	z	P>|z|	[95% Conf. Interval]	
grade	.0717731	.0023341	30.75	0.000	.0671983	.0763479
age	.1077645	.0098097	10.99	0.000	.0885379	.1269911
age2	-.0016381	.0001964	-8.34	0.000	-.002023	-.0012532
_cons	-.9480449	.1195009	-7.93	0.000	-1.182262	-.7138274

In [R] **regress**, we note that `regress, robust cluster()` may produce inefficient coefficient estimates with valid standard errors for random-effects models. These standard errors are robust to model misspecification. The `robust` option of `xtgee`, on the other hand, requires that the model correctly specify the mean.

◁

Saved Results

xtgee saves in e():

Scalars

e(N)	number of observations	e(deviance)	deviance
e(N_g)	number of groups	e(chi2_dev)	χ^2 test of deviance
e(df_m)	model degrees of freedom	e(dispers)	deviance dispersion
e(g_max)	largest group size	e(chi2_dis)	χ^2 test of deviance dispersion
e(g_min)	smallest group size	e(tol)	target tolerance
e(g_avg)	average group size	e(dif)	achieved tolerance
e(chi2)	χ^2	e(phi)	scale parameter
e(df_pear)	degrees of freedom for Pearson χ^2		

Macros

e(cmd)	xtgee	e(tvar)	time variable
e(depvar)	name of dependent variable	e(vcetype)	title used to label Std. Err.
e(family)	distribution family	e(chi2type)	Wald; type of model χ^2 test
e(link)	link function	e(offset)	offset
e(corr)	correlation structure	e(crittype)	optimization criterion
e(scale)	x2, dev, phi, or #; scale parameter	e(properties)	b V
e(ivar)	variable denoting groups	e(predict)	program used to implement predict

Matrices

e(b)	coefficient vector	e(R)	estimated working correlation matrix
e(V)	variance–covariance matrix of the estimators		

Functions

e(sample)	marks estimation sample

Methods and Formulas

xtgee is implemented as an ado-file.

xtgee fits general linear models for panel data using the GEE approach described in Liang and Zeger (1986). A related method, referred to as GEE2, is described in Zhao and Prentice (1990) and Prentice and Zhao (1991). The GEE2 method attempts to gain efficiency in the estimation of β by specifying a parametric model for α and then assumes that the models for both the mean and dependency parameters are correct. Thus there is a tradeoff in robustness for efficiency. The preliminary work of Liang, Zeger, and Qaqish (1987), however, indicates that there is little efficiency gained with this alternative approach.

In the GLM approach (see McCullagh and Nelder 1989), we assume that

$$h(\boldsymbol{\mu}_{i,j}) = x_{i,j}^{\mathrm{T}}\boldsymbol{\beta}$$

$$\mathrm{Var}(y_{i,j}) = g(\mu_{i,j})\phi$$

$$\boldsymbol{\mu}_i = E(\mathbf{y}_i) = \{h^{-1}(x_{i,1}^{\mathrm{T}}\boldsymbol{\beta}), \ldots, h^{-1}(x_{i,n_i}^{\mathrm{T}}\boldsymbol{\beta})\}^{\mathrm{T}}$$

$$\mathbf{A}_i = \mathrm{diag}\{g(\mu_{i,1}), \ldots, g(\mu_{i,n_i})\}$$

$$\mathrm{Cov}(\mathbf{y}_i) = \phi\mathbf{A}_i \quad \text{for independent observations.}$$

In the absence of a convenient likelihood function with which to work, we can rely on a multivariate analog of the quasi-score function introduced by Wedderburn (1974):

$$\mathbf{S}_{\boldsymbol{\beta}}(\boldsymbol{\beta}, \boldsymbol{\alpha}) = \sum_{i=1}^{m} \left(\frac{\partial \boldsymbol{\mu}_i}{\partial \boldsymbol{\beta}} \right)^{\mathrm{T}} \mathrm{Var}(\mathbf{y}_i)^{-1} (\mathbf{y}_i - \boldsymbol{\mu}_i) = 0$$

We can solve for correlation parameters $\boldsymbol{\alpha}$ by simultaneously solving

$$\mathbf{S}_{\boldsymbol{\alpha}}(\boldsymbol{\beta}, \boldsymbol{\alpha}) = \sum_{i=1}^{m} \left(\frac{\partial \boldsymbol{\eta}_i}{\partial \boldsymbol{\alpha}} \right)^{\mathrm{T}} \mathbf{H}_i^{-1} (\mathbf{W}_i - \boldsymbol{\eta}_i) = 0$$

In the GEE approach to GLM, we let $\mathbf{R}_i(\boldsymbol{\alpha})$ be a "working" correlation matrix depending on the parameters in $\boldsymbol{\alpha}$ (see the *Correlation structures* section for the number of parameters), and we estimate $\boldsymbol{\beta}$ by solving the generalized estimating equation,

$$\mathbf{U}(\boldsymbol{\beta}) = \sum_{i=1}^{m} \frac{\partial \boldsymbol{\mu}_i}{\partial \boldsymbol{\beta}} \mathbf{V}_i^{-1}(\boldsymbol{\alpha}) (\mathbf{y}_i - \boldsymbol{\mu}_i) = 0$$

$$\text{where} \quad \mathbf{V}_i(\boldsymbol{\alpha}) = \mathbf{A}_i^{1/2} \mathbf{R}_i(\boldsymbol{\alpha}) \mathbf{A}_i^{1/2}$$

To solve this equation, we need only a crude approximation of the variance matrix, which we can obtain from a Taylor's series expansion, where

$$\mathrm{Cov}(\mathbf{y}_i) = \mathbf{L}_i \mathbf{Z}_i \mathbf{D}_i \mathbf{Z}_i^{\mathrm{T}} \mathbf{L}_i + \phi \mathbf{A}_i = \widetilde{\mathbf{V}}_i$$
$$\mathbf{L}_i = \mathrm{diag}\{\partial h^{-1}(u)/\partial u, u = x_{i,j}^{\mathrm{T}} \boldsymbol{\beta}, j = 1, \dots, n_i\}$$

which allows that

$$\widehat{\mathbf{D}}_i \approx (\mathbf{Z}_i^{\mathrm{T}} \mathbf{Z}_i)^{-1} \mathbf{Z}_i \widehat{\mathbf{L}}_i^{-1} \left\{ (\mathbf{y}_i - \widehat{\boldsymbol{\mu}}_i)(\mathbf{y}_i - \widehat{\boldsymbol{\mu}}_i)^{\mathrm{T}} - \widehat{\phi} \widehat{\mathbf{A}}_i \right\} \widehat{\mathbf{L}}_i^{-1} \mathbf{Z}_i^{\mathrm{T}} (\mathbf{Z}_i' \mathbf{Z}_i)^{-1}$$
$$\widehat{\phi} = \sum_{i=1}^{m} \sum_{j=1}^{n_i} \frac{(y_{i,j} - \widehat{\mu}_{i,j})^2 - (\widehat{\mathbf{L}}_{i,j})^2 \mathbf{Z}_{i,j}^{\mathrm{T}} \widehat{\mathbf{D}}_i \mathbf{Z}_{i,j}}{g(\widehat{\mu}_{i,j})}$$

Calculating GEE for GLM

Using the notation from Liang and Zeger (1986), let $\mathbf{y}_i = (y_{i,1}, \dots, y_{i,n_i})^{\mathrm{T}}$ be the $n_i \times 1$ vector of outcome values, and let $\mathbf{X}_i = (x_{i,1}, \dots, x_{i,n_i})^{\mathrm{T}}$ be the $n_i \times p$ matrix of covariate values for the ith subject $i = 1, \dots, m$. We assume that the marginal density for $y_{i,j}$ may be written in exponential family notation as

$$f(y_{i,j}) = \exp\left[\{ y_{i,j} \theta_{i,j} - a(\theta_{i,j}) + b(y_{i,j}) \} \phi \right]$$

where $\theta_{i,j} = h(\eta_{i,j}), \eta_{i,j} = x_{i,j} \boldsymbol{\beta}$. Under this formulation, the first two moments are given by

$$E(y_{i,j}) = a'(\theta_{i,j}), \qquad \mathrm{Var}(y_{i,j}) = a''(\theta_{i,j})/\phi$$

We define the quantities, assuming that we have an $n \times n$ working correlation matrix $\mathbf{R}(\boldsymbol{\alpha})$,

$$\boldsymbol{\Delta}_i = \mathrm{diag}(d\theta_{i,j}/d\eta_{i,j}) \quad n \times n \text{ matrix}$$

$$\mathbf{A}_i = \mathrm{diag}\{a''(\theta_{i,j})\} \quad n \times n \text{ matrix}$$

$$\mathbf{S}_i = \mathbf{y}_i - a'(\boldsymbol{\theta}_i) \quad n \times 1 \text{ matrix}$$

$$\mathbf{D}_i = \mathbf{A}_i\boldsymbol{\Delta}_i\mathbf{X}_i \quad n \times p \text{ matrix}$$

$$\mathbf{V}_i = \mathbf{A}_i^{1/2}\mathbf{R}(\boldsymbol{\alpha})\mathbf{A}_i^{1/2} \quad n \times n \text{ matrix}$$

such that the GEE becomes

$$\sum_{i=1}^{m} \mathbf{D}_i^{\mathrm{T}}\mathbf{V}_i^{-1}\mathbf{S}_i = 0$$

We then have that

$$\widehat{\boldsymbol{\beta}}_{j+1} = \widehat{\boldsymbol{\beta}}_j - \left\{\sum_{i=1}^{m} \mathbf{D}_i^{\mathrm{T}}(\widehat{\boldsymbol{\beta}}_j)\widetilde{\mathbf{V}}_i^{-1}(\widehat{\boldsymbol{\beta}}_j)\mathbf{D}_i(\widehat{\boldsymbol{\beta}}_j)\right\}^{-1} \left\{\sum_{i=1}^{m} \mathbf{D}_i^{\mathrm{T}}(\widehat{\boldsymbol{\beta}}_j)\widetilde{\mathbf{V}}_i^{-1}(\widehat{\boldsymbol{\beta}}_j)\mathbf{S}_i(\widehat{\boldsymbol{\beta}}_j)\right\}$$

where the term

$$\left\{\sum_{i=1}^{m} \mathbf{D}_i^{\mathrm{T}}(\widehat{\boldsymbol{\beta}}_j)\widetilde{\mathbf{V}}_i^{-1}(\widehat{\boldsymbol{\beta}}_j)\mathbf{D}_i(\widehat{\boldsymbol{\beta}}_j)\right\}^{-1}$$

is what we call the GLS variance estimate (generalized least squares). It is used to calculate the standard errors if the `robust` option is not specified. See Liang and Zeger (1986) for the calculation of the robust variance estimator.

Define the following:

$$\mathbf{D} = (\mathbf{D}_1^{\mathrm{T}}, \ldots, \mathbf{D}_m^{\mathrm{T}})$$

$$\mathbf{S} = (\mathbf{S}_1^{\mathrm{T}}, \ldots, \mathbf{S}_m^{\mathrm{T}})^{\mathrm{T}}$$

$$\widetilde{\mathbf{V}} = nm \times nm \text{ block diagonal matrix with } \widetilde{\mathbf{V}}_i$$

$$\mathbf{Z} = \mathbf{D}\boldsymbol{\beta} - \mathbf{S}$$

At a given iteration, the correlation parameters $\boldsymbol{\alpha}$ and scale parameter ϕ can be estimated from the current Pearson residuals, defined by

$$\widehat{r}_{i,j} = \{y_{i,j} - a'(\widehat{\theta}_{i,j})\}/\{a''(\widehat{\theta}_{i,j})\}^{1/2}$$

where $\widehat{\theta}_{i,j}$ depends on the current value for $\widehat{\beta}$. We can then estimate ϕ by

$$\widehat{\phi}^{-1} = \sum_{i=1}^{m}\sum_{j=1}^{n_i} \widehat{r}_{i,j}^2/(N - p)$$

As this general derivation is complicated, let's follow the derivation of the Gaussian family with the identity link (regression) to illustrate the generalization. After making appropriate substitutions, we will see a familiar updating equation. First, we rewrite the updating equation for β as

$$\widehat{\boldsymbol{\beta}}_{j+1} = \widehat{\boldsymbol{\beta}}_j - \mathbf{Z}_1^{-1}\mathbf{Z}_2$$

and then derive $\mathbf{Z}_1$ and $\mathbf{Z}_2$.

$$\mathbf{Z}_1 = \sum_{i=1}^{m} \mathbf{D}_i^{\mathrm{T}}(\widehat{\boldsymbol{\beta}}_j)\widetilde{\mathbf{V}}_i^{-1}(\widehat{\boldsymbol{\beta}}_j)\mathbf{D}_i(\widehat{\boldsymbol{\beta}}_j) = \sum_{i=1}^{m} \mathbf{X}_i^{\mathrm{T}}\boldsymbol{\Delta}_i^{\mathrm{T}}\mathbf{A}_i^{\mathrm{T}}\{\mathbf{A}_i^{1/2}\mathbf{R}(\boldsymbol{\alpha})\mathbf{A}_i^{1/2}\}^{-1}\mathbf{A}_i\boldsymbol{\Delta}_i\mathbf{X}_i$$

$$= \sum_{i=1}^{m} \mathbf{X}_i^{\mathrm{T}}\operatorname{diag}\left\{\frac{\partial\theta_{i,j}}{\partial(\mathbf{X}\boldsymbol{\beta})}\right\}\operatorname{diag}\{a''(\theta_{i,j})\}\left[\operatorname{diag}\{a''(\theta_{i,j})\}^{1/2}\mathbf{R}(\boldsymbol{\alpha})\operatorname{diag}\{a''(\theta_{i,j})\}^{1/2}\right]^{-1}$$

$$\operatorname{diag}\{a''(\theta_{i,j})\}\operatorname{diag}\left\{\frac{\partial\theta_{i,j}}{\partial(\mathbf{X}\boldsymbol{\beta})}\right\}\mathbf{X}_i$$

$$= \sum_{i=1}^{m} \mathbf{X}_i^{\mathrm{T}}\mathbf{II}(\mathbf{III})^{-1}\mathbf{IIX}_i = \sum_{i=1}^{m} \mathbf{X}_i^{\mathrm{T}}\mathbf{X}_i = \mathbf{X}^{\mathrm{T}}\mathbf{X}$$

$$\mathbf{Z}_2 = \sum_{i=1}^{m} \mathbf{D}_i^{\mathrm{T}}(\widehat{\boldsymbol{\beta}}_j)\widetilde{\mathbf{V}}_i^{-1}(\widehat{\boldsymbol{\beta}}_j)\mathbf{S}_i(\widehat{\boldsymbol{\beta}}_j) = \sum_{i=1}^{m} \mathbf{X}_i^{\mathrm{T}}\boldsymbol{\Delta}_i^{\mathrm{T}}\mathbf{A}_i^{\mathrm{T}}\{\mathbf{A}_i^{1/2}\mathbf{R}(\boldsymbol{\alpha})\mathbf{A}_i^{1/2}\}^{-1}\left(\mathbf{y}_i - \mathbf{X}_i\widehat{\boldsymbol{\beta}}_j\right)$$

$$= \sum_{i=1}^{m} \mathbf{X}_i^{\mathrm{T}}\operatorname{diag}\left\{\frac{\partial\theta_{i,j}}{\partial(\mathbf{X}\boldsymbol{\beta})}\right\}\operatorname{diag}\{a''(\theta_{i,j})\}\left[\operatorname{diag}\{a''(\theta_{i,j})\}^{1/2}\mathbf{R}(\boldsymbol{\alpha})\operatorname{diag}\{a''(\theta_{i,j})\}^{1/2}\right]^{-1}$$

$$\left(\mathbf{y}_i - \mathbf{X}_i\widehat{\boldsymbol{\beta}}_j\right)$$

$$= \sum_{i=1}^{m} \mathbf{X}_i\mathbf{II}(\mathbf{III})^{-1}(\mathbf{y}_i - \mathbf{X}_i\widehat{\boldsymbol{\beta}}_j) = \sum_{i=1}^{m} \mathbf{X}_i^{\mathrm{T}}(\mathbf{y}_i - \mathbf{X}_i\widehat{\boldsymbol{\beta}}_j) = \mathbf{X}^{\mathrm{T}}\widehat{s}_j$$

So, we may write the update formula as

$$\widehat{\boldsymbol{\beta}}_{j+1} = \widehat{\boldsymbol{\beta}}_j - (\mathbf{X}^{\mathrm{T}}\mathbf{X})^{-1}\mathbf{X}^{\mathrm{T}}\widehat{s}_j$$

which is the same formula for GLS in regression.

Correlation structures

The working correlation matrix $\mathbf{R}$ is a function of $\boldsymbol{\alpha}$ and is more accurately written as $\mathbf{R}(\boldsymbol{\alpha})$. Depending on the assumed correlation structure, $\boldsymbol{\alpha}$ might be

Independent	no parameters to estimate
Exchangeable	$\boldsymbol{\alpha}$ is a scalar
Autoregressive	$\boldsymbol{\alpha}$ is a vector
Stationary	$\boldsymbol{\alpha}$ is a vector
Nonstationary	$\boldsymbol{\alpha}$ is a matrix
Unstructured	$\boldsymbol{\alpha}$ is a matrix

Also note that throughout the estimation of a general unbalanced panel, it is more proper to discuss $\mathbf{R}_i$, which is the upper left $n_i \times n_i$ submatrix of the ultimately saved matrix in e(R), $\max\{n_i\} \times \max\{n_i\}$.

The only panels that enter into the estimation for a lag-dependent correlation structure are those with $n_i > g$ (assuming a lag of g). xtgee drops panels with too few observations (and mentions when it does so).

Independent

The working correlation matrix $\mathbf{R}$ is an identity matrix.

Exchangeable

$$\alpha = \sum_{i=1}^{m} \left\{ \frac{\sum_{j=1}^{n_i} \sum_{k=1}^{n_i} \widehat{r}_{i,j} \widehat{r}_{i,k} - \sum_{j=1}^{n_i} \widehat{r}_{i,j}^2}{n_i(n_i - 1)} \right\} \bigg/ \left(\sum_{i=1}^{m} \frac{\sum_{j=1}^{n_i} \widehat{r}_{i,j}^2}{n_i} \right)$$

and the working correlation matrix is given by

$$\mathbf{R}_{s,t} = \begin{cases} 1 & s = t \\ \alpha & \text{otherwise} \end{cases}$$

Autoregressive and stationary

These two structures require g parameters to be estimated so that α is a vector of length $g + 1$ (the first element of α is 1).

$$\alpha = \sum_{i=1}^{m} \left(\frac{\sum_{j=1}^{n_i} \widehat{r}_{i,j}^2}{n_i} , \frac{\sum_{j=1}^{n_i-1} \widehat{r}_{i,j} \widehat{r}_{i,j+1}}{n_i} , \ldots , \frac{\sum_{j=1}^{n_i-g} \widehat{r}_{i,j} \widehat{r}_{i,j+g}}{n_i} \right) \bigg/ \left(\sum_{i=1}^{m} \frac{\sum_{j=1}^{n_i} \widehat{r}_{i,j}^2}{n_i} \right)$$

The working correlation matrix for the AR model is calculated as a function of Toeplitz matrices formed from the α vector; see Newton (1988). The working correlation matrix for the stationary model is given by

$$\mathbf{R}_{s,t} = \begin{cases} \alpha_{1,|s-t|} & \text{if } |s - t| \leq g \\ 0 & \text{otherwise} \end{cases}$$

Nonstationary and unstructured

These two correlation structures require a matrix of parameters. α is estimated (where we replace $\widehat{r}_{i,j} = 0$ whenever $i > n_i$ or $j > n_i$) as

$$\alpha = \sum_{i=1}^{m} m \begin{pmatrix} N_{1,1}^{-1} \widehat{r}_{i,1}^2 & N_{1,2}^{-1} \widehat{r}_{i,1} \widehat{r}_{i,2} & \cdots & N_{1,n}^{-1} \widehat{r}_{i,1} \widehat{r}_{i,n} \\ N_{2,1}^{-1} \widehat{r}_{i,2} \widehat{r}_{i,1} & N_{2,2}^{-1} \widehat{r}_{i,2}^2 & \cdots & N_{2,n}^{-1} \widehat{r}_{i,2} \widehat{r}_{i,n} \\ \vdots & \vdots & \ddots & \vdots \\ N_{n,1}^{-1} \widehat{r}_{i,n_i} \widehat{r}_{i,1} & N_{n,2}^{-1} \widehat{r}_{i,n_i} \widehat{r}_{i,2} & \cdots & N_{n,n}^{-1} \widehat{r}_{i,n}^2 \end{pmatrix} \bigg/ \left(\sum_{i=1}^{m} \frac{\sum_{j=1}^{n_i} \widehat{r}_{i,j}^2}{n_i} \right)$$

where $N_{p,q} = \sum_{i=1}^{m} I(i, p, q)$ and

$$I(i, p, q) = \begin{cases} 1 & \text{if panel } i \text{ has valid observations at times p and q} \\ 0 & \text{otherwise} \end{cases}$$

where $N_{i,j} = \min(N_i, N_j)$, $N_i =$ number of panels observed at time i, and $n = \max(n_1, n_2, \ldots, n_m)$.

The working correlation matrix for the nonstationary model is given by

$$\mathbf{R}_{s,t} = \begin{cases} 1 & \text{if } s = t \\ \alpha_{s,t} & \text{if } 0 < |s - t| \leq g \\ 0 & \text{otherwise} \end{cases}$$

The working correlation matrix for the unstructured model is given by

$$\mathbf{R}_{s,t} = \begin{cases} 1 & \text{if } s = t \\ \alpha_{s,t} & \text{otherwise} \end{cases}$$

such that the unstructured model is equal to the nonstationary model at lag $g = n - 1$, where the panels are balanced with $n_i = n$ for all i.

References

Hardin, J. W. 2002. The robust variance estimator for two-stage models. *Stata Journal* 2: 253–266.

Hardin, J. W. and J. M. Hilbe. 2003. *Generalized Estimating Equations*. Boca Raton, FL: Chapman & Hall/CRC.

Hosmer, D. W., Jr., and S. Lemeshow. 2002. *Applied Logistic Regression*. 2nd ed. New York: Wiley.

Kleinbaum, D. G. and M. Klein. 2002. *Logistic Regression: A Self-Learning Text*. 2nd ed. New York: Springer.

Liang, K.-Y. 1987. Estimating functions and approximate conditional likelihood. *Biometrika* 4: 695–702.

Liang, K.-Y. and S. L. Zeger. 1986. Longitudinal data analysis using generalized linear models. *Biometrika* 73: 13–22.

Liang, K.-Y., S. L. Zeger, and B. Qaqish. 1987. Multivariate regression analyses for categorical data. *Journal of the Royal Statistical Society, Series B* 54: 3–40.

McCullagh, P. and J. A. Nelder. 1989. *Generalized Linear Models*. 2nd ed. London: Chapman & Hall/CRC.

Nelder, J. A. and R. W. M. Wedderburn. 1972. Generalized linear models. *Journal of the Royal Statistical Society, Series A* 135: 370–384.

Newton, H. J. 1988. *TIMESLAB: A Time Series Analysis Laboratory*, Belmont, CA: Brooks/Cole.

Pendergast, J. F., S. J. Gange, M. A. Newton, M. J. Lindstrom, M. Palta, and M. R. Fisher. 1996. A survey of methods for analyzing clustered binary response data. *International Statistical Review* 64: 89–118.

Prentice, R. L. and L. P. Zhao. 1991. Estimating equations for parameters in means and covariances of multivariate discrete and continuous responses. *Biometrics* 47: 825–839.

Rabe-Hesketh, S., A. Pickles, and C. Taylor. 2000. sg129: Generalized linear latent and mixed models. *Stata Technical Bulletin* 53: 47–57. Reprinted in *Stata Technical Bulletin Reprints*, vol. 9, pp. 293–307.

Rabe-Hesketh, S., A. Skrondal, and A. Pickles. 2002 Reliable estimation of generalized linear mixed models using adaptive quadrature. *Stata Journal* 2: 1–21.

Twisk, J. W. R. 2003. *Applied Longitudinal Data Analysis for Epidemiology: A Practical Guide*. Cambridge: Cambridge University Press.

Wedderburn, R. W. M. 1974. Quasi-likelihood functions, generalized linear models, and the Gauss–Newton method. *Biometrika* 61: 439–447.

Zeger, S. L. and K.-Y. Liang. 1986. Longitudinal data analysis for discrete and continuous outcomes. *Biometrics* 42: 121–130.

Zeger, S. L., K.-Y. Liang, and P. S. Albert. 1988. Models for longitudinal data: a generalized estimating equation approach *Biometrics* 44: 1049–1060.

Zhao, L. P. and R. L. Prentice. 1990. Correlated binary regression using a quadratic exponential model. *Biometrika* 77: 642–648.

Also See

Complementary:	[XT] **xtgee postestimation**; [XT] **xtdata**, [XT] **xtdes**, [XT] **xtsum**, [XT] **xttab**
Related:	[XT] **xtcloglog**, [XT] **xtgls**, [XT] **xtintreg**, [XT] **xtlogit**, [XT] **xtnbreg**, [XT] **xtpcse**, [XT] **xtpoisson**, [XT] **xtprobit**, [XT] **xtreg**, [XT] **xtregar**, [XT] **xttobit**, [R] **glm**, [R] **logistic**, [R] **regress**, [SVY] **svy**, [TS] **prais**
Background:	[U] **11.1.10 Prefix commands**, [U] **20 Estimation and postestimation commands**, [XT] **estimation options**, [XT] **xt**, [R] *vce_option*

Title

> **xtgee postestimation** — Postestimation tools for xtgee

Description

The following postestimation command is of special interest after `xtgee`:

command	description
estat wcorrelation	estimated matrix of the within-group correlations

For information about `estat wcorrelation`, see below.

In addition, the following standard postestimation commands are available:

command	description
adjust[1]	adjusted predictions of $\mathbf{x}\beta$, probabilities, or $\exp(\mathbf{x}\beta)$
estat	VCE and estimation sample summary
estimates	cataloging estimation results
hausman	Hausman's specification test
lincom	point estimates, standard errors, testing, and inference for linear combinations of coefficients
mfx	marginal effects or elasticities
nlcom	point estimates, standard errors, testing, and inference for nonlinear combinations of coefficients
predict	predictions, residuals, influence statistics, and other diagnostic measures
predictnl	point estimates, standard errors, testing, and inference for generalized predictions
test	Wald tests for simple and composite linear hypotheses
testnl	Wald tests of nonlinear hypotheses

[1] `adjust` does not work with time-series operators.

See the corresponding entries in the *Stata Base Reference Manual* for details.

Special-interest postestimation commands

`estat wcorrelation` displays the estimated matrix of the within-group correlations.

Syntax for predict

predict [*type*] *newvar* [*if*] [*in*] [, *statistic* <u>nooff</u>set]

statistic	description
mu	predicted probability of *depvar*; considers the offset() or exposure(); the default
rate	calculate predicted probability of *depvar*
xb	linear prediction
stdp	standard error of the linear prediction
score	first derivative of the log likelihood with respect to $\mathbf{x}_j\beta$

These statistics are available both in and out of sample; type predict ... if e(sample) ... if wanted only for the estimation sample.

Options for predict

mu, the default, and rate calculate the predicted value of *depvar*. mu takes into account the offset() or exposure() together with the denominator if the family is binomial; rate ignores those adjustments. mu and rate are equivalent if (1) you did not specify offset() or exposure() when you fitted the xtgee model and (2) you did not specify family(binomial #) or family(binomial *varname*), meaning the binomial family and a denominator not equal to one.

Thus mu and rate are the same for link(identity) family(gaussian).

mu and rate are not equivalent for link(logit) family(binomial pop). In that case, mu would predict the number of positive outcomes, and rate would predict the probability of a positive outcome.

mu and rate are not equivalent for link(log) family(poisson) exposure(time). In that case, mu would predict the number of events given exposure time, and rate would calculate the incidence rate—the number of events given an exposure time of 1.

xb calculates the linear prediction.

stdp calculates the standard error of the linear prediction.

score calculates the equation-level score, $u_j = \partial \ln L_j(\mathbf{x}_j\beta)/\partial(\mathbf{x}_j\beta)$.

nooffset is relevant only if you specified offset(*varname*), exposure(*varname*), family(binomial #), or family(binomial *varname*) when you fitted the model. It modifies the calculations made by predict so that they ignore the offset or exposure variable and the binomial denominator. Thus predict ..., mu nooffset produces the same results as predict ..., rate.

Syntax for estat wcorrelation

> estat wcorrelation [, compact format(%*fmt*)]

Options for estat wcorrelation

compact specifies that only the parameters (alpha) of the estimated matrix of within-group correlations be displayed rather than the entire matrix.

format(%*fmt*) overrides the display format; see [D] **format**.

Remarks

▷ Example 1

xtgee can estimate rich correlation structures. In [XT] **xtgee**, we fitted the model

. xtgee ln_w grade age age2, i(id)

After estimation, estat wcorrelations reports the working correlation matrix **R**:

. estat wcorrelations

Estimated within-idcode correlation matrix R:

	c1	c2	c3	c4	c5	c6	c7	c8	c9
r1	1.0000								
r2	0.4851	1.0000							
r3	0.4851	0.4851	1.0000						
r4	0.4851	0.4851	0.4851	1.0000					
r5	0.4851	0.4851	0.4851	0.4851	1.0000				
r6	0.4851	0.4851	0.4851	0.4851	0.4851	1.0000			
r7	0.4851	0.4851	0.4851	0.4851	0.4851	0.4851	1.0000		
r8	0.4851	0.4851	0.4851	0.4851	0.4851	0.4851	0.4851	1.0000	
r9	0.4851	0.4851	0.4851	0.4851	0.4851	0.4851	0.4851	0.4851	1.0000

The equal-correlation model corresponds to an exchangeable correlation structure, meaning that the correlation of observations within person is a constant. The working correlation estimated by xtgee is 0.4851. (xtreg, re, by comparison, reports .5140.) We constrained the model to have this simple correlation structure. What if we relaxed the constraint? To go to the other extreme, let's place no constraints on the matrix (other than it being symmetric). We do this by specifying correlation(unstructured), although we can abbreviate the option.

. xtgee ln_w grade age age2, i(id) t(year) corr(unstr) nolog

GEE population-averaged model		Number of obs	=	16085
Group and time vars:	idcode year	Number of groups	=	3913
Link:	identity	Obs per group: min =		1
Family:	Gaussian	avg =		4.1
Correlation:	unstructured	max =		9
		Wald chi2(3)	=	2405.20
Scale parameter:	.1418513	Prob > chi2	=	0.0000

ln_wage	Coef.	Std. Err.	z	P>|z|	[95% Conf. Interval]
grade	.0720684	.002151	33.50	0.000	.0678525 .0762843
age	.1008095	.0081471	12.37	0.000	.0848416 .1167775
age2	-.0015104	.0001617	-9.34	0.000	-.0018272 -.0011936
_cons	-.8645484	.1009488	-8.56	0.000	-1.062404 -.6666923

. estat wcorrelations

Estimated within-idcode correlation matrix R:

	c1	c2	c3	c4	c5	c6	c7	c8	c9
r1	1.0000								
r2	0.4355	1.0000							
r3	0.4280	0.5597	1.0000						
r4	0.3772	0.5012	0.5475	1.0000					
r5	0.4031	0.5301	0.5027	0.6216	1.0000				
r6	0.3664	0.4519	0.4783	0.5685	0.7306	1.0000			
r7	0.2820	0.3606	0.3918	0.4012	0.4643	0.5022	1.0000		
r8	0.3162	0.3446	0.4285	0.4389	0.4697	0.5223	0.6476	1.0000	
r9	0.2149	0.3078	0.3337	0.3584	0.4866	0.4613	0.5791	0.7387	1.0000

This correlation matrix looks quite different from the previously constrained one and shows, in particular, that the serial correlation of the residuals diminishes as the lag increases, although residuals separated by small lags are more correlated than, say, AR(1) would imply.

◁

▷ Example 2

In [XT] **xtprobit**, we showed a random-effects model of unionization using the union data described in [XT] **xt**. We performed the estimation using xtprobit but said we could have used xtgee as well. Here we fit a population-averaged (equal-correlation) model for comparison:

```
. use http://www.stata-press.com/data/r9/union
(NLS Women 14-24 in 1968)
. xtgee union age grade not_smsa south southXt, i(id) fam(bin) link(probit)
Iteration 1: tolerance = .04796083
Iteration 2: tolerance = .00352657
Iteration 3: tolerance = .00017886
Iteration 4: tolerance = 8.654e-06
Iteration 5: tolerance = 4.150e-07
```

GEE population-averaged model		Number of obs	=	26200
Group variable:	idcode	Number of groups	=	4434
Link:	probit	Obs per group: min =		1
Family:	binomial	avg =		5.9
Correlation:	exchangeable	max =		12
		Wald chi2(5)	=	241.66
Scale parameter:	1	Prob > chi2	=	0.0000

union	Coef.	Std. Err.	z	P>|z|	[95% Conf. Interval]	
age	.0031597	.0014678	2.15	0.031	.0002829	.0060366
grade	.0329992	.0062334	5.29	0.000	.020782	.0452163
not_smsa	-.0721799	.0275189	-2.62	0.009	-.1261159	-.0182439
south	-.409029	.0372213	-10.99	0.000	-.4819815	-.3360765
southXt	.0081828	.002545	3.22	0.001	.0031946	.0131709
_cons	-1.184799	.0890117	-13.31	0.000	-1.359259	-1.01034

Let us look at the correlation structure and then relax it:

```
. estat wcorrelations
Estimated within-idcode correlation matrix R:
        c1      c2      c3      c4      c5      c6      c7      c8      c9
 r1  1.0000
 r2  0.4630  1.0000
 r3  0.4630  0.4630  1.0000
 r4  0.4630  0.4630  0.4630  1.0000
 r5  0.4630  0.4630  0.4630  0.4630  1.0000
 r6  0.4630  0.4630  0.4630  0.4630  0.4630  1.0000
 r7  0.4630  0.4630  0.4630  0.4630  0.4630  0.4630  1.0000
 r8  0.4630  0.4630  0.4630  0.4630  0.4630  0.4630  0.4630  1.0000
 r9  0.4630  0.4630  0.4630  0.4630  0.4630  0.4630  0.4630  0.4630  1.0000
r10  0.4630  0.4630  0.4630  0.4630  0.4630  0.4630  0.4630  0.4630  0.4630
r11  0.4630  0.4630  0.4630  0.4630  0.4630  0.4630  0.4630  0.4630  0.4630
r12  0.4630  0.4630  0.4630  0.4630  0.4630  0.4630  0.4630  0.4630  0.4630
        c10     c11     c12
r10  1.0000
r11  0.4630  1.0000
r12  0.4630  0.4630  1.0000
```

We estimate the fixed correlation between observations within person to be 0.4630. We have a lot of data (an average of 5.9 observations on 4,434 women), so estimating the full correlation matrix is feasible. Let's do that and then examine the results:

```
. xtgee union age grade not_smsa south southXt, i(id) t(t) fam(bin) link(probit)
> corr(unstr) nolog

GEE population-averaged model                    Number of obs      =       26200
Group and time vars:              idcode t0      Number of groups   =        4434
Link:                                 probit     Obs per group: min =           1
Family:                             binomial                    avg =         5.9
Correlation:                    unstructured                    max =          12
                                                 Wald chi2(5)       =      196.76
Scale parameter:                           1     Prob > chi2        =      0.0000
```

union	Coef.	Std. Err.	z	P>|z|	[95% Conf. Interval]	
age	.0020207	.0019768	1.02	0.307	−.0018539	.0058952
grade	.0349572	.0065627	5.33	0.000	.0220946	.0478198
not_smsa	−.0951058	.0291532	−3.26	0.001	−.152245	−.0379665
south	−.3891526	.0434868	−8.95	0.000	−.4743853	−.30392
southXt	.0078823	.0034032	2.32	0.021	.0012121	.0145524
_cons	−1.194276	.1000155	−11.94	0.000	−1.390303	−.9982495

```
. estat wcorrelations

Estimated within-idcode correlation matrix R:
         c1      c2      c3      c4      c5      c6      c7      c8      c9
 r1  1.0000
 r2  0.6796  1.0000
 r3  0.6272  0.6628  1.0000
 r4  0.5365  0.5800  0.6170  1.0000
 r5  0.3377  0.3716  0.4037  0.4810  1.0000
 r6  0.3079  0.3771  0.4283  0.4591  0.6435  1.0000
 r7  0.3053  0.3630  0.3887  0.4299  0.4949  0.6407  1.0000
 r8  0.2807  0.3062  0.3251  0.3762  0.4691  0.5610  0.7000  1.0000
 r9  0.3045  0.3013  0.3042  0.3822  0.4620  0.5101  0.6093  0.6709  1.0000
r10  0.2324  0.2630  0.2779  0.3655  0.3987  0.4921  0.5878  0.5957  0.6308
r11  0.2369  0.2321  0.2716  0.3265  0.3555  0.4425  0.5094  0.5607  0.5740
r12  0.2400  0.2374  0.2561  0.3153  0.3478  0.3835  0.4782  0.4985  0.5404
         c10     c11     c12
r10  1.0000
r11  0.5706  1.0000
r12  0.5302  0.6406  1.0000
```

As before, we find that the correlation of residuals decreases as the lag increases, but more slowly than an AR(1) process.

◁

▷ Example 3

In this example, we examine injury incidents among 20 airlines in each of 4 years. The data are fictional, and, as a matter of fact, are really from a random-effects model.

```
. use http://www.stata-press.com/data/r9/airacc
. generate lnpm = ln(pmiles)
```

```
. xtgee i_cnt inprog, f(pois) i(airline) t(time) eform off(lnpm) nolog
```

GEE population-averaged model			Number of obs	=	80
Group variable:		airline	Number of groups	=	20
Link:		log	Obs per group: min =		4
Family:		Poisson	avg =		4.0
Correlation:		exchangeable	max =		4
			Wald chi2(1)	=	5.27
Scale parameter:		1	Prob > chi2	=	0.0217

i_cnt	IRR	Std. Err.	z	P>|z|	[95% Conf. Interval]	
inprog	.9059936	.0389528	-2.30	0.022	.8327758	.9856487
lnpm	(offset)					

```
. estat wcorrelations
Estimated within-airline correlation matrix R:
        c1      c2      c3      c4
r1  1.0000
r2  0.4606  1.0000
r3  0.4606  0.4606  1.0000
r4  0.4606  0.4606  0.4606  1.0000
```

Now there are not really enough data here to reliably estimate the correlation without any constraints of structure, but here is what happens if we try:

```
. use http://www.stata-press.com/data/r9/airacc

. generate lnpm = ln(pmiles)

. xtgee i_cnt inprog, f(pois) i(airline) t(time) eform off(lnpm) corr(unstr) nolog
```

GEE population-averaged model			Number of obs	=	80
Group and time vars:		airline time	Number of groups	=	20
Link:		log	Obs per group: min =		4
Family:		Poisson	avg =		4.0
Correlation:		unstructured	max =		4
			Wald chi2(1)	=	0.36
Scale parameter:		1	Prob > chi2	=	0.5496

i_cnt	IRR	Std. Err.	z	P>|z|	[95% Conf. Interval]	
inprog	.9791082	.0345486	-0.60	0.550	.9136826	1.049219
lnpm	(offset)					

```
. estat wcorrelations
Estimated within-airline correlation matrix R:
        c1      c2      c3      c4
r1  1.0000
r2  0.5700  1.0000
r3  0.7164  0.4192  1.0000
r4  0.2383  0.3840  0.3521  1.0000
```

There is no sensible pattern to the correlations.

We created this dataset from a random-effects Poisson model. We reran our data-creation program, and this time had it create 400 airlines rather than 20, still with four years of data each. Here are the equal-correlation model and estimated correlation structure

```
. use http://www.stata-press.com/data/r9/airacc2

. xtgee i_cnt inprog, f(pois) i(airline) eform off(lnpm) nolog
```

GEE population-averaged model		Number of obs	=	1600
Group variable:	airline	Number of groups	=	400
Link:	log	Obs per group: min =		4
Family:	Poisson	avg =		4.0
Correlation:	exchangeable	max =		4
		Wald chi2(1)	=	111.80
Scale parameter:	1	Prob > chi2	=	0.0000

i_cnt	IRR	Std. Err.	z	P>|z|	[95% Conf. Interval]	
inprog	.8915304	.0096807	-10.57	0.000	.8727571	.9107076
lnpm	(offset)					

```
. estat wcorrelations

Estimated within-airline correlation matrix R:
        c1      c2      c3      c4
r1  1.0000
r2  0.5292  1.0000
r3  0.5292  0.5292  1.0000
r4  0.5292  0.5292  0.5292  1.0000
```

The following estimation results assume unstructured correlation:

```
. use http://www.stata-press.com/data/r9/airacc2

. xtgee i_cnt inprog, f(pois) i(airline) corr(unstr) t(time) eform off(lnpm) nolog
```

GEE population-averaged model		Number of obs	=	1600
Group and time vars:	airline time	Number of groups	=	400
Link:	log	Obs per group: min =		4
Family:	Poisson	avg =		4.0
Correlation:	unstructured	max =		4
		Wald chi2(1)	=	113.43
Scale parameter:	1	Prob > chi2	=	0.0000

i_cnt	IRR	Std. Err.	z	P>|z|	[95% Conf. Interval]	
inprog	.8914155	.0096208	-10.65	0.000	.8727572	.9104728
lnpm	(offset)					

```
. estat wcorrelations

Estimated within-airline correlation matrix R:
        c1      c2      c3      c4
r1  1.0000
r2  0.4733  1.0000
r3  0.5241  0.5749  1.0000
r4  0.5140  0.5049  0.5841  1.0000
```

The equal-correlation model estimated a fixed correlation of .5292, and above we have correlations ranging between .4733 and .5841 with little pattern in their structure.

◁

Methods and Formulas

All postestimation commands listed above are implemented as ado-files.

Also See

Complementary:	[XT] **xtgee**,
	[R] **adjust**, [R] **estimates**, [R] **hausman**, [R] **lincom**, [R] **mfx**,
	[R] **nlcom**, [R] **predictnl**, [R] **test**, [R] **testnl**
Background:	[U] **13.5 Accessing coefficients and standard errors**,
	[U] **20 Estimation and postestimation commands**,
	[R] **estat**, [R] **predict**

Title

---

xtgls — Fit panel-data models using GLS

Syntax

xtgls *depvar* [*indepvars*] [*if*] [*in*] [*weight*] [, *options*]

options	description
Model	
i(*varname$_i$*)	use *varname$_i$* as the panel ID variable
t(*varname$_t$*)	use *varname$_t$* as the time variable
<u>nocon</u>stant	suppress constant term
panels(<u>iid</u>)	use i.i.d. error structure
panels(<u>h</u>eteroskedastic)	use heteroskedastic but uncorrelated error structure
panels(<u>c</u>orrelated)	use heteroskedastic and correlated error structure
corr(<u>in</u>dependent)	use independent autocorrelation structure
<u>c</u>orr(<u>ar</u>1)	use AR1 autocorrelation structure
<u>c</u>orr(<u>p</u>sar1)	use panel-specific AR1 autocorrelation structure
<u>rho</u>type(*calc*)	specify method to compute autocorrelation parameter; see *Options* for details; seldom used
igls	use iterated GLS estimator instead of two-step GLS estimator
force	estimate even if observations unequally spaced in time
SE	
nmk	normalize standard error by $N - k$ instead of N
Reporting	
<u>l</u>evel(#)	set confidence level; default is level(95)
Opt options	
optimize_options	control the optimization process; seldom used

depvar and *indepvars* may contain time-series operators; see [U] **11.4.3 Time-series varlists**.
bootstrap, by, jackknife, statsby, and xi may be used with xtgls; see [U] **11.1.10 Prefix commands**.
aweights are allowed; see [U] **11.1.6 weight**.
See [U] **20 Estimation and postestimation commands** for additional capabilities of estimation commands.

Description

xtgls fits panel data linear models using feasible generalized least squares. This command allows estimation in the presence of AR(1) autocorrelation within panels and cross-sectional correlation and heteroskedasticity across panels.

Options

```
                Model
```

i($varname_i$), t($varname_t$); see [XT] **estimation options**.

xtgls does not need to know t() in all cases, and, in those cases, specifying t() makes no difference. We note in the descriptions of the panels() and corr() options when t() is required. When t() is required, the observations must be spaced equally over time; however, see option force below.

noconstant; see [XT] **estimation options**.

panels(*pdist*) specifies the error structure across panels.

panels(iid) specifies a homoskedastic error structure with no cross-sectional correlation. This is the default.

panels(heteroskedastic) specifies a heteroskedastic error structure with no cross-sectional correlation.

panels(correlated) specifies a heteroskedastic error structure with cross-sectional correlation. If p(c) is specified, you must also specify t(). Note that the results will be based on a generalized inverse of a singular matrix unless $T \geq m$ (the number of time periods is greater than or equal to the number of panels).

corr(*corr*) specifies the assumed autocorrelation within panels.

corr(independent) specifies that there is no autocorrelation. This is the default.

corr(ar1) specifies that, within panels, there is AR(1) autocorrelation and that the coefficient of the AR(1) process is common to all the panels. If c(ar1) is specified, you must also specify t().

corr(psar1) specifies that, within panels, there is AR(1) autocorrelation and that the coefficient of the AR(1) process is specific to each panel. psar1 stands for panel-specific AR(1). If c(psar1) is specified, t() must also be specified.

rhotype(*calc*) specifies the method to be used to calculate the autocorrelation parameter:

regress	regression using lags; the default
dw	Durbin–Watson calculation
freg	regression using leads
nagar	Nagar calculation
theil	Theil calculation
tscorr	time-series autocorrelation calculation

All the calculations are asymptotically equivalent and consistent; this is a rarely used option.

igls requests an iterated GLS estimator instead of the two-step GLS estimator in the case of a nonautocorrelated model, or instead of the three-step GLS estimator in the case of an autocorrelated model. The iterated GLS estimator converges to the MLE for the corr(independent) models but does not for the other corr() models.

force specifies that estimation be forced even though t() is not equally spaced. This is relevant only for correlation structures that require knowledge of t() and that require observations be equally spaced.

⎡ SE ⎤

nmk specifies standard errors are to be normalized by $N - k$, where k is the number of parameters estimated, rather than N, the number of observations. Greene (2003, 322) recommends N, and remarks that whether you use N or $N - k$ does not make the variance calculation unbiased in these models.

⎡ Reporting ⎤

level(#); see [XT] **estimation options**.

⎡ Opt options ⎤

optimize_options control the iterative optimization process. These options are seldom used.

iterate(#) specifies the maximum number of iterations. When the number of iterations equals #, the optimization stops and presents the current results, even if convergence has not been reached. The default is iterate(100).

tolerance(#) specifies the tolerance for the coefficient vector. When the relative change in the coefficient vector from one iteration to the next is less than or equal to #, the optimization process is stopped. tolerance(1e-7) is the default.

nolog suppresses display of the iteration log.

Remarks

Remarks are presented under the headings

> *Introduction*
> *Heteroskedasticity across panels*
> *Correlation across panels (cross-sectional correlation)*
> *Autocorrelation within panels*

Introduction

Information on GLS can be found in Greene (2003), Maddala (2001), Davidson and MacKinnon (1993), and Judge et al. (1985).

If you have a large number of panels relative to time periods, see [XT] **xtreg** and [XT] **xtgee**. xtgee, in particular, provides capabilities similar to those of xtgls but does not allow cross-sectional correlation. On the other hand, xtgee allows a richer description of the correlation within panels as long as the same correlations apply to all panels. xtgls provides two unique features:

1. Cross-sectional correlation may be modeled (panels(correlated)).

2. Within panels, the AR(1) correlation coefficient may be unique (corr(psar1)).

xtgls allows models with heteroskedasticity and no cross-sectional correlation, but, strictly speaking, xtgee does not. xtgee with the robust option relaxes the assumption of equal variances, at least as far as the standard error calculation is concerned.

In addition, xtgls, panels(iid) corr(independent) nmk is equivalent to regress.

The nmk option uses $n - k$ rather than n to normalize the variance calculation.

To fit a model with autocorrelated errors (corr(ar1) or corr(psar1)), the data must be equally spaced in time. To fit a model with cross-sectional correlation (panels(correlated)), panels must have the same number of observations (be balanced).

The equation from which the models are developed is given by

$$y_{it} = \mathbf{x}_{it}\boldsymbol{\beta} + \epsilon_{it}$$

where $i = 1, \ldots, m$ is the number of units (or panels) and $t = 1, \ldots, T_i$ is the number of observations for panel i. This model can equally be written as

$$\begin{bmatrix} \mathbf{y}_1 \\ \mathbf{y}_2 \\ \vdots \\ \mathbf{y}_m \end{bmatrix} = \begin{bmatrix} \mathbf{X}_1 \\ \mathbf{X}_2 \\ \vdots \\ \mathbf{X}_m \end{bmatrix} \boldsymbol{\beta} + \begin{bmatrix} \epsilon_1 \\ \epsilon_2 \\ \vdots \\ \epsilon_m \end{bmatrix}$$

The variance matrix of the disturbance terms can be written as

$$E[\epsilon\epsilon'] = \boldsymbol{\Omega} = \begin{bmatrix} \sigma_{1,1}\boldsymbol{\Omega}_{1,1} & \sigma_{1,2}\boldsymbol{\Omega}_{1,2} & \cdots & \sigma_{1,m}\boldsymbol{\Omega}_{1,m} \\ \sigma_{2,1}\boldsymbol{\Omega}_{2,1} & \sigma_{2,2}\boldsymbol{\Omega}_{2,2} & \cdots & \sigma_{2,m}\boldsymbol{\Omega}_{2,m} \\ \vdots & \vdots & \ddots & \vdots \\ \sigma_{m,1}\boldsymbol{\Omega}_{m,1} & \sigma_{m,2}\boldsymbol{\Omega}_{m,2} & \cdots & \sigma_{m,m}\boldsymbol{\Omega}_{m,m} \end{bmatrix}$$

For the $\boldsymbol{\Omega}_{i,j}$ matrices to be parameterized to model cross-sectional correlation, they must be square (balanced panels).

In these models, we assume that the coefficient vector $\boldsymbol{\beta}$ is the same for all panels and consider a variety of models by changing the assumptions on the structure of $\boldsymbol{\Omega}$.

For the classic OLS regression model, we have

$$E[\epsilon_{i,t}] = 0$$
$$\text{Var}[\epsilon_{i,t}] = \sigma^2$$
$$\text{Cov}[\epsilon_{i,t}, \epsilon_{j,s}] = 0 \qquad \text{if } t \neq s \text{ or } i \neq j$$

This amounts to assuming that $\boldsymbol{\Omega}$ has the structure given by

$$\boldsymbol{\Omega} = \begin{bmatrix} \sigma^2\mathbf{I} & \mathbf{0} & \cdots & \mathbf{0} \\ \mathbf{0} & \sigma^2\mathbf{I} & \cdots & \mathbf{0} \\ \vdots & \vdots & \ddots & \vdots \\ \mathbf{0} & \mathbf{0} & \cdots & \sigma^2\mathbf{I} \end{bmatrix}$$

whether or not the panels are balanced (the $\mathbf{0}$ matrices may be rectangular). The classic OLS assumptions are the default panels(uncorrelated) and corr(independent) options for this command.

Heteroskedasticity across panels

In many cross-sectional datasets, the variance for each of the panels differs. It is common to have data on countries, states, or other units that have variation of scale. The heteroskedastic model is specified by including the panels(heteroskedastic) option, which assumes that

$$\Omega = \begin{bmatrix} \sigma_1^2\mathbf{I} & \mathbf{0} & \cdots & \mathbf{0} \\ \mathbf{0} & \sigma_2^2\mathbf{I} & \cdots & \mathbf{0} \\ \vdots & \vdots & \ddots & \vdots \\ \mathbf{0} & \mathbf{0} & \cdots & \sigma_m^2\mathbf{I} \end{bmatrix}$$

▷ Example 1

Greene (2003, 329) reprints data in a classic study of investment demand by Grunfeld and Griliches (1960). Below we allow the variances to differ for each of the five companies.

```
. use http://www.stata-press.com/data/r9/invest2

. xtgls invest market stock, i(company) panels(hetero)

Cross-sectional time-series FGLS regression

Coefficients:  generalized least squares
Panels:        heteroskedastic
Correlation:   no autocorrelation

Estimated covariances      =          5        Number of obs      =        100
Estimated autocorrelations =          0        Number of groups   =          5
Estimated coefficients     =          3        Time periods       =         20
                                               Wald chi2(2)       =     865.38
Log likelihood             = -570.1305         Prob > chi2        =     0.0000
```

invest	Coef.	Std. Err.	z	P>|z|	[95% Conf. Interval]	
market	.0949905	.007409	12.82	0.000	.0804692	.1095118
stock	.3378129	.0302254	11.18	0.000	.2785722	.3970535
_cons	-36.2537	6.124363	-5.92	0.000	-48.25723	-24.25017

◁

Correlation across panels (cross-sectional correlation)

We may wish to assume that the error terms of panels are correlated, in addition to having different scale variances. The variance structure is specified by including the panels(correlated) option and is given by

$$\Omega = \begin{bmatrix} \sigma_1^2\mathbf{I} & \sigma_{1,2}\mathbf{I} & \cdots & \sigma_{1,m}\mathbf{I} \\ \sigma_{2,1}\mathbf{I} & \sigma_2^2\mathbf{I} & \cdots & \sigma_{2,m}\mathbf{I} \\ \vdots & \vdots & \ddots & \vdots \\ \sigma_{m,1}\mathbf{I} & \sigma_{m,2}\mathbf{I} & \cdots & \sigma_m^2\mathbf{I} \end{bmatrix}$$

Note that, since we must estimate cross-sectional correlation in this model, the panels must be balanced (and $T \geq m$ for valid results). In addition, we must now specify the t() option so that xtgls knows how the observations within panels are ordered.

▷ Example 2

```
. xtgls invest market stock, i(company) t(time) panels(correlated)
Cross-sectional time-series FGLS regression
Coefficients:  generalized least squares
Panels:        heteroskedastic with cross-sectional correlation
Correlation:   no autocorrelation
Estimated covariances      =         15          Number of obs      =        100
Estimated autocorrelations =          0          Number of groups   =          5
Estimated coefficients     =          3          Time periods       =         20
                                                 Wald chi2(2)       =    1285.19
Log likelihood             =  -537.8045          Prob > chi2        =     0.0000
```

invest	Coef.	Std. Err.	z	P>|z|	[95% Conf. Interval]	
market	.0961894	.0054752	17.57	0.000	.0854583	.1069206
stock	.3095321	.0179851	17.21	0.000	.2742819	.3447822
_cons	-38.36128	5.344871	-7.18	0.000	-48.83703	-27.88552

The estimated cross-sectional covariances are stored in e(Sigma).

```
. matrix list e(Sigma)
symmetric e(Sigma)[5,5]
             _ee        _ee2        _ee3        _ee4        _ee5
 _ee    9410.9061
_ee2  -168.04631    755.85077
_ee3  -1915.9538  -4163.3434    34288.49
_ee4  -1129.2896  -80.381742   2259.3242   633.42367
_ee5   258.50132    4035.872  -27898.235  -1170.6801   33455.511
```

◁

▷ Example 3

We can obtain the MLE results by specifying the igls option, which iterates the GLS estimation technique to convergence:

```
. xtgls invest market stock, i(company) t(time) panels(correlated) igls
Iteration 1: tolerance = .2127384
Iteration 2: tolerance = .22817
  (output omitted )
Iteration 1046: tolerance = 1.000e-07

Cross-sectional time-series FGLS regression
Coefficients:  generalized least squares
Panels:        heteroskedastic with cross-sectional correlation
Correlation:   no autocorrelation
Estimated covariances      =         15          Number of obs      =        100
Estimated autocorrelations =          0          Number of groups   =          5
Estimated coefficients     =          3          Time periods       =         20
                                                 Wald chi2(2)       =     558.51
Log likelihood             =  -515.4222          Prob > chi2        =     0.0000
```

invest	Coef.	Std. Err.	z	P>|z|	[95% Conf. Interval]	
market	.023631	.004291	5.51	0.000	.0152207	.0320413
stock	.1709472	.0152526	11.21	0.000	.1410526	.2008417
_cons	-2.216508	1.958845	-1.13	0.258	-6.055774	1.622759

◁

Autocorrelation within panels

The individual identity matrices along the diagonal of Ω may be replaced with more general structures to allow for serial correlation. xtgls allows three options so that you may assume a structure with corr(independent) (no autocorrelation); corr(ar1) (serial correlation where the correlation parameter is common for all panels); or corr(psar1) (serial correlation where the correlation parameter is unique for each panel).

The restriction of a common autocorrelation parameter is reasonable when the individual correlations are nearly equal and the time series are short.

If the restriction of a common autocorrelation parameter is reasonable, this allows us to use more information in estimating the autocorrelation parameter to produce a more reasonable estimate of the regression coefficients.

▷ Example 4

If corr(ar1) is specified, each group is assumed to have errors that follow the same AR(1) process; that is, the autocorrelation parameter is the same for all groups.

```
. xtgls invest market stock, i(company) t(time) panels(hetero) corr(ar1)

Cross-sectional time-series FGLS regression

Coefficients:  generalized least squares
Panels:        heteroskedastic
Correlation:   common AR(1) coefficient for all panels  (0.8651)

Estimated covariances      =         5       Number of obs      =        100
Estimated autocorrelations =         1       Number of groups   =          5
Estimated coefficients     =         3       Time periods       =         20
                                             Wald chi2(2)       =     119.69
Log likelihood             = -506.0909       Prob > chi2        =     0.0000
```

invest	Coef.	Std. Err.	z	P>|z|	[95% Conf. Interval]	
market	.0744315	.0097937	7.60	0.000	.0552362	.0936268
stock	.2874294	.0475391	6.05	0.000	.1942545	.3806043
_cons	-18.96238	17.64943	-1.07	0.283	-53.55464	15.62987

◁

▷ Example 5

If corr(psar1) is specified, each group is assumed to have errors that follow a different AR(1) process.

```
. xtgls invest market stock, i(company) t(time) panels(iid) corr(psar1)

Cross-sectional time-series FGLS regression

Coefficients:  generalized least squares
Panels:        homoskedastic
Correlation:   panel-specific AR(1)
```

Estimated covariances = 1	Number of obs =	100
Estimated autocorrelations = 5	Number of groups =	5
Estimated coefficients = 3	Time periods =	20
	Wald chi2(2) =	252.93
Log likelihood = -543.1888	Prob > chi2 =	0.0000

invest	Coef.	Std. Err.	z	P>|z|	[95% Conf. Interval]	
market	.0934343	.0097783	9.56	0.000	.0742693	.1125993
stock	.3838814	.0416775	9.21	0.000	.302195	.4655677
_cons	-10.1246	34.06675	-0.30	0.766	-76.8942	56.64499

◁

Saved Results

xtgls saves in e():

Scalars

e(N)	number of observations	e(df)	degrees of freedom
e(N_g)	number of groups	e(ll)	log likelihood
e(N_t)	number of time periods	e(g_max)	largest group size
e(N_miss)	number of missing observations	e(g_min)	smallest group size
e(n_cf)	number of estimated coefficients	e(g_avg)	average group size
e(n_cv)	number of estimated covariances	e(chi2)	χ^2
e(n_cr)	number of estimated correlations	e(df_pear)	degrees of freedom for Pearson χ^2

Macros

e(cmd)	xtgls	e(ivar)	variable denoting groups
e(depvar)	name of dependent variable	e(tvar)	variable denoting time
e(title)	title in estimation output	e(wtype)	weight type
e(coefftype)	estimation scheme	e(wexp)	weight expression
e(corr)	correlation structure	e(rho)	ρ
e(vt)	panel option	e(properties)	b V
e(rhotype)	type of estimated correlation	e(predict)	program used to implement predict
e(chi2type)	Wald; type of model χ^2 test		

Matrices

e(b)	coefficient vector	e(Sigma)	$\widehat{\Sigma}$ matrix
e(V)	variance–covariance matrix of the estimators		

Functions

e(sample)	marks estimation sample

Methods and Formulas

`xtgls` is implemented as an ado-file.

The GLS results are given by

$$\widehat{\beta}_{\text{GLS}} = (\mathbf{X}'\widehat{\Omega}^{-1}\mathbf{X})^{-1}\mathbf{X}'\widehat{\Omega}^{-1}\mathbf{y}$$
$$\widehat{\text{Var}}(\widehat{\beta}_{\text{GLS}}) = (\mathbf{X}'\widehat{\Omega}^{-1}\mathbf{X})^{-1}$$

For all our models, the Ω matrix may be written in terms of the Kronecker product:

$$\Omega = \Sigma_{m \times m} \otimes \mathbf{I}_{T_i \times T_i}$$

The estimated variance matrix is obtained by substituting the estimator $\widehat{\Sigma}$ for Σ, where

$$\widehat{\Sigma}_{i,j} = \frac{\widehat{\epsilon}_i{}'\widehat{\epsilon}_j}{T}$$

The residuals used in estimating Σ are first obtained from OLS regression. If the estimation is iterated, residuals are obtained from the last fitted model.

Maximum likelihood estimates may be obtained by iterating the FGLS estimates to convergence for models with no autocorrelation, `corr(0)`.

Note that the GLS estimates and their associated standard errors are calculated using $\widehat{\Sigma}^{-1}$. As Beck and Katz (1995) point out, the Σ matrix is of rank at most $\min(T, m)$ when you use the `panels(correlated)` option. For the GLS results to be valid (not based on a generalized inverse), T must be at least as large as m, as you need at least as many time period observations as there are panels.

Beck and Katz (1995) suggest using OLS parameter estimates with asymptotic standard errors that are corrected for correlation between the panels. This estimation can be performed with the `xtpcse` command; see [XT] **xtpcse**.

References

Baum, C. F. 2001. Residual diagnostics. *Stata Journal* 1: 101–104.

Beck, N. and J. N. Katz. 1995. What to do (and not to do) with time-series cross-section data. *American Political Science Review* 89: 634–647.

Davidson, R. and J. G. MacKinnon. 1993. *Estimation and Inference in Econometrics*. New York: Oxford University Press.

Greene, W. H. 2003. *Econometric Analysis*. 5th ed. Upper Saddle River, NJ: Prentice Hall.

Grunfeld, Y. and Z. Griliches. 1960. Is aggregation necessarily bad? *Review of Economics and Statistics* 42: 1–13.

Judge, G. G., W. E. Griffiths, R. C. Hill, H. Lütkepohl, and T.-C. Lee. 1985. *The Theory and Practice of Econometrics*. 2nd ed. New York: Wiley.

Maddala, G. S. 2001. *Introduction to Econometrics*. 3rd ed. New York: Wiley.

Also See

Complementary:	[XT] **xtgls postestimation**; [XT] **xtdata**, [XT] **xtdes**, [XT] **xtsum**, [XT] **xttab**
Related:	[XT] **xtpcse**, [XT] **xtreg**, [XT] **xtregar**,
	[R] **regress**, [SVY] **svy: regress**, [TS] **newey**, [TS] **prais**
Background:	[U] **11.1.10 Prefix commands**,
	[U] **20 Estimation and postestimation commands**,
	[XT] **estimation options**, [XT] **xt**

Title

xtgls postestimation — Postestimation tools for xtgls

Description

The following postestimation commands are available for xtgls:

command	description
adjust[1]	adjusted predictions of $\mathbf{x}\beta$
estat	AIC, BIC, VCE, and estimation sample summary
estimates	cataloging estimation results
hausman	Hausman's specification test
lincom	point estimates, standard errors, testing, and inference for linear combinations of coefficients
lrtest	likelihood-ratio test
mfx	marginal effects or elasticities
nlcom	point estimates, standard errors, testing, and inference for nonlinear combinations of coefficients
predict	predictions, residuals, influence statistics, and other diagnostic measures
predictnl	point estimates, standard errors, testing, and inference for generalized predictions
test	Wald tests for simple and composite linear hypotheses
testnl	Wald tests of nonlinear hypotheses

[1] adjust does not work with time-series operators.

See the corresponding entries in the *Stata Base Reference Manual* for details.

Syntax for predict

predict [*type*] *newvar* [*if*] [*in*] [, [xb|stdp]]

These statistics are available both in and out of sample; type predict ... if e(sample) ... if wanted only for the estimation sample.

Options for predict

xb, the default, calculates the linear prediction.

stdp calculates the standard error of the linear prediction.

Also See

Complementary: [XT] **xtgls**,

[R] **adjust**, [R] **estimates**, [R] **hausman**, [R] **lincom**, [R] **lrtest**,

[R] **mfx**, [R] **nlcom**, [R] **predictnl**, [R] **test**, [R] **testnl**

Background: [U] **13.5 Accessing coefficients and standard errors**,

[U] **20 Estimation and postestimation commands**,

[R] **estat**, [R] **predict**

Title

> **xthtaylor** — Hausman–Taylor estimator for error components models

Syntax

> xthtaylor *depvar* *indepvars* $[$ *if* $]$ $[$ *in* $]$ $[$ *weight* $]$, <u>endog</u>(*varlist*) $[$ *options* $]$

options	description
Main	
<u>i</u>(*varname$_i$*)	use *varname$_i$* as the panel ID variable
<u>t</u>(*varname$_t$*)	use *varname$_t$* as the time variable; required if **amacurdy** specified
<u>no</u>constant	suppress constant term
*<u>endog</u>(*varlist*)	explanatory variables in *indepvars* to be treated as endogenous
<u>c</u>onstant(*varlist$_{ti}$*)	independent variables that are constant within panel
<u>vary</u>ing(*varlist$_{tv}$*)	independent variables that are time varying within panel
<u>ama</u>curdy	fit model based on Amemiya and MaCurdy estimator
SE	
<u>vce</u>(*vcetype*)	*vcetype* may be <u>boot</u>strap or <u>jack</u>knife
Reporting	
<u>level</u>(#)	set confidence level; default is **level(95)**
<u>small</u>	report small-sample statistics

*endog(*varlist*) is required.

You must **tsset** your data before using **xthtaylor**; see [TS] **tsset**.

depvar, *indepvars*, and all *varlist*s may contain time-series operators; see [U] **11.4.3 Time-series varlists**.

bootstrap, **by**, **jackknife**, **statsby**, and **xi** may be used with **xthtaylor**; see [U] **11.1.10 Prefix commands**.

iweights and **fweights** are allowed unless the **amacurdy** option is specified; **fweights** must be constant within panel; see [U] **11.1.6 weight**.

See [U] **20 Estimation and postestimation commands** for additional capabilities of estimation commands.

Description

xthtaylor fits panel-data random-effects models in which some of the covariates are correlated with the unobserved individual-level random effect. The estimators, originally proposed by Hausman and Taylor (1981) and by Amemiya and MaCurdy (1986), are based on instrumental variables. By default, **xthtaylor** uses the Hausman–Taylor estimator. When the **amacurdy** option is specified, **xthtaylor** uses the Amemiya–MaCurdy estimator.

Although the estimators implemented in **xthtaylor** and **xtivreg** (see [XT] **xtivreg**) use the method of instrumental variables, each command is designed for very different problems. The estimators implemented in **xtivreg** assume that a subset of the explanatory variables in the model are correlated with the idiosyncratic error ϵ_{it}. In contrast, the Hausman–Taylor and Amemiya–MaCurdy estimators that are implemented in **xthtaylor** assume that some of the explanatory variables are correlated with the individual-level random-effects, u_i, but that none of the explanatory variables are correlated with the idiosyncratic error, ϵ_{it}.

Options

i(*varname$_i$*), t(*varname$_t$*), noconstant; see [XT] **estimation options**.

endog(*varlist*) specifies a subset of explanatory variables in *indepvars* be treated as endogenous variables, i.e., the explanatory variables that are assumed to be correlated with the unobserved random effect. endog() is required.

constant(*varlist$_{ti}$*) specifies the subset of variables in *indepvars* that are time invariant, that is, constant within panel. By using this option, you not only assert that the variables specified in *varlist$_{ti}$* are time invariant but also that all other variables in *indepvars* are time varying. If this assertion is false, xthtaylor does not perform the estimation and will issue an error message. xthtaylor automatically detects which variables are time invariant and which are not. However, users may want to check their understanding of the data and specify which variables are time invariant and which are not.

varying(*varlist$_{tv}$*) specifies the subset of variables in *indepvars* that are time varying. By using this option, you not only assert that the variables specified in *varlist$_{tv}$* are time varying but also that all other variables in *indepvars* are time invariant. If this assertion is false, xthtaylor does not perform the estimation and issues an error message. xthtaylor automatically detects which variables are time varying and which are not. However, users may want to check their understanding of the data and specify which variables are time varying and which are not.

amacurdy specifies that the Amemiya–MaCurdy estimator be used. This estimator uses extra instruments to gain efficiency at the cost of additional assumptions on the data-generating process. This option may only be specified for samples containing balanced panels, and weights may not be specified. The panels must also have a common initial time period.

vce(*vcetype*); see [R] **vce_option**.

level(#); see [XT] **estimation options**.

small specifies that the p-values from the Wald tests in the output and all subsequent Wald tests obtained via test use t and F distributions instead of the large-sample normal and χ^2 distributions. By default, the p-values are obtained using the normal and χ^2 distributions.

Remarks

If you have not read [XT] **xt**, please do so.

Consider a random-effects model of the form

$$y_{it} = \mathbf{X}_{1it}\boldsymbol{\beta}_1 + \mathbf{X}_{2it}\boldsymbol{\beta}_2 + \mathbf{Z}_{1i}\boldsymbol{\delta}_1 + \mathbf{Z}_{2i}\boldsymbol{\delta}_2 + \mu_i + \epsilon_{it}$$

where

$\mathbf{X}_{1it}$ is a $1 \times k_1$ vector of observations on exogenous, time-varying variables assumed to be uncorrelated with μ_i and ϵ_{it};

$\mathbf{X}_{2it}$ is a $1 \times k_2$ vector of observations on endogenous, time-varying variables assumed to be (possibly) correlated with μ_i but orthogonal to ϵ_{it};

$\mathbf{Z}_{1i}$ is a $1 \times g_1$ vector of observations on exogenous, time-invariant variables assumed to be uncorrelated with μ_i and ϵ_{it};

$\mathbf{Z}_{2i}$ is a $1 \times g_2$ vector of observations on endogenous, time-invariant variables assumed to be (possibly) correlated μ_i but orthogonal to ϵ_{it};

μ_i is the unobserved, panel-level random effect that is assumed to have zero mean and finite variance σ_μ^2 and to be independently and identically distributed (i.i.d.) over the panels;

ϵ_{it} is the idiosyncratic error that is assumed to have zero mean and finite variance σ_ϵ^2 and to be i.i.d. over all the observations in the data;

$\beta_1, \beta_2, \delta_1$, and δ_2 are $k_1 \times 1$, $k_2 \times 1$, $g_1 \times 1$, and $g_2 \times 1$ coefficient vectors, respectively; and

$i = 1, \ldots, n$, where n is the number of panels in the sample and, for each i, $t = 1, \ldots, T_i$.

Since $\mathbf{X}_{2it}$ and $\mathbf{Z}_{2i}$ may be correlated with μ_i, the simple random-effects estimators—xtreg, re and xtreg, mle—are generally not consistent for the parameters in this model. Since the within estimator, xtreg, fe, removes the μ_i by mean-differencing the data before estimating β_1 and β_2, it is consistent for these parameters. However, in the process of removing the μ_i, the within estimator also eliminates the $\mathbf{Z}_{1i}$ and the $\mathbf{Z}_{2i}$. Thus it cannot estimate δ_1 nor δ_2. The Hausman–Taylor and Amemiya–MaCurdy estimators implemented in xthtaylor are designed to resolve this problem.

As mentioned previously, the within estimator consistently estimates β_1 and β_2. Using these estimates, we can obtain the within-residuals, called $\widehat{d}_i$. Intermediate, albeit consistent, estimates of δ_1 and δ_2—called $\widehat{\delta}_{1\mathrm{IV}}$ and $\widehat{\delta}_{2\mathrm{IV}}$, respectively—are obtained by regressing the within-residuals on $\mathbf{Z}_{1i}$ and $\mathbf{Z}_{2i}$, using $\mathbf{X}_{1it}$ and $\mathbf{Z}_{1i}$ as instruments. The order condition for identification requires that the number of variables in $\mathbf{X}_{1it}$, k_1, be at least as large as the number of elements in $\mathbf{Z}_{2i}$, g_2, and that there be sufficient correlation between the instruments and $\mathbf{Z}_{2i}$ to avoid a weak instrument problem.

The within estimates of β_1 and β_2 and the intermediate estimates $\widehat{\delta}_{1\mathrm{IV}}$ and $\widehat{\delta}_{2\mathrm{IV}}$ can be used to obtain sets of within and overall residuals. These two sets of residuals can be used to estimate the variance components (see *Methods and Formulas* for details).

The estimated variance components can then be used to perform a GLS transform on each of the variables. For what follows, define the general notation $\breve{w}_{it}$ to represent the GLS transform of the variable w_{it}, $\overline{w}_i$ to represent the within-panel mean of w_{it}, and $\widetilde{w}_{it}$ to represent the within transform of w_{it}. Using this notational convention, the Hausman–Taylor (1981) estimator of the coefficients of interest can be obtained by the instrumental variables regression

$$\breve{y}_{it} = \breve{\mathbf{X}}_{1it}\beta_1 + \breve{\mathbf{X}}_{2it}\beta_2 + \breve{\mathbf{Z}}_{1i}\delta_1 + \breve{\mathbf{Z}}_{2i}\delta_2 + \breve{\mu}_i + \breve{\epsilon}_{it} \tag{1}$$

using $\widetilde{\mathbf{X}}_{1it}, \widetilde{\mathbf{X}}_{2it}, \overline{\mathbf{X}}_{1i}, \overline{\mathbf{X}}_{2i}$, and $\mathbf{Z}_{1i}$ as instruments.

For the instruments to be valid, this estimator requires that $\overline{\mathbf{X}}_{1i.}$ and $\mathbf{Z}_{1i}$ be uncorrelated with the random-effect μ_i. More precisely, the instruments are valid when

$$\mathrm{plim}_{n \to \infty} \frac{1}{n} \sum_{i=1}^{n} \overline{\mathbf{X}}_{1i.}\mu_i = 0$$

and

$$\mathrm{plim}_{n \to \infty} \frac{1}{n} \sum_{i=1}^{n} \mathbf{Z}_{1i}\mu_i = 0$$

Amemiya and MaCurdy (1986) place stricter requirements on the instruments that vary within panels to obtain a more efficient estimator. Specifically, Amemiya and MaCurdy (1986) assume that $\mathbf{X}_{1it}$ is orthogonal to μ_i in every time period; i.e., $\text{plim}_{n\to\infty} \frac{1}{n}\sum_{i=1}^{n}\mathbf{X}_{1it}\mu_i = 0$ for $t = 1,\ldots,T$. With this restriction, they derive the Amemiya–MaCurdy estimator as the instrumental variables regression of (1) using instruments $\widetilde{\mathbf{X}}_{1it}$, $\widetilde{\mathbf{X}}_{2it}$, $\mathbf{X}_{1it}^*$, and $\mathbf{Z}_{1i}$. Note that the order condition for the Amemiya–MaCurdy estimator is now $Tk_1 > g_2$. xthtaylor uses the Amemiya–MaCurdy estimator when the amacurdy option is specified.

▷ Example 1

This example replicates the results of Baltagi and Khanti-Akom (1990, table II, column HT) using 595 observations on individuals over the period 1976–1982 that were extracted from the Panel Study of Income Dynamics (PSID). In the model, the log-transformed wage lwage is assumed to be a function of how long the person has worked for a firm, wks; binary variables indicating whether a person lives in a large metropolitan area or in the south, smsa and south; marital status is ms; years of education, ed; a quadratic of work experience, exp and exp2; occupation, occ; a binary variable indicating employment in a manufacture industry, ind; a binary variable indicating that wages are set by a union contract, union; a binary variable indicating gender, fem; and a binary variable indicating whether the individual is African-American, blk.

We suspect that the time-varying variables exp, exp2, wks, ms, and union are all correlated with the unobserved individual random effect. We can inspect these variables to see if they exhibit sufficient within-panel variation to serve as their own instruments.

```
. use http://www.stata-press.com/data/r9/psidextract
. xtsum exp exp2 wks ms union, i(id)
```

Variable		Mean	Std. Dev.	Min	Max		Observations
exp	overall	19.85378	10.96637	1	51	N =	4165
	between		10.79018	4	48	n =	595
	within		2.00024	16.85378	22.85378	T =	7
exp2	overall	514.405	496.9962	1	2601	N =	4165
	between		489.0495	20	2308	n =	595
	within		90.44581	231.405	807.405	T =	7
wks	overall	46.81152	5.129098	5	52	N =	4165
	between		3.284016	31.57143	51.57143	n =	595
	within		3.941881	12.2401	63.66867	T =	7
ms	overall	.8144058	.3888256	0	1	N =	4165
	between		.3686109	0	1	n =	595
	within		.1245274	-.0427371	1.671549	T =	7
union	overall	.3639856	.4812023	0	1	N =	4165
	between		.4543848	0	1	n =	595
	within		.1593351	-.4931573	1.221128	T =	7

We are also going to assume that the exogenous variables occ, south, smsa, ind, fem, and blk are instruments for the endogenous, time-invariant variable ed. The output below indicates that while fem appears to be a weak instrument, the remaining instruments are probably sufficiently correlated to identify the coefficient on ed. (See Baltagi and Khanti-Akom [1990] for further discussion.)

```
. correlate fem blk occ south smsa ind ed
(obs=4165)
```

	fem	blk	occ	south	smsa	ind	ed
fem	1.0000						
blk	0.2086	1.0000					
occ	-0.0847	0.0837	1.0000				
south	0.0516	0.1218	0.0413	1.0000			
smsa	0.1044	0.1154	-0.2018	-0.1350	1.0000		
ind	-0.1778	-0.0475	0.2260	-0.0769	-0.0689	1.0000	
ed	-0.0012	-0.1196	-0.6194	-0.1216	0.1843	-0.2365	1.0000

We will assume that the correlations are strong enough and proceed with the estimation. The output below gives the Hausman–Taylor estimates for this model.

```
. xthtaylor lwage occ south smsa ind exp exp2 wks ms union fem blk ed,
> endog(exp exp2 wks ms union ed)
```

Hausman-Taylor estimation			Number of obs	=	4165
Group variable (i): id			Number of groups	=	595

		Obs per group: min =	7
		avg =	7
		max =	7

Random effects u_i ~ i.i.d.		Wald chi2(12)	=	6891.87
		Prob > chi2	=	0.0000

lwage	Coef.	Std. Err.	z	P>|z|	[95% Conf. Interval]	
TVexogenous						
occ	-.0207047	.0137809	-1.50	0.133	-.0477149	.0063055
south	.0074398	.031955	0.23	0.816	-.0551908	.0700705
smsa	-.0418334	.0189581	-2.21	0.027	-.0789906	-.0046761
ind	.0136039	.0152374	0.89	0.372	-.0162608	.0434686
TVendogenous						
exp	.1131328	.002471	45.79	0.000	.1082898	.1179758
exp2	-.0004189	.0000546	-7.67	0.000	-.0005259	-.0003119
wks	.0008374	.0005997	1.40	0.163	-.0003381	.0020129
ms	-.0298508	.01898	-1.57	0.116	-.0670508	.0073493
union	.0327714	.0149084	2.20	0.028	.0035514	.0619914
TIexogenous						
fem	-.1309236	.126659	-1.03	0.301	-.3791707	.1173234
blk	-.2857479	.1557019	-1.84	0.066	-.5909179	.0194221
TIendogenous						
ed	.137944	.0212485	6.49	0.000	.0962977	.1795902
_cons	2.912726	.2836522	10.27	0.000	2.356778	3.468674

sigma_u	.94180304	
sigma_e	.15180273	
rho	.97467788	(fraction of variance due to u_i)

note: TV refers to time varying; TI refers to time invariant.

The estimated σ_μ and σ_ϵ are 0.9418 and 0.1518, respectively, indicating that a very large fraction of the total error variance is attributed to μ_i. The z statistics indicate that a number of the coefficients may not be significantly different from zero. Note that, while the coefficients on the time-invariant variables fem and blk have relatively large standard errors, the standard error for the coefficient on ed is relatively small.

Baltagi and Khanti-Akom (1990) also present evidence that the efficiency gains of the Amemiya–MaCurdy estimator over the Hausman–Taylor estimator are small for these data. This point is especially important given the additional restrictions that the estimator places on the data-generating process. The output below replicates the Baltagi and Khanti-Akom (1990) results from column AM of table II.

```
. set matsize 100
. xthtaylor lwage occ south smsa ind exp exp2 wks ms union fem blk ed,
> endog(exp exp2 wks ms union ed) amacurdy t(t)
```

Amemiya-MaCurdy estimation			Number of obs	=	4165
Group variable (i): id			Number of groups	=	595
			Obs per group: min =		7
			avg =		7
			max =		7
Random effects u_i ~ i.i.d.			Wald chi2(12)	=	6879.20
			Prob > chi2	=	0.0000

lwage	Coef.	Std. Err.	z	P>|z|	[95% Conf. Interval]	
TVexogenous						
occ	-.0208498	.0137653	-1.51	0.130	-.0478292	.0061297
south	.0072818	.0319365	0.23	0.820	-.0553126	.0698761
smsa	-.0419507	.0189471	-2.21	0.027	-.0790864	-.0048149
ind	.0136289	.015229	0.89	0.371	-.0162194	.0434771
TVendogenous						
exp	.1129704	.0024688	45.76	0.000	.1081316	.1178093
exp2	-.0004214	.0000546	-7.72	0.000	-.0005283	-.0003145
wks	.0008381	.0005995	1.40	0.162	-.0003368	.002013
ms	-.0300894	.0189674	-1.59	0.113	-.0672649	.0070861
union	.0324752	.0148939	2.18	0.029	.0032837	.0616667
TIexogenous						
fem	-.132008	.1266039	-1.04	0.297	-.380147	.1161311
blk	-.2859004	.1554857	-1.84	0.066	-.5906468	.0188459
TIendogenous						
ed	.1372049	.0205695	6.67	0.000	.0968894	.1775205
_cons	2.927338	.2751274	10.64	0.000	2.388098	3.466578
sigma_u	.94180304					
sigma_e	.15180273					
rho	.97467788	(fraction of variance due to u_i)				

```
note:  TV refers to time varying; TI refers to time invariant.
```

◁

❏ Technical Note

We mentioned earlier that insufficient correlation between an endogenous variable and the instruments can give rise to a weak instrument problem. For example, suppose that we simulate data for a model of the form

$$y = 3 + 3x_{1a} + 3x_{1b} + 3x_2 + 3z_1 + 3z_2 + u_i + e_{it}$$

and purposely construct the instruments so that they exhibit very little correlation with the endogenous variable z_2.

```
. use http://www.stata-press.com/data/r9/xthtaylor1
. correlate ui z1 z2 x1a x1b x2 eit
(obs=10000)
```

	ui	z1	z2	x1a	x1b	x2	eit
ui	1.0000						
z1	0.0268	1.0000					
z2	0.8777	0.0286	1.0000				
x1a	-0.0145	0.0065	-0.0034	1.0000			
x1b	0.0026	0.0079	0.0038	-0.0030	1.0000		
x2	0.8765	0.0191	0.7671	-0.0192	0.0037	1.0000	
eit	0.0060	-0.0198	0.0123	-0.0100	-0.0138	0.0092	1.0000

In the output below, weak instruments have serious consequences on the estimates produced by xthtaylor. Note that the estimate of the coefficient on z2 is three times larger than its true value and that its standard error is rather large. Without sufficient correlation between the endogenous variable and its instruments in a given sample, there is insufficient information for identifying the parameter. Also, given the results of Stock, Wright, and Yojo (2002), weak instruments will cause serious size distortions in any tests performed.

```
. xthtaylor yit x1a x1b x2 z1 z2, endog(x2 z2) i(id)
```

Hausman–Taylor estimation	Number of obs	=	10000
Group variable (i): id	Number of groups	=	1000
	Obs per group: min =		10
	avg =		10
	max =		10
Random effects u_i ~ i.i.d.	Wald chi2(5)	=	24172.91
	Prob > chi2	=	0.0000

yit	Coef.	Std. Err.	z	P>|z|	[95% Conf. Interval]	
TVexogenous						
x1a	2.959736	.0330233	89.63	0.000	2.895011	3.02446
x1b	2.953891	.0333051	88.69	0.000	2.888614	3.019168
TVendogenous						
x2	3.022685	.033085	91.36	0.000	2.957839	3.08753
TIexogenous						
z1	2.709179	.587031	4.62	0.000	1.55862	3.859739
TIendogenous						
z2	9.525973	8.572966	1.11	0.266	-7.276732	26.32868
_cons	2.837072	.4276595	6.63	0.000	1.998875	3.675269

sigma_u	8.729479	
sigma_e	3.1657492	
rho	.88377062	(fraction of variance due to u_i)

note: TV refers to time varying; TI refers to time invariant.

$\square$

▷ Example 2

Now let's consider why we might want to specify the constant (*varlist*$_{ti}$) option. For this example, we will use simulated data. In the output below, we fit a model over the full sample. Note the placement in the output of the coefficient on the exogenous variable x1c.

```
. use http://www.stata-press.com/data/r9/xthtaylor2
. xthtaylor yit x1a x1b x1c x2 z1 z2, endog(x2 z2) i(id)
```

Hausman-Taylor estimation		Number of obs	=	10000
Group variable (i): id		Number of groups	=	1000
		Obs per group: min =		10
		avg =		10
		max =		10
Random effects u_i ~ i.i.d.		Wald chi2(6)	=	10341.63
		Prob > chi2	=	0.0000

yit	Coef.	Std. Err.	z	P>|z|	[95% Conf. Interval]	
TVexogenous						
x1a	3.023647	.0570274	53.02	0.000	2.911875	3.135418
x1b	2.966666	.0572659	51.81	0.000	2.854427	3.078905
x1c	.2355318	.123502	1.91	0.057	-.0065276	.4775912
TVendogenous						
x2	14.17476	3.128385	4.53	0.000	8.043234	20.30628
TIexogenous						
z1	1.741709	.4280022	4.07	0.000	.9028398	2.580578
TIendogenous						
z2	7.983849	.6970903	11.45	0.000	6.617577	9.350121
_cons	2.146038	.3794179	5.66	0.000	1.402393	2.889684
sigma_u	5.6787791					
sigma_e	3.1806188					
rho	.76120931	(fraction of variance due to u_i)				

```
note:  TV refers to time varying; TI refers to time invariant.
```

Now suppose that we want to fit the model using only the first eight periods. Notice in the output below that x1c now appears under the TIexogenous heading rather than the TVexogenous heading because x1c is time invariant in the subsample defined by t<9.

(*Continued on next page*)

```
. xthtaylor yit x1a x1b x1c x2 z1 z2 if t<9, endog(x2 z2) i(id)
Hausman-Taylor estimation                 Number of obs      =      8000
Group variable (i): id                    Number of groups   =      1000

                                          Obs per group: min =         8
                                                         avg =         8
                                                         max =         8
Random effects u_i ~ i.i.d.               Wald chi2(6)       =  15354.87
                                          Prob > chi2        =    0.0000
```

yit	Coef.	Std. Err.	z	P>|z|	[95% Conf. Interval]	
TVexogenous						
x1a	3.051966	.0367026	83.15	0.000	2.98003	3.123901
x1b	2.967822	.0368144	80.62	0.000	2.895667	3.039977
TVendogenous						
x2	.7361217	3.199764	0.23	0.818	-5.5353	7.007543
TIexogenous						
x1c	3.215907	.5657191	5.68	0.000	2.107118	4.324696
z1	3.347644	.5819756	5.75	0.000	2.206992	4.488295
TIendogenous						
z2	2.010578	1.143982	1.76	0.079	-.231586	4.252742
_cons	3.257004	.5295828	6.15	0.000	2.219041	4.294967
sigma_u	15.445594					
sigma_e	3.175083					
rho	.95945606	(fraction of variance due to u_i)				

```
note:  TV refers to time varying; TI refers to time invariant.
```

To prevent a variable from becoming time invariant, you can use either constant(*varlist*$_{ti}$) or varying(*varlist*$_{tv}$). Recall that constant(*varlist*$_{ti}$) specifies the subset of variables in *varlist* that are time invariant and requires the remaining variables in *varlist* to be time varying. If you specify constant(*varlist*$_{ti}$) and any of the variables contained in *varlist*$_{ti}$ are time varying, or if any of the variables not contained in *varlist*$_{ti}$ are time invariant, xthtaylor will not perform the estimation and will issue an error message.

```
. xthtaylor yit x1a x1b x1c x2 z1 z2 if t<9, endog(x2 z2) i(id) constant(z1 z2)
x1c not included in -constant()-.
```

The same thing happens when you use the varying(*varlist*$_{tv}$) option.

◁

Saved Results

xthtaylor saves in e():

Scalars

e(N)	number of observations	e(chi2)	χ^2
e(N_g)	number of groups	e(rho)	ρ
e(df_m)	model degrees of freedom	e(sigma_u)	panel-level standard deviation
e(def_r)	residual degrees of freedom	e(sigma_e)	standard deviation of ϵ_{it}
e(g_max)	largest group size	e(F)	model F (small only)
e(g_min)	smallest group size	e(Tbar)	harmonic mean of group sizes
e(g_avg)	average group size		

Macros

e(cmd)	xthtaylor	e(TVexogenous)	exog. time-varying variables
e(depvar)	name of dependent variable	e(TIexogenous)	exog. time-invariant variables
e(title)	Hausman-Taylor or	e(TVendogenous)	endog. time-varying variables
	Amemiya-MaCurdy	e(TIendogenous)	endog. time-invariant variables
e(wtype)	weight type	e(chi2type)	Wald; type of model χ^2 test
e(wexp)	weight expression	e(vcetype)	covariance estimation method
e(ivar)	variable denoting groups	e(properties)	b V
e(tvar)	time variable, amacurdy only	e(predict)	program used to implement predict

Matrices

e(b)	coefficient vector	e(V)	variance–covariance matrix of the estimators

Functions

e(sample)	marks estimation sample

Methods and Formulas

xthtaylor is implemented as an ado-file.

Consider an error components model of the form

$$y_{it} = \mathbf{X}_{1it}\boldsymbol{\beta}_1 + \mathbf{X}_{2it}\boldsymbol{\beta}_2 + \mathbf{Z}_{1i}\delta_1 + \mathbf{Z}_{2i}\delta_2 + \mu_i + \epsilon_{it} \qquad (2)$$

for $i = 1, \ldots, n$ and, for each i, $t = 1, \ldots, T_i$, of which T_i periods are observed; n is the number of panels in the sample. The covariates in $\mathbf{X}$ are time varying, and the covariates in $\mathbf{Z}$ are time invariant. Both $\mathbf{X}$ and $\mathbf{Z}$ are decomposed into two parts. The covariates in $\mathbf{X}_1$ and $\mathbf{Z}_1$ are assumed to be uncorrelated with μ_i and e_{it}, while the covariates in $\mathbf{X}_2$ and $\mathbf{Z}_2$ are allowed to be correlated with μ_i but not with ϵ_{it}. Hausman and Taylor (1981) suggest an instrumental variable estimator for this model.

Recall that, for some variable w, the within transformation of w is defined as

$$\widetilde{w}_{it} = w_{it} - \overline{w}_{i.} \qquad \overline{w}_{i.} = \frac{1}{n} \sum_{t=1}^{T_i} w_{it}$$

Since the within estimator removes $\mathbf{Z}$, the within transformation reduces the model to

$$\widetilde{y}_{it} = \widetilde{\mathbf{X}}_{1it}\boldsymbol{\beta}_1 + \widetilde{\mathbf{X}}_{2it}\boldsymbol{\beta}_2 + \widetilde{\epsilon}_{it}$$

The within estimators $\widehat{\beta}_{1w}$ and $\widehat{\beta}_{2w}$ are consistent for $\boldsymbol{\beta}_1$ and $\boldsymbol{\beta}_2$, but they may not be efficient. Also, note that the within estimator cannot estimate $\boldsymbol{\delta}_1$ and $\boldsymbol{\delta}_2$.

The within estimator can be used to obtain the within residuals

$$\widetilde{d}_{it} = \widetilde{y}_{it} - \widetilde{\mathbf{X}}_{1it}\widehat{\beta}_{1w} - \widetilde{\mathbf{X}}_{2it}\widehat{\beta}_{2w}$$

allowing us to estimate the variance of the idiosyncratic error component, σ_ϵ^2, as

$$\widehat{\sigma}_\epsilon^2 = \frac{RSS}{N - n}$$

where RSS is the residual sum of squares from the within regression and N is the total number of observations in the sample.

Regressing $\widetilde{d}_{it}$ on $\mathbf{Z}_1$ and $\mathbf{Z}_2$, using $\mathbf{X}_1$ and $\mathbf{Z}_1$ as instruments, provides intermediate, consistent estimates of $\boldsymbol{\delta}_1$ and $\boldsymbol{\delta}_2$, which we will call $\widehat{\boldsymbol{\delta}}_{1IV}$ and $\widehat{\boldsymbol{\delta}}_{2IV}$.

Using the within estimates, $\widehat{\boldsymbol{\delta}}_{1IV}$, and $\widehat{\boldsymbol{\delta}}_{2IV}$, we can obtain an estimate of the variance of the random effect, σ_μ^2. First, let

$$\widehat{e}_{it} = \left(y_{it} - \mathbf{X}_{1it}\widehat{\beta}_{1w} - \mathbf{X}_{2it}\widehat{\beta}_{2w} - \mathbf{Z}_{1it}\widehat{\boldsymbol{\delta}}_{1IV} - \mathbf{Z}_{2it}\widehat{\boldsymbol{\delta}}_{2IV} \right)$$

Then define

$$s^2 = \frac{1}{N} \sum_{i=1}^{n} \sum_{t=1}^{T_i} \left(\frac{1}{T_i} \sum_{t=1}^{T_i} \widehat{e}_i \right)^2$$

Hausman and Taylor (1981) showed that, in the case of balanced panels,

$$\text{plim}_{n \to \infty} s^2 = T\sigma_\mu^2 + \sigma_\epsilon^2$$

In the case of unbalanced panels,

$$\text{plim}_{n \to \infty} s^2 = \overline{T}\sigma_\mu^2 + \sigma_\epsilon^2$$

where

$$\overline{T} = \frac{n}{\sum_{i=1}^{n} \frac{1}{T_i}}$$

After plugging in $\widehat{\sigma}_\epsilon^2$, our consistent estimate for σ_ϵ^2, a little algebra suggests the estimate

$$\widehat{\sigma}_\mu^2 = (s^2 - \widehat{\sigma}_\epsilon^2)(\overline{T})^{-1}$$

Define $\widehat{\theta}_i$ as

$$\widehat{\theta}_i = 1 - \left(\frac{\widehat{\sigma}_\epsilon^2}{\widehat{\sigma}_\epsilon^2 + T_i \widehat{\sigma}_\mu^2} \right)^{\frac{1}{2}}$$

With $\widehat{\theta}_i$ in hand, we can perform the standard random-effects GLS transform on each of the variables. The transform is given by

$$w_{it}^* = w_{it} - \widehat{\theta}_i \overline{w}_{i.}$$

where $\overline{w}_{i.}$ is the within-panel mean.

We can then obtain the Hausman–Taylor estimates of the coefficients in (2) by fitting an instrumental variables regression of the GLS-transformed y_{it}^* on $\mathbf{X}_{it}^*$ and $\mathbf{Z}_{it}^*$, with instruments $\widetilde{\mathbf{X}}_{it}$, $\overline{\mathbf{X}}_{1i.}$, and $\mathbf{Z}_{1i}$.

We can obtain Amemiya–MaCurdy estimates of the coefficients in (2) by confirming an instrumental variables regression of the GLS-transformed y_{it}^* on $\mathbf{X}_{it}^*$ and $\mathbf{Z}_{it}^*$, using $\widetilde{\mathbf{X}}_{it}$, $\check{\mathbf{X}}_{1it}$, and $\mathbf{Z}_{1i}$ as instruments, where $\check{\mathbf{X}}_{1it} = \mathbf{X}_{1i1}, \mathbf{X}_{1i2}, \ldots, \mathbf{X}_{1iT_i}$. The order condition for the Amemiya–MaCurdy estimator is $T k_1 > g_2$, and this estimator is only available for balanced panels.

References

Amemiya, T. and T. MaCurdy. 1986. Instrumental-variable estimation of an error-components model. *Econometrica* 54(4): 869–880.

Baltagi, B. H. 2001. *Econometric Analysis of Panel Data*. 2nd ed. New York: Wiley.

Baltagi, B. H. and S. Khanti-Akom. 1990. On efficient estimation with panel data: an empirical comparison of instrumental variables estimators. *Journal of Applied Econometrics* 5: 401–406.

Hausman, J. A. and W. E. Taylor. 1981. Panel data and unobservable individual effects. *Econometrica* 49: 1377–1398.

Stock, J. H., J. H. Wright, and M. Yogo. 2002. A survey of weak instruments and weak identification in generalized method of moments. *Journal of Business & Economic Statistics* 20(4): 518–529.

Also See

Complementary:	[XT] **xthtaylor postestimation**; [XT] **xtdata**, [XT] **xtdes**, [XT] **xtsum**,
	[XT] **xttab**,
	[TS] **tsset**
Related:	[XT] **xtivreg**, [XT] **xtreg**
Background:	[U] **11.1.10 Prefix commands**,
	[U] **20 Estimation and postestimation commands**,
	[XT] **estimation options**, [XT] **xt**,
	[R] *vce_option*

Title

> **xthtaylor postestimation** — Postestimation tools for xthtaylor

Description

The following postestimation commands are available for `xthtaylor`:

command	description
adjust[1]	adjusted predictions of $\mathbf{x}\beta$
estat	VCE and estimation sample summary
estimates	cataloging estimation results
lincom	point estimates, standard errors, testing, and inference for linear combinations of coefficients
mfx	marginal effects or elasticities
nlcom	point estimates, standard errors, testing, and inference for nonlinear combinations of coefficients
predict	predictions, residuals, influence statistics, and other diagnostic measures
predictnl	point estimates, standard errors, testing, and inference for generalized predictions
test	Wald tests for simple and composite linear hypotheses
testnl	Wald tests of nonlinear hypotheses

[1] `adjust` does not work with time-series operators.

See the corresponding entries in the *Stata Base Reference Manual* for details.

Syntax for predict

> predict [*type*] *newvar* [*if*] [*in*] [, *statistic*]

statistic	description
xb	$\mathbf{X}_{it}\widehat{\beta} + \mathbf{Z}_i\widehat{\delta}$, fitted values; the default
stdp	standard error of the fitted values
ue	$\widehat{\mu}_i + \widehat{\epsilon}_{it}$, the combined residual
*xbu	$\mathbf{X}_{it}\widehat{\beta} + \mathbf{Z}_i\widehat{\delta} + \widehat{\mu}_i$, prediction including effect
*u	$\widehat{\mu}_i$, the random error component
*e	$\widehat{\epsilon}_{it}$, prediction of the idiosyncratic error component

Unstarred statistics are available both in and out of sample; type `predict ... if e(sample) ...` if wanted only for the estimation sample. Starred statistics are calculated only for the estimation sample, even when `if e(sample)` is not specified.

Options for predict

xb, the default, calculates the linear prediction; that is, $\mathbf{X}_{it}\widehat{\beta} + \mathbf{Z}_{it}\widehat{\delta}$.

126

stdp calculates the standard error of the linear prediction.

ue calculates the prediction of $\widehat{\mu}_i + \widehat{\epsilon}_{it}$.

xbu calculates the prediction of $\mathbf{X}_{it}\widehat{\boldsymbol{\beta}} + \mathbf{Z}_{it}\widehat{\boldsymbol{\delta}} + \widehat{\nu}_i$, the prediction including the random effect.

u calculates the prediction of $\widehat{\mu}_i$, the estimated random effect.

e calculates the prediction of $\widehat{\epsilon}_{it}$.

Methods and Formulas

All postestimation commands listed above are implemented as ado-files.

Also See

Complementary:	[XT] **xthtaylor**,
	[R] **adjust**, [R] **estimates**, [R] **lincom**, [R] **mfx**, [R] **nlcom**,
	[R] **predictnl**, [R] **test**, [R] **testnl**
Background:	[U] **13.5 Accessing coefficients and standard errors**,
	[U] **20 Estimation and postestimation commands**,
	[R] **estat**, [R] **predict**

Title

> **xtintreg** — Random-effects interval data regression models

Syntax

xtintreg *depvar*~lower~ *depvar*~upper~ [*indepvars*] [*if*] [*in*] [*weight*] [, *options*]

options	description
Model	
i(*varname*$_i$)	use *varname*$_i$ as the panel ID variable
<u>nocon</u>stant	suppress constant term
<u>off</u>set(*varname*)	include *varname* in model with coefficient constrained to 1
<u>constraints</u>(*constraints*)	apply specified linear constraints
Int opts	
intmethod(*intmethod*)	integration method; *intmethod* may be <u>agh</u>ermite or <u>gh</u>ermite
<u>intp</u>oints(*#*)	use *#* quadrature points; default is intpoints(12)
SE	
vce(*vcetype*)	*vcetype* may be <u>boot</u>strap or <u>jack</u>knife
Reporting	
<u>level</u>(*#*)	set confidence level; default is level(95)
noskip	perform overall model test as a likelihood-ratio test
intreg	perform likelihood-ratio test against pooled model
Max options	
maximize_options	control the maximization process; see [R] **maximize**

depvar~lower~, *depvar*~upper~, and *indepvars* may contain time-series operators; see [U] **11.4.3 Time-series varlists**.
bootstrap, by, jackknife, statsby, and xi may be used with xtintreg; see [U] **11.1.10 Prefix commands**.
iweights are allowed; see [U] **11.1.6 weight**. Weights must be constant within panels.
See [U] **20 Estimation and postestimation commands** for additional capabilities of estimation commands.

Description

xtintreg fits random-effects interval data regression models. There is no command for a conditional fixed-effects model, as there does not exist a sufficient statistic allowing the fixed effects to be conditioned out of the likelihood. Unconditional fixed-effects intreg models may be fitted with the intreg command, with indicator variables for the panels. The appropriate indicator variables can be generated using tabulate or xi. However, unconditional fixed-effects estimates are biased.

xtintreg is slow because the likelihood function is calculated by adaptive Gauss–Hermite quadrature; see *Methods and Formulas*. Computation time is roughly proportional to the number of points used for the quadrature. The default is intpoints(12). Simulations indicate that increasing the number of points does not appreciably change the estimates for the coefficients or their standard errors. See [XT] **quadchk**.

Options

i(*varname$_i$*), noconstant, offset(*varname*), constraints(*constraints*); see [XT] **estimation options**.

intmethod(*intmethod*) specifies the integration method to be used for the random-effects model. It accepts one of two arguments: the first is a̲g̲hermite, the default, which specifies adaptive Gauss–Hermite quadrature; the second is g̲hermite, which specifies nonadaptive Gauss–Hermite quadrature.

intpoints(*#*) specifies the number of points to use for Gauss–Hermite quadrature. The default is 12. Increasing this value slightly improves the accuracy but also increases computation time. Computation time is roughly proportional to its value.

vce(*vcetype*); see [R] ***vce_option***.

level(*#*), noskip; see [XT] **estimation options**.

intreg specifies that a likelihood-ratio test comparing the random-effects model with the pooled (intreg) model be included in the output.

maximize_options: di̲f̲ficult, te̲chnique(*algorithm_spec*), it̲erate(*#*), [no̲]log̲, tra̲ce, gra̲dient, showstep, hes̲sian, shownr̲tolerance, to̲lerance(*#*), lt̲olerance(*#*), gt̲olerance(*#*), nr̲tolerance(*#*), nonr̲tolerance, from̲(*init_specs*); see [R] **maximize**. Some of these options are not available if intmethod(ghermite) is specified. These options are seldom used.

Remarks

Consider the linear regression model with panel-level random effects

$$y_{it} = \mathbf{x}_{it}\boldsymbol{\beta} + \nu_i + \epsilon_{it}$$

for $i = 1, \ldots, n$ panels, where $t = 1, \ldots, n_i$. The random effects, ν_i, are i.i.d., $N(0, \sigma_\nu^2)$, and ϵ_{it} are i.i.d., $N(0, \sigma_\epsilon^2)$ independently of ν_i. The observed data consist of the couples, (y_{1it}, y_{2it}), such that all that is known is that $y_{1it} \leq y_{it} \leq y_{2it}$, where y_{1it} is possibly $-\infty$ and y_{2it} is possibly $+\infty$.

▷ Example 1

We begin with the dataset nlswork described in [XT] **xt** and create two fictional dependent variables, where the wages are instead reported sometimes as ranges. The wages have been adjusted to 1988 dollars and have further been recoded such that some of the observations are known exactly, some are left-censored, some are right-censored, and some are known only in an interval.

We wish to fit a random-effects interval regression model of adjusted (log) wages:

```
. use http://www.stata-press.com/data/r9/nlswork3
(National Longitudinal Survey.  Young Women 14-26 years of age in 1968)

. xtintreg ln_wage1 ln_wage2 union age grade not_smsa south southXt occ_code,
> i(id) noskip intreg nolog
```

Random-effects interval regression	Number of obs	=	19095
Group variable (i): idcode	Number of groups	=	4139

Random effects u_i ~ Gaussian	Obs per group: min =	1
	avg =	4.6
	max =	12

	LR chi2(7)	=	3471.91
Log likelihood = -14844.293	Prob > chi2	=	0.0000

	Coef.	Std. Err.	z	P>|z|	[95% Conf. Interval]	
union	.1387145	.0067417	20.58	0.000	.1255009	.151928
age	.012555	.0005133	24.46	0.000	.0115489	.0135612
grade	.0780209	.0020281	38.47	0.000	.0740459	.0819959
not_smsa	-.1277259	.0089253	-14.31	0.000	-.1452191	-.1102327
south	-.1155264	.0121582	-9.50	0.000	-.139356	-.0916968
southXt	.0022144	.0008293	2.67	0.008	.0005891	.0038397
occ_code	-.0180571	.0010574	-17.08	0.000	-.0201295	-.0159847
_cons	.453434	.0313198	14.48	0.000	.3920482	.5148197
/sigma_u	.287013	.0039877	71.98	0.000	.2791973	.2948287
/sigma_e	.2684381	.0016246	165.23	0.000	.2652539	.2716224
rho	.5334037	.0078726			.5179525	.5488047

```
Likelihood-ratio test of sigma_u=0: chibar2(01)= 6655.18 Prob>=chibar2 = 0.000
```

Observation summary:	157	left-censored observations
	14372	uncensored observations
	718	right-censored observations
	3848	interval observations

The output includes the overall and panel-level variance components (labeled `sigma_e` and `sigma_u`, respectively) together with ρ (labeled `rho`),

$$\rho = \frac{\sigma_\nu^2}{\sigma_\epsilon^2 + \sigma_\nu^2}$$

which is the proportion of the total variance contributed by the panel-level variance component.

When `rho` is zero, the panel-level variance component is unimportant, and the panel estimator is not different from the pooled estimator. A likelihood-ratio test of this is included at the bottom of the output. This test formally compares the pooled estimator (intreg) with the panel estimator.

◁

❑ Technical Note

The random-effects model is calculated using quadrature. As the panel sizes (or ρ) increase, the quadrature approximation becomes less accurate. We can use the `quadchk` command to see if changing the number of quadrature points affects the results. If the results change, the quadrature approximation is not accurate, and the results of the model should not be interpreted. See [XT] **quadchk** for details and [XT] **xtprobit** for an example.

❑

Saved Results

xtintreg saves in e():

Scalars

e(N)	# of observations	e(chi2_c)	χ^2 for comparison test
e(N_g)	# of groups	e(rho)	ρ
e(N_unc)	# of uncensored observations	e(sigma_u)	panel-level standard deviation
e(N_lc)	# of left-censored observations	e(sigma_e)	standard deviation of ϵ_{it}
e(N_rc)	# of right-censored observations	e(n_quad)	# of quadrature points
e(N_int)	# of interval observations	e(rc)	return code
e(N_cd)	# of completely determined obs.	e(rank)	rank of e(V)
e(df_m)	model degrees of freedom	e(rank0)	rank of e(V) for constant-only model
e(ll)	log likelihood	e(k)	# of parameters
e(ll_0)	log likelihood, constant-only model	e(k_eq)	# of equations
e(g_max)	largest group size	e(k_dv)	# of dependent variables
e(g_min)	smallest group size	e(ic)	# of iterations
e(g_avg)	average group size	e(p)	significance
e(chi2)	χ^2	e(converged)	1 if converged, 0 otherwise

Macros

e(cmd)	xtintreg	e(distrib)	Gaussian; the distribution of the random effect
e(depvar)	names of dependent variables		
e(title)	title in estimation output	e(vce)	vcetype specified in vce()
e(ivar)	variable denoting groups	e(vcetype)	title used to label Std. Err.
e(wtype)	weight type	e(opt)	type of optimization
e(wexp)	weight expression	e(ml_method)	type of ml method
e(offset1)	offset	e(user)	name of likelihood-evaluator program
e(chi2type)	Wald or LR; type of model χ^2 test	e(technique)	maximization technique
e(chi2_ct)	Wald or LR; type of model χ^2 test corresponding to e(chi2_c)	e(crittype)	optimization criterion
		e(properties)	b V
e(intmethod)	integration method	e(predict)	program used to implement predict

Matrices

e(b)	coefficient vector	e(ilog)	iteration log
e(V)	variance–covariance matrix of the estimators	e(gradient)	gradient vector

Functions

e(sample)	marks estimation sample

Methods and Formulas

xtintreg is implemented as an ado-file.

Assuming a normal distribution, $N(0, \sigma_\nu^2)$, for the random effects ν_i, we have the joint (unconditional of ν_i) density of the observed data for the ith panel

$$f\left\{(y_{1i1}, y_{2i1}), \ldots, (y_{1in_i}, y_{2in_i}) | \mathbf{x}_{1i}, \ldots, \mathbf{x}_{in_i}\right\} =$$

$$\int_{-\infty}^{\infty} \frac{e^{-\nu_i^2/2\sigma_\nu^2}}{\sqrt{2\pi}\sigma_\nu} \left\{\prod_{t=1}^{n_i} F(y_{1it}, y_{2it}, \mathbf{x}_{it}\boldsymbol{\beta} + \nu_i)\right\} d\nu_i$$

where

$$
F(y_{1it}, y_{2it}, \Delta_{it}) = \begin{cases} \left(\sqrt{2\pi}\sigma_\epsilon\right)^{-1} e^{-(y_{1it}-\Delta_{it})^2/(2\sigma_\epsilon^2)} & \text{if } (y_{1it}, y_{2it}) \in C \\[2mm] \Phi\left(\frac{y_{2it}-\Delta_{it}}{\sigma_\epsilon}\right) & \text{if } (y_{1it}, y_{2it}) \in L \\[2mm] 1 - \Phi\left(\frac{y_{1it}-\Delta_{it}}{\sigma_\epsilon}\right) & \text{if } (y_{1it}, y_{2it}) \in R \\[2mm] \Phi\left(\frac{y_{2it}-\Delta_{it}}{\sigma_\epsilon}\right) - \Phi\left(\frac{y_{1it}-\Delta_{it}}{\sigma_\epsilon}\right) & \text{if } (y_{1it}, y_{2it}) \in I \end{cases}
$$

where C is the set of noncensored observations ($y_{1it} = y_{2it}$ and both nonmissing), L is the set of left-censored observations (y_{1it} missing and y_{2it} nonmissing), R is the set of right-censored observations (y_{1it} nonmissing and y_{2it} missing), I is the set of interval observations ($y_{1it} < y_{2it}$ and both nonmissing), and $\Phi()$ is the cumulative normal distribution. The integral can be approximated with M-point Gauss–Hermite quadrature

$$
\int_{-\infty}^{\infty} e^{-x^2} g(x)dx \approx \sum_{m=1}^{M} w_m^* g(a_m^*)
$$

where the w_m^* denote the quadrature weights and the a_m^* denote the quadrature abscissas. The log likelihood, L, can be calculated using the quadrature

$$
L = \sum_{i=1}^{n} w_i \log f\left\{(y_{1i1}, y_{2i1}), \ldots, (y_{1in_i}, y_{2in_i})|\mathbf{x}_{1i}, \ldots, \mathbf{x}_{in_i}\right\}
$$

$$
\approx \sum_{i=1}^{n} w_i \log\left\{\frac{1}{\sqrt{\pi}} \sum_{m=1}^{M} w_m^* \prod_{t=1}^{n_i} F\left(y_{1it}, y_{2it}, \mathbf{x}_{it}\boldsymbol{\beta} + \sqrt{2}\sigma_\nu a_m^*\right)\right\}
$$

where w_i is the user-specified weight for panel i; if no weights are specified, $w_i = 1$.

The above is the formula for nonadaptive Gauss–Hermite quadrature. The default is to calculate the log likelihood, L, using adaptive Gauss–Hermite quadrature, which transforms the integrand

$$
g(y_{1it}, y_{2it}, x_{it}, \nu_i) = \frac{e^{-\nu_i^2/2\sigma_\nu^2}}{\sqrt{2\pi}\sigma_\nu}\left\{\prod_{t=1}^{n_i} F(y_{1it}, y_{2it}, \mathbf{x}_{it}\boldsymbol{\beta} + \nu_i)\right\}
$$

so that it is sampled on a suitable range; see Liu (1994).

Both quadrature formulas require that the integrated function be well approximated by a polynomial. The number of time periods (panel size) affects whether

$$
\prod_{t=1}^{n_i} F(y_{1it}, y_{2it}, \mathbf{x}_{it}\boldsymbol{\beta} + \nu_i)
$$

is well approximated by a polynomial. As panel size (or ρ) increases, the quadrature approximation becomes less accurate. Adaptive quadrature gives better results for correlated data and large panels than nonadaptive quadrature; however we recommend that you use the quadchk command to investigate the applicability of the numeric technique used in this command.

References

Liu, Qing and D. A. Pierce 1994. A note on Gauss–Hermite quadrature. *Biometrika* 81: 624–629.

Neuhaus, J. M. 1992. Statistical methods for longitudinal and clustered designs with binary responses. *Statistical Methods in Medical Research* 1: 249–273.

Pendergast, J. F., S. J. Gange, M. A. Newton, M. J. Lindstrom, M. Palta, and M. R. Fisher. 1996. A survey of methods for analyzing clustered binary response data. *International Statistical Review* 64: 89–118.

Also See

Complementary:	[XT] **xtintreg postestimation**; [XT] **quadchk**, [XT] **xtdata**, [XT] **xtdes**, [XT] **xtsum**, [XT] **xttab**
Related:	[XT] **xtreg**, [XT] **xttobit**, [R] **intreg**, [R] **tobit**
Background:	[U] **11.1.10 Prefix commands**, [U] **20 Estimation and postestimation commands**, [XT] **estimation options**, [XT] **xt**, [R] **maximize**, [R] *vce_option*

Title

> **xtintreg postestimation** — Postestimation tools for xtintreg

Description

The following postestimation commands are available for `xtintreg`:

command	description
adjust[1]	adjusted predictions of $\mathbf{x}\beta$
estat	AIC, BIC, VCE, and estimation sample summary
estimates	cataloging estimation results
lincom	point estimates, standard errors, testing, and inference for linear combinations of coefficients
lrtest	likelihood-ratio test
mfx	marginal effects or elasticities
nlcom	point estimates, standard errors, testing, and inference for nonlinear combinations of coefficients
predict	predictions, residuals, influence statistics, and other diagnostic measures
predictnl	point estimates, standard errors, testing, and inference for generalized predictions
test	Wald tests for simple and composite linear hypotheses
testnl	Wald tests of nonlinear hypotheses

[1] `adjust` does not work with time-series operators.

See the corresponding entries in the *Stata Base Reference Manual* for details.

Syntax for predict

> predict [*type*] *newvar* [*if*] [*in*] [, *statistic* <u>nooff</u>set]

statistic	description
xb	linear prediction assuming $\nu_i = 0$, the default
<u>pr</u>0(*a*,*b*)	$\Pr(a < y < b)$ assuming $\nu_i = 0$
<u>e</u>0(*a*,*b*)	$E(y \mid a < y < b)$ assuming $\nu_i = 0$
<u>ystar</u>0(*a*,*b*)	$E(y^*)$, $y^* = \max\{a, \min(y_j, b)\}$ assuming $\nu_i = 0$
stdp	standard error of the linear prediction
stdf	standard error of the linear forecast

These statistics are available both in and out of sample; type `predict ... if e(sample) ...` if wanted only for the estimation sample.

where *a* and *b* may be numbers or variables; *a* missing ($a \geq .$) means $-\infty$, and *b* missing ($b \geq .$) means $+\infty$; see [U] **12.2.1 Missing values**.

Options for predict

xb, the default, calculates the linear prediction.

pr0(*a,b*) calculates estimates of $\Pr(a < y < b | \mathbf{x} = \mathbf{x}_{it}, \nu_i = 0)$, which is the probability that y would be observed in the interval (a, b), given the current values of the predictors, $\mathbf{x}_{it}$, and given a zero random effect. In the discussion that follows, these two conditions are implied.

a and *b* may be specified as numbers or variable names; *lb* and *ub* are variable names;
pr0(20,30) calculates $\Pr(20 < y < 30)$;
pr0(*lb,ub*) calculates $\Pr(lb < y < ub)$; and
pr0(20,*ub*) calculates $\Pr(20 < y < ub)$.

a missing ($a \geq .$) means $-\infty$; pr0(.,30) calculates $\Pr(-\infty < y < 30)$;
pr0(*lb*,30) calculates $\Pr(-\infty < y < 30)$ in observations for which $lb \geq .$
(and calculates $\Pr(lb < y < 30)$ elsewhere).

b missing ($b \geq .$) means $+\infty$; pr0(20,.) calculates $\Pr(+\infty > y > 20)$;
pr0(20,*ub*) calculates $\Pr(+\infty > y > 20)$ in observations for which $ub \geq .$
(and calculates $\Pr(20 < y < ub)$ elsewhere).

e0(*a,b*) calculates estimates of $E(y \mid a < y < b, \mathbf{x} = \mathbf{x}_{it}, \nu_i = 0)$, which is the expected value of y conditional on y being in the interval (a, b), meaning that y is censored. *a* and *b* are specified as they are for pr0().

ystar0(*a,b*) calculates estimates of $E(y^* | \mathbf{x} = \mathbf{x}_{it}, \nu_i = 0)$, where $y^* = a$ if $y \leq a$, $y^* = b$ if $y \geq b$, and $y^* = y$ otherwise, meaning that y^* is the truncated version of y. *a* and *b* are specified as they are for pr0().

stdp calculates the standard error of the prediction. It can be thought of as the standard error of the predicted expected value or mean for the observation's covariate pattern. This is also referred to as the standard error of the fitted value.

stdf calculates the standard error of the forecast. This is the standard error of the point prediction for a single observation. It is commonly referred to as the standard error of the future or forecast value. By construction, the standard errors produced by stdf are always larger than those produced by stdp; see [R] **regress** *Methods and Formulas*.

nooffset is relevant only if you specified offset(*varname*) for xtintreg. It modifies the calculations made by predict so that they ignore the offset variable; the linear prediction is treated as $\mathbf{x}_{it}\beta$ rather than $\mathbf{x}_{it}\beta + \text{offset}_{it}$.

Methods and Formulas

All postestimation commands listed above are implemented as ado-files.

Also See

Title

> **xtivreg** — Instrumental variables and two-stage least squares for panel-data models

Syntax

GLS Random-effects (RE) model

> xtivreg *depvar* $\left[\textit{varlist}_1\right]$ (*varlist*$_2$ = *varlist*$_{iv}$) $\left[\textit{if}\right]$ $\left[\textit{in}\right]$ $\left[\text{, re }\textit{RE\_options}\right]$

Between-effects (BE) model

> xtivreg *depvar* $\left[\textit{varlist}_1\right]$ (*varlist*$_2$ = *varlist*$_{iv}$) $\left[\textit{if}\right]$ $\left[\textit{in}\right]$, be $\left[\textit{BE\_options}\right]$

Fixed-effects (FE) model

> xtivreg *depvar* $\left[\textit{varlist}_1\right]$ (*varlist*$_2$ = *varlist*$_{iv}$) $\left[\textit{if}\right]$ $\left[\textit{in}\right]$, fe $\left[\textit{FE\_options}\right]$

First-differenced (FD) estimator

> xtivreg *depvar* $\left[\textit{varlist}_1\right]$ (*varlist*$_2$ = *varlist*$_{iv}$) $\left[\textit{if}\right]$ $\left[\textit{in}\right]$, fd $\left[\textit{FD\_options}\right]$

RE_options	description
Model	
i(*varname$_i$*)	use *varname* as the panel ID variable
re	use random-effects estimator; the default
ec2sls	use Baltagi's EC2SLS random-effects estimator
nosa	use the Baltagi–Chang estimators of the variance components
regress	treat covariates as exogenous and ignore instrument variables
SE	
vce(*vcetype*)	*vcetype* may be bootstrap or jackknife
Reporting	
level(#)	set confidence level; default is level(95)
first	report first-stage estimates
small	report t and F statistics instead of Z and chi-squared statistics
theta	report θ

BE_options	description
Model	
i(*varname_i*)	use *varname* as the panel ID variable
be	use between-effects estimator
<u>reg</u>ress	treat covariates as exogenous and ignore instrument variables
SE	
vce(*vcetype*)	*vcetype* may be <u>boot</u>strap or jackknife
Reporting	
<u>l</u>evel(#)	set confidence level; default is level(95)
first	report first-stage estimates
<u>sm</u>all	report t and F statistics instead of Z and chi-squared statistics

FE_options	description
Model	
i(*varname_i*)	use *varname* as the panel ID variable
fe	use fixed-effects estimator
<u>reg</u>ress	treat covariates as exogenous and ignore instrument variables
SE	
vce(*vcetype*)	*vcetype* may be <u>boot</u>strap or jackknife
Reporting	
<u>l</u>evel(#)	set confidence level; default is level(95)
first	report first-stage estimates
<u>sm</u>all	report t and F statistics instead of Z and chi-squared statistics

FD_options	description
Model	
<u>no</u>constant	suppress constant term
fd	first-differenced estimator
<u>reg</u>ress	treat covariates as exogenous and ignore instrument variables
SE	
vce(*vcetype*)	*vcetype* may be <u>boot</u>strap or jackknife
Reporting	
<u>l</u>evel(#)	set confidence level; default is level(95)
first	report first-stage estimates
<u>sm</u>all	report t and F statistics instead of Z and chi-squared statistics

You must tsset your data before using xtivreg, fd; see [TS] **tsset**.

depvar, *varlist*$_1$, *varlist*$_2$, and *varlist*$_{iv}$ may contain time-series operators; see [U] **11.4.3 Time-series varlists**.

bootstrap, by, jackknife, statsby, and xi may be used with xtivreg; see [U] **11.1.10 Prefix commands**.

See [U] **20 Estimation and postestimation commands** for additional capabilities of estimation commands.

Description

xtivreg offers five different estimators for fitting panel-data models in which some of the right-hand-side covariates are endogenous. These estimators are two-stage least-squares generalizations of simple panel-data estimators for the case of exogenous variables. xtivreg with the be option uses the two-stage least-squares between estimator. xtivreg with the fe option uses the two-stage least-squares within estimator. xtivreg with the re option uses a two-stage least-squares random-effects estimator. There are two implementations: G2SLS due to Balestra and Varadharajan-Krishnakumar (1987) and EC2SLS due to Baltagi. The Balestra and Varadharajan-Krishnakumar G2SLS is the default because it is computationally less expensive. Baltagi's EC2SLS can be obtained by specifying the ec2sls option. xtivreg with the fd option requests the two-stage least-squares first-differenced estimator.

See Baltagi (2001) for an introduction to panel-data models with endogenous covariates. For the derivation and application of the first-differenced estimator, see Anderson and Hsiao (1981).

Options for RE model

⌐ Model ⌐

i($varname_i$); see [XT] **estimation options**.

re requests the G2SLS random-effects estimator. re is the default.

ec2sls requests Baltagi's EC2SLS random-effects estimator instead of the default Balestra and Varadharajan-Krishnakumar estimator.

nosa specifies that the Baltagi–Chang estimators of the variance components be used instead of the default adapted Swamy–Arora estimators.

regress specifies that all the covariates be treated as exogenous and that the instrument list be ignored. In other words, specifying regress causes xtivreg to fit the requested panel-data regression model of *depvar* on *varlist*$_1$ and *varlist*$_2$, ignoring *varlist*$_{iv}$.

⌐ SE ⌐

vce(*vcetype*); see [R] **vce_option**.

⌐ Reporting ⌐

level(#); see [XT] **estimation options**.

first specifies that the first-stage regressions be displayed.

small specifies that t statistics be reported instead of Z statistics, and that F statistics be reported instead of chi-squared statistics.

theta specifies that the output include the estimated value of θ used in combining the between and fixed estimators. For balanced data, this is a constant, and for unbalanced data, a summary of the values is presented in the header of the output.

Options for BE model

⌐ Model ⌐

i($varname_i$); see [XT] **estimation options**.

be requests the between regression estimator.

regress specifies that all the covariates are to be treated as exogenous and that the instrument list is to be ignored. In other words, specifying regress causes xtivreg to fit the requested panel-data regression model of *depvar* on *varlist₁* and *varlist₂*, ignoring *varlist*$_{\text{iv}}$.

___ SE ___

vce(*vcetype*); see [R] ***vce_option***.

___ Reporting ___

level(*#*); see [XT] **estimation options**.

first specifies that the first-stage regressions be displayed.

small specifies that t statistics be reported instead of Z statistics, and that F statistics be reported instead of chi-squared statistics.

Options for FE model

___ Model ___

i(*varname*$_i$); see [XT] **estimation options**.

fe requests the fixed-effects (within) regression estimator.

regress specifies that all the covariates are to be treated as exogenous and that the instrument list is to be ignored. In other words, specifying regress causes xtivreg to fit the requested panel-data regression model of *depvar* on *varlist₁* and *varlist₂*, ignoring *varlist*$_{\text{iv}}$.

___ SE ___

vce(*vcetype*); see [R] ***vce_option***.

___ Reporting ___

level(*#*); see [XT] **estimation options**.

first specifies that the first-stage regressions be displayed.

small specifies that t statistics be reported instead of Z statistics, and that F statistics be reported instead of chi-squared statistics.

Options for FD model

___ Model ___

noconstant; see [XT] **estimation options**.

fd requests the first-differenced regression estimator.

regress specifies that all the covariates are to be treated as exogenous and that the instrument list is to be ignored. In other words, specifying regress causes xtivreg to fit the requested panel-data regression model of *depvar* on *varlist₁* and *varlist₂*, ignoring *varlist*$_{\text{iv}}$.

vce(*vcetype*); see [R] *vce_option*.

level(*#*); see [XT] **estimation options**.

first specifies that the first-stage regressions be displayed.

small specifies that t statistics be reported instead of Z statistics, and that F statistics be reported instead of chi-squared statistics.

Remarks

If you have not read [XT] **xt**, please do so.

Consider an equation of the form

$$y_{it} = \mathbf{Y}_{it}\boldsymbol{\gamma} + \mathbf{X}_{1it}\boldsymbol{\beta} + \mu_i + \nu_{it} = \mathbf{Z}_{it}\boldsymbol{\delta} + \mu_i + \nu_{it} \qquad (1)$$

where

y_{it} is the dependent variable

$\mathbf{Y}_{it}$ is an $1 \times g_2$ vector of observations on g_2 endogenous variables included as covariates, and these variables are allowed to be correlated with the ν_{it}

$\mathbf{X}_{1it}$ is an $1 \times k_1$ vector of observations on the exogenous variables included as covariates

$\mathbf{Z}_{it} = [\mathbf{Y}_{it}\ \mathbf{X}_{it}]$

$\boldsymbol{\gamma}$ is a $g_2 \times 1$ vector of coefficients

$\boldsymbol{\beta}$ is a $k_1 \times 1$ vector of coefficients

$\boldsymbol{\delta}$ is a $K \times 1$ vector of coefficients, and $K = g_2 + k_1$

Assume that there is a $1 \times k_2$ vector of observations on the k_2 instruments in $\mathbf{X}_{2it}$. The order condition is satisfied if $k_2 \geq g_2$. Let $\mathbf{X}_{it} = [\mathbf{X}_{1it}\ \mathbf{X}_{2it}]$. xtivreg handles exogenously unbalanced panel data. Thus define T_i to be the number of observations on panel i, n to be the number of panels, and N to be the total number of observations; i.e., $N = \sum_{i=1}^{n} T_i$.

xtivreg offers five different estimators, which may be applied to models having the form of (1). The first-differenced estimator (FD2SLS) removes the μ_i by fitting the model in first differences. The within estimator (FE2SLS) fits the model after sweeping out the μ_i by removing the panel-level means from each variable. The between estimator (BE2SLS) models the panel averages. The two random-effects estimators, G2SLS and EC2SLS, treat the μ_i as random variables that are independent and identically distributed (i.i.d.) over the panels. Except for (FD2SLS), all these estimators are generalizations of estimators in xtreg. See [XT] **xtreg** for a discussion of these estimators in the case of exogenous covariates.

While the estimators allow for different assumptions about the μ_i, all the estimators assume that the idiosyncratic error term ν_{it} has zero mean and is uncorrelated with the variables in $\mathbf{X}_{it}$. Just as when there are no endogenous covariates, as discussed in [XT] **xtreg**, there are varying perspectives on what assumptions should be placed on the μ_i. If they are assumed to be fixed, the μ_i may be correlated with the variables in $\mathbf{X}_{it}$, and the within estimator is efficient within a class of limited information estimators. Alternatively, if the μ_i are assumed to be random, they are also assumed to be independent and identically distributed (i.i.d.) over the panels. If the μ_i are assumed to be uncorrelated with the variables in $\mathbf{X}_{it}$, the GLS random-effects estimators are more efficient than the within estimator. However, if the μ_i are correlated with the variables in $\mathbf{X}_{it}$, the random-effects estimators are inconsistent, but the within estimator is consistent. The price of using the within estimator is that it is not possible to estimate coefficients on time-invariant variables, and all inference is conditional on the μ_i in the sample. See Mundlak (1978) and Hsiao (1986) for discussions of this interpretation of the within estimator.

▷ Example 1

The two-stage least-squares first-differenced estimator (FD2SLS) has been used to fit both fixed-effect and random-effect models. If the μ_i are truly fixed-effects, the FD2SLS estimator is not as efficient as the two-stage least-squares within estimator for finite T_i. Similarly, if none of the endogenous variables are lagged dependent variables, the exogenous variables are all strictly exogenous, and the random effects are i.i.d. and independent of the $\mathbf{X}_{it}$, the two-stage GLS estimators are more efficient than the FD2SLS estimator. However, the FD2SLS estimator has been used to obtain consistent estimates when one of these conditions fails. Anderson and Hsiao (1981) used a version of the FD2SLS estimator to fit a panel-data model with a lagged dependent variable.

Arellano and Bond (1991) develop new one-step and two-step GMM estimators for dynamic panel data. See [XT] **xtabond** for a discussion of these estimators and Stata's implementation of them. In their article, Arellano and Bond (1991) apply their new estimators to a model of dynamic labor demand that had previously been considered by Layard and Nickell (1986). They also compare the results of their estimators with those from the Anderson–Hsiao estimator using data from an unbalanced panel of firms from the United Kingdom. As is conventional, all variables are indexed over the firm i and time t. In this dataset, $\mathbf{n}_{it}$ is the log of employment in firm i inside the U.K. at time t, $\mathbf{w}_{it}$ is the natural log of the real product wage, $\mathbf{k}_{it}$ is the natural log of the gross capital stock, and $\mathbf{ys}_{it}$ is the natural log of industry output. The model also includes time dummies yr1980, yr1981, yr1982, yr1983, and yr1984. In Arellano and Bond (1991, table 5, column e), the authors present the results from applying one version of the Anderson–Hsiao estimator to these data. This example reproduces their results for the coefficients, though standard errors are different because Arellano and Bond are using robust standard errors.

(Continued on next page)

```
. use http://www.stata-press.com/data/r9/abdata

. xtivreg n l2.n l(0/1).w l(0/2).(k ys) yr1981-yr1984 (l.n = l3.n), fd
```

First-differenced IV regression					Number of obs	=	471
Group variable: id					Number of groups	=	140

R-sq:	within	= 0.0141			Obs per group: min =	3
	between	= 0.9165			avg =	3.4
	overall	= 0.9892			max =	5

				chi2(14)	=	122.53
corr(u_i, Xb)	= 0.9239			Prob > chi2	=	0.0000

d.n	Coef.	Std. Err.	z	P>|z|	[95% Conf. Interval]	
n						
LD.	1.422765	1.583053	0.90	0.369	-1.679962	4.525493
L2D.	-.1645517	.1647179	-1.00	0.318	-.4873928	.1582894
w						
D1.	-.7524675	.1765733	-4.26	0.000	-1.098545	-.4063902
LD.	.9627611	1.086506	0.89	0.376	-1.166752	3.092275
k						
D1.	.3221686	.1466086	2.20	0.028	.0348211	.6095161
LD.	-.3248778	.5800599	-0.56	0.575	-1.461774	.8120187
L2D.	-.0953947	.1960883	-0.49	0.627	-.4797207	.2889314
ys						
D1.	.7660906	.369694	2.07	0.038	.0415037	1.490678
LD.	-1.361881	1.156835	-1.18	0.239	-3.629237	.9054744
L2D.	.3212993	.5440403	0.59	0.555	-.745	1.387599
yr1981						
D1.	-.0574197	.0430158	-1.33	0.182	-.1417291	.0268896
yr1982						
D1.	-.0882952	.0706214	-1.25	0.211	-.2267106	.0501203
yr1983						
D1.	-.1063153	.10861	-0.98	0.328	-.319187	.1065563
yr1984						
D1.	-.1172108	.15196	-0.77	0.441	-.4150468	.1806253
_cons	.0161204	.0336264	0.48	0.632	-.0497861	.082027

sigma_u	.29069213	
sigma_e	.18855982	
rho	.70384993	(fraction of variance due to u_i)

```
Instrumented:  L.n
Instruments:   L2.n w L.w k L.k L2.k ys L.ys L2.ys yr1981 yr1982 yr1983 yr1984
               L3.n
```

                                                                              ◁

▷ Example 2

For the within estimator, consider another version of the wage equation discussed in [XT] **xtreg**. The data for this example come from an extract of women from the National Longitudinal Survey of Youth that was described in detail in [XT] **xt**. Restricting ourselves to only time-varying covariates, we might suppose that the log of the real wage was a function of the individual's age, age^2, her tenure in the observed place of employment, whether or not she belonged to union, whether or not she lives in metropolitan area, and whether or not she lives in the south. The variables for these are, respectively, age, age2, tenure, union, not_smsa, and south. If we treat all the variables as exogenous, we can use the one-stage within estimator from xtreg, yielding

```
. use http://www.stata-press.com/data/r9/nlswork
(National Longitudinal Survey. Young Women 14-26 years of age in 1968)
```

```
. generate age2 = age^2
(24 missing values generated)

. xtreg ln_w age* tenure not_smsa union south, fe i(idcode)
```

Fixed-effects (within) regression	Number of obs	=	19007
Group variable (i): idcode	Number of groups	=	4134

R-sq:	within = 0.1333	Obs per group: min =	1
	between = 0.2375	avg =	4.6
	overall = 0.2031	max =	12
		F(6,14867) =	381.19
corr(u_i, Xb)	= 0.2074	Prob > F =	0.0000

ln_wage	Coef.	Std. Err.	t	P>|t|	[95% Conf. Interval]	
age	.0311984	.0033902	9.20	0.000	.0245533	.0378436
age2	-.0003457	.0000543	-6.37	0.000	-.0004522	-.0002393
tenure	.0176205	.0008099	21.76	0.000	.0160331	.0192079
not_smsa	-.0972535	.0125377	-7.76	0.000	-.1218289	-.072678
union	.0975672	.0069844	13.97	0.000	.0838769	.1112576
south	-.0620932	.013327	-4.66	0.000	-.0882158	-.0359706
_cons	1.091612	.0523126	20.87	0.000	.9890729	1.194151
sigma_u	.3910683					
sigma_e	.25545969					
rho	.70091004	(fraction of variance due to u_i)				

```
F test that all u_i=0:     F(4133,14867) =       8.31           Prob > F = 0.0000
```

All the coefficients are statistically significant and have the expected signs.

Now suppose that we wish to model tenure as a function of union and south, and that we believe that the errors in the two equations are correlated. Since we are still interested in the within estimates, we now need a two-stage least-squares estimator. The following output shows the command and the results from fitting this model:

```
. xtivreg ln_w age* not_smsa (tenure = union south), fe i(idcode)
```

Fixed-effects (within) IV regression	Number of obs	=	19007
Group variable: idcode	Number of groups	=	4134

R-sq:	within = .	Obs per group: min =	1
	between = 0.1304	avg =	4.6
	overall = 0.0897	max =	12
		Wald chi2(4) =	147926.58
corr(u_i, Xb)	= -0.6843	Prob > chi2 =	0.0000

ln_wage	Coef.	Std. Err.	z	P>|z|	[95% Conf. Interval]	
tenure	.2403531	.0373419	6.44	0.000	.1671643	.3135419
age	.0118437	.0090032	1.32	0.188	-.0058023	.0294897
age2	-.0012145	.0001968	-6.17	0.000	-.0016003	-.0008286
not_smsa	-.0167178	.0339236	-0.49	0.622	-.0832069	.0497713
_cons	1.678287	.1626657	10.32	0.000	1.359468	1.997106
sigma_u	.70661941					
sigma_e	.63029359					
rho	.55690561	(fraction of variance due to u_i)				

```
F  test that all u_i=0:     F(4133,14869) =       1.44        Prob > F  = 0.0000
```

```
Instrumented:   tenure
Instruments:    age age2 not_smsa union south
```

Although all the coefficients still have the expected signs, the coefficients on `age` and `not_smsa` are no longer statistically significant. Given that these variables have been found to be important in many other studies, we might want to rethink our specification.

◁

If we are willing to assume that the μ_i are uncorrelated with the other covariates, we can fit a random-effects model. The model is frequently known as the variance-components or error-components model. `xtivreg` has estimators for two-stage least-squares one-way error component models. In the one-way framework, there are two variance components to estimate, the variance of the μ_i and the variance of the ν_{it}. Since the variance components are unknown, consistent estimates are required to implement feasible GLS. `xtivreg` offers two choices: a Swamy–Arora method and simple consistent estimators due to Baltagi and Chang (2000).

Baltagi and Chang (1994) derived the Swamy–Arora estimators of the variance components for unbalanced panels. By default, `xtivreg` uses estimators that extend these unbalanced Swamy–Arora estimators to the case with instrumental variables. The default Swamy–Arora method contains a degree-of-freedom correction to improve its performance in small samples. Baltagi and Chang (2000) use variance-components estimators, which are based on the ideas of Amemiya (1971) and Swamy and Arora (1972), but do not attempt to make small-sample adjustments. These consistent estimators of the variance components will be used if the `nosa` option is specified.

Using either estimator of the variance components, `xtivreg` offers two GLS estimators of the random-effects model. These two estimators differ only in how they construct the GLS instruments from the exogenous and instrumental variables contained in $\mathbf{X}_{it} = [\mathbf{X}_{1it}\ \mathbf{X}_{2it}]$. The default method, G2SLS, which is due to Balestra and Varadharajan-Krishnakumar, uses the exogenous variables after they have been passed through the feasible GLS transform. In math, G2SLS uses $\mathbf{X}_{it}^{*}$ for the GLS instruments, where $\mathbf{X}_{it}^{*}$ is constructed by passing each variable in $\mathbf{X}_{it}$ through the GLS transform in (3) given in *Methods and Formulas*. If the `ec2sls` option is specified, `xtivreg` performs Baltagi's EC2SLS. In EC2SLS, the instruments are $\widetilde{\mathbf{X}}_{it}$ and $\overline{\mathbf{X}}_{it}$, where $\widetilde{\mathbf{X}}_{it}$ is constructed by passing each of the variables in $\mathbf{X}_{it}$ through the within transform, and $\overline{\mathbf{X}}_{it}$ is constructed by passing each variable through the between transform. The within and between transforms are given in the *Methods and Formulas* section. Baltagi and Li (1992) show that, although the G2SLS instruments are a subset of those contained in EC2SLS, the extra instruments in EC2SLS are redundant in the sense of White (1984). Given the extra computational cost, G2SLS is the default.

(Continued on next page)

▷ Example 3

Here is the output from applying the G2SLS estimator to this model:

```
. generate byte black = (race==2)
. xtivreg ln_w age* not_smsa black (tenure = union birth south), re i(idcode)
```

G2SLS random-effects IV regression				Number of obs	=	19007
Group variable: idcode				Number of groups	=	4134

R-sq:	within	= 0.0664	Obs per group: min =		1
	between	= 0.2098		avg =	4.6
	overall	= 0.1463		max =	12

			Wald chi2(5)	=	1446.37
corr(u_i, X)	= 0 (assumed)		Prob > chi2	=	0.0000

ln_wage	Coef.	Std. Err.	z	P>|z|	[95% Conf. Interval]	
tenure	.1391798	.0078756	17.67	0.000	.123744	.1546157
age	.0279649	.0054182	5.16	0.000	.0173454	.0385843
age2	-.0008357	.0000871	-9.60	0.000	-.0010063	-.000665
not_smsa	-.2235103	.0111371	-20.07	0.000	-.2453386	-.2016821
black	-.2078613	.0125803	-16.52	0.000	-.2325183	-.1832044
_cons	1.337684	.0844988	15.83	0.000	1.172069	1.503299

sigma_u	.36582493	
sigma_e	.63031479	
rho	.25197078	(fraction of variance due to u_i)

Instrumented:	tenure
Instruments:	age age2 not_smsa black union birth_yr south

Note that we have included two time-invariant covariates, birth_yr and black. All the coefficients are statistically significant and are of the expected sign.

Applying the EC2SLS estimator yields similar results:

```
. xtivreg ln_w age* not_smsa black (tenure = union birth south), re ec2sls
> i(idcode)
```

EC2SLS random-effects IV regression				Number of obs	=	19007
Group variable: idcode				Number of groups	=	4134

R-sq:	within	= 0.0898	Obs per group: min =		1
	between	= 0.2608		avg =	4.6
	overall	= 0.1926		max =	12

			Wald chi2(5)	=	2721.92
corr(u_i, X)	= 0 (assumed)		Prob > chi2	=	0.0000

ln_wage	Coef.	Std. Err.	z	P>|z|	[95% Conf. Interval]	
tenure	.064822	.0025647	25.27	0.000	.0597953	.0698486
age	.0380048	.0039549	9.61	0.000	.0302534	.0457562
age2	-.0006676	.0000632	-10.56	0.000	-.0007915	-.0005438
not_smsa	-.2298961	.0082993	-27.70	0.000	-.2461625	-.2136297
black	-.1823627	.0092005	-19.82	0.000	-.2003954	-.16433
_cons	1.110564	.0606538	18.31	0.000	.9916849	1.229443

sigma_u	.36582493	
sigma_e	.63031479	
rho	.25197078	(fraction of variance due to u_i)

Instrumented:	tenure
Instruments:	age age2 not_smsa black union birth_yr south

Fitting the same model as above with the G2SLS estimator and the consistent variance components estimators yields

```
. xtivreg ln_w age* not_smsa black (tenure = union birth south), re nosa
> i(idcode)
```

| G2SLS random-effects IV regression | | Number of obs | = | 19007 |
| Group variable: idcode | | Number of groups | = | 4134 |

R-sq:	within = 0.0664	Obs per group: min =	1
	between = 0.2098	avg =	4.6
	overall = 0.1463	max =	12

| | | Wald chi2(5) | = | 1446.93 |
| corr(u_i, X) | = 0 (assumed) | Prob > chi2 | = | 0.0000 |

ln_wage	Coef.	Std. Err.	z	P>|z|	[95% Conf. Interval]
tenure	.1391859	.007873	17.68	0.000	.1237552	.1546166
age	.0279697	.005419	5.16	0.000	.0173486	.0385909
age2	-.0008357	.0000871	-9.60	0.000	-.0010064	-.000665
not_smsa	-.2235738	.0111344	-20.08	0.000	-.2453967	-.2017508
black	-.2078733	.0125751	-16.53	0.000	-.2325201	-.1832265
_cons	1.337522	.0845083	15.83	0.000	1.171889	1.503155

sigma_u	.36535633	
sigma_e	.63020883	
rho	.2515512	(fraction of variance due to u_i)

```
Instrumented:   tenure
Instruments:    age age2 not_smsa black union birth_yr south
```

◁

Acknowledgment

We thank Mead Over of the World Bank, who wrote an early implementation of xtivreg.

(Continued on next page)

Saved Results

xtivreg, re saves in e():

Scalars

e(N)	number of observations	e(r2_o)	R-squared for overall model
e(N_g)	number of groups	e(r2_b)	R-squared for between model
e(df_m)	model degrees of freedom	e(sigma)	ancillary parameter (gamma, lnormal)
e(g_max)	largest group size	e(sigma_u)	panel-level standard deviation
e(g_min)	smallest group size	e(sigma_e)	standard deviation of ϵ_{it}
e(g_avg)	average group size	e(thta_min)	minimum θ
e(chi2)	χ^2	e(thta_5)	θ, 5th percentile
e(rho)	ρ	e(thta_50)	θ, 50th percentile
e(Tbar)	harmonic mean of group sizes	e(thta_95)	θ, 95th percentile
e(F)	model F (small only)	e(thta_max)	maximum θ
e(df_rz)	residual degrees of freedom	e(m_p)	p-value from model test
e(r2_w)	R-squared for within model		

Macros

e(cmd)	xtivreg	e(instd)	instrumented variables
e(depvar)	name of dependent variable	e(vcetype)	title used to label Std. Err.
e(model)	g2sls or ec2sls	e(chi2type)	Wald; type of model χ^2 test
e(ivar)	variable denoting groups	e(predict)	program used to implement predict
e(insts)	instruments		

Matrices

e(b)	coefficient vector	e(V)	variance–covariance matrix of the estimators

Functions

e(sample)	marks estimation sample

xtivreg, be saves in e():

Scalars

e(N)	number of observations	e(g_max)	largest group size
e(N_g)	number of groups	e(g_min)	smallest group size
e(df_m)	model degrees of freedom	e(g_avg)	average group size
e(rss)	residual sum of squares	e(Tcon)	1 if T is constant
e(df_r)	residual degrees of freedom	e(r2)	R-squared
e(chi2)	model Wald	e(r2_w)	R-squared for within model
e(F)	F statistic (small only)	e(r2_o)	R-squared for overall model
e(rmse)	root mean squared error	e(r2_b)	R-squared for between model

Macros

e(cmd)	xtivreg	e(instd)	instrumented variables
e(depvar)	name of dependent variable	e(small)	small if specified
e(model)	be	e(vcetype)	title used to label Std. Err.
e(ivar)	variable denoting groups	e(predict)	program used to implement predict
e(insts)	instruments		

Matrices

e(b)	coefficient vector	e(V)	variance–covariance matrix of the estimators

Functions

e(sample)	marks estimation sample

`xtivreg, fe` saves in `e()`:

Scalars

`e(N)`	number of observations		`e(g_max)`	largest group size
`e(N_g)`	number of groups		`e(g_min)`	smallest group size
`e(mss)`	model sum of squares		`e(g_avg)`	average group size
`e(tss)`	total sum of squares		`e(rho)`	ρ
`e(df_m)`	model degrees of freedom		`e(Tbar)`	harmonic mean of group sizes
`e(rss)`	residual sum of squares		`e(Tcon)`	1 if T is constant
`e(df_r)`	residual d.o.f. (`small` only)		`e(r2_w)`	R-squared for within model
`e(r2)`	R-squared		`e(r2_o)`	R-squared for overall model
`e(r2_a)`	adjusted R-squared		`e(r2_b)`	R-squared for between model
`e(F)`	F statistic (`small` only)		`e(sigma)`	ancillary parameter (`gamma`, `lnormal`)
`e(rmse)`	root mean squared error		`e(corr)`	corr(u_i, Xb)
`e(chi2)`	model Wald (not `small`)		`e(sigma_u)`	panel-level standard deviation
`e(df_a)`	degrees of freedom for absorbed effect		`e(sigma_e)`	standard deviation of ϵ_{it}
`e(F_f)`	F for H_0: $u_i{=}0$			

Macros

`e(cmd)`	xtivreg		`e(insts)`	instruments
`e(depvar)`	name of dependent variable		`e(instd)`	instrumented variables
`e(model)`	fe		`e(vcetype)`	title used to label Std. Err.
`e(ivar)`	variable denoting groups		`e(predict)`	program used to implement `predict`

Matrices

`e(b)`	coefficient vector		`e(V)`	variance–covariance matrix of the estimators

Functions

`e(sample)`	marks estimation sample

(Continued on next page)

`xtivreg, fd` saves in `e()`:

Scalars

`e(N)`	number of observations	`e(g_max)`	largest group size
`e(N_g)`	number of groups	`e(g_min)`	smallest group size
`e(mss)`	model sum of squares	`e(g_avg)`	average group size
`e(tss)`	total sum of squares	`e(rho)`	ρ
`e(df_m)`	model degrees of freedom	`e(Tbar)`	harmonic mean of group sizes
`e(rss)`	residual sum of squares	`e(Tcon)`	1 if T is constant
`e(df_r)`	residual d.o.f. (`small` only)	`e(r2_w)`	R-squared for within model
`e(r2)`	R-squared	`e(r2_o)`	R-squared for overall model
`e(r2_a)`	adjusted R-squared	`e(r2_b)`	R-squared for between model
`e(F)`	F statistic (`small` only)	`e(sigma)`	ancillary parameter (`gamma`, `lnormal`)
`e(rmse)`	root mean squared error	`e(corr)`	$\text{corr}(u_i, \text{Xb})$
`e(chi2)`	model Wald (not `small`)	`e(sigma_u)`	panel-level standard deviation
`e(df_a)`	degrees of freedom for absorbed effect	`e(sigma_e)`	standard deviation of ϵ_{it}
`e(F_f)`	F for H_0: $u_i=0$		

Macros

`e(cmd)`	`xtivreg`	`e(insts)`	instruments
`e(depvar)`	name of dependent variable	`e(instd)`	instrumented variables
`e(model)`	`fd`	`e(vcetype)`	title used to label Std. Err.
`e(ivar)`	variable denoting groups	`e(predict)`	program used to implement `predict`
`e(tvar)`	time variable		

Matrices

`e(b)`	coefficient vector	`e(V)`	variance–covariance matrix of the estimators

Functions

`e(sample)`	marks estimation sample

Methods and Formulas

Consider an equation of the form

$$y_{it} = \mathbf{Y}_{it}\boldsymbol{\gamma} + \mathbf{X}_{1it}\boldsymbol{\beta} + \mu_i + \nu_{it} = \mathbf{Z}_{it}\boldsymbol{\delta} + \mu_i + \nu_{it} \qquad (2)$$

where

y_{it} is the dependent variable;

$\mathbf{Y}_{it}$ is an $1 \times g_2$ vector of observations on g_2 endogenous variables included as covariates, and these variables are allowed to be correlated with the ν_{it};

$\mathbf{X}_{1it}$ is an $1 \times k_1$ vector of observations on the exogenous variables included as covariates;

$\mathbf{Z}_{it} = [\mathbf{Y}_{it} \ \mathbf{X}_{it}]$;

$\boldsymbol{\gamma}$ is a $g_2 \times 1$ vector of coefficients;

$\boldsymbol{\beta}$ is a $k_1 \times 1$ vector of coefficients;

$\boldsymbol{\delta}$ is a $K \times 1$ vector of coefficients, where $K = g_2 + k_1$.

Assume that there is a $1 \times k_2$ vector of observations on the k_2 instruments in $\mathbf{X}_{2it}$. The order condition is satisfied if $k_2 \geq g_2$. Let $\mathbf{X}_{it} = [\mathbf{X}_{1it} \ \mathbf{X}_{2it}]$. `xtivreg` handles exogenously unbalanced panel data. Thus define T_i to be the number of observations on panel i, n to be the number of panels, and N to be the total number of observations, i.e., $N = \sum_{i=1}^{n} T_i$.

xtivreg, fd

As the name implies, this estimator obtains its estimates from an instrumental-variables regression on the first-differenced data. Specifically, first differencing the data yields

$$y_{it} - y_{it-1} = (\mathbf{Z}_{it} - \mathbf{Z}_{i,t-1})\,\delta + \nu_{it} - \nu_{i,t-1}$$

With the μ_i removed by differencing, we can obtain the estimated coefficients and their estimated variance–covariance matrix from a standard two-stage least-squares regression of Δy_{it} on $\Delta \mathbf{Z}_{it}$ with instruments $\Delta \mathbf{X}_{it}$.

R^2 within is reported as $\left[\operatorname{corr}\{(\mathbf{Z}_{it} - \overline{\mathbf{Z}}_i)\widehat{\delta}, y_{it} - \overline{y}_i\}\right]^2$.

R^2 between is reported as $\left\{\operatorname{corr}(\overline{\mathbf{Z}}_i\widehat{\delta}, \overline{y}_i)\right\}^2$.

R^2 overall is reported as $\left\{\operatorname{corr}(\mathbf{Z}_{it}\widehat{\delta}, y_{it})\right\}^2$.

xtivreg, fe

At the heart of this model is the within transformation. The within transform of a variable w is

$$\widetilde{w}_{it} = w_{it} - \overline{w}_{i.} + \overline{w}$$

where

$$\overline{w}_{i.} = \frac{1}{n}\sum_{t=1}^{T_i} w_{it}$$

$$\overline{w} = \frac{1}{N}\sum_{i=1}^{n}\sum_{t=1}^{T_i} w_{it}$$

and n is the number of groups and N is the total number of observations on the variable.

The within transform of (2) is

$$\widetilde{y}_{it} = \widetilde{\mathbf{Z}}_{it} + \widetilde{\nu}_{it}$$

Note that the within transform has removed the μ_i. With the μ_i gone, the within 2SLS estimator can be obtained from a two-stage least-squares regression of $\widetilde{y}_{it}$ on $\widetilde{\mathbf{Z}}_{it}$ with instruments $\widetilde{\mathbf{X}}_{it}$.

Suppose that there are K variables in $\mathbf{Z}_{it}$, including the mandatory constant. There are $K + n - 1$ parameters estimated in the model, and the VCE for the within estimator is

$$\frac{N - K}{N - n - K + 1} V_{IV}$$

where V_{IV} is the VCE from the above two-stage least-squares regression.

From the estimate of $\widehat{\delta}$, estimates $\widehat{\mu}_i$ of μ_i are obtained as $\widehat{\mu}_i = \overline{y}_i - \overline{\mathbf{Z}}_i\widehat{\delta}$. Reported from the calculated $\widehat{\mu}_i$ is its standard deviation and its correlation with $\overline{\mathbf{Z}}_i\widehat{\delta}$. Reported as the standard deviation of ν_{it} is the regression's estimated root mean squared error, s^2, which is adjusted (as previously stated) for the $n - 1$ estimated means.

R^2 within is reported as the R^2 from the mean-deviated regression.

R^2 between is reported as $\left\{ \operatorname{corr}(\overline{\mathbf{Z}}_i \widehat{\boldsymbol{\delta}}, \overline{y}_i) \right\}^2$.

R^2 overall is reported as $\left\{ \operatorname{corr}(\mathbf{Z}_{it} \widehat{\boldsymbol{\delta}}, y_{it}) \right\}^2$.

At the bottom of the output, an F statistic against the null hypothesis that all the μ_i are zero is reported. This F statistic is an application of the results in Wooldridge (1990).

xtivreg, be

After passing (2) through the between transform, we are left with

$$\overline{y}_i = \alpha + \overline{\mathbf{Z}}_i \boldsymbol{\delta} + \mu_i + \overline{\nu}_i \tag{3}$$

where

$$\overline{w}_i = \frac{1}{T_i} \sum_{t=1}^{T_i} w_{it} \quad \text{for } w \in \{y, \mathbf{Z}, \nu\}$$

Similarly, define $\overline{\mathbf{X}}_i$ as the matrix of instruments $\mathbf{X}_{it}$ after they have been passed through the between transform.

The BE2SLS estimator of (3) obtains its coefficient estimates and its VCE, a two-stage least-squares regression of $\overline{y}_i$ on $\overline{\mathbf{Z}}_i$ with instruments $\overline{\mathbf{X}}_i$ in which each average appears T_i times.

R^2 between is reported as the R^2 from the fitted regression.

R^2 within is reported as $\left[\operatorname{corr}\{ (\mathbf{Z}_{it} - \overline{\mathbf{Z}}_i) \widehat{\boldsymbol{\delta}}, y_{it} - \overline{y}_i \} \right]^2$.

R^2 overall is reported as $\left\{ \operatorname{corr}(\mathbf{Z}_{it} \widehat{\boldsymbol{\delta}}, y_{it}) \right\}^2$.

xtivreg, re

Following Baltagi and Chang (2000), let

$$u = \mu_i + \nu_{it}$$

be the $N \times 1$ vector of combined errors. Then under the assumptions of the random-effects model,

$$E(uu') = \sigma_\nu^2 \operatorname{diag}\left[I_{T_i} - \frac{1}{T_i} \boldsymbol{\iota}_{T_i} \boldsymbol{\iota}'_{T_i} \right] + \operatorname{diag}\left[w_i \frac{1}{T_i} \boldsymbol{\iota}_{T_i} \boldsymbol{\iota}'_{T_i} \right]$$

where

$$\omega_i = T_i \sigma_\mu^2 + \sigma_\nu^2$$

and $\boldsymbol{\iota}_{T_i}$ is a vector of ones of dimension T_i.

Since the variance components are unknown, consistent estimates are required to implement feasible GLS. xtivreg offers two choices. The default is a simple extension of the Swamy–Arora method for unbalanced panels.

Let

$$u_{it}^w = \widetilde{y}_{it} - \widetilde{\mathbf{Z}}_{it} \widehat{\boldsymbol{\delta}}_w$$

be the combined residuals from the within estimator. Let $\widetilde{u}_{it}$ be the within transformed u_{it}. Then

$$\widehat{\sigma}_\nu = \frac{\sum_{i=1}^n \sum_{t=1}^{T_i} \widetilde{u}_{it}^2}{N - n - K + 1}$$

Let

$$u_{it}^b = y_{it} - \mathbf{Z}_{it}\boldsymbol{\delta}_b$$

be the combined residual from the between estimator. Let $\overline{u}_{i.}^b$ be the between residuals after they have been passed through the between transform. Then

$$\widehat{\sigma}_\mu^2 = \frac{\sum_{i=1}^n \sum_{t=1}^{T_i} \overline{u}_{it}^2 - (n-K)\widehat{\sigma}_\nu^2}{N - r}$$

where

$$r = \text{trace}\left\{ \left(\overline{\mathbf{Z}}_i'\overline{\mathbf{Z}}_i\right)^{-1} \overline{\mathbf{Z}}_i'\mathbf{Z}_\mu \mathbf{Z}_\mu'\overline{\mathbf{Z}}_i \right\}$$

where

$$\mathbf{Z}_\mu = \text{diag}\left(\iota_{T_i}\iota_{T_i}'\right)$$

If the `nosa` option is specified, the consistent estimators described in Baltagi and Chang (2000) are used. These are given by

$$\widehat{\sigma}_\nu = \frac{\sum_{i=1}^n \sum_{t=1}^{T_i} \widetilde{u}_{it}^2}{N - n}$$

and

$$\widehat{\sigma}_\mu^2 = \frac{\sum_{i=1}^n \sum_{t=1}^{T_i} \overline{u}_{it}^2 - n\widehat{\sigma}_\nu^2}{N}$$

Note that the default Swamy–Arora method contains a degree-of-freedom correction to improve its performance in small samples.

Given estimates of the variance components, $\widehat{\sigma}_\nu^2$ and $\widehat{\sigma}_\mu^2$, the feasible GLS transform of a variable w is

$$w^* = w_{it} - \widehat{\theta}_{it}\overline{w}_{i.} \tag{4}$$

where

$$\overline{w}_{i.} = \frac{1}{T_i}\sum_{t=1}^{T_i} w_{it}$$

$$\widehat{\theta}_{it} = 1 - \left(\frac{\widehat{\sigma}_\nu^2}{\widehat{\omega}_i}\right)^{-\frac{1}{2}}$$

and

$$\widehat{\omega}_i = T_i\widehat{\sigma}_\mu^2 + \widehat{\sigma}_\nu^2$$

Using either estimator of the variance components, `xtivreg` contains two GLS estimators of the random-effects model. These two estimators differ only in how they construct the GLS instruments from the exogenous and instrumental variables contained in $\mathbf{X}_{it} = [\mathbf{X}_{1it}\mathbf{X}_{2it}]$. The default method, G2SLS, which is due to Balestra and Varadharajan-Krishnakumar, uses the exogenous variables after they have been passed through the feasible GLS transform. Mathematically, G2SLS uses $\mathbf{X}^*$ for the GLS instruments, where $\mathbf{X}^*$ is constructed by passing each variable in $\mathbf{X}$ though the GLS transform in (4). The G2SLS estimator obtains its coefficient estimates and VCE from an instrumental variable regression of y_{it}^* on $\mathbf{Z}_{it}^*$ with instruments $\mathbf{X}_{it}^*$.

If the `ec2sls` option is specified, `xtivreg` performs Baltagi's EC2SLS. In EC2SLS, the instruments are $\widetilde{\mathbf{X}}_i t$ and $\overline{\mathbf{X}}_{it}$, where $\widetilde{X}_{it}$ is constructed by each of the variables in $\mathbf{X}_{it}$ throughout the GLS transform in (4), and $\overline{\mathbf{X}}_{it}$ is made of the group means of each variable in $\mathbf{X}_{it}$. The EC2SLS estimator obtains its coefficient estimates and its VCE from an instrumental variables regression of y_{it}^* on $\mathbf{Z}_{it}^*$ with instruments $\widetilde{\mathbf{X}}_{it}$ and $\overline{\mathbf{X}}_{it}$.

Baltagi and Li (1992) show that although the G2SLS instruments are a subset of those in EC2SLS, the extra instruments in EC2SLS are redundant in the sense of White (1984). Given the extra computational cost, G2SLS is the default.

The standard deviation of $\mu_i + \nu_{it}$ is calculated as $\sqrt{\widehat{\sigma}_\mu^2 + \widehat{\sigma}_\nu^2}$.

R^2 between is reported as $\left\{ \operatorname{corr}(\overline{\mathbf{Z}}_i \widehat{\boldsymbol{\delta}}, \overline{y}_i) \right\}^2$.

R^2 within is reported as $\left[\operatorname{corr}\left\{ (\mathbf{Z}_{it} - \overline{\mathbf{Z}}_i)\widehat{\boldsymbol{\delta}}, y_{it} - \overline{y}_i \right\} \right]^2$.

R^2 overall is reported as $\left\{ \operatorname{corr}(\mathbf{Z}_{it}\widehat{\boldsymbol{\delta}}, y_{it}) \right\}^2$.

References

Amemiya, T. 1971. The estimation of the variances is a variance-components model. *International Economic Review* 12: 1–13.

Anderson, T. W. and C. Hsiao. 1981. Estimation of dynamic models with error components. *Journal of the American Statistical Association* 76: 598–606.

Balestra, P. and J. Varadharajan-Krishnakumar. 1987. Full-information estimations of a system of simultaneous equations with error component structure. *Econometric Theory* 3: 223–246.

Baltagi, B. H. 2001. *Econometric Analysis of Panel Data*. 2nd ed. New York: Wiley.

Baltagi, B. H. and Y. Chang. 1994. Incomplete panels: A comparative study of alternative estimators for the unbalanced one-way error component regression model. *Journal of Econometrics* 62: 67–89.

———. 2000. Simultaneous equations with incomplete panels. *Econometric Theory* 16: 269–279.

Baltagi, B. H. and Q. Li. 1992. A note on the estimation of simultaneous equations with error components. *Econometric Theory* 8: 113–119.

Swamy, P. A. V. B. and S. S. Arora. 1972. The exact finite sample properties of the estimators of coefficients in the error components regression models. *Econometrica* 40: 261–275.

White, H. 2000. *Asymptotic Theory for Econometricians*. rev. ed. New York: Academic Press.

Wooldridge, J. M. 1990. A note on the Lagrange multiple and F statistics for two-stage least squares regressions. *Economics Letters* 34: 151–155.

Also See

Complementary:	[XT] **xtivreg postestimation**; [XT] **xtdata**, [XT] **xtdes**, [XT] **xtsum**, [XT] **xttab**, [TS] **tsset**
Related:	[XT] **xtreg**; [XT] **xtabond**, [XT] **xtgee**, [XT] **xthtaylor**, [XT] **xtintreg**, [XT] **xtregar**, [XT] **xttobit**
Background:	[U] **11.1.10 Prefix commands**, [U] **20 Estimation and postestimation commands**, [XT] **estimation options**, [XT] **xt**, [R] *vce_option*

Title

> **xtivreg postestimation** — Postestimation tools for xtivreg

Description

The following postestimation commands are available for `xtivreg`:

command	description
adjust[1]	adjusted predictions of $\mathbf{x}\beta$
estat	VCE and estimation sample summary
estimates	cataloging estimation results
hausman	Hausman's specification test
lincom	point estimates, standard errors, testing, and inference for linear combinations of coefficients
mfx	marginal effects or elasticities
nlcom	point estimates, standard errors, testing, and inference for nonlinear combinations of coefficients
predict	predictions, residuals, influence statistics, and other diagnostic measures
predictnl	point estimates, standard errors, testing, and inference for generalized predictions
test	Wald tests for simple and composite linear hypotheses
testnl	Wald tests of nonlinear hypotheses

[1] `adjust` does not work with time-series operators.

See the corresponding entries in the *Stata Base Reference Manual* for details.

Syntax for predict

For all but the first-differenced estimator

> predict [*type*] *newvar* [*if*] [*in*] [, *statistic*]

First-differenced estimator

> predict [*type*] *newvar* [*if*] [*in*] [, *FD_statistic*]

statistic	description
xb	$\mathbf{Z}_{it}\widehat{\delta}$, fitted values; the default
ue	$\widehat{\mu}_i + \widehat{\nu}_{it}$, the combined residual
*xbu	$\mathbf{Z}_{it}\widehat{\delta} + \widehat{\mu}_i$, prediction including effect
*u	$\widehat{\mu}_i$, the fixed or random error component
*e	$\widehat{\nu}_{it}$, the overall error component

Unstarred statistics are available both in and out of sample; type `predict ... if e(sample) ...` if wanted only for the estimation sample. Starred statistics are calculated only for the estimation sample, even when `if e(sample)` is not specified.

FD_statistic	description
xb	$\mathbf{x}_j\mathbf{b}$, fitted values for the first-differenced model; the default
e	$e_{it} - e_{it-1}$, the first-differenced overall error component

These statistics are available both in and out of sample; type `predict ... if e(sample) ...` if wanted only for the estimation sample.

Options for predict

xb, the default, calculates the linear prediction, that is, $\mathbf{Z}_{it}\widehat{\boldsymbol{\delta}}$.

ue calculates the prediction of $\widehat{\mu}_i + \widehat{\nu}_{it}$. This is not available after the first-differenced model.

xbu calculates the prediction of $\mathbf{Z}_{it}\widehat{\boldsymbol{\delta}} + \widehat{\mu}_i$, the prediction including the fixed or random component. This is not available after the first-differenced model.

u calculates the prediction of $\widehat{\mu}_i$, the estimated fixed or random effect. This is not available after the first-differenced model.

e calculates the prediction of $\widehat{\nu}_{it}$.

Also See

Complementary:	[XT] **xtivreg**,
	[R] **adjust**, [R] **estimates**, [R] **hausman**, [R] **lincom**, [R] **mfx**,
	[R] **nlcom**, [R] **predictnl**, [R] **test**, [R] **testnl**
Background:	[U] **13.5 Accessing coefficients and standard errors**,
	[U] **20 Estimation and postestimation commands**,
	[R] **estat**, [R] **predict**

Title

> **xtline** — Panel-data line plots

Syntax

Graph by panel

>   xtline *varlist* [*if*] [*in*] [, *panel_options*]

Overlaid panels

>   xtline *varname* [*if*] [*in*], <u>ov</u>erlay [*overlaid_options*]

panel_options	description
Plot	
cline_options	affect rendition of the plotted points connected by lines
Add plot	
addplot(*plot*)	add other plots to the generated graph
Y-Axis, T-Axis, Title, Caption, Legend, Overall	
twoway_options	any options other than by() documented in [G] *twoway_options*
By	
<u>by</u>opts(*by_suboptions*)	affect appearance of the combined graph

overlaid_options	description
Main	
<u>ov</u>erlay	overlay each panel on the same graph
Plot 1, Plot 2, Plot 3, Plot 4	
plot#opts(*cline_options*)	affect rendition of the # panel line
Add plot	
addplot(*plot*)	add other plots to the generated graph
Y-Axis, T-Axis, Title, Caption, Legend, Overall	
twoway_options	any options other than by() documented in [G] *twoway_options*

Description

xtline draws line plots for panel data.

Options

<u>Main</u>

overlay causes the plot from each panel to be overlaid on the same graph. The default is to generate plots by panel. This option may not be combined with byopts() or be specified when there are multiple variables in *varlist*.

<u>Plot</u>

cline_options affect the rendition of the plotted points connected by lines; see [G] *cline_options*.

<u>Plot 1, Plot 2, Plot 3, Plot 4</u>

plot#opts(*cline_options*) affect the rendition of the #th panel (in sorted order). The *cline_options* can affect whether and how the points are connected; see [G] *cline_options*.

<u>Add plot</u>

addplot(*plot*) provides a way to add other plots to the generated graph; see [G] *addplot_option*.

<u>Y-Axis, T-Axis, Title, Caption, Legend, Overall</u>

twoway_options are any of the options documented in [G] *twoway_options* excluding by(). These include options for titling the graph (see [G] *title_options*) and saving the graph to disk (see [G] *saving_option*).

<u>By</u>

byopts(*by_suboptions*) allows all the options documented in [G] *by_option*. These options affect the appearance of the by-graph. byopts() may not be combined with overlay.

Remarks

▷ Example 1

Suppose that Tess, Sam, and Arnold kept a calorie log for an entire calendar year. At the end of the year, if they pooled their data together, they would have a dataset (e.g., xtline1.dta) that contains the amount of calories each of them consumed for 365 days. They could then use tsset to identify the date variable and treat each person as a panel and use xtline to plot the calories versus time for each person separately.

```
. use http://www.stata-press.com/data/r9/xtline1, clear

. tsset person day
        panel variable:  person, 1 to 3
         time variable:  day, 01jan2002 to 31dec2002
```

```
. xtline calories, tlabel(#3)
```

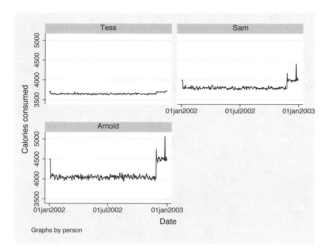

Specify the `overlay` option so that the values are plotted on the same graph to provide a better comparison between Tess, Sam, and Arnold.

```
. use http://www.stata-press.com/data/r9/xtline1, clear
. tsset person day
       panel variable:  person, 1 to 3
        time variable:  day, 01jan2002 to 31dec2002
. xtline calories, overlay
```

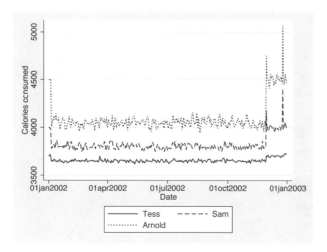

◁

Methods and Formulas

`xtline` is implemented as an ado-file.

Also See

Complementary:	[G] **graph twoway**, [TS] **tsset**
Related:	[TS] **tsline**
Background:	[XT] **xt**

Title

> **xtlogit** — Fixed-effects, random-effects, and population-averaged logit models

Syntax

Random-effects (RE) model

    xtlogit *depvar* [*indepvars*] [*if*] [*in*] [*weight*] [, re *RE_options*]

Conditional fixed-effects (FE) model

    xtlogit *depvar* [*indepvars*] [*if*] [*in*] [*weight*] , fe [*FE_options*]

Population-averaged (PA) model

    xtlogit *depvar* [*indepvars*] [*if*] [*in*] [*weight*] , pa [*PA_options*]

RE_options	description
Model	
i(*varname$_i$*)	use *varname$_i$* as the panel ID variable
<u>nocon</u>stant	suppress constant term
re	use random-effects estimator; the default
<u>off</u>set(*varname*)	include *varname* in model with coefficient constrained to 1
<u>constraints</u>(*constraints*)	apply specified linear constraints
Int opts (RE)	
<u>intm</u>ethod(*intmethod*)	integration method; *intmethod* may be <u>agh</u>ermite or <u>gh</u>ermite
<u>intp</u>oints(#)	use # quadrature points; default is intpoints(12)
SE	
vce(*vcetype*)	*vcetype* may be <u>boot</u>strap or jackknife
Reporting	
<u>level</u>(#)	set confidence level; default is level(95)
or	report odds ratios
noskip	perform overall model test as a likelihood-ratio test
Max options	
maximize_options	control the maximization process; seldom used
† <u>nodis</u>play	suppress display of header and coefficients

FE_options	description
Model	
i(*varname$_i$*)	use *varname$_i$* as the panel ID variable
fe	use fixed-effects estimator
<u>off</u>set(*varname*)	include *varname* in model with coefficient constrained to 1
<u>constra</u>ints(*constraints*)	apply specified linear constraints
SE	
vce(*vcetype*)	*vcetype* may be <u>boot</u>strap or <u>jack</u>knife
Reporting	
<u>l</u>evel(#)	set confidence level; default is level(95)
or	report odds ratios
noskip	perform overall model test as a likelihood-ratio test
Max options	
maximize_options	control the maximization process; seldom used
†<u>nodis</u>play	suppress display of header and coefficients

PA_options	description
Model	
i(*varname$_i$*)	use *varname$_i$* as the panel ID variable
<u>nocon</u>stant	suppress constant term
pa	use population-averaged estimator
<u>off</u>set(*varname*)	include *varname* in model with coefficient constrained to 1
PA options	
<u>c</u>orr(*correlation*)	within-group correlation structure
force	estimate even if observations unequally spaced in time
SE/Robust	
vce(*vcetype*)	*vcetype* may be <u>r</u>obust, <u>boot</u>strap, or <u>jack</u>knife
robust	synonym for vce(robust)
nmp	use divisor $N - P$ instead of the default N
<u>s</u>cale(x2)	set scale parameter to Pearson chi-squared statistic
<u>s</u>cale(dev)	set scale parameter to deviance divided by degrees of freedom
<u>s</u>cale(phi)	do not rescale the variance
<u>s</u>cale(#)	set scale parameter to #
Reporting	
<u>l</u>evel(#)	set confidence level; default is level(95)
or	report odds ratios
Opt options	
optimize_options	control the optimization process; seldom used
†<u>nodis</u>play	do not display the header and coefficients

† nodisplay is not shown in the dialog box.

correlation	description
<u>exc</u>hangeable	exchangeable
<u>ind</u>ependent	independent
<u>uns</u>tructured	unstructured
<u>fix</u>ed *matname*	user-specified
ar *#*	autoregressive of order *#*
<u>sta</u>tionary *#*	stationary of order *#*
<u>non</u>stationary *#*	nonstationary of order *#*

depvar and *indepvars* may contain time-series operators; see [U] **11.4.3 Time-series varlists**.

bootstrap, by, jackknife, statsby, and xi may be used with xtlogit; see [U] **11.1.10 Prefix commands**.

iweights, fweights, and pweights are allowed for the population-averaged model, and iweights are allowed for the fixed-effects and random-effects models; see [U] **11.1.6 weight**. Weights must be constant within panels.

See [U] **20 Estimation and postestimation commands** for additional capabilities of estimation commands.

Description

xtlogit fits random-effects, conditional fixed-effects, and population-averaged logit models. Whenever we refer to a fixed-effects model, we mean the conditional fixed-effects model.

Note: xtlogit, re is slow because the likelihood function is calculated by adaptive Gauss–Hermite quadrature; see *Methods and Formulas*. Computation time is roughly proportional to the number of points used for the quadrature; the default is intpoints(12). Simulations indicate that increasing the number of points does not appreciably change the estimates for the coefficients or their standard errors. See [XT] **quadchk**.

By default, the population-averaged model is an equal-correlation model; xtlogit, pa assumes corr(exchangeable). See [XT] **xtgee** for details on how to fit other population-averaged models.

See [R] **logistic** for a list of related estimation commands.

Options for RE model

⌐──── Model ⌐──

i(*varname$_i$*), noconstant; see [XT] **estimation options**.

re requests the random-effects estimator, which is the default.

offset(*varname*) constraints(*constraints*); see [XT] **estimation options**.

⌐──── Int opts (RE) ⌐──

intmethod(*intmethod*) specifies the integration method to be used for the random-effects model. It accepts one of two arguments: the first is <u>agh</u>ermite, the default, which specifies adaptive Gauss–Hermite quadrature; the second is <u>gh</u>ermite, which specifies nonadaptive Gauss–Hermite quadrature.

intpoints(*#*) specifies the number of points to use for Gauss–Hermite quadrature. The default is 12. Increasing this value slightly improves the accuracy but also increases computation time. Computation time is roughly proportional to its value.

⌐ SE ⌐

vce(*vcetype*); see [R] ***vce_option***.

⌐ Reporting ⌐

level(*#*); see [XT] **estimation options**.

or reports the estimated coefficients transformed to odds ratios; i.e., e^b rather than b. Standard errors and confidence intervals are similarly transformed. This option affects how results are displayed, not how they are estimated. or may be specified at estimation or when replaying previously estimated results.

noskip; see [XT] **estimation options**.

⌐ Max options ⌐

maximize_options: difficult, technique(*algorithm_spec*), iterate(*#*), [no]log, trace, gradient, showstep, hessian, shownrtolerance, tolerance(*#*), ltolerance(*#*), gtolerance(*#*), nrtolerance(*#*), nonrtolerance, from(*init_specs*); see [R] **maximize**. Some of these options are not available if intmethod(ghermite) is specified. These options are seldom used.

The following option is available with xtlogit but is not shown in the dialog box:

nodisplay is for programmers. It suppresses the display of the header and the coefficients.

Options for FE model

⌐ Model ⌐

i(*varname$_i$*); see [XT] **estimation options**.

fe requests the fixed-effects estimator.

offset(*varname*) constraints(*constraints*); see [XT] **estimation options**.

⌐ SE ⌐

vce(*vcetype*); see [R] ***vce_option***.

⌐ Reporting ⌐

level(*#*); see [XT] **estimation options**.

or reports the estimated coefficients transformed to odds ratios, i.e., e^b rather than b. Standard errors and confidence intervals are similarly transformed. This option affects how results are displayed, not how they are estimated. or may be specified at estimation or when replaying previously estimated results.

noskip; see [XT] **estimation options**.

⌐ Max options ⌐

maximize_options: difficult, technique(*algorithm_spec*), iterate(*#*), [no]log, trace, gradient, showstep, hessian, shownrtolerance, tolerance(*#*), ltolerance(*#*), gtolerance(*#*), nrtolerance(*#*), nonrtolerance, from(*init_specs*); see [R] **maximize**. These options are seldom used.

The following option is available with `xtlogit` but is not shown in the dialog box:

`nodisplay` is for programmers. It suppresses the display of the header and the coefficients.

Options for PA model

⌐───┌ Model ┐──

`i(`*varname*$_i$`)`, `noconstant`; see [XT] **estimation options**.

`pa` requests the population-averaged estimator.

`offset(`*varname*`)`; see [XT] **estimation options**.

⌐───┌ Correlation ┐───

`corr(`*correlation*`)`, `force`; see [XT] **estimation options**.

⌐───┌ SE/Robust ┐──

`vce(`*vcetype*`)`; see [R] ***vce_option***.

`robust`, `nmp`; see [XT] **estimation options**.

`scale(x2`|`dev`|`phi`|`#)` overrides the default scale parameter of `scale(1)`; see [XT] **estimation options**.

⌐───┌ Reporting ┐──

`level(#)`; see [XT] **estimation options**.

`or` reports the estimated coefficients transformed to odds ratios; i.e., e^b rather than b. Standard errors and confidence intervals are similarly transformed. This option affects how results are displayed, not how they are estimated. `or` may be specified at estimation or when replaying previously estimated results.

⌐───┌ Opt options ┐───

optimize_options control the iterative optimization process. These options are seldom used.

    `iterate(#)` specifies the maximum number of iterations. When the number of iterations equals #, the optimization stops and presents the current results, even if convergence has not been reached. The default is `iterate(100)`.

    `tolerance(#)` specifies the tolerance for the coefficient vector. When the relative change in the coefficient vector from one iteration to the next is less than or equal to #, the optimization process is stopped. `tolerance(1e-6)` is the default.

    `nolog` suppresses display of the iteration log.

    `trace` specifies that the current estimates be printed at each iteration.

The following option is available with `xtlogit` but is not shown in the dialog box:

`nodisplay` is for programmers. It suppresses the display of the header and the coefficients.

Remarks

xtlogit is a convenience command if you want the population-averaged model. Typing

   . xtlogit ..., pa ...

is equivalent to typing

   . xtgee ..., ... family(binomial) link(logit) corr(exchangeable)

It is also a convenience command if you want the fixed-effects model. Typing

   . xtlogit ..., fe i(*varname_i*) ...

is equivalent to typing

   . clogit ..., group(*varname_i*) ...

See also [XT] **xtgee** and [R] **clogit** for information about xtlogit.

By default or when re is specified, xtlogit fits via maximum likelihood the random-effects model

$$\Pr(y_{it} \neq 0 | \mathbf{x}_{it}) = P(\mathbf{x}_{it}\boldsymbol{\beta} + \nu_i)$$

for $i = 1, \ldots, n$ panels, where $t = 1, \ldots, n_i$, ν_i are i.i.d., $N(0, \sigma_\nu^2)$, and $P(z) = \{1 + \exp(-z)\}^{-1}$.

Underlying this model is the variance components model

$$y_{it} \neq 0 \iff \mathbf{x}_{it}\boldsymbol{\beta} + \nu_i + \epsilon_{it} > 0$$

where ϵ_{it} are i.i.d. logistic distributed with mean zero and variance $\sigma_\epsilon^2 = \pi^2/3$, independently of ν_i.

▷ Example 1

We are studying unionization of women in the United States and are using the union dataset; see [XT] **xt**. We wish to fit a random-effects model of union membership:

```
. use http://www.stata-press.com/data/r9/union
(NLS Women 14-24 in 1968)
. xtlogit union age grade not_smsa south southXt, i(id) nolog
Random-effects logistic regression        Number of obs      =      26200
Group variable (i): idcode                Number of groups   =       4434
Random effects u_i ~ Gaussian             Obs per group: min =          1
                                                         avg =        5.9
                                                         max =         12
                                          Wald chi2(5)       =     261.32
Log likelihood  = -10590.007              Prob > chi2        =     0.0000
```

union	Coef.	Std. Err.	z	P>|z|	[95% Conf. Interval]	
age	.0094584	.004259	2.22	0.026	.0011109	.017806
grade	.0804722	.0153909	5.23	0.000	.0503065	.1106378
not_smsa	-.2644412	.0752125	-3.52	0.000	-.411855	-.1170273
south	-1.104838	.1029103	-10.74	0.000	-1.306538	-.9031374
southXt	.0213871	.0075565	2.83	0.005	.0065767	.0361975
_cons	-3.118484	.2309515	-13.50	0.000	-3.571141	-2.665828
/lnsig2u	1.488964	.03507			1.420228	1.5577
sigma_u	2.10535	.0369173			2.034223	2.178965
rho	.5739819	.0085755			.5570949	.5906981

Likelihood-ratio test of rho=0: chibar2(01) = 5911.46 Prob >= chibar2 = 0.000

The output includes the additional panel-level variance component. This is parameterized as the log of the variance $\ln(\sigma_\nu^2)$ (labeled `lnsig2u` in the output). The standard deviation σ_ν is also included in the output and labeled `sigma_u` together with ρ (labeled `rho`),

$$\rho = \frac{\sigma_\nu^2}{\sigma_\nu^2 + \sigma_\epsilon^2}$$

which is the proportion of the total variance contributed by the panel-level variance component.

When `rho` is zero, the panel-level variance component is unimportant, and the panel estimator is no different from the pooled estimator. A likelihood-ratio test of this is included at the bottom of the output. This test formally compares the pooled estimator (logit) with the panel estimator.

As an alternative to the random-effects specification, we might want to fit an equal-correlation logit model:

```
. xtlogit union age grade not_smsa south southXt, i(id) pa

Iteration 1: tolerance = .07495101
Iteration 2: tolerance = .00626455
Iteration 3: tolerance = .00030986
Iteration 4: tolerance = .00001432
Iteration 5: tolerance = 6.699e-07

GEE population-averaged model              Number of obs      =       26200
Group variable:                  idcode    Number of groups   =        4434
Link:                             logit    Obs per group: min =           1
Family:                        binomial                   avg =         5.9
Correlation:                exchangeable                  max =          12
                                           Wald chi2(5)       =      233.60
Scale parameter:                      1    Prob > chi2        =      0.0000
```

union	Coef.	Std. Err.	z	P>|z|	[95% Conf. Interval]	
age	.0053241	.0024988	2.13	0.033	.0004265	.0102216
grade	.0595076	.0108311	5.49	0.000	.0382791	.0807361
not_smsa	-.1224955	.0483137	-2.54	0.011	-.2171887	-.0278024
south	-.7270863	.0675522	-10.76	0.000	-.8594861	-.5946865
southXt	.0151984	.0045586	3.33	0.001	.0062638	.024133
_cons	-2.01111	.15439	-13.03	0.000	-2.313709	-1.708512

◁

▷ Example 2

`xtlogit` with the `pa` option allows a `robust` option, so we can obtain the population-averaged logit estimator with the robust variance calculation by typing

```
. xtlogit union age grade not_smsa south southXt, i(id) pa robust nolog
```

GEE population-averaged model			Number of obs	=	26200
Group variable:		idcode	Number of groups	=	4434
Link:		logit	Obs per group: min =		1
Family:		binomial	avg =		5.9
Correlation:		exchangeable	max =		12
			Wald chi2(5)	=	152.01
Scale parameter:		1	Prob > chi2	=	0.0000

(Std. Err. adjusted for clustering on idcode)

union	Coef.	Semi-robust Std. Err.	z	P>|z|	[95% Conf. Interval]	
age	.0053241	.0037494	1.42	0.156	-.0020246	.0126727
grade	.0595076	.0133482	4.46	0.000	.0333455	.0856697
not_smsa	-.1224955	.0613646	-2.00	0.046	-.2427678	-.0022232
south	-.7270863	.0870278	-8.35	0.000	-.8976577	-.5565149
southXt	.0151984	.006613	2.30	0.022	.0022371	.0281596
_cons	-2.01111	.2016405	-9.97	0.000	-2.406319	-1.615902

These standard errors are somewhat larger than those obtained without the robust option.

◁

Finally, we can also fit a fixed-effects model to these data (see also [R] **clogit** for details):

```
. xtlogit union age grade not_smsa south southXt, i(id) fe
note: multiple positive outcomes within groups encountered.
note: 2744 groups (14165 obs) dropped due to all positive or
      all negative outcomes.
Iteration 0:   log likelihood = -4541.9044
Iteration 1:   log likelihood = -4511.1353
Iteration 2:   log likelihood = -4511.1042
```

Conditional fixed-effects logistic regression		Number of obs	=	12035
Group variable (i): idcode		Number of groups	=	1690
		Obs per group: min =		2
		avg =		7.1
		max =		12
		LR chi2(5)	=	78.16
Log likelihood = -4511.1042		Prob > chi2	=	0.0000

union	Coef.	Std. Err.	z	P>|z|	[95% Conf. Interval]	
age	.0079706	.0050283	1.59	0.113	-.0018848	.0178259
grade	.0811808	.0419137	1.94	0.053	-.0009686	.1633302
not_smsa	.0210368	.113154	0.19	0.853	-.2007411	.2428146
south	-1.007318	.1500491	-6.71	0.000	-1.301409	-.7132271
southXt	.0263495	.0083244	3.17	0.002	.010034	.0426649

Saved Results

xtlogit, re saves in e():

Scalars

e(N)	# of observations	e(rho)	ρ
e(N_g)	# of groups	e(sigma_u)	panel-level standard deviation
e(N_cd)	# of completely determined obs.	e(n_quad)	# of quadrature points
e(df_m)	model degrees of freedom	e(k)	# of parameters
e(ll)	log likelihood	e(k_eq)	# of equations
e(ll_0)	log likelihood, constant-only model	e(k_dv)	# of dependent variables
e(ll_c)	log likelihood, comparison model	e(p)	significance
e(g_max)	largest group size	e(rank)	rank of e(V)
e(g_min)	smallest group size	e(rank0)	rank of e(V) for constant-only model
e(g_avg)	average group size	e(ic)	# of iterations
e(chi2)	χ^2	e(rc)	return code
e(chi2_c)	χ^2 for comparison test	e(converged)	1 if converged, 0 otherwise

Macros

e(cmd)	xtlogit	e(distrib)	Gaussian; the distribution of the random effect
e(depvar)	name of dependent variable		
e(title)	title in estimation output	e(vce)	*vcetype* specified in vce()
e(ivar)	variable denoting groups	e(vcetype)	title used to label Std. Err.
e(wtype)	weight type	e(opt)	type of optimization
e(wexp)	weight expression	e(ml_method)	type of ml method
e(offset)	offset	e(user)	name of likelihood-evaluator program
e(chi2type)	Wald or LR; type of model χ^2 test	e(technique)	maximization technique
e(chi2_ct)	Wald or LR; type of model χ^2 test corresponding to e(chi2_c)	e(crittype)	optimization criterion
		e(properties)	b V
e(intmethod)	integration method	e(predict)	program used to implement predict

Matrices

e(b)	coefficient vector	e(ilog)	iteration log
e(V)	variance–covariance matrix of the estimators	e(gradient)	gradient vector

Functions

e(sample)	marks estimation sample

`xtlogit, fe` saves in `e()`:

Scalars

e(N)	number of observations	e(chi2)	χ^2
e(N_g)	number of groups	e(k)	# of parameters
e(df_m)	model degrees of freedom	e(k_eq)	# of equations
e(ll)	log likelihood	e(k_dv)	# of dependent variables
e(ll_0)	log likelihood, constant-only model	e(p)	significance
e(g_max)	largest group size	e(rank)	rank of e(V)
e(g_min)	smallest group size	e(ic)	# of iterations
e(g_avg)	average group size	e(rc)	return code
e(r2_p)	pseudo R-squared	e(converged)	1 if converged, 0 otherwise

Macros

e(cmd)	clogit	e(vce)	*vcetype* specified in vce()
e(cmd2)	xtlogit	e(vcetype)	title used to label Std. Err.
e(depvar)	name of dependent variable	e(opt)	type of optimization
e(title)	title in estimation output	e(ml_method)	type of ml method
e(ivar)	variable denoting groups	e(user)	name of likelihood-evaluator program
e(offset)	offset	e(technique)	maximization technique
e(wtype)	weight type	e(crittype)	optimization criterion
e(wexp)	weight expression	e(properties)	b V
e(chi2type)	LR; type of model χ^2 test	e(predict)	program used to implement predict
e(group)	name of group() variable		

Matrices

e(b)	coefficient vector	e(ilog)	iteration log
e(V)	variance–covariance matrix of the estimators	e(gradient)	gradient vector

Functions

e(sample)	marks estimation sample

(Continued on next page)

`xtlogit, pa` saves in `e()`:

Scalars

e(N)	number of observations	e(deviance)	deviance
e(N_g)	number of groups	e(chi2_dev)	χ^2 test of deviance
e(df_m)	model degrees of freedom	e(dispers)	deviance dispersion
e(g_max)	largest group size	e(chi2_dis)	χ^2 test of deviance dispersion
e(g_min)	smallest group size	e(tol)	target tolerance
e(g_avg)	average group size	e(dif)	achieved tolerance
e(chi2)	χ^2	e(phi)	scale parameter
e(df_pear)	degrees of freedom for Pearson χ^2	e(rc)	return code

Macros

e(cmd)	xtgee	e(ivar)	variable denoting groups
e(cmd2)	xtlogit	e(vce)	*vcetype* specified in vce()
e(depvar)	name of dependent variable	e(vcetype)	title used to label Std. Err.
e(family)	binomial	e(chi2type)	Wald; type of model χ^2 test
e(link)	logit; link function	e(offset)	offset
e(corr)	correlation structure	e(properties)	b V
e(crittype)	optimization criterion	e(predict)	program used to implement predict
e(scale)	x2, dev, phi, or #; scale parameter		

Matrices

e(b)	coefficient vector	e(R)	estimated working correlation matrix
e(V)	variance–covariance matrix of the estimators		

Functions

e(sample)	marks estimation sample

Methods and Formulas

`xtlogit` is implemented as an ado-file.

`xtlogit` reports the population-averaged results obtained by using `xtgee, family(binomial) link(logit)` to obtain estimates. The fixed-effects results are obtained using `clogit`. See [XT] **xtgee** and [R] **clogit** for details on the methods and formulas.

Assuming a normal distribution, $N(0, \sigma_\nu^2)$, for the random effects ν_i,

$$\Pr(y_{i1}, \ldots, y_{in_i} | \mathbf{x}_{i1}, \ldots, \mathbf{x}_{in_i}) = \int_{-\infty}^{\infty} \frac{e^{-\nu_i^2/2\sigma_\nu^2}}{\sqrt{2\pi}\sigma_\nu} \left\{ \prod_{t=1}^{n_i} F(y_{it}, \mathbf{x}_{it}\boldsymbol{\beta} + \nu_i) \right\} d\nu_i$$

where

$$F(y, z) = \begin{cases} \dfrac{1}{1 + \exp(-z)} & \text{if } y \neq 0 \\ \dfrac{1}{1 + \exp(z)} & \text{otherwise} \end{cases}$$

The integral can be approximated with M-point Gauss–Hermite quadrature

$$\int_{-\infty}^{\infty} e^{-x^2} g(x)dx \approx \sum_{m=1}^{M} w_m^* g(a_m^*)$$

where the w_m^* denote the quadrature weights and the a_m^* denote the quadrature abscissas. The log likelihood, L, where $\rho = \sigma_\nu^2/(\sigma_\nu^2 + \pi^2/3)$, is then calculated using the quadrature

$$L = \sum_{i=1}^{n} w_i \log\Big\{ \Pr(y_{i1}, \ldots, y_{in_i} | \mathbf{x}_{i1}, \ldots, \mathbf{x}_{in_i}) \Big\}$$

$$\approx \sum_{i=1}^{n} w_i \log \left[\frac{1}{\sqrt{\pi}} \sum_{m=1}^{M} w_m^* \prod_{t=1}^{n_i} F \left\{ y_{it}, \mathbf{x}_{it}\boldsymbol{\beta} + a_m^* \left(\frac{2\rho}{1-\rho} \right)^{1/2} \right\} \right]$$

where w_i is the user-specified weight for panel i; if no weights are specified, $w_i = 1$.

The above is the formula for nonadaptive Gauss–Hermite quadrature. The default is to calculate the log likelihood, L, using adaptive Gauss–Hermite quadrature, which transforms the integrand

$$g(y_{it}, x_{it}, \nu_i) = \frac{e^{-\nu_i^2/2\sigma_\nu^2}}{\sqrt{2\pi}\sigma_\nu} \left\{ \prod_{t=1}^{n_i} F(y_{it}, \mathbf{x}_{it}\boldsymbol{\beta} + \nu_i) \right\}$$

so that it is sampled on a suitable range; see Liu (1994).

Both quadrature formulas require that the integrated function be well approximated by a polynomial. The number of time periods (panel size) affects whether

$$\prod_{t=1}^{n_i} F(y_{it}, \mathbf{x}_{it}\boldsymbol{\beta} + \nu_i)$$

is well approximated by a polynomial. As panel size (or ρ) increases, the quadrature approximation becomes less accurate. Adaptive quadrature gives better results for correlated data and large panels than nonadaptive quadrature; however we recommend that you use the `quadchk` command to investigate the applicability of the numeric technique used in this command.

References

Conway, M. R. 1990. A random effects model for binary data. *Biometrics* 46: 317–328.

Liang, K.-Y. and S. L. Zeger. 1986. Longitudinal data analysis using generalized linear models. *Biometrika* 73: 13–22.

Liu, Qing and D. A. Pierce 1994. A note on Gauss–Hermite quadrature. *Biometrika* 81: 624–629.

Neuhaus, J. M. 1992. Statistical methods for longitudinal and clustered designs with binary responses. *Statistical Methods in Medical Research* 1: 249–273.

Neuhaus, J. M., J. D. Kalbfleisch, and W. W. Hauck. 1991. A comparison of cluster-specific and population-averaged approaches for analyzing correlated binary data. *International Statistical Review* 59: 25–35.

Pendergast, J. F., S. J. Gange, M. A. Newton, M. J. Lindstrom, M. Palta, and M. R. Fisher. 1996. A survey of methods for analyzing clustered binary response data. *International Statistical Review* 64: 89–118.

Twisk, J. W. R. 2003. *Applied Longitudinal Data Analysis for Epidemiology: A Practical Guide.* Cambridge: Cambridge University Press.

Also See

Complementary: [XT] **xtlogit postestimation**; [XT] **quadchk**, [XT] **xtdata**, [XT] **xtdes**,
[XT] **xtsum**, [XT] **xttab**,
[R] **constraint**

Related: [XT] **xtcloglog**, [XT] **xtgee**, [XT] **xtprobit**,
[R] **clogit**, [R] **logit**, [R] **logistic**

Background: [U] **11.1.10 Prefix commands**,
[U] **20 Estimation and postestimation commands**,
[XT] **estimation options**, [XT] **xt**,
[R] **maximize**, [R] *vce_option*

Title

xtlogit postestimation — Postestimation tools for xtlogit

Description

The following postestimation commands are available for xtlogit:

command	description
adjust[1]	adjusted predictions of $\mathbf{x}\beta$, probabilities, or $\exp(\mathbf{x}\beta)$ predictions
*estat	AIC, BIC, VCE, and estimation sample summary
estimates	cataloging estimation results
lincom	point estimates, standard errors, testing, and inference for linear combinations of coefficients
lrtest	likelihood-ratio test
mfx	marginal effects or elasticities
nlcom	point estimates, standard errors, testing, and inference for nonlinear combinations of coefficients
predict	predictions, residuals, influence statistics, and other diagnostic measures
predictnl	point estimates, standard errors, testing, and inference for generalized predictions
test	Wald tests for simple and composite linear hypotheses
testnl	Wald tests of nonlinear hypotheses

[1] adjust does not work with time-series operators.
* estat ic may not be used after xtlogit, pa.
See the corresponding entries in the *Stata Base Reference Manual* for details.

Syntax for predict

Random-effects model

> predict [*type*] *newvar* [*if*] [*in*] [, *RE_statistic* nooffset]

Fixed-effects model

> predict [*type*] *newvar* [*if*] [*in*] [, *FE_statistic* nooffset]

Population-averaged model

> predict [*type*] *newvar* [*if*] [*in*] [, *PA_statistic* nooffset]

RE_statistic	description
xb	linear prediction; the default
pu0	probability of a positive outcome assuming that the random effect is zero
stdp	standard error of the linear prediction

FE_statistic	description
p	predicted probability of a positive outcome conditional on one positive outcome within group; the default
pu0	probability of a positive outcome assuming that the fixed effect is zero
xb	linear prediction
stdp	standard error of the linear prediction

PA_statistic	description
mu	predicted probability of *depvar*; considers the offset()
rate	predicted probability of *depvar*
xb	calculate linear prediction
stdp	calculate standard error of the linear prediction
<u>sc</u>ore	first derivative of the log likelihood with respect to $x_j\beta$

These statistics are available both in and out of sample; type predict ... if e(sample) ... if wanted only for the estimation sample.

Note that the predicted probability for the fixed-effects model is conditional on there being only one outcome per group. See [R] **clogit** for details.

Options for predict

xb calculates the linear prediction. This is the default for the random-effects model.

p calculates the predicted probability of a positive outcome conditional on one positive outcome within group. This is the default for the fixed-effects model.

mu and rate both calculate the predicted probability of *depvar*. mu takes into account the offset(), and rate ignores those adjustments. mu and rate are equivalent if you did not specify offset(). mu is the default for the population-averaged model.

pu0 calculates the probability of a positive outcome, assuming that the fixed or random effect for that observation's panel is zero ($\nu = 0$). Note that this may not be similar to the proportion of observed outcomes in the group.

stdp calculates the standard error of the linear prediction.

score calculates the equation-level score, $u_j = \partial \ln L_j(x_j\beta)/\partial(x_j\beta)$.

nooffset is relevant only if you specified offset(*varname*) for xtlogit. This option modifies the calculations made by predict so that they ignore the offset variable; the linear prediction is treated as $x_{it}\beta$ rather than $x_{it}\beta + \text{offset}_{it}$.

Methods and Formulas

All postestimation commands listed above are implemented as ado-files.

Also See

Complementary: [XT] **xtlogit**,

[R] **adjust**, [R] **estimates**, [R] **lincom**, [R] **lrtest**, [R] **mfx**,

[R] **nlcom**, [R] **predictnl**, [R] **test**, [R] **testnl**

Background: [U] **13.5 Accessing coefficients and standard errors**,

[U] **20 Estimation and postestimation commands**,

[R] **estat**, [R] **predict**

Title

xtmixed — Multilevel mixed-effects linear regression

Syntax

> xtmixed *depvar fe_equation* [|| *re_equation*] [|| *re_equation* ...] [, *options*]

where the syntax of *fe_equation* is

> [*indepvars*] [*if*] [*in*] [, *fe_options*]

and the syntax of *re_equation* is one of the following:

for random coefficients and intercepts

> *levelvar*: [*varlist*] [, *re_options*]

for random effects among the values of a factor variable

> *levelvar*: R.*varname* [, *re_options*]

levelvar is a variable identifying the group structure for the random effects at that level, or _all representing a single group comprised of all observations.

fe_options	description
Model	
no<u>c</u>onstant	suppress the constant term from the fixed-effects equation

re_options	description
Model	
no<u>c</u>onstant	suppress the constant term from the random-effects equation
<u>cov</u>ariance(*vartype*)	variance–covariance structure of the random effects

options	description
Estimation	
<u>reml</u>	fit model via maximum restricted likelihood; the default
<u>mle</u>	fit model via maximum likelihood
<u>nostderr</u>	do not estimate standard errors of random-effects parameters
<u>nolrtest</u>	do not perform LR test comparing to linear regression

Reporting

noheader	suppress output header
nogroup	suppress table summarizing groups
nofetable	suppress fixed-effects table
noretable	suppress random-effects table
variance	show random-effects parameter estimates as variances and covariances
estmetric	show parameter estimates in the estimation metric
level(#)	set confidence level; default is level(95)

EM Options

emiterate(#)	number of EM iterations; default is 20
emtolerance(#)	EM convergence tolerance; default is 1e−10
emonly	fit model exclusively using EM
emlog	show EM iteration log
emdots	show EM iterations as dots

Max options

maximize_options	control the maximization process

vartype	description
independent	one unique variance parameter per random effect, all covariances zero; the default unless a factor variable is specified
exchangeable	equal variances for random effects, and one common pairwise covariance
identity	equal variances for random effects, all covariances zero
unstructured	all variances/covariances distinctly estimated

depvar and *indepvars* may contain time-series operators; see [U] **11.4.3 Time-series varlists**.

bootstrap, by, jackknife, statsby, and xi may be used with xtmixed; see [U] **11.1.10 Prefix commands**.

See [U] **20 Estimation and postestimation commands** for additional capabilities of estimation commands.

Description

xtmixed fits linear mixed models. Mixed models are characterized as containing both *fixed effects* and *random effects*. The fixed effects are analogous to standard regression coefficients and are estimated directly. The random effects are not directly estimated, but are summarized according to their estimated variances and covariances. Although random effects are not directly estimated, you can form best linear unbiased predictions (BLUPs) of them using predict after xtmixed; see [XT] **xtmixed postestimation**. Random effects may take the form of either random intercepts or random coefficients, and the grouping structure of the data may consist of multiple levels of nested groups. The error distribution of the linear mixed model is assumed to be Gaussian.

Options

⌐ Model ⌐

noconstant suppresses the constant (intercept) term and may be specified for the fixed-effects equation and for any or all of the random-effects equations.

covariance(*vartype*), where *vartype* is

independent | exchangeable | identity | unstructured

specifies the structure of the covariance matrix for the random effects and may be specified for each random-effects equation. An independent covariance structure allows for a distinct variance for each random effect within a random-effects equation and assumes that all covariances are zero. exchangeable structure specifies one common variance for all random effects and one common pairwise covariance. identity is short for "multiple of the identity"; that is, all variances are equal, and all covariances are zero. unstructured allows for all variances and covariances to be distinct. If an equation consists of p random-effects terms, the unstructured covariance matrix will have $p(p+1)/2$ unique parameters.

covariance(independent) is the default, except for when the random-effects equation is a factor-variable specification R.*varname*, in which case covariance(identity) is the default.

Only covariance(identity) and covariance(exchangeable) are allowed with the factor-variable specification.

⌐ Estimation ⌐

reml and mle specify the statistical method for fitting the model.

reml, the default, specifies that the model be fitted using maximum restricted likelihood (REML), also known as maximum residual likelihood.

mle specifies that the model be fitted using maximum likelihood (ML).

nostderr prevents xtmixed from calculating standard errors for the estimated random-effects parameters, although standard errors are still provided for the fixed-effects parameters. Specifying this option will result in faster computation times.

nolrtest prevents xtmixed from fitting a reference linear regression model and using this model to calculate a likelihood-ratio test comparing the mixed model to ordinary regression. This option may also be specified on replay to suppress this test from the output.

⌐ Reporting ⌐

noheader suppresses the output header, either at estimation or upon replay.

nogroup suppresses the display of group summary information (number of groups, average group size, minimum, and maximum) from the output header.

nofetable suppresses the table of fixed effects.

noretable suppresses the table of random effects.

variance displays the random-effects parameter estimates as variances and covariances. The default is to display them as standard deviations and correlations.

estmetric displays all parameter estimates in the estimation metric. Fixed-effects estimates are unchanged from those normally displayed, but random-effects parameter estimates are displayed as log-standard deviations and hyperbolic arctangents of correlations, with equations names that organize them by model level.

level(#); see [XT] **estimation options**.

___ EM options ___

emiter(#) specifies the number of EM (expectation-maximization) iterations to perform. The default is 20.

emtolerance(#) specifies the convergence tolerance for the EM algorithm. The default is 1e-10. EM iterations stop once the log (restricted) likelihood changes by a relative amount less than #. At that point, maximization switches to a gradient-based method, unless emonly is specified, in which case maximization stops.

emonly specifies that the likelihood be maximized exclusively using EM. The advantage of specifying emonly is that EM iterations are typically much faster than those for gradient-based methods. The disadvantages are that EM iterations can be slow to converge (if at all), and EM provides no facility for estimating standard errors for the random-effects parameters.

emlog specifies that the EM iteration log be shown. The EM iteration log is, by default, not displayed unless option emonly is specified.

emdots specifies that the EM iterations be shown as dots.

___ Max options ___

maximize_options: <u>diff</u>icult, <u>tech</u>nique(*algorithm_spec*), <u>iter</u>ate(#), [<u>no</u>]log, trace, gradient, showstep, hessian, shownrtolerance, <u>tol</u>erance(#), <u>ltol</u>erance(#), <u>gtol</u>erance(#), <u>nrtol</u>erance(#), nonrtolerance; see [R] **maximize**.

For option technique(), the default is technique(nr), and algorithm bhhh is not allowed.

Remarks

Remarks are presented under the headings

> *Introduction*
> *One-level models*
> *Covariance structures*
> *Likelihood versus restricted likelihood*
> *Two-level models*
> *Blocked-diagonal covariance structures*
> *Factor notation and crossed-effects models*
> *Diagnosing convergence problems*
> *Distribution theory for likelihood-ratio tests*

Introduction

Linear mixed models are models containing both fixed effects and random effects. They are a generalization of linear regression allowing for the inclusion of random deviations (effects) other than those associated with the overall error term. In matrix notation,

$$\mathbf{y} = \mathbf{X}\boldsymbol{\beta} + \mathbf{Z}\mathbf{u} + \boldsymbol{\epsilon} \tag{1}$$

where $\mathbf{y}$ is the $n \times 1$ vector of responses, $\mathbf{X}$ is a $n \times p$ design/covariate matrix for the fixed effects β, and $\mathbf{Z}$ is the $n \times q$ design/covariate matrix for the random effects $\mathbf{u}$. The $n \times 1$ vector of errors, ϵ, is assumed to be multivariate normal with mean zero and variance matrix $\sigma_\epsilon^2 \mathbf{I}_n$.

The fixed portion of (1), $\mathbf{X}\beta$, is analogous to the linear predictor from a standard OLS regression model with β the regression coefficients to be estimated. For the random portion of (1), $\mathbf{Z}\mathbf{u} + \epsilon$, we assume that $\mathbf{u}$ has variance–covariance matrix $\mathbf{G}$ and that $\mathbf{u}$ is orthogonal to ϵ so that

$$\mathrm{Var}\begin{bmatrix} \mathbf{u} \\ \epsilon \end{bmatrix} = \begin{bmatrix} \mathbf{G} & 0 \\ 0 & \sigma_\epsilon^2 \mathbf{I}_n \end{bmatrix}$$

The random effects $\mathbf{u}$ are not directly estimated (although they may be predicted), but instead are characterized by the elements of $\mathbf{G}$, known as *variance components*, that are estimated along with the residual variance σ_ϵ^2.

The general forms of the design matrices $\mathbf{X}$ and $\mathbf{Z}$ allow estimation for a broad class of linear models; blocked designs, split-plot designs, growth curves, multilevel or hierarchical designs, etc. They also allow a flexible method of modeling within-panel correlation. Subjects within the same panel can be correlated as a result of a shared random intercept, or through a shared random slope on (say) age, or both. The general specification of $\mathbf{G}$ also provides additional flexibility—the random intercept and random slope could themselves be modeled as independent, or correlated, or independent with equal variances, and so forth.

Overviews of mixed models are provided by, among others, Searle, Casella, and McCulloch (1992); McCulloch and Searle (2001); Verbeke and Molenberghs (2000); Raudenbush and Bryk (2002); and Pinheiro and Bates (2000). In particular, chapter 2 of Searle, Casella, and McCulloch (1992) provides an excellent history.

The key to fitting mixed models lies in estimating the variance components, and for that, there exist a multitude of methods. Most of the early literature in mixed models dealt with estimating variance components in ANOVA models. For simple models with balanced data, estimating variance components amounts to solving a system of equations obtained by setting expected mean-squares expressions equal to their observed counterparts. Much of the work in extending the "ANOVA method" to unbalanced data for general ANOVA designs is due to Henderson (1953).

The ANOVA method is, however, not without its shortcomings. Among these is a lack of uniqueness in that alternative, unbiased estimates of variance components could be derived using other quadratic forms of the data in place of observed mean squares (Searle, Casella, and McCulloch 1992, 38–39). As a result, ANOVA methods gave way to more modern methods, such as minimum norm quadratic unbiased estimation (MINQUE) and minimum variance quadratic unbiased estimation (MIVQUE); see Rao (1973) for MINQUE and Lamotte (1973) for MIVQUE. Both methods involve finding optimal quadratic forms of the data that are unbiased for the variance components.

The most popular methods, however, are maximum likelihood (ML) and restricted maximum-likelihood (REML), and these are the two methods that are supported by xtmixed. The ML estimates are based on the usual application of likelihood theory, given the distributional assumptions of the model. The basic idea behind REML (Thompson 1962) is that you can form a set of linear contrasts of the response that do not depend on the fixed effects, β, but instead depend only on the variance components to be estimated. You then apply ML methods using the distribution of the linear contrasts to form the likelihood.

Returning to (1), note that in panel-data situations it is convenient not to consider all n observations at once, but instead organize the mixed model as a series of M independent panels

$$\mathbf{y}_i = \mathbf{X}_i\boldsymbol{\beta} + \mathbf{Z}_i\mathbf{u}_i + \boldsymbol{\epsilon}_i \tag{2}$$

for $i = 1, \ldots, M$, with panel i consisting of n_i observations. The response, $\mathbf{y}_i$, is comprised of the rows of $\mathbf{y}$ corresponding to the ith panel, with $\mathbf{X}_i$ and $\boldsymbol{\epsilon}_i$ defined analogously. The random effects, $\mathbf{u}_i$, can now be thought of as M realizations of a $q \times 1$ vector that is normally distributed with mean $\mathbf{0}$ and $q \times q$ variance matrix $\boldsymbol{\Sigma}$. The matrix $\mathbf{Z}_i$ is the $n_i \times q$ design matrix for the ith panel random effects. Relating this to (1), note that

$$\mathbf{Z} = \begin{bmatrix} \mathbf{Z}_1 & \mathbf{0} & \cdots & \mathbf{0} \\ \mathbf{0} & \mathbf{Z}_2 & \cdots & \mathbf{0} \\ \vdots & \vdots & \ddots & \vdots \\ \mathbf{0} & \mathbf{0} & \mathbf{0} & \mathbf{Z}_M \end{bmatrix}; \quad \mathbf{u} = \begin{bmatrix} \mathbf{u}_1 \\ \vdots \\ \mathbf{u}_M \end{bmatrix}; \quad \mathbf{G} = \mathbf{I}_M \otimes \boldsymbol{\Sigma}$$

The mixed-model formulation (2) is due to Laird and Ware (1982) and offers two key advantages. First, it makes specifications of random-effects terms easier. If the panels are schools, you can simply specify a random effect "at the school level", as opposed to thinking of what a school-level random effect would mean when all the data are considered as a whole (if it helps, think Kronecker products). Second, representing a mixed-model with (2) generalizes easily to more than one level of random variation. For example, if classes are nested within schools, then (2) can be generalized to allow random effects at both the school and at the class-within-school levels. This we demonstrate later.

Finally, using formulation (2) and its multilevel extensions requires one important convention of terminology. Model (2) is what we call a *one-level* model, with extensions to two, three, or any number of levels. In our hypothetical two-level model with classes nested within schools, the schools are considered the first level, and classes the second level of the model. This is generally accepted terminology but differs from that of the literature on hierarchical models, e.g., Skrondal and Rabe-Hesketh (2004). In that literature, our schools and classes model would be considered a three-level model, with the students comprising the first level, classes the second, and schools the third. Not only is there one more level, students, but the order is reversed.

One-level models

We begin with a simple application of (2).

▷ Example 1

Consider a longitudinal dataset used by both Ruppert, Wand, and Carroll (2003) and Diggle et al. (2002), consisting of weight measurements of 48 pigs on 9 successive weeks. Pigs are identified by variable id. Below is a plot of the growth curves for the first 10 pigs.

```
. use http://www.stata-press.com/data/r9/pig
(Longitudinal analysis of pig weights)
```

```
. twoway connected weight week if id<=10, connect(L)
```

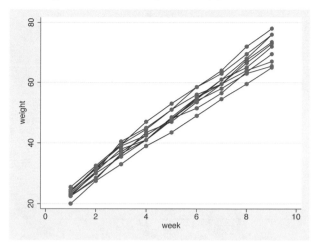

It seems clear that each pig experiences a linear trend in growth and that overall weight measurements vary from pig to pig. Because we are not really interested in these particular 48 pigs *per se*, we instead treat them as a random sample from a larger population and model the between-pig variability as a random effect or, in the terminology of (2), as a random intercept term at the pig level. We thus wish to fit the following model

$$\texttt{weight}_{ij} = \beta_0 + \beta_1 \texttt{week}_{ij} + u_i + \epsilon_{ij} \tag{3}$$

for $i = 1, \ldots, 48$ pigs and $j = 1, \ldots, 9$ weeks. The fixed portion of the model, $\beta_0 + \beta_1 \texttt{week}_{ij}$, simply states that we want one overall regression line representing the population average. The random effect u_i serves to shift this regression line up or down according to each pig. Since the random effects occur at the pig level (`id`), we fit the model by typing

Charles Roy Henderson (1911–1989) was born in Iowa and grew up on the family farm. His education in animal husbandry, animal nutrition, and statistics at Iowa State was interspersed with jobs in the Iowa Extension Service, Ohio University, and the U.S. Army. After completing his Ph.D., Henderson joined the Animal Science faculty at Cornell. He developed and applied statistical methods in the improvement of farm livestock productivity through genetic selection, with particular focus on dairy cattle. His methods are general and have been used worldwide in livestock breeding and beyond agriculture. Henderson's work on variance components and best linear unbiased prediction has proved to be one of the main roots of current mixed-model methodology.

```
. xtmixed weight week || id:

Performing EM optimization:

Performing gradient-based optimization:

Iteration 0:    log restricted-likelihood = -1016.8984
Iteration 1:    log restricted-likelihood = -1016.8984

Computing standard errors:

Mixed-effects REML regression                   Number of obs      =        432
Group variable: id                              Number of groups   =         48

                                                Obs per group: min =          9
                                                               avg =        9.0
                                                               max =          9

                                                Wald chi2(1)       =   25271.50
Log restricted-likelihood = -1016.8984          Prob > chi2        =     0.0000
```

weight	Coef.	Std. Err.	z	P>|z|	[95% Conf. Interval]	
week	6.209896	.0390633	158.97	0.000	6.133333	6.286458
_cons	19.35561	.603139	32.09	0.000	18.17348	20.53774

Random-effects Parameters	Estimate	Std. Err.	[95% Conf. Interval]	
id: Identity				
sd(_cons)	3.891253	.4143198	3.158334	4.794252
sd(Residual)	2.096356	.0757444	1.953034	2.250195

```
LR test vs. linear regression: chibar2(01) =    473.15 Prob >= chibar2 = 0.0000
```

At this point, a guided tour of the model specification and output is in order:

1. By typing "weight week", we specified the response, weight, and the fixed portion of the model in the same way we would if we were using regress or any other estimation command. Our fixed effects are a coefficient on week and a constant term.

2. When we added "|| id:", we specified random effects at the level identified by group variable id, i.e., the pig level. Since we only wanted a random intercept, that is all we had to type.

3. The estimation log consists of three parts:

   (a) A set of expectation-maximization (EM) iterations used to refine starting values. By default, the iterations themselves are not displayed, but you can display them with option emlog.

   (b) A set of "gradient-based" iterations. By default, these are Newton–Raphson iterations, but other methods are available by specifying the appropriate maximize options; see [R] **maximize**.

   (c) The message "Computing standard errors:". This is just to inform you that xtmixed has finished its iterative maximization and is now reparameterizing from a matrix-based parameterization (see *Methods and Formulas*) to the natural metric of variance components and their estimated standard errors.

4. The output title, "Mixed-effects REML regression", informs us that our model was fitted using REML, the default. For ML estimates, use option mle.

   Since this model is a simple random-intercept model, specifying option mle would be equivalent to using xtreg, also with option mle.

5. The first estimation table reports the fixed effects. We estimate $\beta_0 = 19.36$ and $\beta_1 = 6.21$.

6. The second estimation table shows the estimated variance components. The first section of the table is labeled "id: Identity", meaning that these are random effects at the id (pig) level and that their variance–covariance matrix is a multiple of the identity matrix; that is, $\Sigma = \sigma_u^2 I$. Since we only have one random effect at this level, xtmixed knew that Identity is the only possible covariance structure. In any case, σ_u is estimated as 3.89 with standard error 0.414.

   If you prefer variance estimates, $\widehat{\sigma}_u^2$, to standard deviation estimates, $\widehat{\sigma}_u$, specify option variance either at estimation or on replay.

7. The row labeled "sd(Residual)" displays the estimated standard deviation of the overall error term; i.e., $\widehat{\sigma}_\epsilon = 2.10$.

8. Finally, a likelihood-ratio test comparing the model to ordinary linear regression, model (3) without u_i, is provided and is highly significant for these data.

   We now store our estimates for later use.

   ```
   . estimates store randint
   ```

   ◁

▷ Example 2

Extending (3) to allow for a random slope on week yields the model

$$\text{weight}_{ij} = \beta_0 + \beta_1 \text{week}_{ij} + u_{0i} + u_{1i}\text{week}_{ij} + \epsilon_{ij} \tag{4}$$

fitted using xtmixed:

```
. xtmixed weight week || id: week

Performing EM optimization:

Performing gradient-based optimization:

Iteration 0:   log restricted-likelihood = -870.51473
Iteration 1:   log restricted-likelihood = -870.51473

Computing standard errors:
```

Mixed-effects REML regression				Number of obs	=	432
Group variable: id				Number of groups	=	48
				Obs per group: min =		9
				avg =		9.0
				max =		9
				Wald chi2(1)	=	4592.10
Log restricted-likelihood = -870.51473				Prob > chi2	=	0.0000

weight	Coef.	Std. Err.	z	P>|z|	[95% Conf. Interval]	
week	6.209896	.0916386	67.77	0.000	6.030287	6.389504
_cons	19.35561	.4021142	48.13	0.000	18.56748	20.14374

Random-effects Parameters	Estimate	Std. Err.	[95% Conf. Interval]	
id: Independent				
sd(week)	.6135471	.0673971	.4947035	.7609409
sd(_cons)	2.630132	.302883	2.098719	3.296105
sd(Residual)	1.26443	.0487971	1.172317	1.363781

```
LR test vs. linear regression:        chi2(2) =   765.92   Prob > chi2 = 0.0000
Note: LR test is conservative and provided only for reference
. estimates store randslope
```

Since we didn't specify a covariance structure for the random effects $(u_{0i}, u_{1i})'$, xtmixed used the default Independent structure; that is

$$\Sigma = \text{Var}\begin{bmatrix} u_{0i} \\ u_{1i} \end{bmatrix} = \begin{bmatrix} \sigma_{u0}^2 & 0 \\ 0 & \sigma_{u1}^2 \end{bmatrix} \tag{5}$$

with $\widehat{\sigma}_{u0} = 2.63$ and $\widehat{\sigma}_{u1} = 0.61$. Our point estimates of the fixed affects are for all intents and purposes identical to those from model (3), but note that this does not hold generally. Given the 95% confidence interval for $\widehat{\sigma}_{u1}$, it would seem that the random slope is significant, and we can use lrtest and our two saved estimation results to verify this fact

```
. lrtest randslope randint
Likelihood-ratio test                           LR chibar2(01)  =   292.77
(Assumption: randint nested in randslope)       Prob > chibar2  =   0.0000
Note: LR tests based on REML are valid only when the fixed-effects
        specification is identical for both models
```

❏ Technical Note

As stated at the bottom of our lrtest output, LR tests with REML require identical fixed-effects specifications for both models. As stated in Ruppert, Wand, and Carroll (2003), "The reason for this is that restricted likelihood is the likelihood of the residuals after fitting the fixed effects and so is not appropriate when there is more than one fixed effects model under consideration." To compare models with different fixed-effects specifications, use a Wald test, or fit the models by ML (option mle).

In our example, the fixed-effects specifications for both models are identical ($\beta_0 + \beta_1 \text{week}$), so our REML-based test is valid.

❏

The results thus favor the model that allows for a random pig-specific regression line over the model that only allows for a pig-specific shift.

Finally, we also note the message at the bottom of our xtmixed output informing us that our overall LR test comparing to linear regression is conservative. For an explanation, see *Distribution theory for likelihood-ratio tests* later in this entry.

◁

Covariance structures

In example 2, we fit a model using the default Independent covariance given in (5). Within any random-effects level specification, we can override this default by specifying an alternative covariance structure via option covariance().

▷ Example 3

We generalize (5) to allow u_{0i} and u_{1i} to be correlated; that is

$$\Sigma = \mathrm{Var}\begin{bmatrix} u_{0i} \\ u_{1i} \end{bmatrix} = \begin{bmatrix} \sigma_{u0}^2 & \sigma_{01} \\ \sigma_{01} & \sigma_{u1}^2 \end{bmatrix}$$

```
. xtmixed weight week || id: week, covariance(unstructured) variance
```
  (*output omitted*)

```
Mixed-effects REML regression                   Number of obs      =        432
Group variable: id                              Number of groups   =         48

                                                Obs per group: min =          9
                                                               avg =        9.0
                                                               max =          9

                                                Wald chi2(1)       =    4552.31
Log restricted-likelihood = -870.43562          Prob > chi2        =     0.0000
```

weight	Coef.	Std. Err.	z	P>|z|	[95% Conf. Interval]
week	6.209896	.0920382	67.47	0.000	6.029504 6.390287
_cons	19.35561	.4038677	47.93	0.000	18.56405 20.14718

Random-effects Parameters	Estimate	Std. Err.	[95% Conf. Interval]
id: Unstructured			
var(week)	.3799957	.0839023	.2465103 .5857635
var(_cons)	6.986465	1.616357	4.439432 10.99481
cov(week,_cons)	-.1033632	.2627309	-.6183063 .41158
var(Residual)	1.596829	.1231981	1.372736 1.857506

```
LR test vs. linear regression:       chi2(3) =    766.07   Prob > chi2 = 0.0000
Note: LR test is conservative and provided only for reference
```

But we don't find the correlation to be at all significant.

```
. lrtest . randslope
Likelihood-ratio test                           LR chi2(1)    =       0.16
(Assumption: randslope nested in .)             Prob > chi2   =     0.6908
Note: LR tests based on REML are valid only when the fixed-effects
      specification is identical for both models
```

Note that in addition to specifying an alternate covariance structure, we specified option `variance` to display variance components in the variance–covariance metric, rather than the default, which displays them as standard deviations and correlations.

◁

Alternatively, we could have also specified `covariance(identity)`, restricting u_{0i} and u_{1i} to not only be independent but also to have common variance, or we could have specified `covariance(exchangeable)`, which imposes a common variance but allows for a nonzero correlation.

Likelihood versus restricted likelihood

Thus far, all our examples have used restricted maximum likelihood (REML) to estimate variance components. We could have just as easily asked for ML estimates. Refitting the model in example 2 by ML, we get

```
. xtmixed weight week || id: week, ml
  (output omitted)
```

Mixed-effects ML regression	Number of obs	=	432
Group variable: id	Number of groups	=	48

	Obs per group: min =	9
	avg =	9.0
	max =	9

	Wald chi2(1)	=	4689.52
Log likelihood = -869.03825	Prob > chi2	=	0.0000

weight	Coef.	Std. Err.	z	P>|z|	[95% Conf. Interval]
week	6.209896	.0906818	68.48	0.000	6.032163 6.387629
_cons	19.35561	.3979158	48.64	0.000	18.57571 20.13551

Random-effects Parameters	Estimate	Std. Err.	[95% Conf. Interval]
id: Independent			
sd(week)	.6066848	.0660293	.4901415 .7509392
sd(_cons)	2.599299	.2969071	2.077912 3.251513
sd(Residual)	1.264441	.0487958	1.172331 1.363789

LR test vs. linear regression: chi2(2) =   764.42   Prob > chi2 = 0.0000

Note: LR test is conservative and provided only for reference

While ML estimators are based on the usual likelihood theory, the idea behind REML is to transform the response into a set of linear contrasts whose distribution is free of the fixed effects β. The restricted likelihood is then formed by considering the distribution of the linear contrasts. Not only does this make the maximization problem free of β, it also incorporates the degrees of freedom used to estimate β into the estimation of the variance components. This follows since, by necessity, the rank of the linear contrasts must be less than the number of observations.

As a very simple example, consider a constant-only regression where $y_i \sim N(\mu, \sigma^2)$ for $i = 1, \ldots, n$. The ML estimate of σ^2 can be derived theoretically as the n-divided sample variance. The REML estimate can be derived by considering the first $n - 1$ error contrasts, $y_i - \bar{y}$, whose joint distribution is free of μ. Applying maximum-likelihood to this distribution results in an estimate of σ^2 that is the $(n - 1)$ divided sample variance, which is unbiased for σ^2.

The unbiasedness property of REML extends to all mixed models when the data are balanced, and thus REML would seem the clear choice in balanced-data problems, although in large samples the difference between ML and REML is negligible. One disadvantage of REML is that LR tests based on REML are inappropriate for comparing models with different fixed-effects specifications. ML is appropriate for such LR tests and has the advantage of being easy to explain and being the method of choice for other estimators. As such, the question of which method to use remains a matter of personal taste.

Examining the ML output, we find that the estimates of the variance components are slightly smaller than the REML estimates. This is typical, since ML estimates, which do not incorporate the degrees of freedom used to estimate the fixed effects, tend to be biased downward.

Two-level models

The panel-data representation of the mixed model given in (2) can be extended to two nested levels. Formally

$$\mathbf{y}_{ij} = \mathbf{X}_{ij}\boldsymbol{\beta} + \mathbf{Z}_{ij}^{(1)}\mathbf{u}_i^{(1)} + \mathbf{Z}_{ij}^{(2)}\mathbf{u}_{ij}^{(2)} + \boldsymbol{\epsilon}_{ij} \tag{6}$$

for $i = 1, \ldots, M$ first-level groups and $j = 1, \ldots, M_i$ second-level groups that are nested within group i. Group i, j consists of n_{ij} observations, so $\mathbf{y}_{ij}$, $\mathbf{X}_{ij}$, and $\boldsymbol{\epsilon}_{ij}$ each have row dimension n_{ij}. $\mathbf{Z}_{ij}^{(1)}$ is the $n_{ij} \times q_1$ design matrix for the first-level random effects $\mathbf{u}_i^{(1)}$, and $\mathbf{Z}_{ij}^{(2)}$ is the $n_{ij} \times q_2$ design matrix for the second-level random effects $\mathbf{u}_{ij}^{(2)}$. Furthermore, assume that

$$\mathbf{u}_i^{(1)} \sim N(\mathbf{0}, \boldsymbol{\Sigma}_1); \quad \mathbf{u}_{ij}^{(2)} \sim N(\mathbf{0}, \boldsymbol{\Sigma}_2); \quad \boldsymbol{\epsilon}_{ij} \sim N(\mathbf{0}, \sigma_\epsilon^2 \mathbf{I})$$

and that $\mathbf{u}_i^{(1)}$, $\mathbf{u}_{ij}^{(2)}$, and $\boldsymbol{\epsilon}_{ij}$ are independent.

Fitting a two-level model requires you to specify two random-effects "equations", one for each level. The variable list for the first equation represents $\mathbf{Z}_{ij}^{(1)}$, and the second equation, $\mathbf{Z}_{ij}^{(2)}$.

▷ Example 4

Baltagi, Song, and Jung (2001) estimate a Cobb–Douglas production function examining the productivity of public capital in each state's private output. Originally provided by Munnell (1990), the data were recorded over the period 1970–1986 for 48 states grouped into nine regions.

```
. use http://www.stata-press.com/data/r9/productivity, clear
(Public Capital Productivity)

. describe

Contains data from productivity.dta
  obs:            816                          Public Capital Productivity
  vars:            11                          28 Mar 2005 17:16
  size:         32,640 (99.7% of memory free)  (_dta has notes)
```

variable name	storage type	display format	value label	variable label
state	byte	%9.0g		states 1-48
region	byte	%9.0g		regions 1-9
year	int	%9.0g		years 1970-1986
public	float	%9.0g		public capital stock
hwy	float	%9.0g		log(highway component of public)
water	float	%9.0g		log(water component of public)
other	float	%9.0g		log(bldg/other component of public)
private	float	%9.0g		log(private capital stock)
gsp	float	%9.0g		log(gross state product)
emp	float	%9.0g		log(nonagriculture payrolls)
unemp	float	%9.0g		state unemployment rate

```
Sorted by:
```

Since the states are nested within regions, we fit a two-level mixed model with random intercepts at both the region and at the state-within-region levels. That is, we use (6) with both $\mathbf{Z}_{ij}^{(1)}$ and $\mathbf{Z}_{ij}^{(2)}$ set to the $n_{ij} \times 1$ column of ones, and $\boldsymbol{\Sigma}_1 = \sigma_1^2$ and $\boldsymbol{\Sigma}_2 = \sigma_2^2$ are both scalars.

```
. xtmixed gsp private emp hwy water other unemp || region: || state:
  (output omitted)
```

Mixed-effects REML regression   Number of obs   =   816

Group Variable	No. of Groups	Observations per Group		
		Minimum	Average	Maximum
region	9	51	90.7	136
state	48	17	17.0	17

Log restricted-likelihood = 1404.7101

Wald chi2(6)   =   18382.39
Prob > chi2   =   0.0000

gsp	Coef.	Std. Err.	z	P>|z|	[95% Conf. Interval]	
private	.2660308	.0215471	12.35	0.000	.2237993	.3082624
emp	.7555059	.0264556	28.56	0.000	.7036539	.8073579
hwy	.0718857	.0233478	3.08	0.002	.0261249	.1176464
water	.0761552	.0139952	5.44	0.000	.0487251	.1035853
other	-.1005396	.0170173	-5.91	0.000	-.1338929	-.0671862
unemp	-.0058815	.0009093	-6.47	0.000	-.0076636	-.0040994
_cons	2.126995	.1574864	13.51	0.000	1.818327	2.435663

Random-effects Parameters	Estimate	Std. Err.	[95% Conf. Interval]	
region: Identity				
sd(_cons)	.0435471	.0186292	.0188287	.1007161
state: Identity				
sd(_cons)	.0802737	.0095512	.0635762	.1013567
sd(Residual)	.0368008	.0009442	.034996	.0386987

LR test vs. linear regression: chi2(2) =   1162.40   Prob > chi2 = 0.0000

Note: LR test is conservative and provided only for reference

Some items of note:

1. Our model now has two random-effects equations, separated by ||. The first is a random intercept (constant-only) at the region level, and the second is a random intercept at the state level. The order in which these are specified (from left to right) is significant—xtmixed assumes that state is nested within region.

2. The information on groups is now displayed as a table, with one row for each model level. You can suppress this table with option nogroup or with noheader, which will suppress the rest of the header, as well.

3. The variance-component estimates are now organized and labeled according to level.

After adjusting for the nested-level error structure, we find that the highway and water components of public capital had significant positive effects on private output, while the other public buildings component had a negative effect.

◁

❑ Technical Note

In the previous example, the states are coded 1 through 48 and are nested within 9 regions. xtmixed treated the states as nested within regions, regardless of whether the codes for each state are unique between regions. That is, even if codes for states were duplicated between regions, xtmixed would have enforced the nesting and produced the same results.

The group information at the top of xtmixed output and that produced by the postestimation command estat group (see [XT] **xtmixed postestimation**) take the nesting into account. As such, the statistics are not necessarily what you would get if you instead tabulated each group variable individually.

❑

Model (6) extends in a straightforward manner to more than two nested levels of random effects, as does the specification of such models in xtmixed.

Blocked-diagonal covariance structures

Covariance matrices of random effects within an equation can be modeled either as a multiple of the identity matrix, diagonal (i.e., Independent), exchangeable, or as general symmetric (Unstructured). In addition, these may be combined to produce more complex block-diagonal covariance structures, effectively placing constraints on the variance components.

▷ Example 5

Returning to our productivity data, we now add random coefficients on hwy and unemp at the region level. This only slightly changes the estimates of the fixed effects, so we focus our attention on the variance components

```
. xtmixed gsp private emp hwy water other unemp || region: hwy unemp || state:,
> nolog nogroup nofetable
Mixed-effects REML regression                  Number of obs    =        816
                                               Wald chi2(6)     =   16803.51
Log restricted-likelihood =  1423.3455         Prob > chi2      =     0.0000
```

Random-effects Parameters	Estimate	Std. Err.	[95% Conf. Interval]	
region: Independent				
sd(hwy)	.0052752	.0108846	.0000925	.3009897
sd(unemp)	.0052895	.001545	.002984	.0093764
sd(_cons)	.0596008	.0758296	.0049235	.721487
state: Identity				
sd(_cons)	.0807543	.009887	.0635259	.1026551
sd(Residual)	.0353932	.000914	.0336464	.0372307

```
LR test vs. linear regression:        chi2(4) =   1199.67   Prob > chi2 = 0.0000
Note: LR test is conservative and provided only for reference
. estimates store prodrc
```

This model is the same as that fitted in example 4, except that $\mathbf{Z}_{ij}^{(1)}$ is now the $n_{ij} \times 3$ matrix with columns determined by the values of hwy, unemp, and an intercept term (one), in that order, and (since we used the default Independent structure) $\boldsymbol{\Sigma}_1$ is

$$
\boldsymbol{\Sigma}_1 = \begin{matrix} & \text{hwy} & \text{unemp} & \text{\_cons} \\ & \begin{pmatrix} \sigma_a^2 & 0 & 0 \\ 0 & \sigma_b^2 & 0 \\ 0 & 0 & \sigma_c^2 \end{pmatrix} \end{matrix}
$$

The random-effects specification at the state level remains unchanged; i.e., $\boldsymbol{\Sigma}_2$ is still treated as the scalar variance of the random intercepts at the state level.

An LR test comparing this model with that from example 4 favors the inclusion of the two random coefficients, a fact we leave to the interested reader to verify.

Examination of the estimated variance components reveals that the variances of the random coefficients on hwy and unemp could be treated as equal. That is

$$
\boldsymbol{\Sigma}_1 = \begin{matrix} & \text{hwy} & \text{unemp} & \text{\_cons} \\ & \begin{pmatrix} \sigma_a^2 & 0 & 0 \\ 0 & \sigma_a^2 & 0 \\ 0 & 0 & \sigma_c^2 \end{pmatrix} \end{matrix}
$$

looks quite plausible. We can impose this equality constraint by treating $\boldsymbol{\Sigma}_1$ as blocked-diagonal: the first block is a 2×2 multiple of the identity matrix, i.e., $\sigma_a^2 \mathbf{I}_2$; the second is a scalar, equivalently a 1×1 multiple of the identity.

We construct blocked-diagonal covariances by repeating level specifications

```
. xtmixed gsp private emp hwy water other unemp || region: hwy unemp,
> cov(identity) || region: || state:, nolog nogroup nofetable
Mixed-effects REML regression                  Number of obs      =        816
                                                Wald chi2(6)       =   16803.41
Log restricted-likelihood =  1423.3455          Prob > chi2        =     0.0000
```

Random-effects Parameters	Estimate	Std. Err.	[95% Conf. Interval]	
region: Identity				
sd(hwy unemp)	.0052896	.0015446	.0029844	.0093752
region: Identity				
sd(_cons)	.0595029	.0318238	.0208589	.1697401
state: Identity				
sd(_cons)	.080752	.0097453	.0637425	.1023006
sd(Residual)	.0353932	.0009139	.0336465	.0372306

```
LR test vs. linear regression:       chi2(3) =   1199.67    Prob > chi2 = 0.0000
Note: LR test is conservative and provided only for reference
```

Note that we specified two equations for the region level: the first for the random coefficients on hwy and unemp with covariance set to Identity, and the second for the random intercept _cons, whose covariance defaults to Identity because it is of dimension one. xtmixed labeled the estimate of σ_a as "sd(hwy unemp)" to designate that it is common to the random coefficients on both hwy and unemp.

An LR test shows that the constrained model fits equally well.

```
. lrtest . prodrc
Likelihood-ratio test                     LR chibar2(01)   =      0.00
(Assumption: . nested in prodrc)          Prob > chibar2   =    1.0000
Note: LR tests based on REML are valid only when the fixed-effects
      specification is identical for both models
```

◁

You can repeat level specifications as often as you like, defining successive blocks of a blocked-diagonal covariance matrix. However, repeated level equations must be listed consecutively; otherwise, xtmixed will give an error.

❏ Technical Note

In the previous estimation output, note that there was no constant term included in the first region equation, even though we did not use option noconstant. When you specify repeated level equations, xtmixed knows not to put constant terms in each equation since such a model would be unidentified. By default, it places the constant in the last repeated level equation, but you can use noconstant creatively to override this.

❏

Factor notation and crossed-effects models

Not all mixed models contain nested levels of random effects.

▷ Example 6

Returning to our longitudinal analysis of pig weights, suppose that instead of (4) we wish to fit

$$\texttt{weight}_{ij} - \beta_0 + \beta_1 \texttt{week}_{ij} + u_i + v_j + \epsilon_{ij} \qquad (7)$$

for the $i = 1, \ldots, 48$ pigs and $j = 1, \ldots, 9$ weeks and

$$u_i \sim N(0, \sigma_u^2); \quad v_j \sim N(0, \sigma_v^2); \quad \epsilon_{ij} \sim N(0, \sigma_\epsilon^2)$$

all independently. Both (4) and (7) assume an overall population-average growth curve $\beta_0 + \beta_1 \texttt{week}$ and a random pig-specific shift.

The models differ in how week enters into the random part of the model. In (4), we assume that the effect due to week is linear and pig-specific (a random slope); in (7), we assume that the effect due to week, v_j, is systematic to that week and common to all pigs. The rationale behind (7) could be that, assuming that the pigs were measured contemporaneously, we might be concerned that week-specific random factors such as weather and feeding patterns had significant systematic effects on all pigs.

Model (7) is a an example of a two-way *crossed-effects* model, with the pig effects u_i being crossed with the week effects v_j. One way to fit such models is to consider all the data as one big panel and treat the u_i and v_j as a series of $48 + 9 = 57$ random coefficients on indicator variables for pig and week. In the notation of (1),

$$
\mathbf{u} = \begin{bmatrix} u_1 \\ \vdots \\ u_{48} \\ v_1 \\ \vdots \\ v_9 \end{bmatrix} \sim N(\mathbf{0}, \mathbf{G}); \quad \mathbf{G} = \begin{bmatrix} \sigma_u^2 \mathbf{I}_{48} & \mathbf{0} \\ \mathbf{0} & \sigma_v^2 \mathbf{I}_9 \end{bmatrix}
$$

Since **G** is blocked-diagonal, it can be represented in xtmixed as repeated level equations. All we need is an ID variable to identify all the observations as one big group and a way to tell xtmixed to treat pig and week as factor variables (or equivalently, as two sets of overparameterized indicator variables identifying pigs and weeks, respectively). xtmixed supports the special group designation _all for the former and the factor notation R.*varname* for the latter.

```
. use http://www.stata-press.com/data/r9/pig, clear
(Longitudinal analysis of pig weights)

. xtmixed weight week || _all: R.id || _all: R.week

Performing EM optimization:

Performing gradient-based optimization:

Iteration 0:   log restricted-likelihood = -1015.4214
Iteration 1:   log restricted-likelihood = -1015.4214

Computing standard errors:
```

Mixed-effects REML regression   Number of obs   =   432
Group variable: _all   Number of groups   =   1

Obs per group: min =	432
avg =	432.0
max =	432

Log restricted-likelihood = -1015.4214   Wald chi2(1)   =   11516.16
                                        Prob > chi2   =   0.0000

weight	Coef.	Std. Err.	z	P>|z|	[95% Conf. Interval]	
week	6.209896	.0578669	107.31	0.000	6.096479	6.323313
_cons	19.35561	.6493996	29.81	0.000	18.08281	20.62841

Random-effects Parameters	Estimate	Std. Err.	[95% Conf. Interval]	
_all: Identity				
sd(R.id)	3.892648	.4141707	3.15994	4.795252
_all: Identity				
sd(R.week)	.3337581	.1611824	.1295268	.8600111
sd(Residual)	2.072917	.0755915	1.929931	2.226496

LR test vs. linear regression: chi2(2) =   476.10   Prob > chi2 = 0.0000

Note: LR test is conservative and provided only for reference

```
. estimates store crossed
```

and thus we estimate $\hat{\sigma}_u = 3.89$ and $\hat{\sigma}_v = 0.33$. Both (4) and (7) estimate a total of five parameters, two fixed effects and three variance components. The models, however, are not nested within each other, which precludes the use of an LR test to compare both models. Refitting model (4) and looking at the AIC values using estimates stats

```
. quietly xtmixed weight week || id:week

. estimates stats crossed .
```

Model	Obs	ll(null)	ll(model)	df	AIC	BIC
crossed	432	.	-1015.421	5	2040.843	2061.185
.	432	.	-870.5147	5	1751.029	1771.372

definitely favors model (4). This is not surprising, given that our rationale behind (7) was somewhat fictitious. Note that in our estimates stats output, the values of ll(null) are missing. xtmixed does not fit a constant-only model as part of its usual estimation of the full model, but we can use xtmixed to fit a constant-only model directly.

◁

The R.*varname* notation is equivalent to giving a list of overparameterized (none dropped) indicator variables for use in a random-effects specification. When you use R.*varname*, xtmixed handles the calculations internally rather than creating the indicators in the data. Since the set of indicators is overparameterized, R.*varname* implies noconstant. To include indicator variables in the fixed-effects specification, use xi; see [R] **xi**.

❑ Technical Note

Although we were able to fit the crossed-effects model (7), it came at the expense of increasing the column dimension of our random-effects design from two in model (4) to 57 in model (7). Computation time and memory requirements grow (roughly) quadratically with the dimension of the random effects. As a result, fitting such crossed-effects models is feasible only when the total column dimension is small to moderate.

Re-examining model (7), we note that if we drop v_j, we end up with a model equivalent to (3), meaning that we could have fitted (3) by typing

```
. xtmixed weight week || _all: R.id
```

instead of

```
. xtmixed weight week || id:
```

as we did when we originally fitted the model. The results of both estimations are identical, but the latter specification, organized at the panel (pig) level with random-effects dimension one (a random-intercept) is much more computationally efficient. Whereas with the first form we are limited as to how many pigs we can analyze, with the second form there is no such limitation.

Furthermore, we fit model (7) using

```
. xtmixed weight week || _all: R.id || _all: R.week
```

as a direct way to demonstrate factor notation. However, we can technically treat pigs as nested within the "_all" group, yielding the equivalent and more efficient (total column dimension 10) way to fit (7)

```
. xtmixed weight week || _all: R.week || id:
```

We leave it to you to verify that both produce identical results.

❑

▷ Example 7

As another example of how the same model may be fitted different ways using `xtmixed` (and also as a way to demonstrate `covariance(exchangeable)`), consider the model used in example 4

$$\mathbf{y}_{ij} = \mathbf{X}_{ij}\boldsymbol{\beta} + u_i^{(1)} + u_{ij}^{(2)} + \epsilon_{ij}$$

where $\mathbf{y}_{ij}$ represents the logarithms of gross state products for the $n_{ij} = 17$ observations from state j in region i, $\mathbf{X}_{ij}$ is a set of regressors, $u_i^{(1)}$ is a random intercept at the region level, and $u_{ij}^{(2)}$ is a random intercept at the state (nested within region) level. We assume that $u_i^{(1)} \sim N(0, \sigma_1^2)$ and $u_{ij}^{(2)} \sim N(0, \sigma_2^2)$ independently. Define

$$\mathbf{v}_i = \begin{bmatrix} u_i^{(1)} + u_{i1}^{(2)} \\ u_i^{(1)} + u_{i2}^{(2)} \\ \vdots \\ u_i^{(1)} + u_{iM_i}^{(2)} \end{bmatrix}$$

where M_i is the number of states in region i. Making this substitution, we can stack the observations for all the states within region i to get

$$\mathbf{y}_i = \mathbf{X}_i\boldsymbol{\beta} + \mathbf{Z}_i\mathbf{v}_i + \epsilon_i$$

where $\mathbf{Z}_i$ is a set of indicators identifying the states within each region; that is

$$\mathbf{Z}_i = \mathbf{I}_{M_i} \otimes \mathbf{J}_{17}$$

for a k-column vector of ones $\mathbf{J}_k$, and

$$\boldsymbol{\Sigma} = \mathrm{Var}(\mathbf{v}_i) = \begin{bmatrix} \sigma_1^2 + \sigma_2^2 & \sigma_1^2 & \cdots & \sigma_1^2 \\ \sigma_1^2 & \sigma_1^2 + \sigma_2^2 & \cdots & \sigma_1^2 \\ \vdots & \vdots & \ddots & \vdots \\ \sigma_1^2 & \sigma_1^2 & \sigma_1^2 & \sigma_1^2 + \sigma_2^2 \end{bmatrix}_{M_i \times M_i}$$

Since $\boldsymbol{\Sigma}$ is an exchangeable matrix, we can fit this alternative form of the model by specifying the `exchangeable` covariance structure.

```
. use http://www.stata-press.com/data/r9/productivity, clear
(Public Capital Productivity)
```

```
. xtmixed gsp private emp hwy water other unemp || region: R.state,
> cov(exchangeable) variance
```

(*output omitted*)

```
Mixed-effects REML regression                  Number of obs      =        816
Group variable: region                         Number of groups   =          9

                                               Obs per group: min =         51
                                                              avg =       90.7
                                                              max =        136

                                               Wald chi2(6)       =   18382.39
Log restricted-likelihood =  1404.7101         Prob > chi2        =     0.0000
```

gsp	Coef.	Std. Err.	z	P>|z|	[95% Conf. Interval]	
private	.2660308	.0215471	12.35	0.000	.2237993	.3082623
emp	.7555059	.0264556	28.56	0.000	.7036539	.8073579
hwy	.0718857	.0233478	3.08	0.002	.0261249	.1176464
water	.0761552	.0139952	5.44	0.000	.0487251	.1035853
other	-.1005396	.0170173	-5.91	0.000	-.1338929	-.0671862
unemp	-.0058815	.0009093	-6.47	0.000	-.0076636	-.0040994
_cons	2.126995	.1574864	13.51	0.000	1.818327	2.435663

Random-effects Parameters	Estimate	Std. Err.	[95% Conf. Interval]	
region: Exchangeable				
var(R.state)	.0083402	.0020718	.0051254	.0135715
cov(R.state)	.0018963	.0016225	-.0012836	.0050763
var(Residual)	.0013543	.0000695	.0012247	.0014976

```
LR test vs. linear regression:        chi2(2) =  1162.40   Prob > chi2 = 0.0000
```
Note: LR test is conservative and provided only for reference

We note that the estimates of the fixed effects and their standard errors are equivalent to those from example 4 and that remapping the variance components from $(\sigma_1^2 + \sigma_2^2, \sigma_1^2, \sigma_\epsilon^2)$, as displayed here, to $(\sigma_1, \sigma_2, \sigma_\epsilon)$, as displayed in example 4, will show that they are equivalent as well.

Of course, given the discussion in the previous *Technical Note*, it is more efficient to fit this model as we did originally, as a two-level model.

◁

Diagnosing convergence problems

Given the flexibility of the class of linear mixed models, you will find that some models "fail to converge" when used with your data. The default gradient-based method used by xtmixed is the Newton–Raphson algorithm, requiring the calculation of a gradient vector and Hessian (second derivative) matrix; see [R] **ml**.

A failure to converge can take any one of three forms:

1. Repeated "nonconcave" or "backed-up" iterations without convergence;

2. A Hessian (second derivative) calculation that has become asymmetric, unstable, or has missing values;

3. The message "standard error calculation has failed" when computing standard errors.

All three situations essentially amount to the same thing: the Hessian calculation has become unstable, most likely due to a ridge in the likelihood function, a subsurface of the likelihood in which all points give the same value of the likelihood and for which there is no unique solution.

Such behavior is usually the result of either

A. A model that is not identified given the data. For example, fitting the two-level nested random intercept model

$$y_{ij} = \mathbf{x}_{ij}\boldsymbol{\beta} + u_i^{(1)} + u_{ij}^{(2)} + \epsilon_{ij}$$

without any replicated measurements at the (i, j) level. This model is unidentified for such data since the random intercepts $u_{ij}^{(2)}$ are confounded with the overall errors ϵ_{ij};

B. A model that contains a variance component whose estimate is really close to zero. When this occurs, a ridge is formed by an interval of values near zero, which produce the same likelihood and look equally good to the optimizer.

One useful way to diagnose problems of nonconvergence is to rely on the expectation-maximization (EM) algorithm (Dempster, Laird, and Rubin 1977), normally used by xtmixed only as a means of refining starting values. The advantages of EM are that it does not require a Hessian calculation, each successive EM iteration will result in a larger likelihood, iterations can be calculated very quickly, and iterations will quickly bring parameter estimates into a neighborhood of the solution. The disadvantages of EM are that, once in a neighborhood of the solution, it can be very slow to converge, if at all, and EM provides no facility for estimating standard errors of the estimated variance components.

One useful property of EM is that it is always willing to provide a solution if you allow it to iterate enough times, if you are satisfied with being in a neighborhood of the optimum rather than right on the optimum, and if standard errors of variance components are not crucial to your analysis. If you encounter a nonconvergent model, try using option emonly to bypass gradient-based optimization. Use emiterate(#) to specify the maximum number of EM iterations, which you will usually want to set much higher than the default of 20. If your EM solution shows an estimated variance component that is near zero, this provides evidence that B is the cause of the nonconvergence of the gradient-based method, in which case, the solution would be to drop the offending variance component from the model. If no estimated variance components are near zero, reason A could be the culprit.

If your data and model are nearly unidentified, as opposed to fully unidentified, you may be able to obtain convergence with standard errors by changing some of the settings of the gradient-based optimization. Adding option difficult can be particularly helpful if you are seeing many "nonconcave" messages; you may also consider changing the technique() or using option nonrtolerance, see [R] **maximize**.

Distribution theory for likelihood-ratio tests

When determining the asymptotic distribution of a likelihood-ratio (LR) test comparing two nested models fitted by xtmixed, issues concerning boundary problems imposed by estimating strictly positive quantities (i.e., variances) can complicate the situation. As such, when performing LR tests involving mixed models (whether comparing with linear regression within xtmixed or comparing two separate mixed models with lrtest), you may sometimes see a test labeled as "chibar" rather than the usual "chi2" or see a chi2 test with a note attached stating that the test is conservative.

At the heart of the issue is the number of variances being restricted to zero in the reduced model. If there are none, the usual asymptotic theory holds and the distribution of the test statistic is χ^2 with degrees of freedom equal to the difference in the number of estimated parameters between both models.

In the case where there is only one variance being set to zero in the reduced model, the asymptotic distribution of the likelihood-ratio test statistic is a 50:50 mixture of a χ_k^2 and a χ_{k+1}^2 distribution, where k is the number of other restricted parameters in the reduced model that are unaffected by boundary conditions. Stata labels such test statistics as chibar and adjusts the significance levels accordingly. See Self and Liang (1987) for the appropriate theory or Gutierrez, Carter, and Drukker (2001) for a Stata-specific discussion.

When more than one variance parameter is being set to zero in the reduced model, however, the situation becomes more complicated. For example, consider a comparison test vs. linear regression for a mixed model with two random coefficients and unstructured covariance matrix

$$\Sigma = \begin{bmatrix} \sigma_0^2 & \sigma_{01} \\ \sigma_{01} & \sigma_1^2 \end{bmatrix}$$

Since the random component of the mixed model is comprised of three parameters $(\sigma_0^2, \sigma_{01}^2, \sigma_1^2)$, on the surface it would seem that the LR comparison test would be distributed as χ_3^2. However, two complications need to be considered. First, the variances σ_0^2 and σ_1^2 are restricted to be positive, and second, constraints such as $\sigma_1^2 = 0$ implicitly restrict the covariance σ_{01} to be zero, as well. From a technical standpoint, it is unclear how many parameters must be restricted in order to reduce the model to linear regression.

Because of these complications, appropriate and sufficiently general distribution theory for the more-than-one-variance case has yet to be developed. Theory (e.g., Stram and Lee 1994) and empirical studies (e.g., McLachlan and Basford 1988) have demonstrated that, whatever the distribution of the LR test statistic, its tail probabilities are bounded above by those of the χ^2 distribution with degrees of freedom equal to the full number of restricted parameters (three in the above example).

xtmixed uses this reference distribution, the χ^2 with full degrees of freedom, to produce a conservative test and places a note in the output labeling the test as such. Since the displayed significance level is an upper bound, rejection of the null hypothesis based on the reported level would imply rejection based on the actual level.

❑ Technical Note

It may seem that xtmixed does not follow Stata's standard syntax for multiple-equation models, but it does. In example 2, we typed

    . xtmixed weight week || id:

but we could have used the standard multi-equation syntax:

    . xtmixed (weight week) (id:)

xtmixed will understand either and produce the same results. We prefer the syntax using || because it better emphasizes the nested structure of the levels.

❑

Saved Results

xtmixed saves in e():

Scalars

e(N)	number of observations	e(chi2)	χ^2
e(k)	number of parameters	e(p)	p-value for χ^2
e(k_f)	number of FE parameters	e(ll_c)	log-likelihood, comparison model
e(k_r)	number of RE parameters	e(chi2_c)	χ^2, comparison model
e(k_rs)	number of std. deviations	e(df_c)	degrees of freedom, comparison model
e(k_rc)	number of correlations	e(p_c)	p-value, comparison model
e(df_m)	model degrees of freedom	e(converged)	1 if converged, 0 otherwise
e(ll)	log (restricted)-likelihood	e(rc)	return code

Macros

e(cmd)	xtmixed	e(chi2type)	Wald, type of model χ^2
e(title)	title in estimation output	e(opt)	type of optimization
e(depvar)	name of dependent variable	e(ml_method)	type of ml method
e(method)	ML or REML	e(technique)	maximization technique
e(ivars)	grouping variables	e(crittype)	optimization criterion
e(redim)	random-effects dimensions	e(properties)	b V
e(vartypes)	variance-structure types	e(estat_cmd)	program used to implement estat
e(revars)	random-effects covariates	e(predict)	program used to implement predict

Matrices

e(b)	coefficient vector	e(V)	variance–covariance matrix of the estimator
e(N_g)	group counts		
e(g_min)	group size minimums	e(g_avg)	group size averages
e(g_max)	group size maximums		

Functions

e(sample)	marks estimation sample

Methods and Formulas

xtmixed is implemented as an ado-file.

As given by (1), we have the linear mixed model

$$\mathbf{y} = \mathbf{X}\boldsymbol{\beta} + \mathbf{Z}\mathbf{u} + \boldsymbol{\epsilon}$$

where $\mathbf{y}$ is the $n \times 1$ vector of responses, $\mathbf{X}$ is a $n \times p$ design/covariate matrix for the fixed effects $\boldsymbol{\beta}$, and $\mathbf{Z}$ is the $n \times q$ design/covariate matrix for the random effects $\mathbf{u}$. The $n \times 1$ vector of errors, $\boldsymbol{\epsilon}$, is assumed to be multivariate normal with mean zero and variance matrix $\sigma_{\epsilon}^2 \mathbf{I}_n$. We also assume that $\mathbf{u}$ has variance–covariance matrix $\mathbf{G}$ and that $\mathbf{u}$ is orthogonal to $\boldsymbol{\epsilon}$ so that

$$\text{Var}\begin{bmatrix} \mathbf{u} \\ \boldsymbol{\epsilon} \end{bmatrix} = \begin{bmatrix} \mathbf{G} & \mathbf{0} \\ \mathbf{0} & \sigma_{\epsilon}^2 \mathbf{I}_n \end{bmatrix}$$

Considering the combined error term $\mathbf{Z}\mathbf{u} + \boldsymbol{\epsilon}$, we see that $\mathbf{y}$ is multivariate normal with mean $\mathbf{X}\boldsymbol{\beta}$ and $n \times n$ variance–covariance matrix

$$\mathbf{V} = \mathbf{Z}\mathbf{G}\mathbf{Z}' + \sigma_{\epsilon}^2 \mathbf{I}_n$$

Defining θ as the vector of unique elements of $\mathbf{G}$ results in the log likelihood

$$L(\boldsymbol{\beta}, \boldsymbol{\theta}, \sigma_\epsilon^2) = -\frac{1}{2} \left\{ n \log(2\pi) + \log |\mathbf{V}| + (\mathbf{y} - \mathbf{X}\boldsymbol{\beta})' \mathbf{V}^{-1} (\mathbf{y} - \mathbf{X}\boldsymbol{\beta}) \right\} \tag{8}$$

which is maximized as a function of $\boldsymbol{\beta}$, $\boldsymbol{\theta}$, and σ_ϵ^2. As explained in chapter 6 of Searle, Casella, and McCulloch (1992), considering instead the likelihood of a set of linear contrasts, $\mathbf{Ky}$, that do not depend on $\boldsymbol{\beta}$ results in the restricted log likelihood

$$L_R(\boldsymbol{\beta}, \boldsymbol{\theta}, \sigma_\epsilon^2) = L(\boldsymbol{\beta}, \boldsymbol{\theta}, \sigma_\epsilon^2) - \frac{1}{2} \log |\mathbf{X}' \mathbf{V}^{-1} \mathbf{X}| \tag{9}$$

Given the high dimension of $\mathbf{V}$, however, the log-likelihood and restricted log-likelihood criteria are not usually computed by brute-force application of the above expressions. Instead, you can simplify the problem by subdividing the data into independent panels (and subpanels if possible) and using matrix decomposition methods on the smaller matrices that result from treating each panel one at time.

Consider the one-level model described previously in (2)

$$\mathbf{y}_i = \mathbf{X}_i \boldsymbol{\beta} + \mathbf{Z}_i \mathbf{u}_i + \boldsymbol{\epsilon}_i$$

for $i = 1, \ldots, M$ panels with panel i containing n_i observations, with $\text{Var}(\mathbf{u}_i) = \boldsymbol{\Sigma}$, a $q \times q$ matrix.

Efficient methods for computing (8) and (9) are given in chapter 2 of Pinheiro and Bates (2000). Namely, for the one-level model, define $\boldsymbol{\Delta}$ to be the Cholesky factor of $\sigma_\epsilon^2 \boldsymbol{\Sigma}^{-1}$, such that $\sigma_\epsilon^2 \boldsymbol{\Sigma}^{-1} = \boldsymbol{\Delta}' \boldsymbol{\Delta}$. For $i = 1, \ldots, M$, decompose

$$\begin{bmatrix} \mathbf{Z}_i \\ \boldsymbol{\Delta} \end{bmatrix} = \mathbf{Q}_i \begin{bmatrix} \mathbf{R}_{11i} \\ \mathbf{0} \end{bmatrix}$$

using an orthogonal-triangular (QR) decomposition, with $\mathbf{Q}_i$ a $(n_i + q)$-square matrix and $\mathbf{R}_{11i}$ a q-square matrix. We then apply $\mathbf{Q}_i$ as follows

$$\begin{bmatrix} \mathbf{R}_{10i} \\ \mathbf{R}_{00i} \end{bmatrix} = \mathbf{Q}_i' \begin{bmatrix} \mathbf{X}_i \\ \mathbf{0} \end{bmatrix}; \qquad \begin{bmatrix} \mathbf{c}_{1i} \\ \mathbf{c}_{0i} \end{bmatrix} = \mathbf{Q}_i' \begin{bmatrix} \mathbf{y}_i \\ \mathbf{0} \end{bmatrix}$$

stack the $\mathbf{R}_{00i}$ and $\mathbf{c}_{0i}$ matrices, and perform the additional QR decomposition

$$\begin{bmatrix} \mathbf{R}_{001} & \mathbf{c}_{01} \\ \vdots & \vdots \\ \mathbf{R}_{00M} & \mathbf{c}_{0M} \end{bmatrix} = \mathbf{Q}_0 \begin{bmatrix} \mathbf{R}_{00} & \mathbf{c}_0 \\ \mathbf{0} & \mathbf{c}_1 \end{bmatrix}$$

Pinheiro and Bates (2000) show that ML estimates of $\boldsymbol{\beta}$, σ_ϵ^2, and $\boldsymbol{\Delta}$ (the unique elements of $\boldsymbol{\Delta}$, that is) are obtained by maximizing the profile log-likelihood (profiled in $\boldsymbol{\Delta}$)

$$L(\boldsymbol{\Delta}) = \frac{n}{2} \left\{ \log n - \log(2\pi) - 1 \right\} - n \log \|\mathbf{c}_1\| + \sum_{i=1}^{M} \log \left| \frac{\det(\boldsymbol{\Delta})}{\det(\mathbf{R}_{11i})} \right| \tag{10}$$

where $\| \cdot \|$ denotes the 2-norm, and following this maximization with

$$\widehat{\boldsymbol{\beta}} = \mathbf{R}_{00}^{-1} \mathbf{c}_0; \quad \widehat{\sigma}_\epsilon^2 = n^{-1} \|\mathbf{c}_1\|^2 \tag{11}$$

REML estimates are obtained by maximizing

$$
L_R(\boldsymbol{\Delta}) = \frac{n-p}{2}\left\{\log(n-p) - \log(2\pi) - 1\right\} - (n-p)\log\|\mathbf{c}_1\|
$$

$$
- \log|\det(\mathbf{R}_{00})| + \sum_{i=1}^{M} \log\left|\frac{\det(\boldsymbol{\Delta})}{\det(\mathbf{R}_{11i})}\right|
\tag{12}
$$

followed by

$$
\widehat{\boldsymbol{\beta}} = \mathbf{R}_{00}^{-1}\mathbf{c}_0; \quad \widehat{\sigma}_\epsilon^2 = (n-p)^{-1}\|\mathbf{c}_1\|^2
$$

For purposes of numerical stability, maximization of (10) and (12) is not performed with respect to the unique elements of $\boldsymbol{\Delta}$, but instead with respect to the unique elements of the matrix logarithm of $\boldsymbol{\Sigma}/\sigma_\epsilon^2$; define $\boldsymbol{\gamma}$ to be the vector containing these elements.

Once maximization with respect to $\boldsymbol{\gamma}$ is completed, $(\boldsymbol{\gamma}, \sigma_\epsilon^2)$ is reparameterized to $\{\boldsymbol{\alpha}, \log(\sigma_\epsilon)\}$, where $\boldsymbol{\alpha}$ is a vector containing the unique elements of $\boldsymbol{\Sigma}$, expressed as logarithms of standard deviations for the diagonal elements and hyperbolic arctangents of the correlations for off-diagonal elements. This last step is necessary in order to (a) obtain a joint variance–covariance estimate of the elements of $\boldsymbol{\Sigma}$ and σ_ϵ^2; (b) obtain a parameterization under which parameter estimates can be interpreted individually, rather than as elements of a matrix logarithm; and (c) parameterize these elements such that their ranges each encompass the entire real line.

Obtaining a joint variance–covariance matrix for the estimated $\{\boldsymbol{\alpha}, \log(\sigma_\epsilon)\}$ requires the evaluation of the log likelihood (or log-restricted likelihood) with only $\boldsymbol{\beta}$ profiled out. In the case of ML, we have

$$
L^*\{\boldsymbol{\alpha}, \log(\sigma_\epsilon)\} = L\{\boldsymbol{\Delta}(\boldsymbol{\alpha}, \sigma_\epsilon^2), \sigma_\epsilon^2\}
$$

$$
= -\frac{n}{2}\log(2\pi\sigma_\epsilon^2) - \frac{\|\mathbf{c}_1\|^2}{2\sigma_\epsilon^2} + \sum_{i=1}^{M}\log\left|\frac{\det(\boldsymbol{\Delta})}{\det(\mathbf{R}_{11i})}\right|
$$

with the analogous expression for REML.

The variance–covariance matrix of $\widehat{\boldsymbol{\beta}}$ is estimated as

$$
\widehat{\mathrm{Var}}(\widehat{\boldsymbol{\beta}}) = \widehat{\sigma}_\epsilon^2 \mathbf{R}_{00}^{-1}\left(\mathbf{R}_{00}^{-1}\right)'
$$

but note that this does not mean that $\widehat{\mathrm{Var}}(\widehat{\boldsymbol{\beta}})$ is identical under both ML and REML since $\mathbf{R}_{00}$ depends on $\boldsymbol{\Delta}$. Since $\widehat{\boldsymbol{\beta}}$ is asymptotically uncorrelated with $\{\widehat{\boldsymbol{\alpha}}, \log(\widehat{\sigma}_\epsilon)\}$, the covariance of $\widehat{\boldsymbol{\beta}}$ with the other estimated parameters is treated as zero.

Parameter estimates are stored in e(b) as $\{\widehat{\boldsymbol{\beta}}, \widehat{\boldsymbol{\alpha}}, \log(\widehat{\sigma}_\epsilon)\}$, with the corresponding (block-diagonal) variance–covariance matrix stored in e(V). Parameter estimates can be displayed in this metric by specifying option estmetric. However, in xtmixed output, variance components are most often displayed either as variances and covariances or as standard deviations and correlations.

EM iterations are derived by considering the $\mathbf{u}_i$ in (2) as missing data. Here we describe the procedure for maximizing the log likelihood via EM; the procedure for maximizing the restricted log likelihood is similar. The log likelihood for the full data $(\mathbf{y}, \mathbf{u})$ is

$$
L_F(\boldsymbol{\beta}, \boldsymbol{\Sigma}, \sigma_\epsilon^2) = \sum_{i=1}^{M}\left\{\log f_1(\mathbf{y}_i|\mathbf{u}_i, \boldsymbol{\beta}, \sigma_\epsilon^2) + \log f_2(\mathbf{u}_i|\boldsymbol{\Sigma})\right\}
$$

where $f_1()$ is the density function for multivariate normal with mean $\mathbf{X}_i\boldsymbol{\beta} + \mathbf{Z}_i\mathbf{u}_i$ and variance $\sigma_\epsilon^2\mathbf{I}_{n_i}$, and $f_2()$ is the density for multivariate normal with mean $\mathbf{0}$ and $q \times q$ covariance matrix $\boldsymbol{\Sigma}$. As before, we can profile $\boldsymbol{\beta}$ and σ_ϵ^2 out of the optimization, yielding the following EM iterative procedure:

1. For the current iterated value of $\boldsymbol{\Sigma}^{(t)}$, fix $\widehat{\boldsymbol{\beta}} = \widehat{\boldsymbol{\beta}}(\boldsymbol{\Sigma}^{(t)})$ and $\widehat{\sigma}_\epsilon^2 = \widehat{\sigma}_\epsilon^2(\boldsymbol{\Sigma}^{(t)})$ according to (11).

2. E-step: Calculate

$$
D(\boldsymbol{\Sigma}) \equiv E\left\{ L_F(\widehat{\boldsymbol{\beta}}, \boldsymbol{\Sigma}, \widehat{\sigma}_\epsilon^2)|\mathbf{y} \right\}
$$

$$
= C - \frac{M}{2}\log\det(\boldsymbol{\Sigma}) - \frac{1}{2}\sum_{i=1}^{M} E\left(\mathbf{u}_i'\boldsymbol{\Sigma}^{-1}\mathbf{u}_i|\mathbf{y}\right)
$$

where C is a constant that does not depend on $\boldsymbol{\Sigma}$, and the expected value of the quadratic form $\mathbf{u}_i'\boldsymbol{\Sigma}^{-1}\mathbf{u}_i$ is taken with respect to the conditional density $f(\mathbf{u}_i|\mathbf{y}, \widehat{\boldsymbol{\beta}}, \boldsymbol{\Sigma}^{(t)}, \widehat{\sigma}_\epsilon^2)$.

3. M-step: Maximize $D(\boldsymbol{\Sigma})$ to produce $\boldsymbol{\Sigma}^{(t+1)}$.

For general, symmetric $\boldsymbol{\Sigma}$, the maximizer of $D(\boldsymbol{\Sigma})$ can be derived explicitly, making EM iterations quite fast.

For extensions to two or more nested levels of random effects, see Bates and Pinheiro (1998).

Acknowledgments

We would like to thank Badi Baltagi, Department of Economics, Texas A&M University; and Ray Carroll, Department of Statistics, Texas A&M University, for providing us with the datasets used in this entry.

References

Baltagi, B. H., S. H. Song, and B. C. Jung. 2001. The unbalanced nested error component regression model. *Journal of Econometrics* 101: 357–381.

Bates, D. M. and J. C. Pinheiro. 1998. Computational methods for multilevel models. *Technical Memorandum BL0112140-980226-01TM*. Murray Hill, NJ: Bell Labs, Lucent Technologies.

Dempster, A. P., N. M. Laird, and D. B. Rubin. 1977. Maximum likelihood from incomplete data via the EM algorithm. *Journal of the Royal Statistical Society, Series. B* 39: 1–22.

Diggle, P. J., P. Heagerty, K.-Y. Liang, and S. L. Zeger. 2002. *Analysis of Longitudinal Data.* 2nd ed. Oxford: Oxford University Press.

Gutierrez, R. G., S. L. Carter, and D. M. Drukker. 2001. sg160: On boundary-value likelihood-ratio tests. *Stata Technical Bulletin* 60: 15–18. Reprinted in *Stata Technical Bulletin Reprints*, vol. 10, pp. 269–273.

Harville, D. A. 1977. Maximum likelihood approaches to variance component estimation and to related problems. *Journal of the American Statistical Association* 72: 320–340.

Hocking, R. R. 1985. *The Analysis of Linear Models.* Monterey, CA: Brooks/Cole.

Henderson, C. R. 1953. Estimation of variance and covariance components. *Biometrics* 9: 226–252.

Laird, N. M. and J. H. Ware. 1982. Random-effects models for longitudinal data. *Biometrics* 38: 963–974.

LaMotte, L. R. 1973. Quadratic estimation of variance components. *Biometrics* 29: 311–330.

McCulloch, C. E. and S. R. Searle. 2001. *Generalized, Linear, and Mixed Models.* New York: Wiley.

McLachlan, G. J. and K. E. Basford. 1988. *Mixture Models.* New York: Marcel Dekker.

Munnell, A. 1990. Why has productivity growth declined? Productivity and public investment. *New England Economic Review* Jan./Feb.: 3–22.

Pinheiro, J. C. and D. M. Bates. 2000. *Mixed-Effects Models in S and S-PLUS*. New York: Springer.

Rao, C. R. 1973. *Linear Statistical Inference and Its Applications*, 2nd ed. New York: Wiley.

Raudenbush, S. W. and A. S. Bryk. 2002. *Hierarchical Linear Models: Applications and Data Analysis Methods*, 2nd ed. Thousand Oaks, CA: Sage.

Ruppert, D., M. P. Wand, and R. J. Carroll. 2003. *Semiparametric Regression*. Cambridge: Cambridge University Press.

Searle, S. R. 1989. Charles Roy Henderson 1911–1989. *Biometrics* 45: 1333–1335.

Searle, S. R., G. Casella, and C. E. McCulloch. 1992. *Variance Components*. New York: Wiley.

Self, S. G. and K.-Y. Liang. 1987. Asymptotic properties of maximum likelihood estimators and likelihood ratio tests under nonstandard conditions. *Journal of the American Statistical Association* 82: 605–610.

Skrondal, A. and S. Rabe-Hesketh. 2004. *Generalized Latent Variable Modeling: Multilevel, Longitudinal and Structural Equation Models*. Boca Raton, FL: Chapman & Hall/CRC Press.

Stram, D. O. and J. W. Lee. 1994. Variance components testing in the longitudinal mixed effects model. *Biometrics* 50: 1171–1177.

Thompson, W. A. 1962. The problem of negative estimates of variance components. *Annals of Mathematical Statistics* 33: 273–289.

Verbeke, G. and G. Molenberghs. 2000. *Linear Mixed Models for Longitudinal Data*. New York: Springer.

Also See

Complementary:	[XT] **xtmixed postestimation**
Related:	[XT] **xtreg**; [XT] **xtrc**; [XT] **xtgee**, [XT] **xtregar**
Background:	[U] **11.1.10 Prefix commands**,
	[U] **20 Estimation and postestimation commands**,
	[XT] **estimation options**, [XT] **xt**,
	[R] **maximize**

Title

xtmixed postestimation — Postestimation tools for xtmixed

Description

The following postestimation commands are of special interest after `xtmixed`:

commands	description
estat group	summarizes the composition of the nested groups
estat recovariance	displays the estimated random-effects covariance matrix (or matrices)

For information about these commands, see below.

In addition, the following standard postestimation commands are available:

commands	description
adjust	adjusted predictions of $x\beta$
estat	AIC, BIC, VCE, and estimation sample summary
estimates	cataloging estimation results
lincom	point estimates, standard errors, testing, and inference for linear combinations of coefficients
lrtest	likelihood-ratio test
mfx	marginal effects or elasticities
nlcom	point estimates, standard errors, testing, and inference for nonlinear combinations of coefficients
predict	predicted probabilities, estimated linear predictor and its standard error
predictnl	point estimates, standard errors, testing, and inference for generalized predictions
test	Wald tests for simple and composite linear hypotheses
testnl	Wald tests of nonlinear hypotheses

See the corresponding entries in the *Stata Base Reference Manual* for details.

Special-interest postestimation commands

`estat group` reports number of groups, and minimum, average, and maximum group sizes for each level of the model. Model levels are identified by the corresponding group variable in the data. Since groups are treated as nested, the information in this summary may differ from what you would get if you `tabulate` each group variable individually.

`estat recovariance` displays the estimated variance–covariance matrix of the random effects for each level in the model. Random effects can either be random intercepts, in which case the corresponding rows and columns of the matrix are labeled as `_cons`, or random coefficients, in which case the label is the name of the associated variable in the data.

Syntax for predict

Syntax for obtaining best linear unbiased predictions (BLUPs) of random effects

> predict [*type*] {*stub**|*newvar*₁ ... *newvar_q*} [*if*] [*in*] , <u>ref</u>fects
>
> [<u>level</u>(*levelvar*)]

Syntax for obtaining other predictions

> predict [*type*] *newvar* [*if*] [*in*] [, *statistic* <u>level</u>(*levelvar*)]

statistic	description
xb	linear prediction for the *fixed* portion of the model only; the default
stdp	standard error of the fixed-portion linear prediction
<u>fitted</u>	fitted values, fixed-portion linear prediction plus contributions based on predicted random effects
<u>res</u>iduals	residuals, response minus fitted values
<u>rstan</u>dard	standardized residuals

Statistics are available both in and out of sample; type predict ... if e(sample) ... if wanted only for the estimation sample.

Options for predict

xb, the default, calculates the linear prediction $x\beta$ based on the estimated fixed effects (coefficients) in the model. This is equivalent to fixing all random effects in the model to their theoretical mean value of zero.

stdp calculates the standard error of the linear predictor $x\beta$.

level(*levelvar*) specifies the level in the model at which predictions involving random effects are to be obtained; see the options below for the specifics. *levelvar* is the name of the model level and is either the name of the variable describing the grouping at that level or _all, a special designation for a group comprised of all the estimation data.

reffects calculates best linear unbiased predictions (BLUPs) of the random effects. By default, BLUPs for all random effects in the model are calculated. However, if option level(*levelvar*) is specified, then BLUPs for only level *levelvar* in the model are calculated. For example, if classes are nested within schools, then typing

> . predict b*, reffects level(school)

would produce BLUPs at the school level. You must specify q new variables, where q is the number of random-effects terms in the model (or level). However, it is much easier to just specify *stub** and let Stata name the variables *stub*1 ... *stub*q for you.

fitted calculates fitted values, which are equal to the fixed-portion linear predictor *plus* contributions based on predicted random effects, or in mixed-model notation, $x\beta+Zu$. By default, the fitted values take into account random effects from all levels in the model; however, if option level(*levelvar*) is specified, the fitted values are fitted beginning with the topmost level down to and including level *levelvar*. For example, if classes are nested within schools, then typing

> . predict yhat_school, fitted level(school)

would produce school-level predictions. That is, the predictions would incorporate school-specific random effects but not those for each class nested within each school.

`residuals` calculates residuals, equal to the responses minus fitted values. By default, the fitted values take into account random effects from all levels in the model; however, if option `level(levelvar)` is specified, the fitted values are fitted beginning at the topmost level down to and including level *levelvar*.

`rstandard` calculates standardized residuals, equal to the residuals described above, divided by the estimated residual standard deviation (listed as "sd(Residual)" in `xtmixed` output).

Syntax for estat group

> estat group

Syntax for estat recovariance

> estat recovariance [, level(*levelvar*) correlation *matlist_options*]

Options for estat recovariance

`level(levelvar)` specifies the level in the model for which the random-effects covariance matrix is to be displayed and returned in `r(cov)`. By default, the covariance matrices for all levels in the model are displayed. *levelvar* is the name of the model level and is either the name of variable describing the grouping at that level or `_all`, a special designation for a group comprised of all the estimation data.

`correlation` displays the covariance matrix as a correlation matrix and returns the correlation matrix in `r(corr)`.

matlist_options are style and formatting options that control how the matrix (or matrices) are displayed; see [P] **matlist** for a list of what is available.

Remarks

Various predictions, statistics, and diagnostic measures are available after fitting a mixed model using `xtmixed`. For the most part, calculation centers around obtaining best linear unbiased predictors (BLUPs) of the random effects. Recall that random effects are not estimated when the model is fit but instead need to be predicted after estimation.

▷ Example 1

In example 3 of [XT] **xtmixed**, we modeled the weights of 48 pigs measured on nine successive weeks as

$$\text{weight}_{ij} = \beta_0 + \beta_1 \text{week}_{ij} + u_{0i} + u_{1i}\text{week}_{ij} + \epsilon_{ij} \tag{1}$$

for $i = 1, \ldots, 48$, $j = 1, \ldots, 9$, $\epsilon_{ij} \sim N(0, \sigma_\epsilon^2)$, and u_{0i} and u_{1i} normally distributed with mean zero and variance–covariance matrix

$$\Sigma = \text{Var}\begin{bmatrix} u_{0i} \\ u_{1i} \end{bmatrix} = \begin{bmatrix} \sigma_{u0}^2 & \sigma_{01} \\ \sigma_{01} & \sigma_{u1}^2 \end{bmatrix}$$

```
. use http://www.statapress.com/data/r9/pig
(Longitudinal analysis of pig weights)

. xtmixed weight week || id: week, covariance(unstructured) variance

  (output omitted )
```

Mixed-effects REML regression				Number of obs	=	432
Group variable: id				Number of groups	=	48

		Obs per group: min =	9
		avg =	9.0
		max =	9

	Wald chi2(1)	=	4552.31
Log restricted-likelihood = -870.43562	Prob > chi2	=	0.0000

weight	Coef.	Std. Err.	z	P>|z|	[95% Conf. Interval]	
week	6.209896	.0920382	67.47	0.000	6.029504	6.390287
_cons	19.35561	.4038677	47.93	0.000	18.56405	20.14718

Random-effects Parameters	Estimate	Std. Err.	[95% Conf. Interval]	
id: Unstructured				
var(week)	.3799957	.0839023	.2465103	.5857635
var(_cons)	6.986465	1.616357	4.439432	10.99481
cov(week,_cons)	-.1033632	.2627309	-.6183063	.41158
var(Residual)	1.596829	.1231981	1.372736	1.857506

```
LR test vs. linear regression:      chi2(3) =   766.07   Prob > chi2 = 0.0000
Note: LR test is conservative and provided only for reference
```

Rather than see the estimated variance components listed as above, we can instead see them in matrix form; i.e., we can see $\widehat{\Sigma}$

```
. estat recovariance
Random-effects covariance matrix for level id
```

	week	_cons
week	.3799957	
_cons	-.1033632	6.986465

or we can see $\widehat{\Sigma}$ as a correlation matrix

```
. estat recovariance, correlation
Random-effects correlation matrix for level id
```

	week	_cons
week	1	
_cons	-.0634377	1

We can also obtain BLUPs of the pig-level random effects (u_{0i} and u_{1i}). We need to specify the variables to be created in the order u1 u0 since that is the order in which the corresponding variance components are listed in the output (week _cons). We obtain the predictions and list them for the first ten pigs.

```
. predict u1 u0, reffects
. by id, sort: generate tolist = (_n==1)
```

```
. list id u0 u1 if id <=10 & tolist
```

	id	u0	u1
1.	1	.2402243	-.3964052
10.	2	-1.591519	.5113588
19.	3	-3.537457	.321844
28.	4	1.974493	-.7738019
37.	5	1.308741	-.9259342
46.	6	-1.146433	-.5451292
55.	7	-2.597208	.0405007
64.	8	-1.138727	-.1694532
73.	9	-3.192426	-.7363427
82.	10	1.163175	.0026334

If you forget how to order your variables in predict, or if you use predict *stub**, remember that predict labels the generated variables for you in order to avoid confusion.

```
. describe u0 u1
```

variable name	storage type	display format	value label	variable label
u0	float	%9.0g		BLUP r.e. for id: _cons
u1	float	%9.0g		BLUP r.e. for id: week

Examining (1), we see that, within each pig, the successive weight measurements are modeled as simple linear regression with intercept $\beta_0 + u_{i0}$ and slope $\beta_1 + u_{i1}$. We can generate estimates of the pig-level intercepts and slopes with

```
. gen intercept = _b[_cons] + u0
. gen slope = _b[week] + u1
. list id intercept slope if id<=10 & tolist
```

	id	interc~t	slope
1.	1	19.59584	5.81349
10.	2	17.7641	6.721255
19.	3	15.81816	6.53174
28.	4	21.33011	5.436094
37.	5	20.66435	5.283962
46.	6	18.20918	5.664767
55.	7	16.75841	6.250397
64.	8	18.21689	6.040442
73.	9	16.16319	5.473553
82.	10	20.51879	6.212529

Thus we can plot estimated regression lines for each of the pigs. Equivalently, we can just plot the fitted values since they are based on both the fixed and random effects:

```
. predict fitweight, fitted
. twoway connected fitweight week if id<=10, connect(L)
```

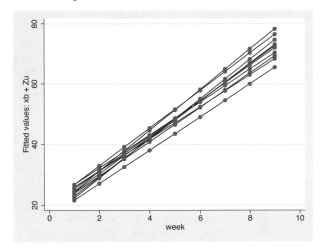

We can also generate standardized residuals and see if they follow a standard normal distribution, as they should in any good-fitting model:

```
. predict rs, rstandard
. sum rs
```

Variable	Obs	Mean	Std. Dev.	Min	Max
rs	432	-4.42e-10	.8925255	-3.620188	2.993914

```
. qnorm rs
```

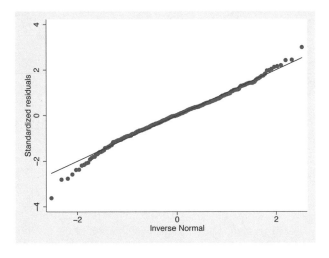

◁

▷ Example 2

In example 4 of [XT] **xtmixed**, we estimated a Cobb–Douglas production function with random intercepts at the region level and at the state-within-region level:

$$\mathbf{y}_{ij} = \mathbf{X}_{ij}\boldsymbol{\beta} + u_i^{(1)} + u_{ij}^{(2)} + \epsilon_{ij}$$

```
. use http://www.statapress.com/data/r9/productivity
(Public Capital Productivity)
. xtmixed gsp private emp hwy water other unemp || region: || state:
(output omitted)
```

We can use `estat group` to see how the data are broken down by state and region

```
. estat group
```

Group Variable	No. of Groups	Observations per Group Minimum	Average	Maximum
region	9	51	90.7	136
state	48	17	17.0	17

and we are reminded that we have balanced productivity data for 17 years for each state.

We can use `predict, fitted` to get the fitted values

$$\widehat{\mathbf{y}}_{ij} = \mathbf{X}_{ij}\widehat{\boldsymbol{\beta}} + \widehat{u}_i^{(1)} + \widehat{u}_{ij}^{(2)}$$

but if we instead want fitted values at the region level, i.e.,

$$\widehat{\mathbf{y}}_{ij} = \mathbf{X}_{ij}\widehat{\boldsymbol{\beta}} + \widehat{u}_i^{(1)}$$

we need to use option `level()`;

```
. predict gsp_region, fitted level(region)
. list gsp gsp_region in 1/10
```

	gsp	gsp_re~n
1.	10.25478	10.40034
2.	10.2879	10.4184
3.	10.35147	10.46851
4.	10.41721	10.52158
5.	10.42671	10.54457
6.	10.4224	10.53043
7.	10.4847	10.60275
8.	10.53111	10.64228
9.	10.59573	10.70008
10.	10.62082	10.72299

◁

❏ Technical Note

Out-of-sample predictions are permitted after `xtmixed`, but if these predictions involve BLUPs of random effects, the integrity of the estimation data must be preserved. If the estimation data have changed since the mixed model was fitted, `predict` will be unable to obtain predicted random effects that are appropriate for the fitted model and will give an error. As such, to obtain out-of-sample predictions that contain random-effects terms, be sure the data for these predictions are in observations that augment the estimation data.

❏

Saved Results

`estat recovariance` saves the last-displayed random-effects covariance matrix in `r(cov)` or in `r(corr)` if it is displayed as a correlation matrix.

Methods and Formulas

Following the notation defined in the *Methods and Formulas* section of [XT] **xtmixed**, best linear unbiased predictions (BLUPs) of random effects $\mathbf{u}$ are obtained as

$$\widetilde{\mathbf{u}} = \widetilde{\mathbf{G}}\mathbf{Z}'\widetilde{\mathbf{V}}^{-1}\left(\mathbf{y} - \mathbf{X}\widehat{\boldsymbol{\beta}}\right)$$

where $\widetilde{\mathbf{G}}$ and $\widetilde{\mathbf{V}}$ are $\mathbf{G}$ and $\mathbf{V}$ with ML or REML estimates of the variance components plugged in. Fitted values are given by $\mathbf{X}\widehat{\boldsymbol{\beta}} + \mathbf{Z}\widetilde{\mathbf{u}}$, residuals as $\mathbf{y} - \mathbf{X}\widehat{\boldsymbol{\beta}} - \mathbf{Z}\widetilde{\mathbf{u}}$, and standardized residuals as residuals divided by $\widehat{\sigma}_\epsilon$.

If option `level`(*levelvar*) is specified, fitted values, residuals, and standardized residuals consider only those random-effects terms up to and including level *levelvar* in the model.

Also See

Complementary:	[XT] **xtmixed**,
	[R] **adjust**, [R] **estimates**, [R] **lincom**, [R] **lrtest**, [R] **mfx**,
	[R] **nlcom**, [R] **predictnl**, [R] **test**, [R] **testnl**
Background:	[U] **13.5 Accessing coefficients and standard errors**,
	[U] **20 Estimation and postestimation commands**,
	[R] **estat**, [R] **predict**

Title

> **xtnbreg** — Fixed-effects, random-effects, & population-averaged negative binomial models

Syntax

Random-effects (RE) and conditional fixed-effects (FE) overdispersion models

     xtnbreg *depvar* [*indepvars*] [*if*] [*in*] [*weight*] [, [re|fe] *RE/FE_options*]

Population-averaged (PA) model

     xtnbreg *depvar* [*indepvars*] [*if*] [*in*] [*weight*] , pa [*PA_options*]

RE/FE_options	description
Model	
i(*varname_i*)	use *varname* as the panel ID variable
<u>nocon</u>stant	suppress constant term; not available with fe
re	use random-effects estimator; the default
fe	use fixed-effects estimator
<u>exp</u>osure(*varname*)	include ln(*varname*) in model with coefficient constrained to 1
<u>off</u>set(*varname*)	include *varname* in model with coefficient constrained to 1
constraints(*constraints*)	apply specified linear constraints
SE	
vce(*vcetype*)	*vcetype* may be <u>boot</u>strap or jackknife
Reporting	
<u>level</u>(#)	set confidence level; default is level(95)
<u>irr</u>	report incidence-rate ratios
noskip	perform overall model test as a likelihood-ratio test
Max options	
maximize_options	control the maximization process; seldom used

PA_options	description
Model	
i(*varname_i*)	use *varname* as the panel ID variable
<u>nocon</u>stant	suppress constant term
pa	use population-averaged estimator
<u>exp</u>osure(*varname*)	include ln(*varname*) in model with coefficient constrained to 1
<u>off</u>set(*varname*)	include *varname* in model with coefficient constrained to 1
PA options	
<u>corr</u>(*correlation*)	within-group correlation structure
force	estimate even if observations unequally spaced in time

SE/Robust

vce(*vcetype*)	*vcetype* may be <u>r</u>obust, <u>boot</u>strap, or <u>jackknife</u>
<u>r</u>obust	synonym for vce(robust)
nmp	use divisor $N - P$ instead of the default N
<u>s</u>cale(x2)	set scale parameter to Pearson chi-squared statistic
<u>s</u>cale(dev)	set scale parameter to deviance divided by degrees of freedom
<u>s</u>cale(phi)	do not rescale the variance
<u>s</u>cale(#)	set scale parameter to #

Reporting

<u>l</u>evel(#)	set confidence level; default is level(95)
<u>irr</u>	report incidence-rate ratios

Opt options

optimize_options	control the optimization process; seldom used

correlation	description
<u>exc</u>hangeable	exchangeable
<u>inde</u>pendent	independent
<u>uns</u>tructured	unstructured
<u>fix</u>ed *matname*	user-specified
ar #	autoregressive of order #
<u>stat</u>ionary #	stationary of order #
<u>non</u>stationary #	nonstationary of order #

depvar and *indepvars* may contain time-series operators; see [U] **11.4.3 Time-series varlists**.
bootstrap, by, jackknife, statsby, and xi may be used with xtnbreg; see [U] **11.1.10 Prefix commands**.
iweights, fweights, and pweights are allowed for the population-averaged model, and iweights are allowed in the random-effects and fixed-effects models; see [U] **11.1.6 weight**. Weights must be constant within panels.
See [U] **20 Estimation and postestimation commands** for additional capabilities of estimation commands.

Description

xtnbreg fits random-effects overdispersion models, conditional fixed-effects overdispersion models, and population-averaged negative binomial models. Here "random effects" and "fixed effects" apply to the distribution of the dispersion parameter, not to the $x\beta$ term in the model. In the random-effects and fixed-effects overdispersion models, the dispersion is the same for all elements in the same group (i.e., elements with the same value of the i() variable). In the random-effects model, the dispersion varies randomly from group to group, such that the inverse of one plus the dispersion follows a Beta(r, s) distribution. In the fixed-effects model, the dispersion parameter in a group can take on any value, since a conditional likelihood is used in which the dispersion parameter drops out of the estimation.

By default, the population-averaged model is an equal-correlation model; xtnbreg, pa assumes corr(exchangeable). See [XT] **xtgee** for details on this option to fit other population-averaged models.

Options for RE/FE models

$\overline{\quad\text{Model}\quad}$

i(*varname*$_i$), noconstant; see [XT] **estimation options**.

re requests the random-effects estimator, which is the default.

fe requests the conditional fixed-effects estimator.

exposure(*varname*), offset(*varname*), constraints(*constraints*); see [XT] **estimation options**.

$\overline{\quad\text{SE}\quad}$

vce(*vcetype*); see [R] *vce_option*.

$\overline{\quad\text{Reporting}\quad}$

level(*#*); see [XT] **estimation options**.

irr reports exponentiated coefficients e^b rather than coefficients b. For the negative binomial model, exponentiated coefficients have the interpretation of incidence-rate ratios.

noskip; see [XT] **estimation options**.

$\overline{\quad\text{Max options}\quad}$

maximize_options: difficult, technique(*algorithm_spec*), iterate(*#*), [no]log, trace, gradient, showstep, hessian, shownrtolerance, tolerance(*#*), ltolerance(*#*), gtolerance(*#*), nrtolerance(*#*), nonrtolerance, from(*init_specs*); see [R] **ml** and [R] **maximize**. These options are seldom used.

Options for PA model

$\overline{\quad\text{Model}\quad}$

i(*varname*$_i$), noconstant; see [XT] **estimation options**.

pa requests the population-averaged estimator.

exposure(*varname*), offset(*varname*); see [XT] **estimation options**.

$\overline{\quad\text{PA options}\quad}$

corr(*correlation*), force; see [XT] **estimation options**.

$\overline{\quad\text{SE/Robust}\quad}$

vce(*vcetype*); see [R] *vce_option*.

robust, nmp; see [XT] **estimation options**.

scale(x2|dev|phi|*#*) overrides the default scale parameter of scale(1); see [XT] **estimation options**.

$\overline{\quad\text{Reporting}\quad}$

level(*#*); see [XT] **estimation options**.

irr reports exponentiated coefficients e^b rather than coefficients b. For the negative binomial model, exponentiated coefficients have the interpretation of incidence-rate ratios.

⌐ Opt options ⌐

optimize_options control the iterative optimization process. These options are seldom used.

iterate(*#*) specifies the maximum number of iterations. When the number of iterations equals *#*, the optimization stops and presents the current results, even if convergence has not been reached. The default is iterate(100).

tolerance(*#*) specifies the tolerance for the coefficient vector. When the relative change in the coefficient vector from one iteration to the next is less than or equal to *#*, the optimization process is stopped. tolerance(1e-6) is the default.

nolog suppresses display of the iteration log.

trace specifies that the current estimates be printed at each iteration.

Remarks

xtnbreg is a convenience command if you want the population-averaged model. Typing

    . xtnbreg ..., ... pa exposure(time)

is equivalent to typing

    . xtgee ..., ... family(nbinom) link(log) corr(exchangeable) exposure(time)

See also [XT] **xtgee** for information about xtnbreg.

By default, or when re is specified, xtnbreg fits a maximum-likelihood random-effects overdispersion model.

▷ Example 1

You have (fictional) data on injury "incidents" incurred among 20 airlines in each of four years. (Incidents range from major injuries to exceedingly minor ones.) The government agency in charge of regulating airlines has run an experimental safety training program, and, in each of the years, some airlines have participated and some have not. You now wish to analyze whether the "incident" rate is affected by the program. You choose to estimate using random-effects negative binomial regression, as the dispersion might vary across the airlines for unidentified airline-specific reasons. Your measure of exposure is passenger miles for each airline in each year.

```
. use http://www.stata-press.com/data/r9/airacc

. xtnbreg i_cnt inprog, i(airline) exposure(pmiles) irr nolog
Random-effects negative binomial regression       Number of obs      =        80
Group variable (i): airline                        Number of groups   =        20

Random effects u_i ~ Beta                          Obs per group: min =         4
                                                                  avg =       4.0
                                                                  max =         4

                                                   Wald chi2(1)       =      2.04
Log likelihood  = -265.38202                       Prob > chi2        =    0.1532
```

i_cnt	IRR	Std. Err.	z	P>|z|	[95% Conf. Interval]	
inprog	.911673	.0590277	-1.43	0.153	.8030206	1.035027
pmiles	(exposure)					
/ln_r	4.794991	.951781			2.929535	6.660448
/ln_s	3.268052	.4709033			2.345098	4.191005
r	120.9033	115.0735			18.71892	780.9007
s	26.26013	12.36598			10.4343	66.08918

```
Likelihood-ratio test vs. pooled: chibar2(01) =     19.03 Prob>=chibar2 = 0.000
```

In the output above, the /ln_r and /ln_s lines refer to $\ln(r)$ and $\ln(s)$, where the inverse of one plus the dispersion is assumed to follow a $\text{Beta}(r, s)$ distribution. The output also includes a likelihood-ratio test, which compares the panel estimator with the pooled estimator (i.e., a negative binomial estimator with constant dispersion).

You find that the incidence rate for accidents is not significantly different for participation in the program, and that the panel estimator is significantly different from the pooled estimator.

We may alternatively fit a fixed-effects overdispersion model:

```
. xtnbreg i_cnt inprog, i(airline) exposure(pmiles) irr fe nolog
Conditional FE negative binomial regression       Number of obs      =        80
Group variable (i): airline                        Number of groups   =        20

                                                   Obs per group: min =         4
                                                                  avg =       4.0
                                                                  max =         4

                                                   Wald chi2(1)       =      2.11
Log likelihood  = -174.25143                       Prob > chi2        =    0.1463
```

i_cnt	IRR	Std. Err.	z	P>|z|	[95% Conf. Interval]	
inprog	.9062669	.0613917	-1.45	0.146	.793587	1.034946
pmiles	(exposure)					

◁

▷ Example 2

We rerun our previous example, but this time we fit a robust equal-correlation population-averaged model:

```
. xtnbreg i_cnt inprog, i(airline) exposure(pmiles) eform robust pa nolog
```

GEE population-averaged model		Number of obs	=	80
Group variable:	airline	Number of groups	=	20
Link:	log	Obs per group: min =		4
Family:	negative binomial(k=1)	avg =		4.0
Correlation:	exchangeable	max =		4
		Wald chi2(1)	=	1.28
Scale parameter:	1	Prob > chi2	=	0.2571

(Std. Err. adjusted for clustering on airline)

i_cnt	IRR	Semi-robust Std. Err.	z	P>|z|	[95% Conf. Interval]	
inprog	.927275	.0617857	-1.13	0.257	.8137513	1.056636
pmiles	(exposure)					

We compare this with a pooled estimator with clustered robust-variance estimates:

```
. nbreg i_cnt inprog, exposure(pmiles) robust cluster(airline) irr nolog
```

Negative binomial regression		Number of obs	=	80
Dispersion	= mean	Wald chi2(1)	=	0.60
Log pseudolikelihood = -274.55077		Prob > chi2	=	0.4369

(Std. Err. adjusted for 20 clusters in airline)

i_cnt	IRR	Robust Std. Err.	z	P>|z|	[95% Conf. Interval]	
inprog	.9429015	.0713091	-0.78	0.437	.8130032	1.093555
pmiles	(exposure)					
/lnalpha	-2.835089	.3351784			-3.492027	-2.178151
alpha	.0587133	.0196794			.0304391	.1132507

◁

Saved Results

xtnbreg, re saves in e():

Scalars

e(N)	# of observations	e(r)	value of r in Beta(r,s)
e(N_g)	number of groups	e(s)	value of s in Beta(r,s)
e(df_m)	model degrees of freedom	e(k)	# of parameters
e(ll)	log likelihood	e(k_eq)	# of equations
e(ll_0)	log likelihood, constant-only model	e(k_dv)	# of dependent variables
e(ll_c)	log likelihood, comparison model	e(p)	significance
e(g_max)	largest group size	e(rank)	rank of e(V)
e(g_min)	smallest group size	e(rank0)	rank of e(V) for constant-only model
e(g_avg)	average group size	e(ic)	# of iterations
e(chi2)	χ^2	e(rc)	return code
e(chi2_c)	χ^2 for comparison test	e(converged)	1 if converged, 0 otherwise

Macros

e(cmd)	xtnbreg	e(distrib)	Beta; the distribution of the random effect
e(cmd2)	xtn_re		
e(depvar)	name of dependent variable	e(vce)	*vcetype* specified in vce()
e(title)	title in estimation output	e(vcetype)	title used to label Std. Err.
e(ivar)	variable denoting groups	e(opt)	type of optimization
e(wtype)	weight type	e(ml_method)	type of ml method
e(wexp)	weight expression	e(user)	name of likelihood-evaluator program
e(offset)	offset	e(technique)	maximization technique
e(chi2type)	Wald or LR; type of model χ^2 test	e(crittype)	optimization criterion
e(chi2_ct)	Wald or LR; type of model χ^2 test corresponding to e(chi2_c)	e(properties)	b V
		e(predict)	program used to implement predict
e(method)	estimation method		

Matrices

e(b)	coefficient vector	e(ilog)	iteration log
e(V)	variance–covariance matrix of the estimators	e(gradient)	gradient vector

Functions

e(sample)	marks estimation sample

(Continued on next page)

`xtnbreg, fe` saves in `e()`:

Scalars

e(N)	number of observations	e(chi2)	χ^2
e(N_g)	number of groups	e(k)	# of parameters
e(df_m)	model degrees of freedom	e(k_eq)	# of equations
e(ll)	log likelihood	e(k_dv)	# of dependent variables
e(ll_0)	log likelihood, constant-only model	e(p)	significance
e(g_max)	largest group size	e(rank)	rank of e(V)
e(g_min)	smallest group size	e(ic)	# of iterations
e(g_avg)	average group size	e(rc)	return code
e(r2_p)	pseudo R-squared	e(converged)	1 if converged, 0 otherwise

Macros

e(cmd)	xtnbreg	e(vce)	*vcetype* specified in vce()
e(cmd2)	xtn_re	e(vcetype)	title used to label Std. Err.
e(depvar)	name of dependent variable	e(opt)	type of optimization
e(title)	title in estimation output	e(ml_method)	type of ml method
e(ivar)	variable denoting groups	e(user)	name of likelihood-evaluator program
e(offset)	offset	e(technique)	maximization technique
e(wtype)	weight type	e(crittype)	optimization criterion
e(wexp)	weight expression	e(properties)	b V
e(chi2type)	LR; type of model χ^2 test	e(predict)	program used to implement predict
e(method)	requested estimation method		

Matrices

e(b)	coefficient vector	e(ilog)	iteration log
e(V)	variance–covariance matrix of the estimators	e(gradient)	gradient vector

Functions

e(sample)	marks estimation sample

```
xtnbreg, pa saves in e():
```

Scalars

e(N)	number of observations	e(deviance)	deviance
e(N_g)	number of groups	e(chi2_dev)	χ^2 test of deviance
e(df_m)	model degrees of freedom	e(dispers)	deviance dispersion
e(g_max)	largest group size	e(chi2_dis)	χ^2 test of deviance dispersion
e(g_min)	smallest group size	e(tol)	target tolerance
e(g_avg)	average group size	e(dif)	achieved tolerance
e(chi2)	χ^2	e(phi)	scale parameter
e(df_pear)	degrees of freedom for Pearson χ^2	e(rc)	return code

Macros

e(cmd)	xtgee	e(nbalpha)	α
e(cmd2)	xtnbreg	e(ivar)	variable denoting groups
e(depvar)	name of dependent variable	e(vce)	*vcetype* specified in vce()
e(family)	negative binomial(k=1)	e(vcetype)	title used to label Std. Err.
e(link)	log; link function	e(chi2type)	Wald; type of model χ^2 test
e(corr)	correlation structure	e(offset)	offset
e(crittype)	optimization criterion	e(properties)	b V
e(scale)	x2, dev, phi, or #; scale parameter	e(predict)	program used to implement predict

Matrices

e(b)	coefficient vector	e(V)	variance–covariance matrix of the
e(R)	estimated working correlation matrix		estimators

Functions

e(sample)	marks estimation sample

Methods and Formulas

xtnbreg is implemented as an ado-file.

xtnbreg, pa reports the population-averaged results obtained by using xtgee, family(nbreg) link(log) to obtain estimates. See [XT] **xtgee** for details on the methods and formulas.

For the random-effects and fixed-effects overdispersion models, let y_{it} be the count for the tth observation in the ith group. We begin with the model $y_{it} \mid \gamma_{it} \sim \text{Poisson}(\gamma_{it})$, where $\gamma_{it} \mid \delta_i \sim \text{gamma}(\lambda_{it}, \delta_i)$ with $\lambda_{it} = \exp(\mathbf{x}_{it}\boldsymbol{\beta} + \text{offset}_{it})$ and δ_i is the dispersion parameter. This yields the model

$$\Pr(Y_{it} = y_{it} \mid \mathbf{x}_{it}, \delta_i) = \frac{\Gamma(\lambda_{it} + y_{it})}{\Gamma(\lambda_{it})\Gamma(y_{it} + 1)} \left(\frac{1}{1 + \delta_i}\right)^{\lambda_{it}} \left(\frac{\delta_i}{1 + \delta_i}\right)^{y_{it}}$$

(See Hausman, Hall, and Griliches [1984, equation 3.1, 922]; note that our δ is the inverse of their δ.) Looking at within-group effects only, we find that this specification yields a negative binomial model for the ith group with dispersion (variance divided by the mean) equal to $1 + \delta_i$, i.e., constant dispersion within group. Note that this parameterization of the negative binomial model differs from the default parameterization of nbreg, which has dispersion equal to $1 + \alpha \exp(\mathbf{x}\boldsymbol{\beta} + \text{offset})$; see [R] **nbreg**.

For a random-effects overdispersion model, we allow δ_i to vary randomly across groups; namely, we assume that $1/(1 + \delta_i) \sim \text{Beta}(r, s)$. The joint probability of the counts for the ith group is

$$\Pr(Y_{i1} = y_{i1}, \ldots, Y_{in_i} = y_{in_i} | \mathbf{X}_i) = \int_0^\infty \prod_{t=1}^{n_i} \Pr(Y_{it} = y_{it} \mid \mathbf{x}_{it}, \delta_i) \, f(\delta_i) \, d\delta_i$$

$$= \frac{\Gamma(r+s)\Gamma(r+\sum_{t=1}^{n_i}\lambda_{it})\Gamma(s+\sum_{t=1}^{n_i}y_{it})}{\Gamma(r)\Gamma(s)\Gamma(r+s+\sum_{t=1}^{n_i}\lambda_{it}+\sum_{t=1}^{n_i}y_{it})} \prod_{t=1}^{n_i} \frac{\Gamma(\lambda_{it}+y_{it})}{\Gamma(\lambda_{it})\Gamma(y_{it}+1)}$$

for $\mathbf{X}_i = (\mathbf{x}_{i1}, \ldots, \mathbf{x}_{in_i})$ and where f is the probability density function for δ_i. The resulting log likelihood is

$$\ln L = \sum_{i=1}^{n} w_i \left[\ln\Gamma(r+s) + \ln\Gamma\left(r+\sum_{k=1}^{n_i}\lambda_{ik}\right) + \ln\Gamma\left(s+\sum_{k=1}^{n_i}y_{ik}\right) - \ln\Gamma(r) - \ln\Gamma(s) \right.$$
$$\left. - \ln\Gamma\left(r+s+\sum_{k=1}^{n_i}\lambda_{ik}+\sum_{k=1}^{n_i}y_{ik}\right) + \sum_{t=1}^{n_i}\left\{\ln\Gamma(\lambda_{it}+y_{it}) - \ln\Gamma(\lambda_{it}) - \ln\Gamma(y_{it}+1)\right\} \right]$$

where $\lambda_{it} = \exp(\mathbf{x}_{it}\boldsymbol{\beta} + \text{offset}_{it})$ and w_i is the weight for the ith group (Hausman, Hall, and Griliches 1984, equation 3.5, 927).

For the fixed-effects overdispersion model, we condition the joint probability of the counts for each group on the sum of the counts for the group (i.e., the observed $\sum_{t=1}^{n_i} y_{it}$). This yields

$$\Pr(Y_{i1} = y_{i1}, \ldots, Y_{in_i} = y_{in_i} \mid \mathbf{X}_i, \textstyle\sum_{t=1}^{n_i} Y_{it} = \sum_{t=1}^{n_i} y_{it})$$

$$= \frac{\Gamma(\sum_{t=1}^{n_i}\lambda_{it})\Gamma(\sum_{t=1}^{n_i}y_{it}+1)}{\Gamma(\sum_{t=1}^{n_i}\lambda_{it}+\sum_{t=1}^{n_i}y_{it})} \prod_{t=1}^{n_i} \frac{\Gamma(\lambda_{it}+y_{it})}{\Gamma(\lambda_{it})\Gamma(y_{it}+1)}$$

The conditional log likelihood is

$$\ln L = \sum_{i=1}^{n} w_i \left[\ln\Gamma\left(\sum_{t=1}^{n_i}\lambda_{it}\right) + \ln\Gamma\left(\sum_{t=1}^{n_i}y_{it}+1\right) - \ln\Gamma\left(\sum_{t=1}^{n_i}\lambda_{it}+\sum_{t=1}^{n_i}y_{it}\right) \right.$$
$$\left. + \sum_{t=1}^{n_i}\left\{\ln\Gamma(\lambda_{it}+y_{it}) - \ln\Gamma(\lambda_{it}) - \ln\Gamma(y_{it}+1)\right\} \right]$$

See Hausman, Hall, and Griliches (1984) for a more thorough development of the random-effects and fixed-effects models. Also, see Cameron and Trivedi (1998) for a good textbook treatment of this model.

References

Cameron, A. C. and P. K. Trivedi. 1998. *Regression Analysis of Count Data*. New York: Cambridge University Press.

Hausman, J., B. H. Hall, and Z. Griliches. 1984. Econometric models for count data with an application to the patents–R & D relationship. *Econometrica* 52: 909–938.

Liang, K.-Y. and S. L. Zeger. 1986. Longitudinal data analysis using generalized linear models. *Biometrika* 73: 13–22.

Also See

Complementary:	[XT] **xtnbreg postestimation**; [XT] **xtdata**, [XT] **xtdes**, [XT] **xtsum**, [XT] **xttab**, [R] **constraint**
Related:	[XT] **xtgee**, [XT] **xtpoisson**, [R] **nbreg**
Background:	[U] **11.1.10 Prefix commands**, [U] **20 Estimation and postestimation commands**, [XT] **estimation options**, [XT] **xt**, [R] **maximize**, [R] *vce_option*

Title

> **xtnbreg postestimation** — Postestimation tools for xtnbreg

Description

The following postestimation commands are available for `xtnbreg`:

command	description
adjust[1]	adjusted predictions of $\mathbf{x}\beta$ or $\exp(\mathbf{x}\beta)$
*estat	AIC, BIC, VCE, and estimation sample summary
estimates	cataloging estimation results
lincom	point estimates, standard errors, testing, and inference for linear combinations of coefficients
lrtest	likelihood-ratio test
mfx	marginal effects or elasticities
nlcom	point estimates, standard errors, testing, and inference for nonlinear combinations of coefficients
predict	predictions, residuals, influence statistics, and other diagnostic measures
predictnl	point estimates, standard errors, testing, and inference for generalized predictions
test	Wald tests for simple and composite linear hypotheses
testnl	Wald tests of nonlinear hypotheses

[1] `adjust` does not work with time-series operators.

* `estat ic` may not be used after `xtnbreg, pa`.

See the corresponding entries in the *Stata Base Reference Manual* for details.

Syntax for predict

Random-effects (RE) and conditional fixed-effects (FE) overdispersion models

>   predict [*type*] *newvar* [*if*] [*in*] [, *RE/FE_statistic* <u>nooff</u>set]

Population-averaged (PA) model

>   predict [*type*] *newvar* [*if*] [*in*] [, *PA_statistic* <u>nooff</u>set]

RE/FE_statistic	description
xb	linear prediction; the default
stdp	standard error of the linear prediction
nu0	predicted number of events; assuming fixed or random effect is zero
iru0	predicted incidence rate; assuming fixed or random effect is zero

PA_statistic	description
mu	predicted value of *depvar*; considers the offset(); the default
rate	predicted value of *depvar*
xb	linear prediction
stdp	standard error of the linear prediction
score	first derivative of the log likelihood with respect to $x_j\beta$

These statistics are available both in and out of sample; type predict ... if e(sample) ... if wanted only for the estimation sample.

Options for predict

xb calculates the linear prediction. This is the default for the random-effects and fixed-effects models.

stdp calculates the standard error of the linear prediction.

nu0 calculates the predicted number of events, assuming a zero fixed or random effect.

iru0 calculates the predicted incidence rate, assuming a zero fixed or random effect.

mu and rate both calculate the predicted value of *depvar* (i.e., the predicted count). mu takes into account the offset(), and rate ignores those adjustments. mu and rate are equivalent if you did not specify offset(). mu is the default for the population-averaged model.

score calculates the equation-level score, $u_j = \partial \ln L_j(x_j\beta)/\partial(x_j\beta)$.

nooffset is relevant only if you specified offset(*varname*) for xtnbreg. It modifies the calculations made by predict so that they ignore the offset variable; the linear prediction is treated as $x_{it}\beta$ rather than $x_{it}\beta + \text{offset}_{it}$.

Methods and Formulas

All postestimation commands listed above are implemented as ado-files.

Also See

Complementary:	[XT] **xtnbreg**,
	[R] **adjust**, [R] **estimates**, [R] **lincom**, [R] **lrtest**, [R] **mfx**,
	[R] **nlcom**, [R] **predictnl**, [R] **test**, [R] **testnl**
Background:	[U] **13.5 Accessing coefficients and standard errors**,
	[U] **20 Estimation and postestimation commands**,
	[R] **estat**, [R] **predict**

Title

> **xtpcse** — OLS or Prais–Winsten models with panel-corrected standard errors

Syntax

xtpcse *depvar* [*indepvars*] [*if*] [*in*] [*weight*] [, *options*]

options	description
Model	
noconstant	suppress constant term
correlation(**independent**)	use independent autocorrelation structure
correlation(**ar**1)	use AR1 autocorrelation structure
correlation(**psar**1)	use panel-specific AR1 autocorrelation structure
rhotype(*calc*)	specify method to compute autocorrelation parameter; seldom used
np1	weight panel-specific autocorrelations by panel sizes
hetonly	assume panel-level heteroskedastic errors
independent	assume independent errors across panels
by/if/in	
casewise	include only observations with complete cases
pairwise	include all available observations with nonmissing pairs
SE	
nmk	normalize standard errors by $N - k$ instead of N
Reporting	
level(#)	set confidence level; default is level(95)
detail	report list of gaps in time series

You must tsset your data before using xtpcse; see [TS] **tsset**.

depvar and *indepvars* may contain time-series operators; see [U] **11.4.3 Time-series varlists**.

bootstrap, by, jackknife, statsby, and xi may be used with xtpcse; see [U] **11.1.10 Prefix commands**.

iweights and aweights are allowed; see [U] **11.1.6 weight**.

See [U] **20 Estimation and postestimation commands** for additional capabilities of estimation commands.

Description

xtpcse calculates panel-corrected standard error (PCSE) estimates for linear cross-sectional time-series models where the parameters are estimated by either OLS or Prais–Winsten regression. When computing the standard errors and the variance–covariance estimates, xtpcse assumes that the disturbances are, by default, heteroskedastic and contemporaneously correlated across panels.

See [XT] **xtgls** for the generalized least-squares estimator for these models.

Options

noconstant; see [XT] **estimation options**.

correlation(*corr*) specifies the form of assumed autocorrelation within panels.

correlation(independent), the default, specifies that there is no autocorrelation.

correlation(ar1) specifies that, within panels, there is first-order autocorrelation AR(1) and that the coefficient of the AR(1) process is common to all the panels.

correlation(psar1) specifies that, within panels, there is first-order autocorrelation and that the coefficient of the AR(1) process is specific to each panel. psar1 stands for panel-specific AR(1).

rhotype(*calc*) specifies the method to be used to calculate the autocorrelation parameter. Allowed for *calc* are

regress	regression using lags; the default
freg	regression using leads
tscorr	time-series autocorrelation calculation
dw	Durbin–Watson calculation

All above methods are consistent and asymptotically equivalent; this is a rarely used option.

np1 specifies that the panel-specific autocorrelations be weighted by T_i rather than by the default $T_i - 1$ when estimating a common ρ for all panels, where T_i is the number of observations in panel i. This option has an effect only when panels are unbalanced and option correlation(ar1) is specified.

hetonly and independent specify alternative forms for the assumed covariance of the disturbances across the panels. If neither is specified, the disturbances are assumed to be heteroskedastic (each panel has its own variance) and contemporaneously correlated across the panels (each pair of panels has its own covariance). This is the standard PCSE model.

hetonly specifies that the disturbances are assumed to be panel-level heteroskedastic only with no contemporaneous correlation across panels.

independent specifies that the disturbances are assumed to be independent across panels; that is, there is a single disturbance variance common to all observations.

casewise and pairwise specify how missing observations in unbalanced panels are to be treated when estimating the interpanel covariance matrix of the disturbances. The default is casewise selection.

casewise specifies that the entire covariance matrix be computed only on the observations (time periods) that are available for all panels. If an observation has missing data, all observations of that time period are excluded when estimating the covariance matrix of disturbances. Specifying casewise ensures that the estimated covariance matrix will be of full rank and will be positive definite.

pairwise specifies that, for each element in the covariance matrix, all available observations (time periods) that are common to the two panels contributing to the covariance be used to compute the covariance.

Options casewise and pairwise have an effect only when the panels are unbalanced and neither hetonly nor independent is specified.

⌐ SE ⌐

nmk specifies that standard errors be normalized by $N - k$, where k is the number of parameters estimated, rather than N, the number of observations. Different authors have used one or the other normalization. Greene (2003, 322) recommends N and notes that using N or $N - k$ does not make the variance calculation unbiased in these models.

⌐ Reporting ⌐

level(#); see [XT] **estimation options**.

detail specifies that a detailed list of any gaps in the series be reported.

Remarks

xtpcse is an alternative to feasible generalized least squares (FGLS)—see [XT] **xtgls**—for fitting linear cross-sectional time-series models when the disturbances are not assumed to be independent and identically distributed (i.i.d.). Instead, the disturbances are assumed to be either heteroskedastic across panels or heteroskedastic and contemporaneously correlated across panels. The disturbances may also be assumed to be autocorrelated within panel, and the autocorrelation parameter may be constant across panels or different for each panel.

We can write such models as

$$y_{it} = \mathbf{x}_{it}\boldsymbol{\beta} + \epsilon_{it}$$

where $i = 1, \ldots, m$ is the number of units (or panels); $t = 1, \ldots, T_i$; T_i is the number of time periods in panel i; and ϵ_{it} is a disturbance that may be autocorrelated along t or contemporaneously correlated across i.

This model can also be written panel by panel as

$$\begin{bmatrix} \mathbf{y}_1 \\ \mathbf{y}_2 \\ \vdots \\ \mathbf{y}_m \end{bmatrix} = \begin{bmatrix} \mathbf{X}_1 \\ \mathbf{X}_2 \\ \vdots \\ \mathbf{X}_m \end{bmatrix} \boldsymbol{\beta} + \begin{bmatrix} \epsilon_1 \\ \epsilon_2 \\ \vdots \\ \epsilon_m \end{bmatrix}$$

For a model with heteroskedastic disturbances and contemporaneous correlation but with no autocorrelation, the disturbance covariance matrix is assumed to be

$$E[\epsilon\epsilon'] = \boldsymbol{\Omega} = \begin{bmatrix} \sigma_{11}\mathbf{I}_{11} & \sigma_{12}\mathbf{I}_{12} & \cdots & \sigma_{1m}\mathbf{I}_{1m} \\ \sigma_{21}\mathbf{I}_{21} & \sigma_{22}\mathbf{I}_{22} & \cdots & \sigma_{2m}\mathbf{I}_{2m} \\ \vdots & \vdots & \ddots & \vdots \\ \sigma_{m1}\mathbf{I}_{m1} & \sigma_{m2}\mathbf{I}_{m2} & \cdots & \sigma_{mm}\mathbf{I}_{mm} \end{bmatrix}$$

where σ_{ii} is the variance of the disturbances for panel i, σ_{ij} is the covariance of the disturbances between panel i and panel j when the panels' time periods are matched, and $\mathbf{I}$ is a T_i by T_i identity matrix with balanced panels. Note that the panels need not be balanced for xtpcse, but the expression for the covariance of the disturbances will be more general if they are unbalanced.

This could also be written as

$$E(\epsilon'\epsilon) = \boldsymbol{\Sigma}_{m \times m} \otimes \mathbf{I}_{T_i \times T_i}$$

where $\boldsymbol{\Sigma}$ is the panel-by-panel covariance matrix and $\mathbf{I}$ is an identity matrix.

See [XT] **xtgls** for a full taxonomy and description of possible disturbance covariance structures.

`xtpcse` and `xtgls` follow two different estimation schemes for this family of models. `xtpcse` produces OLS estimates of the parameters when no autocorrelation is specified, or Prais–Winsten (see [TS] **prais**) estimates when autocorrelation is specified. If autocorrelation is specified, the estimates of the parameters are conditional on the estimates of the autocorrelation parameter(s). The estimate of the variance–covariance matrix of the parameters is asymptotically efficient under the assumed covariance structure of the disturbances and uses the FGLS estimate of the disturbance covariance matrix; see Kmenta (1997, 121).

`xtgls` produces full FGLS parameter and variance–covariance estimates. These estimates are conditional on the estimates of the disturbance covariance matrix and are conditional on any autocorrelation parameters that are estimated; see Kmenta (1997), Greene (2003), Davidson and MacKinnon (1993), or Judge et al. (1985).

Both estimators are consistent, as long as the conditional mean ($\mathbf{x}_{it}\boldsymbol{\beta}$) is correctly specified. If the assumed covariance structure is correct, FGLS estimates produced by `xtgls` are more efficient. Beck and Katz (1995) have shown, however, that the full FGLS variance–covariance estimates are typically unacceptably optimistic (anti-conservative) when used with the type of data analyzed by most social scientists—10 to 20 panels with 10 to 40 time periods per panel. They show that the OLS or Prais–Winsten estimates with PCSEs have coverage probabilities that are closer to nominal.

Since the covariance matrix elements, σ_{ij}, are estimated from panels i and j using those observations that have common time periods, estimators for this model achieve their asymptotic behavior as the T_is approach infinity. In contrast, the random- and fixed-effects estimators assume a different model and are asymptotic in the number of panels m; see [XT] **xtreg** for details of the random- and fixed-effects estimators.

Although `xtpcse` allows other disturbance covariance structures, the term PCSE, as used in the literature, refers specifically to models that are both heteroskedastic and contemporaneously correlated across panels, with or without autocorrelation.

▷ Example 1

Grunfeld and Griliches (1960) analyzed a company's current-year gross investment (`invest`) as determined by the company's prior year market value (`mvalue`) and the prior year's value of the company's plant and equipment (`kstock`). The dataset includes five companies over twenty years, from 1935 through 1954, and is a classic dataset for demonstrating cross-sectional time-series analysis. Greene (2003, 329) reproduces the dataset.

To use `xtpcse`, the data must be organized in "long form"; that is, each observation must represent a record for a specific company at a specific time; see [D] **reshape**. In the Grunfeld data, `company` is a categorical variable identifying the company, and `year` is a variable recording the year. Here are the first few records:

```
. use http://www.stata-press.com/data/r9/grunfeld
. list in 1/5
```

	company	year	invest	mvalue	kstock	time
1.	1	1935	317.6	3078.5	2.8	1
2.	1	1936	391.8	4661.7	52.6	2
3.	1	1937	410.6	5387.1	156.9	3
4.	1	1938	257.7	2792.2	209.2	4
5.	1	1939	330.8	4313.2	203.4	5

To compute PCSEs, Stata must be able to identify the panel to which each observation belongs and be able to match the time periods across the panels. We tell Stata how to do this matching by specifying the time and panel variables using `tsset`; see [TS] **tsset**. Since the data are annual, we specify the `yearly` option.

```
. tsset company year, yearly
        panel variable:  company, 1 to 10
         time variable:  year, 1935 to 1954
```

We can obtain OLS parameter estimates for a linear model of `invest` on `mvalue` and `kstock` while allowing the standard errors (and variance–covariance matrix of the estimates) to be consistent when the disturbances from each observation are not independent. Specifically, we want the standard errors to be robust to each company having a different variance of the disturbances and to each company's observations being correlated with those of the other companies through time.

This model is fitted in Stata by typing

```
. xtpcse invest mvalue kstock

Linear regression, correlated panels corrected standard errors (PCSEs)

Group variable:   company                Number of obs      =       200
Time variable:    year                   Number of groups   =        10
Panels:           correlated (balanced)  Obs per group: min =        20
Autocorrelation:  no autocorrelation                    avg =        20
                                                        max =        20
Estimated covariances      =        55   R-squared          =    0.8124
Estimated autocorrelations =         0   Wald chi2(2)       =    637.41
Estimated coefficients     =         3   Prob > chi2        =    0.0000
```

	Coef.	Panel-corrected Std. Err.	z	P>|z|	[95% Conf. Interval]	
mvalue	.1155622	.0072124	16.02	0.000	.101426	.1296983
kstock	.2306785	.0278862	8.27	0.000	.1760225	.2853345
_cons	-42.71437	6.780965	-6.30	0.000	-56.00482	-29.42392

◁

▷ Example 2

`xtgls` will produce more efficient FGLS estimates of the models' parameters, but with the disadvantage that the standard error estimates are conditional on the estimated disturbance covariance. Beck and Katz (1995) argue that the improvement in power using FGLS with such data is small and that the standard error estimates from FGLS are unacceptably optimistic (anti-conservative).

The FGLS model is fitted by typing

```
. xtgls invest mvalue kstock, panels(correlated)

Cross-sectional time-series FGLS regression

Coefficients:  generalized least squares
Panels:        heteroskedastic with cross-sectional correlation
Correlation:   no autocorrelation

Estimated covariances      =         55      Number of obs      =        200
Estimated autocorrelations =          0      Number of groups   =         10
Estimated coefficients     =          3      Time periods       =         20
                                             Wald chi2(2)       =    3738.07
Log likelihood             =  -879.4274      Prob > chi2        =     0.0000
```

invest	Coef.	Std. Err.	z	P>|z|	[95% Conf. Interval]
mvalue	.1127515	.0022364	50.42	0.000	.1083683 .1171347
kstock	.2231176	.0057363	38.90	0.000	.2118746 .2343605
_cons	-39.84382	1.717563	-23.20	0.000	-43.21018 -36.47746

The coefficients between the two models are very close; the constants differ substantially, but we are generally not interested in the constant. As Beck and Katz observed, the standard errors for the FGLS model are 50 to 100% smaller than those for the OLS model with PCSE.

If we were also concerned about autocorrelation of the disturbances, we could obtain a model with a common AR(1) parameter by specifying `correlation(ar1)`.

```
. xtpcse invest mvalue kstock, correlation(ar1)
(note: estimates of rho outside [-1,1] bounded to be in the range [-1,1])

Prais-Winsten regression, correlated panels corrected standard errors (PCSEs)

Group variable:   company              Number of obs      =        200
Time variable:    year                 Number of groups   =         10
Panels:           correlated (balanced) Obs per group: min =        20
Autocorrelation:  common AR(1)                        avg =         20
                                                      max =         20
Estimated covariances      =         55      R-squared          =     0.5468
Estimated autocorrelations =          1      Wald chi2(2)       =      93.71
Estimated coefficients     =          3      Prob > chi2        =     0.0000
```

	Panel-corrected Coef.	Std. Err.	z	P>|z|	[95% Conf. Interval]
mvalue	.0950157	.0129934	7.31	0.000	.0695492 .1204822
kstock	.306005	.0603718	5.07	0.000	.1876784 .4243317
_cons	-39.12569	30.50355	-1.28	0.200	-98.91154 20.66016
rho	.9059774				

The estimate of the autocorrelation parameter is high (.926), and the standard errors are larger than for the model without autocorrelation, which is to be expected if there is autocorrelation.

◁

▷ Example 3

Let's estimate panel-specific autocorrelation parameters and change the method of estimating the autocorrelation parameter to the one typically used to estimate autocorrelation in time-series analysis.

```
. xtpcse invest mvalue kstock, correlation(psar1) rhotype(tscorr)

Prais-Winsten regression, correlated panels corrected standard errors (PCSEs)

Group variable:    company                Number of obs      =        200
Time variable:     year                   Number of groups   =         10
Panels:            correlated (balanced)  Obs per group: min =         20
Autocorrelation:   panel-specific AR(1)                  avg =         20
                                                          max =         20
Estimated covariances      =        55    R-squared          =     0.8670
Estimated autocorrelations =        10    Wald chi2(2)       =     444.53
Estimated coefficients     =         3    Prob > chi2        =     0.0000
```

	Coef.	Panel-corrected Std. Err.	z	P>|z|	[95% Conf. Interval]	
mvalue	.1052613	.0086018	12.24	0.000	.0884021	.1221205
kstock	.3386743	.0367568	9.21	0.000	.2666322	.4107163
_cons	-58.18714	12.63687	-4.60	0.000	-82.95496	-33.41933

```
     rhos =   .5135627    .87017  .9023497    .63368  .8571502 ...  .8752707
```

Beck and Katz (1995, 121) make a case against estimating panel-specific AR parameters, as opposed to a single AR parameter for all panels.

◁

▷ Example 4

We can also diverge from PCSEs to estimate standard errors that are panel corrected, but only for panel-level heteroskedasticity; that is, each company has a different variance of the disturbances. Allowing also for autocorrelation, we would type

```
. xtpcse invest mvalue kstock, correlation(ar1) hetonly
(note: estimates of rho outside [-1,1] bounded to be in the range [-1,1])

Prais-Winsten regression, heteroskedastic panels corrected standard errors

Group variable:    company                    Number of obs      =        200
Time variable:     year                       Number of groups   =         10
Panels:            heteroskedastic (balanced) Obs per group: min =         20
Autocorrelation:   common AR(1)                              avg =         20
                                                             max =         20
Estimated covariances      =        10    R-squared          =     0.5468
Estimated autocorrelations =         1    Wald chi2(2)       =      91.72
Estimated coefficients     =         3    Prob > chi2        =     0.0000
```

	Coef.	Het-corrected Std. Err.	z	P>|z|	[95% Conf. Interval]	
mvalue	.0950157	.0130872	7.26	0.000	.0693653	.1206661
kstock	.306005	.061432	4.98	0.000	.1856006	.4264095
_cons	-39.12569	26.16935	-1.50	0.135	-90.41666	12.16529

```
      rho |  .9059774
```

With this specification, we do not obtain what are referred to in the literature as PCSEs. These standard errors are in the same spirit as PCSEs but are from the asymptotic covariance estimates of OLS without allowing for contemporaneous correlation.

◁

Saved Results

xtpcse saves in e():

Scalars

e(N)	number of observations	e(rmse)	root mean squared error
e(N_g)	number of groups	e(g_max)	largest group size
e(n_cf)	number of estimated coefficients	e(g_min)	smallest group size
e(n_cv)	number of estimated covariances	e(g_avg)	average group size
e(n_cr)	number of estimated correlations	e(rc)	return code
e(mss)	model sum of squares	e(chi2)	χ^2
e(df)	degrees of freedom	e(p)	significance
e(df_m)	model degrees of freedom	e(N_gaps)	number of gaps
e(rss)	residual sum of squares	e(n_sigma)	obs used to estimate elements
e(r2)	R-squared		of Sigma

Macros

e(cmd)	xtpcse	e(vcetype)	title used to label Std. Err.
e(depvar)	name of dependent variable	e(chi2type)	Wald; type of model χ^2 test
e(title)	title in estimation output	e(rho)	ρ
e(panels)	contemporaneous covariance structure	e(cons)	noconstant or ""
e(corr)	correlation structure	e(missmeth)	casewise or pairwise
e(rhotype)	type of estimated correlation	e(balance)	balanced or unbalanced
e(ivar)	variable denoting groups	e(properties)	b V
e(tvar)	variable denoting time	e(predict)	program used to implement predict

Matrices

e(b)	coefficient vector	e(Sigma)	$\widehat{\Sigma}$ matrix
e(V)	variance–covariance matrix of the estimators	e(rhomat)	vector of autocorrelation parameter estimates

Functions

e(sample)	marks estimation sample

Methods and Formulas

xtpcse is implemented as an ado-file.

If no autocorrelation is specified, the parameters β are estimated by OLS; see [R] **regress**. If autocorrelation is specified, the parameters β are estimated by Prais–Winsten; see [TS] **prais**.

When autocorrelation with panel-specific coefficients of correlation is specified (by using option correlation(psar1)), each panel-level ρ_i is computed from the residuals of an OLS regression across all panels; see [TS] **prais**. When autocorrelation with a common coefficient of correlation is specified (by using option correlation(ar1)), the common correlation coefficient is computed as

$$\rho = \frac{\rho_1 + \rho_2 + \cdots + \rho_m}{m}$$

where ρ_i is the estimated autocorrelation coefficient for panel i and m is the number of panels.

The covariance of the OLS or Prais–Winsten coefficients is

$$\mathrm{Var}(\boldsymbol{\beta}) = (\mathbf{X}'\mathbf{X})^{-1}\mathbf{X}'\boldsymbol{\Omega}\mathbf{X}(\mathbf{X}'\mathbf{X})^{-1}$$

where $\boldsymbol{\Omega}$ is the full covariance matrix of the disturbances.

When the panels are balanced, we can write $\boldsymbol{\Omega}$ as

$$\boldsymbol{\Omega} = \boldsymbol{\Sigma}_{m \times m} \otimes \mathbf{I}_{T_i \times T_i}$$

where $\boldsymbol{\Sigma}$ is the m by m panel-by-panel covariance matrix of the disturbances; see *Remarks*.

xtpcse estimates the elements of $\boldsymbol{\Sigma}$ as

$$\widehat{\boldsymbol{\Sigma}}_{ij} = \frac{\epsilon_i'\epsilon_j}{T_{ij}}$$

where ϵ_i and ϵ_j are the residuals for panels i and j, respectively, that can be matched by time period, and where T_{ij} is the number of residuals between the panels i and j that can be matched by time period.

When the panels are balanced (each panel has the same number of observations and all time periods are common to all panels), $T_{ij} = T$, where T is the number of observations per panel.

When panels are unbalanced, xtpcse by default uses casewise selection, in which only those residuals from time periods that are common to all panels are used to compute $\widehat{S}_{ij}$. In this case, $T_{ij} = T^*$, where T^* is the number of time periods common to all panels. When pairwise is specified, each $\widehat{S}_{ij}$ is computed using all observations that can be matched by time period between the panels i and j.

Acknowledgment

We would like to thank the following people for helpful comments: Nathaniel Beck, Department of Politics, New York University; Jonathan Katz, Division of the Humanities and Social Science, California Institute of Technology; and Robert John Franzese, Jr., Center for Political Studies, Institute for Social Research, University of Michigan.

References

Beck, N. and J. N. Katz. 1995. What to do (and not to do) with time-series cross-section data. *American Political Science Review* 89: 634–647.

Davidson, R. and J. G. MacKinnon. 1993. *Estimation and Inference in Econometrics.* New York: Oxford University Press.

Greene, W. H. 2003. *Econometric Analysis.* 5th ed. Upper Saddle River, NJ: Prentice Hall.

Grunfeld, Y. and Z. Griliches. 1960. Is aggregation necessarily bad? *Review of Economics and Statistics* 42: 1–13.

Judge, G. G., W. E. Griffiths, R. C. Hill, H. Lütkepohl, and T.-C. Lee. 1985. *The Theory and Practice of Econometrics.* 2nd ed. New York: Wiley.

Kmenta, J. 1997. *Elements of Econometrics.* 2nd ed. Ann Arbor: University of Michigan Press.

Also See

Complementary:	[XT] **xtpcse postestimation**; [XT] **xtdata**, [XT] **xtdes**, [XT] **xtsum**, [XT] **xttab**, [TS] **tsset**
Related:	[XT] **xtgls**, [XT] **xtreg**, [XT] **xtregar**, [R] **regress**, [TS] **newey**, [TS] **prais**
Background:	[U] **11.1.10 Prefix commands**, [U] **20 Estimation and postestimation commands**, [XT] **estimation options**, [XT] **xt**

Title

> **xtpcse postestimation** — Postestimation tools for xtpcse

Description

The following postestimation commands are available for `xtpcse`:

command	description
adjust[1]	adjusted predictions of $\mathbf{x}\beta$
estat	VCE and estimation sample summary
estimates	cataloging estimation results
lincom	point estimates, standard errors, testing, and inference for linear combinations of coefficients
mfx	marginal effects or elasticities
nlcom	point estimates, standard errors, testing, and inference for nonlinear combinations of coefficients
predict	predictions, residuals, influence statistics, and other diagnostic measures
predictnl	point estimates, standard errors, testing, and inference for generalized predictions
test	Wald tests for simple and composite linear hypotheses
testnl	Wald tests of nonlinear hypotheses

[1] `adjust` does not work with time-series operators.

See the corresponding entries in the *Stata Base Reference Manual* for details.

Syntax for predict

predict [*type*] *newvar* [*if*] [*in*] [, [xb|stdp]]

These statistics are available both in and out of sample; type `predict ... if e(sample) ...` if wanted only for the estimation sample.

Options for predict

`xb`, the default, calculates the linear prediction.

`stdp` calculates the standard error of the linear prediction.

Methods and Formulas

All postestimation commands listed above are implemented as ado-files.

Also See

Complementary:	[XT] **xtpcse**,
	[R] **adjust**, [R] **estimates**, [R] **lincom**, [R] **mfx**, [R] **nlcom**,
	[R] **predictnl**, [R] **test**, [R] **testnl**
Background:	[U] **13.5 Accessing coefficients and standard errors**,
	[U] **20 Estimation and postestimation commands**,
	[R] **estat**, [R] **predict**

Title

> **xtpoisson** — Fixed-effects, random-effects, and population-averaged Poisson models

Syntax

Random-effects (RE) model

> xtpoisson *depvar* [*indepvars*] [*if*] [*in*] [*weight*] [, re *RE_options*]

Conditional fixed-effects (FE) model

> xtpoisson *depvar* [*indepvars*] [*if*] [*in*] [*weight*] , fe [*FE_options*]

Population-averaged (PA) model

> xtpoisson *depvar* [*indepvars*] [*if*] [*in*] [*weight*] , pa [*PA_options*]

RE_options	description
Model	
i(*varname$_i$*)	use *varname$_i$* as the panel ID variable
noconstant	suppress constant term
re	use random-effects estimator; the default
exposure(*varname*)	include ln(*varname*) in model with coefficient constrained to 1
offset(*varname*)	include *varname* in model with coefficient constrained to 1
normal	use a normal distribution for random effects instead of gamma
constraints(*constraints*)	apply specified linear constraints
Int opts (RE)	
intmethod(*intmethod*)	integration method; *intmethod* may be aghermite or ghermite
intpoints(*#*)	use *#* quadrature points; default is intpoints(12)
SE	
vce(*vcetype*)	*vcetype* may be bootstrap or jackknife
Reporting	
level(*#*)	set confidence level; default is level(95)
irr	report incidence-rate ratios
noskip	perform overall model test as a likelihood-ratio test
Max options	
maximize_options	control the maximization process; seldom used

FE_options	description
Model	
i(*varname_i*)	use *varname_i* as the panel ID variable
fe	use fixed-effects estimator
<u>exp</u>osure(*varname*)	include ln(*varname*) in model with coefficient constrained to 1
<u>off</u>set(*varname*)	include *varname* in model with coefficient constrained to 1
<u>constraints</u>(*constraints*)	apply specified linear constraints
SE	
vce(*vcetype*)	*vcetype* may be <u>boot</u>strap or jackknife
Reporting	
<u>l</u>evel(*#*)	set confidence level; default is level(95)
irr	report incidence-rate ratios
noskip	perform overall model test as a likelihood-ratio test
Max options	
maximize_options	control the maximization process; seldom used

PA_options	description
Model	
i(*varname_i*)	use *varname_i* as the panel ID variable
<u>nocons</u>tant	suppress constant term
pa	use population-averaged estimator
<u>exp</u>osure(*varname*)	include ln(*varname*) in model with coefficient constrained to 1
<u>off</u>set(*varname*)	include *varname* in model with coefficient constrained to 1
Correlation	
<u>corr</u>(*correlation*)	within-group correlation structure
force	estimate if observations unequally spaced in time
SE/Robust	
vce(*vcetype*)	*vcetype* may be <u>r</u>obust, <u>boot</u>strap, or jackknife
<u>r</u>obust	synonym for vce(robust)
<u>s</u>cale(x2)	set scale parameter to Pearson chi-squared statistic
<u>s</u>cale(dev)	set scale parameter to deviance divided by degrees of freedom
<u>s</u>cale(phi)	do not rescale the variance
<u>s</u>cale(*#*)	set scale parameter to *#*
nmp	use divisor $N - P$ instead of the default N
Reporting	
<u>l</u>evel(*#*)	set confidence level; default is level(95)
irr	report incidence-rate ratios
Opt options	
optimize_options	control the optimization process; seldom used

correlation	description
exchangeable	exchangeable
independent	independent
unstructured	unstructured
fixed *matname*	user-specified
ar #	autoregressive
stationary #	stationary
nonstationary #	nonstationary

depvar and *indepvars* may contain time-series operators; see [U] **11.4.3 Time-series varlists**.

bootstrap, by, jackknife, statsby, and xi may be used with xtpoisson; see [U] **11.1.10 Prefix commands**.

iweights, fweights, and pweights are allowed for the population-averaged model and iweights are
   allowed in the random-effects and fixed-effects models; see [U] **11.1.6 weight**. Weights must be constant within panels.

See [U] **20 Estimation and postestimation commands** for additional capabilities of estimation commands.

Description

   xtpoisson fits random-effects, conditional fixed-effects, and population-averaged Poisson models. Whenever we refer to a fixed-effects model, we mean the conditional fixed-effects model.

   xtpoisson, re normal is slow since the likelihood function is calculated by adaptive Gauss–Hermite quadrature; see *Methods and Formulas*. Computation time is roughly proportional to the number of points used for the quadrature. The default is intpoints(12). Simulations indicate that increasing the number of points does not appreciably change the estimates for the coefficients or their standard errors. See [XT] **quadchk**.

   By default, the population-averaged model is an equal-correlation model; xtpoisson, pa assumes corr(exchangeable). See [XT] **xtgee** for information on how to fit other population-averaged models.

Options for RE model

Model

i(*varname$_i$*), noconstant; see [XT] **estimation options**.

re, the default, requests the random-effects estimator.

exposure(*varname*), offset(*varname*),

normal specifies that the random effects follow a normal distribution instead of a gamma distribution.

constraints(*constraints*); see [XT] **estimation options**.

Int opts (RE)

intmethod(*intmethod*) specifies the integration method to be used for the random-effects model. It accepts one of two arguments: the first is aghermite, the default, which specifies adaptive Gauss–Hermite quadrature; the second is ghermite, which specifies nonadaptive Gauss–Hermite quadrature.

intpoints(#) specifies the number of points to use for Gauss–Hermite quadrature. The default is 12. Increasing this value slightly improves the accuracy but also increases computation time. Computation time is roughly proportional to its value.

SE

vce(*vcetype*); see [R] ***vce_option***.

Reporting

level(*#*); see [XT] **estimation options**.

irr reports exponentiated coefficients e^b rather than coefficients b. For the Poisson model, exponentiated coefficients are interpreted as incidence-rate ratios.

noskip; see [XT] **estimation options**.

Max options

maximize_options: <u>dif</u>ficult, <u>tech</u>nique(*algorithm_spec*), <u>iter</u>ate(*#*), $\boxed{\text{no}}$<u>log</u>, <u>trace</u>, <u>grad</u>ient, <u>showstep</u>, <u>hess</u>ian, <u>shownr</u>tolerance, <u>tol</u>erance(*#*), <u>ltol</u>erance(*#*), <u>gtol</u>erance(*#*), <u>nrtol</u>erance(*#*), <u>nonrtol</u>erance, from(*init_specs*); see [R] **maximize**. Some of these options are not available if intmethod(ghermite) is specified. These options are seldom used.

Options for FE model

Model

i(*varname_i*); see [XT] **estimation options**.

fe requests the fixed-effects estimator.

exposure(*varname*), offset(*varname*), constraints(*constraints*); see [XT] **estimation options**.

SE

vce(*vcetype*); see [R] ***vce_option***.

Reporting

level(*#*); see [XT] **estimation options**.

irr reports exponentiated coefficients e^b rather than coefficients b. For the Poisson model, exponentiated coefficients are interpreted as incidence-rate ratios.

noskip; see [XT] **estimation options**.

Max options

maximize_options: <u>dif</u>ficult, <u>tech</u>nique(*algorithm_spec*), <u>iter</u>ate(*#*), $\boxed{\text{no}}$<u>log</u>, <u>trace</u>, <u>grad</u>ient, <u>showstep</u>, <u>hess</u>ian, <u>shownr</u>tolerance, <u>tol</u>erance(*#*), <u>ltol</u>erance(*#*), <u>gtol</u>erance(*#*), <u>nrtol</u>erance(*#*), <u>nonrtol</u>erance, from(*init_specs*); see [R] **maximize**. These options are seldom used.

Options for PA model

Model

i(*varname_i*), noconstant: see [XT] **estimation options**.

pa requests the population-averaged estimator.

exposure(*varname*), offset(*varname*); see [XT] **estimation options**.

⌐ Correlation ⌐

corr(*correlation*), force; see [XT] **estimation options**.

⌐ SE/Robust ⌐

vce(*vcetype*); see [R] *vce_option*.

robust; see [XT] **estimation options**.

scale(x2 | dev | phi | #) overrides the default scale parameter of scale(1); see [XT] **estimation options**.

nmp; see [XT] **estimation options**.

⌐ Reporting ⌐

level(#); see [XT] **estimation options**.

irr reports exponentiated coefficients e^b rather than coefficients b. For the Poisson model, exponentiated coefficients are interpreted as incidence-rate ratios.

⌐ Opt options ⌐

optimize_options control the iterative optimization process. These options are seldom used.

iterate(#) specifies the maximum number of iterations. When the number of iterations equals #, the optimization stops and presents the current results, even if convergence has not been reached. The default is iterate(100).

tolerance(#) specifies the tolerance for the coefficient vector. When the relative change in the coefficient vector from one iteration to the next is less than or equal to #, the optimization process is stopped. tolerance(1e-6) is the default.

nolog suppresses display of the iteration log.

trace specifies that the current estimates be printed at each iteration.

Remarks

xtpoisson is a convenience command if you want the population-averaged model. Typing

    . xtpoisson ..., ... pa exposure(time)

is equivalent to typing

    . xtgee ..., ... family(poisson) link(log) corr(exchangeable) exposure(time)

Also see [XT] **xtgee** for information about xtpoisson.

By default or when `re` is specified, `xtpoisson` fits via maximum likelihood the random-effects model

$$\Pr(Y_{it} = y_{it}|\mathbf{x}_{it}) = F(y_{it}, \mathbf{x}_{it}\boldsymbol{\beta} + \nu_i)$$

for $i = 1, \ldots, n$ panels, where $t = 1, \ldots, n_i$, and $F(x, z) = \Pr(X = x)$, where X is Poisson distributed with mean $\exp(z)$. In the standard random-effects model, ν_i is assumed to be i.i.d. such that $\exp(\nu_i)$ is gamma with mean one and variance α, which is estimated from the data. If `normal` is specified, ν_i is assumed to be i.i.d. $N(0, \sigma_\nu^2)$.

▷ Example 1

We have data on the number of ship accidents for five different types of ships (McCullagh and Nelder 1989, 205). We wish to analyze whether the "incident" rate is affected by the period in which the ship was constructed and operated. Our measure of exposure is months of service for the ship, and in this model, we assume that the exponentiated random effects are distributed as gamma with mean one and variance α.

```
. use http://www.stata-press.com/data/r9/ships
. xtpoisson accident op_75_79 co_65_69 co_70_74 co_75_79, i(ship) ex(service) irr
Fitting comparison Poisson model:
Iteration 0:   log likelihood = -147.37993
Iteration 1:   log likelihood = -80.372714
Iteration 2:   log likelihood = -80.116093
Iteration 3:   log likelihood = -80.115916
Iteration 4:   log likelihood = -80.115916
Fitting full model:
Iteration 0:   log likelihood = -79.653186
Iteration 1:   log likelihood = -76.990836  (not concave)
Iteration 2:   log likelihood = -74.824942
Iteration 3:   log likelihood = -74.811243
Iteration 4:   log likelihood = -74.811217
Iteration 5:   log likelihood = -74.811217
Random-effects Poisson regression          Number of obs      =         34
Group variable (i) : ship                  Number of groups   =          5
Random effects u_i ~ Gamma                 Obs per group: min =          6
                                                          avg =        6.8
                                                          max =          7
                                           Wald chi2(4)       =      50.90
Log likelihood  = -74.811217               Prob > chi2        =     0.0000
```

accident	IRR	Std. Err.	z	P>|z|	[95% Conf. Interval]
op_75_79	1.466305	.1734005	3.24	0.001	1.162957 1.848777
co_65_69	2.032543	.304083	4.74	0.000	1.515982 2.72512
co_70_74	2.356853	.3999259	5.05	0.000	1.690033 3.286774
co_75_79	1.641913	.3811398	2.14	0.033	1.04174 2.58786
service	(exposure)				
/lnalpha	-2.368406	.8474597			-4.029397 -.7074155
alpha	.0936298	.0793475			.0177851 .4929165

```
Likelihood-ratio test of alpha=0: chibar2(01) =    10.61 Prob>=chibar2 = 0.001
```

The output also includes a likelihood-ratio test of $\alpha = 0$, which compares the panel estimator with the pooled (Poisson) estimator.

We find that the incidence rate for accidents is significantly different for the periods of construction and operation of the ships and that the random-effects model is significantly different from the pooled model.

We may alternatively fit a fixed-effects specification instead of a random-effects specification:

```
. xtpoisson accident op_75_79 co_65_69 co_70_74 co_75_79, i(ship) ex(service)
> irr fe
Iteration 0:   log likelihood = -80.738973
Iteration 1:   log likelihood = -54.857546
Iteration 2:   log likelihood = -54.641897
Iteration 3:   log likelihood = -54.641859
Iteration 4:   log likelihood = -54.641859
Conditional fixed-effects Poisson regression    Number of obs      =        34
Group variable (i): ship                         Number of groups   =         5

                                                 Obs per group: min =         6
                                                                avg =       6.8
                                                                max =         7

                                                 Wald chi2(4)       =     48.44
Log likelihood  = -54.641859                     Prob > chi2        =    0.0000
```

accident	IRR	Std. Err.	z	P>|z|	[95% Conf. Interval]	
op_75_79	1.468831	.1737218	3.25	0.001	1.164926	1.852019
co_65_69	2.008003	.3004803	4.66	0.000	1.497577	2.692398
co_70_74	2.26693	.384865	4.82	0.000	1.625274	3.161912
co_75_79	1.573695	.3669393	1.94	0.052	.9964273	2.485397
service	(exposure)					

Both of these models fit the same thing but will differ in efficiency, depending on whether the assumptions of the random-effects model are true.

Note that we could have assumed that the random effects followed a normal distribution, $N(0, \sigma_\nu^2)$, instead of a "log-gamma" distribution, and obtained

```
. xtpoisson accident op_75_79 co_65_69 co_70_74 co_75_79, i(ship) ex(service)
> irr normal nolog
Random-effects Poisson regression               Number of obs      =        34
Group variable (i): ship                         Number of groups   =         5

Random effects u_i ~ Gaussian                    Obs per group: min =         6
                                                                avg =       6.8
                                                                max =         7

                                                 LR chi2(4)         =     55.25
Log likelihood  = -74.781731                     Prob > chi2        =    0.0000
```

accident	IRR	Std. Err.	z	P>|z|	[95% Conf. Interval]	
op_75_79	1.466695	.173441	3.24	0.001	1.163276	1.849255
co_65_69	2.032729	.3040807	4.74	0.000	1.516164	2.72529
co_70_74	2.357714	.3992821	5.06	0.000	1.691761	3.285816
co_75_79	1.647449	.3817246	2.15	0.031	1.046124	2.594423
service	(exposure)					
/lnsig2u	-2.353033	.8583269	-2.74	0.006	-4.035323	-.6707431
sigma_u	.308351	.132333			.1329661	.7150724

```
Likelihood-ratio test of sigma_u=0: chibar2(01) =    10.67 Pr>=chibar2 = 0.001
```

The output includes the additional panel-level variance component. This is parameterized as the log of the variance $\ln(\sigma_\nu^2)$ (labeled lnsig2u in the output). The standard deviation σ_ν is also included in the output labeled sigma_u.

When sigma_u is zero, the panel-level variance component is unimportant and the panel estimator is no different from the pooled estimator. A likelihood-ratio test of this is included at the bottom of the output. This test formally compares the pooled estimator (poisson) with the panel estimator. In this case, σ_ν is significantly greater than zero, so a panel estimator is indicated.

◁

▷ Example 2

We rerun our previous example, but this time we fit a robust equal-correlation population-averaged model:

```
. xtpoisson accident op_75_79 co_65_69 co_70_74 co_75_79, i(ship) ex(service)
> pa robust eform

Iteration 1: tolerance = .04083192
Iteration 2: tolerance = .00270188
Iteration 3: tolerance = .00030663
Iteration 4: tolerance = .00003466
Iteration 5: tolerance = 3.891e-06
Iteration 6: tolerance = 4.359e-07

GEE population-averaged model          Number of obs      =         34
Group variable:                ship    Number of groups   =          5
Link:                           log    Obs per group: min =          6
Family:                     Poisson                   avg =        6.8
Correlation:            exchangeable                  max =          7
                                       Wald chi2(3)       =     181.55
Scale parameter:                  1    Prob > chi2        =     0.0000

                          (Std. Err. adjusted for clustering on ship)
```

accident	IRR	Semi-robust Std. Err.	z	P>|z|	[95% Conf. Interval]	
op_75_79	1.483299	.1197901	4.88	0.000	1.266153	1.737685
co_65_69	2.038477	.1809524	8.02	0.000	1.712955	2.425059
co_70_74	2.643467	.4093947	6.28	0.000	1.951407	3.580962
co_75_79	1.876656	.33075	3.57	0.000	1.328511	2.650966
service	(exposure)					

We may compare this with a pooled estimator with clustered robust-variance estimates:

(Continued on next page)

```
. poisson accident op_75_79 co_65_69 co_70_74 co_75_79, ex(service) robust
> cluster(ship) irr

Iteration 0:   log pseudolikelihood = -147.37993
Iteration 1:   log pseudolikelihood = -80.372714
Iteration 2:   log pseudolikelihood = -80.116093
Iteration 3:   log pseudolikelihood = -80.115916
Iteration 4:   log pseudolikelihood = -80.115916

Poisson regression                              Number of obs   =         34
                                                Wald chi2(3)    =          .
Log pseudolikelihood = -80.115916               Prob > chi2     =          .

                     (Std. Err. adjusted for 5 clusters in ship)
```

accident	IRR	Robust Std. Err.	z	P>|z|	[95% Conf. Interval]	
op_75_79	1.47324	.1287036	4.44	0.000	1.2414	1.748377
co_65_69	2.125914	.2850531	5.62	0.000	1.634603	2.764897
co_70_74	2.860138	.6213563	4.84	0.000	1.868384	4.378325
co_75_79	2.021926	.4265285	3.34	0.001	1.337221	3.057227
service	(exposure)					

◁

(Continued on next page)

Saved Results

xtpoisson, re saves in e():

Scalars

e(N)	# of observations	e(sigma_u)	panel-level standard deviation
e(N_g)	# of groups	e(alpha)	the value of alpha
e(N_cd)	# of completely determined obs.	e(k)	# of parameters
e(df_m)	model degrees of freedom	e(k_eq)	# of equations
e(ll)	log likelihood	e(k_dv)	# of dependent variables
e(ll_0)	log likelihood, constant-only model	e(p)	significance
e(ll_c)	log likelihood, comparison model	e(rank)	rank of e(V)
e(g_max)	largest group size	e(rank0)	rank of e(V) for constant-only model
e(g_min)	smallest group size	e(ic)	# of iterations
e(g_avg)	average group size	e(rc)	return code
e(chi2)	χ^2	e(converged)	1 if converged, 0 otherwise
e(chi2_c)	χ^2 for comparison test		

Macros

e(cmd)	xtpoisson	e(distrib)	Gamma; the distribution of the
e(depvar)	name of dependent variable		random effect
e(title)	title in estimation output	e(vce)	*vcetype* specified in vce()
e(ivar)	variable denoting groups	e(vcetype)	title used to label Std. Err.
e(wtype)	weight type	e(opt)	type of optimization
e(wexp)	weight expression	e(ml_method)	type of ml method
e(offset)	offset	e(user)	name of likelihood-evaluator program
e(chi2type)	Wald or LR; type of model χ^2 test	e(technique)	maximization technique
e(chi2_ct)	Wald or LR; type of model χ^2 test	e(crittype)	optimization criterion
	corresponding to e(chi2_c)	e(properties)	b V
e(method)	requested estimation method	e(predict)	program used to implement predict

Matrices

e(b)	coefficient vector	e(ilog)	iteration log
e(V)	variance–covariance matrix of the estimators	e(gradient)	gradient vector

Functions

e(sample)	marks estimation sample

(Continued on next page)

`xtpoisson, re normal` saves in `e()`:

Scalars

e(N)	# of observations	e(sigma_u)	panel-level standard deviation
e(N_g)	# of groups	e(n_quad)	# of quadrature points
e(N_cd)	# of completely determined obs.	e(k)	# of parameters
e(df_m)	model degrees of freedom	e(k_eq)	# of equations
e(ll)	log likelihood	e(k_dv)	# of dependent variables
e(ll_0)	log likelihood, constant-only model	e(p)	significance
e(ll_c)	log likelihood, comparison model	e(rank)	rank of e(V)
e(g_max)	largest group size	e(rank0)	rank of e(V) for constant-only model
e(g_min)	smallest group size	e(ic)	# of iterations
e(g_avg)	average group size	e(rc)	return code
e(chi2)	χ^2	e(converged)	1 if converged, 0 otherwise
e(chi2_c)	χ^2 for comparison test		

Macros

e(cmd)	xtpoisson	e(distrib)	Gaussian; the distribution of the random effect
e(depvar)	name of dependent variable		
e(title)	title in estimation output	e(vce)	*vcetype* specified in vce()
e(ivar)	variable denoting groups	e(vcetype)	title used to label Std. Err.
e(wtype)	weight type	e(opt)	type of optimization
e(wexp)	weight expression	e(ml_method)	type of ml method
e(offset)	offset	e(user)	name of likelihood-evaluator program
e(chi2type)	Wald or LR; type of model χ^2 test	e(technique)	maximization technique
e(chi2_ct)	Wald or LR; type of model χ^2 test corresponding to e(chi2_c)	e(crittype)	optimization criterion
		e(properties)	b V
e(intmethod)	integration method	e(predict)	program used to implement predict

Matrices

e(b)	coefficient vector	e(ilog)	iteration log
e(V)	variance–covariance matrix of the estimators	e(gradient)	gradient vector

Functions

e(sample)	marks estimation sample

`xtpoisson, fe` saves in `e()`:

Scalars

e(N)	number of observations	e(k)	# of parameters
e(N_g)	number of groups	e(k_eq)	# of equations
e(df_m)	model degrees of freedom	e(k_dv)	# of dependent variables
e(ll)	log likelihood	e(p)	significance
e(ll_0)	log likelihood, constant-only model	e(rank)	rank of e(V)
e(g_max)	largest group size	e(ic)	# of iterations
e(g_min)	smallest group size	e(rc)	return code
e(g_avg)	average group size	e(converged)	1 if converged, 0 otherwise
e(chi2)	χ^2		

Macros

e(cmd)	xtpoisson	e(vcetype)	title used to label Std. Err.
e(depvar)	name of dependent variable	e(opt)	type of optimization
e(title)	title in estimation output	e(ml_method)	type of ml method
e(ivar)	variable denoting groups	e(user)	name of likelihood-evaluator program
e(offset)	offset	e(technique)	maximization technique
e(wtype)	weight type	e(crittype)	optimization criterion
e(wexp)	weight expression	e(properties)	b V
e(chi2type)	LR; type of model χ^2 test	e(predict)	program used to implement predict
e(vce)	*vcetype* specified in vce()		

Matrices

e(b)	coefficient vector	e(ilog)	iteration log
e(V)	variance–covariance matrix of the estimators	e(gradient)	gradient vector

Functions

e(sample)	marks estimation sample

(Continued on next page)

xtpoisson, pa saves in e():

Scalars

e(N)	number of observations	e(chi2_dev)	χ^2 test of deviance
e(N_g)	number of groups	e(chi2_dis)	χ^2 test of deviance dispersion
e(df_m)	model degrees of freedom	e(deviance)	deviance
e(df_pear)	degrees of freedom for Pearson χ^2	e(dispers)	deviance dispersion
e(g_max)	largest group size	e(tol)	target tolerance
e(g_min)	smallest group size	e(dif)	achieved tolerance
e(g_avg)	average group size	e(phi)	scale parameter
e(chi2)	χ^2	e(rc)	return code

Macros

e(cmd)	xtgee	e(ivar)	variable denoting groups
e(cmd2)	xtpoisson	e(vce)	*vcetype* specified in vce()
e(depvar)	name of dependent variable	e(vcetype)	covariance estimation method
e(family)	Poisson	e(chi2type)	Wald; type of model χ^2 test
e(link)	log; link function	e(offset)	offset
e(corr)	correlation structure	e(predict)	program used to implement predict
e(crittype)	optimization criterion	e(properties)	b V
e(scale)	scale parameter x2, dev, phi, or #		

Matrices

e(b)	coefficient vector	e(R)	estimated working correlation matrix
e(V)	variance–covariance matrix of the estimators		

Functions

e(sample)	marks estimation sample

Methods and Formulas

xtpoisson is implemented as an ado-file.

xtpoisson, pa reports the population-averaged results obtained by using xtgee, family(poisson) link(log) to obtain estimates. See [XT] **xtgee** for details about the methods and formulas.

While Hausman, Hall, and Griliches (1984) wrote the seminal article on the random-effects and fixed-effects models, Cameron and Trivedi (1998) provide a good textbook treatment.

For a random-effects specification, we know that

$$\Pr(y_{i1}, \ldots, y_{in_i} | \alpha_i, \mathbf{x}_{i1}, \ldots, \mathbf{x}_{in_i}) = \left(\prod_{t=1}^{n_i} \frac{\lambda_{it}^{y_{it}}}{y_{it}!} \right) \exp \left\{ -\exp(\alpha_i) \sum_{t=1}^{n_i} \lambda_{it} \right\} \exp \left(\alpha_i \sum_{t=1}^{n_i} y_{it} \right)$$

where $\lambda_{it} = \exp(\mathbf{x}_{it}\boldsymbol{\beta})$. We may rewrite the above as (defining $\epsilon_i = \exp(\alpha_i)$)

$$\Pr(y_{i1},\ldots,y_{in_i}|\epsilon_i,\mathbf{x}_{i1},\ldots,\mathbf{x}_{in_i}) = \left\{\prod_{t=1}^{n_i}\frac{(\lambda_{it}\epsilon_i)^{y_{it}}}{y_{it}!}\right\}\exp\left(-\sum_{t=1}^{n_i}\lambda_{it}\epsilon_i\right)$$

$$= \left(\prod_{t=1}^{n_i}\frac{\lambda_{it}^{y_{it}}}{y_{it}!}\right)\exp\left(-\epsilon_i\sum_{t=1}^{n_i}\lambda_{it}\right)\epsilon_i^{\sum_{t=1}^{n_i}y_{it}}$$

We now assume that ϵ_i follows a gamma distribution with mean one and variance θ so that unconditional on ϵ_i

$$\Pr(y_{i1},\ldots,y_{in_i}|\mathbf{X}_i) = \frac{\theta^\theta}{\Gamma(\theta)}\left(\prod_{t=1}^{n_i}\frac{\lambda_{it}^{y_{it}}}{y_{it}!}\right)\int_0^\infty \exp\left(-\epsilon_i\sum_{t=1}^{n_i}\lambda_{it}\right)\epsilon_i^{\sum_{t=1}^{n_i}y_{it}}\epsilon_i^{\theta-1}\exp(-\theta\epsilon_i)d\epsilon_i$$

$$= \frac{\theta^\theta}{\Gamma(\theta)}\left(\prod_{t=1}^{n_i}\frac{\lambda_{it}^{y_{it}}}{y_{it}!}\right)\int_0^\infty \exp\left\{-\epsilon_i\left(\theta+\sum_{t=1}^{n_i}\lambda_{it}\right)\right\}\epsilon_i^{\theta+\sum_{t=1}^{n_i}y_{it}-1}d\epsilon_i$$

$$= \left(\prod_{t=1}^{n_i}\frac{\lambda_{it}^{y_{it}}}{y_{it}!}\right)\frac{\Gamma\left(\theta+\sum_{t=1}^{n_i}y_{it}\right)}{\Gamma(\theta)}\left(\frac{\theta}{\theta+\sum_{t=1}^{n_i}\lambda_{it}}\right)^\theta\left(\frac{1}{\theta+\sum_{t=1}^{n_i}\lambda_{it}}\right)^{\sum_{t=1}^{n_i}y_{it}}$$

for $\mathbf{X}_i = (\mathbf{x}_{i1},\ldots,\mathbf{x}_{in_i})$.

The log likelihood (assuming Gamma heterogeneity) is then derived using

$$u_i = \frac{\theta}{\theta+\sum_{t=1}^{n_i}\lambda_{it}} \qquad \lambda_{it} = \exp(\mathbf{x}_{it}\boldsymbol{\beta})$$

$$\Pr(Y_{i1}=y_{i1},\ldots,Y_{in_i}=y_{in_i}|\mathbf{X}_i) = \frac{\prod_{t=1}^{n_i}\lambda_{it}^{y_{it}}\Gamma\left(\theta+\sum_{t=1}^{n_i}y_{it}\right)}{\prod_{t=1}^{n_i}y_{it}!\Gamma(\theta)\left(\sum_{t=1}^{n_i}\lambda_{it}\right)^{\sum_{t=1}^{n_i}y_{it}}}u_i^\theta(1-u_i)^{\sum_{t=1}^{n_i}y_{it}}$$

such that the log likelihood may be written as

$$L = \sum_{i=1}^n w_i\left\{\log\Gamma\left(\theta+\sum_{t=1}^{n_i}y_{it}\right) - \sum_{t=1}^{n_i}\log\Gamma(1+y_{it}) - \log\Gamma(\theta) + \theta\log u_i\right.$$

$$\left. + \log(1-u_i)\sum_{t=1}^{n_i}y_{it} + \sum_{t=1}^{n_i}y_{it}(\mathbf{x}_{it}\boldsymbol{\beta}) - \left(\sum_{t=1}^{n_i}y_{it}\right)\log\left(\sum_{t=1}^{n_i}\lambda_{it}\right)\right\}$$

where w_i is the user-specified weight for panel i; if no weights are specified, $w_i = 1$.

Alternatively, if we assume a normal distribution, $N(0, \sigma_\nu^2)$, for the random effects ν_i

$$\Pr(y_{i1}, \ldots, y_{in_i}|\mathbf{X}_i) = \int_{-\infty}^{\infty} \frac{e^{-\nu_i^2/2\sigma_\nu^2}}{\sqrt{2\pi}\sigma_\nu} \left\{ \prod_{t=1}^{n_i} F(y_{it}, \mathbf{x}_{it}\boldsymbol{\beta} + \nu_i) \right\} d\nu_i$$

where

$$F(y, z) = \exp\left\{ -\exp(z) + yz - \log(y!) \right\}.$$

The integral can be approximated with M-point Gauss–Hermite quadrature

$$\int_{-\infty}^{\infty} e^{-x^2} g(x) dx \approx \sum_{m=1}^{M} w_m^* g(a_m^*)$$

where the w_m^* denote the quadrature weights and the a_m^* denote the quadrature abscissas. The log likelihood, L, where $\rho = \sigma_\nu^2/(\sigma_\nu^2 + 1)$, is then calculated using the quadrature

$$L = \sum_{i=1}^{n} w_i \log\left\{ \Pr(y_{i1}, \ldots, y_{in_i}|\mathbf{X}_i) \right\}$$

$$\approx \sum_{i=1}^{n} w_i \log \left[\frac{1}{\sqrt{\pi}} \sum_{m=1}^{M} w_m^* \prod_{t=1}^{n_i} F\left\{ y_{it}, \mathbf{x}_{it}\boldsymbol{\beta} + a_m^* \left(\frac{2\rho}{1-\rho} \right)^{1/2} \right\} \right]$$

The above is the formula for nonadaptive Gauss–Hermite quadrature. The default is to calculate the log likelihood, L, using adaptive Gauss–Hermite quadrature, which transforms the integrand

$$g(y_{it}, x_{it}, \nu_i) = \frac{e^{-\nu_i^2/2\sigma_\nu^2}}{\sqrt{2\pi}\sigma_\nu} \left\{ \prod_{t=1}^{n_i} F(y_{it}, \mathbf{x}_{it}\boldsymbol{\beta} + \nu_i) \right\}$$

so that it is sampled on a suitable range; see Liu (1994).

Both quadrature formulas require that the integrated function be well approximated by a polynomial. The number of time periods (panel size) affects whether

$$\prod_{t=1}^{n_i} F(y_{it}, \mathbf{x}_{it}\boldsymbol{\beta} + \nu_i)$$

is well approximated by a polynomial. As panel size (or ρ) increases, the quadrature approximation becomes less accurate. Adaptive quadrature gives better results for correlated data and large panels than nonadaptive quadrature; however we recommend that you use the `quadchk` command to investigate the applicability of the numeric technique used in this command.

For a fixed-effects specification, we know that

$$\Pr(Y_{it} = y_{it}|\mathbf{x}_{it}) = \exp\{-\exp(\alpha_i + \mathbf{x}_{it}\boldsymbol{\beta})\}\exp(\alpha_i + \mathbf{x}_{it}\boldsymbol{\beta})^{y_{it}}/y_{it}!$$

$$= \frac{1}{y_{it}!}\exp\{-\exp(\alpha_i)\exp(\mathbf{x}_{it}\boldsymbol{\beta}) + \alpha_i y_{it}\}\exp(\mathbf{x}_{it}\boldsymbol{\beta})^{y_{it}}$$

$$\equiv F_{it}$$

Since we know that the observations are independent, we may write the joint probability for the observations within a panel as

$$\Pr\left(Y_{i1} = y_{i1}, \ldots, Y_{in_i} = y_{in_i}|\mathbf{X}_i\right)$$

$$= \prod_{t=1}^{n_i}\frac{1}{y_{it}!}\exp\{-\exp(\alpha_i)\exp(\mathbf{x}_{it}\boldsymbol{\beta}) + \alpha_i y_{it}\}\exp(\mathbf{x}_{it}\boldsymbol{\beta})^{y_{it}}$$

$$= \left(\prod_{t=1}^{n_i}\frac{\exp(\mathbf{x}_{it}\boldsymbol{\beta})^{y_{it}}}{y_{it}!}\right)\exp\left\{-\exp(\alpha_i)\sum_t\exp(\mathbf{x}_{it}\boldsymbol{\beta}) + \alpha_i\sum_t y_{it}\right\}$$

and we also know that the sum of n_i Poisson independent random variables, each with parameter λ_{it} for $t = 1, \ldots, n_i$, is distributed as Poisson with parameter $\sum_t \lambda_{it}$. Thus

$$\Pr\left(\sum_t Y_{it} = \sum_t y_{it}\bigg|\mathbf{X}_i\right) =$$

$$\frac{1}{(\sum_t y_{it})!}\exp\left\{-\exp(\alpha_i)\sum_t\exp(\mathbf{x}_{it}\boldsymbol{\beta}) + \alpha_i\sum_t y_{it}\right\}\left\{\sum_t\exp(\mathbf{x}_{it}\boldsymbol{\beta})\right\}^{\sum_t y_{it}}$$

So, the conditional likelihood is conditioned on the sum of the outcomes in the set (panel). The appropriate function is given by

$$\Pr\left(Y_{i1} = y_{i1}, \ldots, Y_{in_i} = y_{in_i}\bigg|\mathbf{X}_i, \sum_t Y_{it} = \sum_t y_{it}\right) =$$

$$\left[\left(\prod_{t=1}^{n_i}\frac{\exp(\mathbf{x}_{it}\boldsymbol{\beta})^{y_{it}}}{y_{it}!}\right)\exp\left\{-\exp(\alpha_i)\sum_t\exp(\mathbf{x}_{it}\boldsymbol{\beta}) + \alpha_i\sum_t y_{it}\right\}\right] \Big/$$

$$\left[\frac{1}{(\sum_t y_{it})!}\exp\left\{-\exp(\alpha_i)\sum_t\exp(\mathbf{x}_{it}\boldsymbol{\beta}) + \alpha_i\sum_t y_{it}\right\}\left\{\sum_t\exp(\mathbf{x}_{it}\boldsymbol{\beta})\right\}^{\sum_t y_{it}}\right]$$

$$= \left(\sum_t y_{it}\right)!\prod_{t=1}^{n_i}\frac{\exp(\mathbf{x}_{it}\boldsymbol{\beta})^{y_{it}}}{y_{it}!\{\sum_k\exp(\mathbf{x}_{ik}\boldsymbol{\beta})\}^{y_{it}}}$$

which is free of α_i.

The conditional log likelihood is given by

$$
L = \log \prod_{i=1}^{n} \left[\left(\sum_{t=1}^{n_i} y_{it} \right)! \prod_{t=1}^{n_i} \frac{\exp(\mathbf{x}_{it}\boldsymbol{\beta})^{y_{it}}}{y_{it}! \left\{ \sum_{\ell=1}^{n_\ell} \exp(\mathbf{x}_{i\ell}\boldsymbol{\beta}) \right\}^{y_{it}}} \right]^{w_i}
$$

$$
= \log \prod_{i=1}^{n} \left\{ \frac{\left(\sum_t y_{it} \right)!}{\prod_{t=1}^{n_i} y_{it}!} \prod_{t=1}^{n_i} p_{it}^{y_{it}} \right\}^{w_i}
$$

$$
= \sum_{i=1}^{n} w_i \left\{ \log \Gamma \left(\sum_{t=1}^{n_i} y_{it} + 1 \right) - \sum_{t=1}^{n_i} \log \Gamma(y_{it} + 1) + \sum_{t=1}^{n_i} y_{it} \log p_{it} \right\}
$$

where

$$
p_{it} = e^{\mathbf{x}_{it}\boldsymbol{\beta}} \Big/ \sum_{\ell} e^{\mathbf{x}_{i\ell}\boldsymbol{\beta}}
$$

References

Cameron, A. C. and P. K. Trivedi. 1998. *Regression Analysis of Count Data*. New York: Cambridge University Press.

Greene, W. H. 2003. *Econometric Analysis*. 5th ed. Upper Saddle River, NJ: Prentice Hall.

Hardin, J. and J. Hilbe. 2001. *Generalized Linear Models and Extensions*. College Station, TX: Stata Press.

Hausman, J., B. H. Hall, and Z. Griliches. 1984. Econometric models for count data with an application to the patents–R & D relationship. *Econometrica* 52: 909–938.

Liang, K.-Y. and S. L. Zeger. 1986. Longitudinal data analysis using generalized linear models. *Biometrika* 73: 13–22.

Liu, Qing and D. A. Pierce 1994. A note on Gauss–Hermite quadrature. *Biometrika* 81: 624–629.

McCullagh, P. and J. A. Nelder. 1989. *Generalized Linear Models*. 2nd ed. London: Chapman & Hall/CRC.

Also See

Complementary:	[XT] **xtpoisson postestimation**; [XT] **quadchk**, [XT] **xtdata**, [XT] **xtdes**, [XT] **xtsum**, [XT] **xttab**, [R] **constraint**
Related:	[XT] **xtgee**, [XT] **xtnbreg**, [R] **poisson**
Background:	[U] **11.1.10 Prefix commands**, [U] **20 Estimation and postestimation commands**, [XT] **estimation options**, [XT] **xt**, [R] **maximize**, [R] *vce_option*

Title

> **xtpoisson postestimation** — Postestimation tools for xtpoisson

Description

The following postestimation commands are available for `xtpoisson`:

command	description
adjust[1]	adjusted predictions of $\mathbf{x}\beta$ and $\exp(\mathbf{x}\beta)$
*estat	AIC, BIC, VCE, and estimation sample summary
estimates	cataloging estimation results
hausman	Hausman's specification test
lincom	point estimates, standard errors, testing, and inference for linear combinations of coefficients
lrtest	likelihood-ratio test
mfx	marginal effects or elasticities
nlcom	point estimates, standard errors, testing, and inference for nonlinear combinations of coefficients
predict	predictions, residuals, influence statistics, and other diagnostic measures
predictnl	point estimates, standard errors, testing, and inference for generalized predictions
test	Wald tests for simple and composite linear hypotheses
testnl	Wald tests of nonlinear hypotheses

[1] `adjust` does not work with time-series operators.

* `estat ic` may not be used after `xtpoisson, pa`.

See the corresponding entries in the *Stata Base Reference Manual* for details.

Syntax for predict

Random-effects (RE) and fixed-effects (FE) models

> predict [*type*] *newvar* [*if*] [*in*] [, *RE/FE_statistic* <u>nooff</u>set]

Population-averaged (PA) model

> predict [*type*] *newvar* [*if*] [*in*] [, *PA_statistic* <u>nooff</u>set]

RE/FE_statistic	description
xb	linear prediction; the default
stdp	standard error of the linear prediction
nu0	predicted number of events; assumes zero
iru0	predicted incidence rate; assumes zero

PA_statistic	description
mu	predicted value of *depvar*; considers the offset(); the default
rate	predicted value of *depvar*
xb	linear prediction
stdp	standard error of the linear prediction
score	first derivative of the log likelihood with respect to $\mathbf{x}_j\beta$

These statistics are available both in and out of sample; type predict ... if e(sample) ... if wanted only for the estimation sample.

Options for predict

xb calculates the linear prediction. This is the default for the random-effects and fixed-effects models.

mu and rate both calculate the predicted value of *depvar*, i.e., the predicted count. mu takes into account the offset(), and rate ignores those adjustments. mu and rate are equivalent if you did not specify offset(). mu is the default for the population-averaged model.

stdp calculates the standard error of the linear prediction.

nu0 calculates the predicted number of events assuming a zero random or fixed effect.

iru0 calculates the predicted incidence rate assuming a zero random or fixed effect.

score calculates the equation-level score, $u_j = \partial \ln L_j(\mathbf{x}_j\beta)/\partial(\mathbf{x}_j\beta)$.

nooffset is relevant only if you specified offset(*varname*) for xtpoisson. It modifies the calculations made by predict so that they ignore the offset variable; the linear prediction is treated as $\mathbf{x}_{it}\beta$ rather than $\mathbf{x}_{it}\beta + \text{offset}_{it}$.

Methods and Formulas

All postestimation commands listed above are implemented as ado-files.

Also See

Complementary:	[XT] **xtpoisson**,
	[R] **adjust**, [R] **estimates**, [R] **hausman**, [R] **lincom**, [R] **lrtest**,
	[R] **mfx**, [R] **nlcom**, [R] **predictnl**, [R] **test**, [R] **testnl**
Background:	[U] **13.5 Accessing coefficients and standard errors**
	[U] **20 Estimation and postestimation commands**,
	[R] **estat**, [R] **predict**

Title

> **xtprobit** — Random-effects and population-averaged probit models

Syntax

Random-effects (RE) model

> xtprobit *depvar* [*indepvars*] [*if*] [*in*] [*weight*] [, re *RE_options*]

Population-averaged (PA) model

> xtprobit *depvar* [*indepvars*] [*if*] [*in*] [*weight*] , pa [*PA_options*]

RE_options	description
Model	
i(*varname$_i$*)	use *varname* as the panel ID variable
<u>nocon</u>stant	suppress constant term
re	use random-effects estimator; the default
<u>off</u>set(*varname*)	include *varname* in model with coefficient constrained to 1
constraints(*constraints*)	apply specified linear constraints
Int opts (RE)	
<u>intm</u>ethod(*intmethod*)	integration method; *intmethod* may be <u>agh</u>ermite or <u>gh</u>ermite
<u>intp</u>oints(#)	use # quadrature points; default is intpoints(12)
SE	
vce(*vcetype*)	*vcetype* may be <u>boot</u>strap or <u>jack</u>knife
Reporting	
<u>l</u>evel(#)	set confidence level; default is level(95)
noskip	perform overall model test as a likelihood-ratio test
Max options	
maximize_options	control the maximization process; seldom used

PA_options	description
Model	
i(*varname$_i$*)	use *varname* as the panel ID variable
noconstant	suppress constant term
pa	use population-averaged estimator
offset(*varname*)	include *varname* in model with coefficient constrained to 1
Correlation	
corr(*correlation*)	within-group correlation structure
force	estimate even if observations unequally spaced in time
SE/Robust	
vce(*vcetype*)	*vcetype* may be bootstrap or jackknife
robust	compute standard errors using the robust/sandwich estimator
scale(x2)	set scale parameter to Pearson chi-squared statistic
scale(dev)	set scale parameter to deviance divided by degrees of freedom
scale(phi)	do not rescale the variance
scale(#)	set scale parameter to #
nmp	use divisor $N - P$ instead of the default N
Reporting	
level(#)	set confidence level; default is level(95)
Opt options	
optimize_options	control the optimization process; seldom used

correlation	description
exchangeable	exchangeable
independent	independent
unstructured	unstructured
fixed *matname*	user-specified
ar #	autoregressive of order #
stationary #	stationary of order #
nonstationary #	nonstationary of order #

depvar and *indepvars* may contain time-series operators; see [U] **11.4.3 Time-series varlists**.

bootstrap, by, jackknife, statsby, and xi may be used with xtprobit; see [U] **11.1.10 Prefix commands**.

iweights, fweights, and pweights are allowed for the population-averaged model, and iweights are allowed in the random-effects model; see [U] **11.1.6 weight**. Weights must be constant within panels.

See [U] **20 Estimation and postestimation commands** for additional capabilities of estimation commands.

Description

xtprobit fits random-effects and population-averaged probit models. There is no command for a conditional fixed-effects model, as there does not exist a sufficient statistic allowing the fixed effects to be conditioned out of the likelihood. Unconditional fixed-effects probit models may be fitted with the probit command with indicator variables for the panels. The appropriate indicator variables can be generated using tabulate or xi. However, unconditional fixed-effects estimates are biased.

xtprobit, re, the default, is slow because the likelihood function is calculated by adaptive Gauss–Hermite quadrature; see *Methods and Formulas*. Computation time is roughly proportional to the number of points used for the quadrature. The default is intpoints(12). Simulations indicate that increasing the number of points does not appreciably change the estimates for the coefficients or their standard errors. See [XT] **quadchk**.

By default, the population-averaged model is an equal-correlation model; xtprobit assumes the within-group correlation structure corr(exchangeable). See [XT] **xtgee** for information about how to fit other population-averaged models.

See [R] **logistic** for a list of related estimation commands.

Options for RE model

_____ Model _____

i(*varname$_i$*), noconstant; see [XT] **estimation options**.

re requests the random-effects estimator. re is the default if neither re nor pa is specified.

offset(*varname*), constraints(*constraints*); see [XT] **estimation options**.

_____ Int opts (RE) _____

intmethod(*intmethod*) specifies the integration method to be used for the random-effects model. It accepts one of two arguments: the first is aghermite, the default, which specifies adaptive Gauss–Hermite quadrature; the second is ghermite, which specifies nonadaptive Gauss–Hermite quadrature.

intpoints(#) specifies the number of points to use for Gauss–Hermite quadrature. The default is 12. Increasing this value slightly improves the accuracy but also increases computation time. Computation time is roughly proportional to its value.

_____ SE _____

vce(*vcetype*); see [R] *vce_option*.

_____ Reporting _____

level(#), noskip; see [XT] **estimation options**.

_____ Max options _____

maximize_options: difficult, technique(*algorithm_spec*), iterate(#), [no]log, trace, gradient, showstep, hessian, shownrtolerance, tolerance(#), ltolerance(#), gtolerance(#), nrtolerance(#), nonrtolerance, from(*init_specs*); see [R] **maximize**. Some of these options are not available if intmethod(ghermite) is specified. These options are seldom used.

Options for PA model

_____ Model _____

i(*varname$_i$*), noconstant; see [XT] **estimation options**.

pa requests the population-averaged estimator.

offset(*varname*); see [XT] **estimation options**.

corr(*correlation*), force; see [XT] **estimation options**.

vce(*vcetype*); see [R] *vce_option*.

robust; see [XT] **estimation options**.

scale(x2 | dev | phi | #) overrides the default scale parameter of scale(1); see [XT] **estimation options**.

nmp; see [XT] **estimation options**.

level(#); see [XT] **estimation options**.

optimize_options control the iterative optimization process. These options are seldom used.

iterate(#) specifies the maximum number of iterations. When the number of iterations equals #, the optimization stops and presents the current results, even if convergence has not been reached. The default is iterate(100).

tolerance(#) specifies the tolerance for the coefficient vector. When the relative change in the coefficient vector from one iteration to the next is less than or equal to #, the optimization process is stopped. tolerance(1e-6) is the default.

nolog suppresses display of the iteration log.

trace specifies that the current estimates be printed at each iteration.

Remarks

xtprobit is a convenience command for obtaining the population-averaged model. Typing

> . xtprobit ..., pa ...

is equivalent to typing

> . xtgee ..., ... family(binomial) link(probit) corr(exchangeable)

See also [XT] **xtgee** for information about xtprobit.

By default or when re is specified, xtprobit fits via maximum likelihood the random-effects model

$$\Pr(y_{it} \neq 0 | \mathbf{x}_{it}) = \Phi(\mathbf{x}_{it}\boldsymbol{\beta} + \nu_i)$$

for $i = 1, \ldots, n$ panels, where $t = 1, \ldots, n_i$, ν_i are i.i.d., $N(0, \sigma_\nu^2)$, and Φ is the standard normal cumulative distribution function.

Underlying this model is the variance components model

$$y_{it} \neq 0 \iff \mathbf{x}_{it}\boldsymbol{\beta} + \nu_i + \epsilon_{it} > 0$$

where ϵ_{it} are i.i.d. Gaussian distributed with mean zero and variance $\sigma_\epsilon^2 = 1$, independently of ν_i.

▷ Example 1

We are studying unionization of women in the United States and are using the `union` dataset; see [XT] **xt**. We wish to fit a random-effects model of union membership:

```
. use http://www.stata-press.com/data/r9/union
(NLS Women 14-24 in 1968)
. xtprobit union age grade not_smsa south southXt, i(id) nolog
```

Random-effects probit regression   Number of obs   =   26200
Group variable (i): idcode   Number of groups   =   4434

Random effects u_i ~ Gaussian   Obs per group: min =   1
                                                               avg =   5.9
                                                               max =   12

                                                Wald chi2(5)   =   220.73
Log likelihood = -10553.458   Prob > chi2   =   0.0000

union	Coef.	Std. Err.	z	P>|z|	[95% Conf. Interval]	
age	.0046535	.0025097	1.85	0.064	-.0002655	.0095724
grade	.0479245	.0099058	4.84	0.000	.0285094	.0673395
not_smsa	-.1402927	.0459599	-3.05	0.002	-.2303725	-.050213
south	-.6413919	.0618841	-10.36	0.000	-.7626824	-.5201014
southXt	.0130018	.004386	2.96	0.003	.0044054	.0215981
_cons	-1.864926	.1450472	-12.86	0.000	-2.149213	-1.580639
/lnsig2u	.5962036	.0440178			.5099304	.6824769
sigma_u	1.347299	.0296526			1.290417	1.406689
rho	.6447873	.0100817			.6247902	.6642913

Likelihood-ratio test of rho=0: chibar2(01) = 5987.70 Prob >= chibar2 = 0.000

The output includes the additional panel-level variance component, which is parameterized as the log of the variance $\ln(\sigma_\nu^2)$ (labeled `lnsig2u` in the output). The standard deviation σ_ν is also included in the output (labeled `sigma_u`) together with ρ (labeled `rho`), where

$$\rho = \frac{\sigma_\nu^2}{\sigma_\nu^2 + 1}$$

which is the proportion of the total variance contributed by the panel-level variance component.

When `rho` is zero, the panel-level variance component is unimportant, and the panel estimator is not different from the pooled estimator. A likelihood-ratio test of this is included at the bottom of the output. This test formally compares the pooled estimator (probit) with the panel estimator.

◁

❑ Technical Note

The random-effects model is calculated using quadrature. As the panel sizes (or ρ) increase, the quadrature approximation becomes less accurate. We can use the `quadchk` command to see if changing the number of quadrature points affects the results. If the results do change, the quadrature approximation is not accurate, and the results of the model should not be interpreted.

```
. quadchk, nooutput
Refitting model intpoints() =  8
Refitting model intpoints() = 16
```

	Quadrature check			
	Fitted quadrature 12 points	Comparison quadrature 8 points	Comparison quadrature 16 points	
Log likelihood	-10553.458	-10557.492	-10552.562	
		-4.0341797	.89648438	Difference
		.00038226	-.00008495	Relative difference
union: age	.00465346	.00464225	.00465542	
		-.00001121	1.962e-06	Difference
		-.00240996	.00042167	Relative difference
union: grade	.04792446	.04746149	.04809003	
		-.00046297	.00016557	Difference
		-.00966041	.0034548	Relative difference
union: not_smsa	-.14029273	-.14097586	-.14006602	
		-.00068313	.00022672	Difference
		.00486931	-.00161602	Relative difference
union: south	-.6413919	-.63751794	-.64268918	
		.00387396	-.00129727	Difference
		-.00603992	.00202259	Relative difference
union: southXt	.01300176	.01288318	.01304342	
		-.00011858	.00004166	Difference
		-.00911999	.00320414	Relative difference
union: _cons	-1.864926	-1.8479994	-1.8710721	
		.01692658	-.00614611	Difference
		-.00907628	.00329563	Relative difference
lnsig2u: _cons	.59620364	.55763739	.60899691	
		-.03856626	.01279326	Difference
		-.06468638	.02145788	Relative difference

Note that the results obtained for 12 quadrature points were closer to the results using 16 points than to the results using 8 points. While the relative and absolute differences are a bit larger than we'd like, they are not very large. We can increase the number of quadrature points with the `intpoints()` option; if we choose `intpoints(20)` and do another `quadchk` we will get acceptable results, with relative differences around .01%.

This is not the case if we use nonadaptive quadrature. In this case, the results we obtain are

```
. xtprobit union age grade not_smsa south southXt, i(id) intmethod(gh) nolog
```

Random-effects probit regression   Number of obs   =   26200
Group variable (i): idcode   Number of groups   =   4434

Random effects u_i ~ Gaussian   Obs per group: min =   1
                                                         avg =   5.9
                                                         max =   12

                                          Wald chi2(5)   =   218.90
Log likelihood = -10561.065   Prob > chi2   =   0.0000

union	Coef.	Std. Err.	z	P>|z|	[95% Conf. Interval]	
age	.0044483	.0025027	1.78	0.076	-.000457	.0093535
grade	.0482482	.0100413	4.80	0.000	.0285677	.0679287
not_smsa	-.1370699	.0462961	-2.96	0.003	-.2278087	-.0463312
south	-.6305824	.0614827	-10.26	0.000	-.7510863	-.5100785
southXt	.0131853	.0043819	3.01	0.003	.004597	.0217737
_cons	-1.846838	.1458222	-12.67	0.000	-2.132644	-1.561032
/lnsig2u	.5612193	.0431875			.4765733	.6458653
sigma_u	1.323937	.0285888			1.269073	1.381172
rho	.6367346	.0099894			.6169384	.6560781

Likelihood-ratio test of rho=0: chibar2(01) = 5972.49 Prob >= chibar2 = 0.000

We now check the stability of the quadrature technique for this nonadaptive quadrature model. We expect it to be less stable.

(Continued on next page)

```
. quadchk, nooutput
Refitting model intpoints() =  8
Refitting model intpoints() = 16
```

Quadrature check

	Fitted quadrature 12 points	Comparison quadrature 8 points	Comparison quadrature 16 points	
Log likelihood	-10561.065	-10574.78	-10555.853	
		-13.714764	5.2126898	Difference
		.00129862	-.00049358	Relative difference
union: age	.00444829	.00478943	.00451117	
		.00034115	.00006288	Difference
		.07669143	.01413662	Relative difference
union: grade	.04824822	.05629525	.04411081	
		.00804704	-.00413741	Difference
		.16678412	-.0857525	Relative difference
union: not_smsa	-.13706993	-.1314541	-.14109796	
		.00561584	-.00402803	Difference
		-.04097061	.02938665	Relative difference
union: south	-.63058241	-.62309654	-.64546968	
		.00748587	-.01488727	Difference
		-.01187136	.02360876	Relative difference
union: southXt	.01318534	.01194434	.01341723	
		-.001241	.00023189	Difference
		-.09411977	.01758658	Relative difference
union: _cons	-1.8468379	-1.9306422	-1.8066853	
		-.08380426	.0401526	Difference
		.04537716	-.02174127	Relative difference
lnsig2u: _cons	.56121927	.49078989	.58080961	
		-.07042938	.01959034	Difference
		-.12549352	.03490674	Relative difference

Once again, the results obtained for 12 quadrature points were closer to the results using 16 points than to the results using 8 points. However, in this case the convergence point seems to be sensitive to the number of quadrature points, so we should not trust these results. We should not use the results of a random-effects specification when there is evidence that the numeric technique for calculating the model is not stable (as shown by quadchk).

Generally, the relative differences in the coefficients should not change by more than 1% if the quadrature technique is stable. See [XT] **quadchk** for details. When the quadrature technique is not stable, we cannot merely increase the number of quadrature points to fix the problem. We can switch between adaptive and nonadaptive quadrature. As a rule, adaptive quadrature, which is the default integration method, is much more flexible and robust.   ❑

▷ Example 2

As an alternative to the random-effects specification, we can fit an equal-correlation probit model:

```
. xtprobit union age grade not_smsa south southXt, i(id) pa
Iteration 1: tolerance = .04796083
Iteration 2: tolerance = .00352657
Iteration 3: tolerance = .00017886
Iteration 4: tolerance = 8.654e-06
Iteration 5: tolerance = 4.150e-07
```

```
GEE population-averaged model              Number of obs      =      26200
Group variable:                     idcode Number of groups   =       4434
Link:                               probit Obs per group: min =          1
Family:                           binomial                avg =        5.9
Correlation:                   exchangeable                max =         12
                                           Wald chi2(5)       =     241.66
Scale parameter:                         1 Prob > chi2        =     0.0000
```

union	Coef.	Std. Err.	z	P>|z|	[95% Conf. Interval]	
age	.0031597	.0014678	2.15	0.031	.0002829	.0060366
grade	.0329992	.0062334	5.29	0.000	.020782	.0452163
not_smsa	-.0721799	.0275189	-2.62	0.009	-.1261159	-.0182439
south	-.409029	.0372213	-10.99	0.000	-.4819815	-.3360765
southXt	.0081828	.002545	3.22	0.001	.0031946	.0131709
_cons	-1.184799	.0890117	-13.31	0.000	-1.359259	-1.01034

◁

▷ Example 3

In [R] **probit**, we showed the above results and compared them with probit, robust cluster(). xtprobit with the pa option allows a robust option (the random-effects estimator does not allow the robust specification), so we can obtain the population-averaged probit estimator with the robust variance calculation by typing

```
. xtprobit union age grade not_smsa south southXt, i(id) pa robust nolog
GEE population-averaged model              Number of obs      =      26200
Group variable:                     idcode Number of groups   =       4434
Link:                               probit Obs per group: min =          1
Family:                           binomial                avg =        5.9
Correlation:                   exchangeable                max =         12
                                           Wald chi2(5)       =     154.00
Scale parameter:                         1 Prob > chi2        =     0.0000
              (Std. Err. adjusted for clustering on idcode)
```

union	Coef.	Semi-robust Std. Err.	z	P>|z|	[95% Conf. Interval]	
age	.0031597	.0022027	1.43	0.151	-.0011575	.007477
grade	.0329992	.0076631	4.31	0.000	.0179797	.0480186
not_smsa	-.0721799	.0348772	-2.07	0.038	-.140538	-.0038218
south	-.409029	.0482545	-8.48	0.000	-.5036061	-.3144519
southXt	.0081828	.0037108	2.21	0.027	.0009097	.0154558
_cons	-1.184799	.116457	-10.17	0.000	-1.413051	-.9565479

These standard errors are similar to those shown for probit, robust cluster() in [R] **probit**.

◁

▷ Example 4

In a previous example, we showed how `quadchk` indicated that the quadrature technique was numerically unstable. Here we present an example in which the quadrature is stable.

In this example, we have (synthetic) data on whether workers complain to managers at a fast-food restaurant. The covariates are `age` (in years of the worker), `grade` (years of schooling completed by the worker), `south` (equal to 1 if the restaurant is located in the South), `tenure` (the number of years spent on the job by the worker), `gender` (of the worker), `race` (of the worker), `income` (in thousands of dollars by the restaurant), `genderm` (gender of the manager), `burger` (equal to 1 if the restaurant specializes in hamburgers), and `chicken` (equal to 1 if the restaurant specializes in chicken). The model is given by

```
. use http://www.stata-press.com/data/r9/chicken
. xtprobit complain age grade south tenure gender race income genderm burger
> chicken, i(person) nolog
```

Random-effects probit regression   Number of obs   =   5952
Group variable (i): person   Number of groups   =   1076

Random effects u_i ~ Gaussian   Obs per group: min =   3
                                                                 avg =   5.5
                                                                 max =   8

                                                  Wald chi2(10)   =   65.04
Log likelihood = -2574.1169   Prob > chi2   =   0.0000

complain	Coef.	Std. Err.	z	P>|z|	[95% Conf. Interval]	
age	-.0003202	.0762509	-0.00	0.997	-.1497692	.1491287
grade	-.0411101	.0647714	-0.63	0.526	-.1680598	.0858395
south	-.0346268	.0723736	-0.48	0.632	-.1764764	.1072227
tenure	-.3835949	.0550427	-6.97	0.000	-.4914766	-.2757133
gender	.0668019	.0734584	0.91	0.363	-.0771739	.2107776
race	.0834891	.0557721	1.50	0.134	-.0258222	.1928003
income	-.2111534	.0730111	-2.89	0.004	-.3542525	-.0680543
genderm	.1306414	.0557123	2.34	0.019	.0214473	.2398354
burger	-.0616441	.0729721	-0.84	0.398	-.2046669	.0813786
chicken	.0635853	.0557632	1.14	0.254	-.0457085	.1728791
_cons	-1.12381	.033004	-34.05	0.000	-1.188497	-1.059124
/lnsig2u	-1.03059	.12909			-1.283601	-.7775779
sigma_u	.5973245	.0385543			.5263438	.6778773
rho	.2629698	.0250198			.2169378	.3148421

Likelihood-ratio test of rho=0: chibar2(01) =   166.88 Prob >= chibar2 = 0.000

Again we would like to check the stability of the quadrature technique of the model before interpreting the results. Given the estimate of ρ and the small size of the panels (between 3 and 8), we should find that the quadrature technique is numerically stable.

```
. quadchk, nooutput
```
Refitting model intpoints() = 8
Refitting model intpoints() = 16

	Fitted quadrature 12 points	Comparison quadrature 8 points	Comparison quadrature 16 points	
Log likelihood	-2574.1169	-2574.1179 -.00097656 3.794e-07	-2574.1165 .00048828 -1.897e-07	Difference Relative difference
complain: age	-.00032023	-.00032334 -3.106e-06 .00970046	-.00031847 1.760e-06 -.00549491	Difference Relative difference
complain: grade	-.04111014	-.04110948 6.603e-07 -.00001606	-.04111053 -3.851e-07 9.368e-06	Difference Relative difference
complain: south	-.03462684	-.03462236 4.475e-06 -.00012922	-.03462937 -2.529e-06 .00007303	Difference Relative difference
complain: tenure	-.38359494	-.38358538 9.559e-06 -.00002492	-.38360033 -5.394e-06 .00001406	Difference Relative difference
complain: gender	.06680187	.06680166 -2.128e-07 -3.186e-06	.06680199 1.259e-07 1.885e-06	Difference Relative difference
complain: race	.08348907	.08348598 -3.088e-06 -.00003699	.08349082 1.755e-06 .00002101	Difference Relative difference
complain: income	-.2111534	-.21114867 4.726e-06 -.00002238	-.21115602 -2.626e-06 .00001244	Difference Relative difference
complain: genderm	.13064137	.13063682 -4.552e-06 -.00003485	.13064397 2.602e-06 .00001992	Difference Relative difference
complain: burger	-.06164412	-.06163759 6.538e-06 -.00010606	-.06164778 -3.656e-06 .0000593	Difference Relative difference
complain: chicken	.06358531	.06358217 -3.147e-06 -.00004949	.06358711 1.793e-06 .0000282	Difference Relative difference
complain: _cons	-1.1238104	-1.1237801 .0000303 -.00002696	-1.1238279 -.00001753 .00001559	Difference Relative difference
lnsig2u: _cons	-1.0305896	-1.0308562 -.00026657 .00025866	-1.0304385 .00015108 -.0001466	Difference Relative difference

Quadrature check

The relative differences are all very small between the default 12 quadrature points and the result with 16 points. We don't have any coefficients that have a large relative difference between the default 12 quadrature points and 8 quadrature points. In looking again at the absolute differences, we see that the absolute differences between 12 and 16 quadrature points are also small.

We conclude that the quadrature technique is stable. We may wish to rerun the above model with quad(16) or even higher (but we do not have to do this since the results will not significantly differ) and interpret those results for our presentation.

◁

Saved Results

xtprobit, re saves in e():

Scalars

e(N)	# of observations	e(rho)	ρ
e(N_g)	# of groups	e(sigma_u)	panel-level standard deviation
e(N_cd)	# of completely determined obs.	e(n_quad)	# of quadrature points
e(df_m)	model degrees of freedom	e(k)	# of parameters
e(ll)	log likelihood	e(k_eq)	# of equations
e(ll_0)	log likelihood, constant-only model	e(k_dv)	# of dependent variables
e(ll_c)	log likelihood, comparison model	e(p)	significance
e(g_max)	largest group size	e(rank)	rank of e(V)
e(g_min)	smallest group size	e(rank0)	rank of e(V) for constant-only model
e(g_avg)	average group size	e(ic)	# of iterations
e(chi2)	χ^2	e(rc)	return code
e(chi2_c)	χ^2 for comparison test	e(converged)	1 if converged, 0 otherwise

Macros

e(cmd)	xtprobit	e(distrib)	Gaussian; the distribution of the random effect
e(depvar)	name of dependent variable		
e(title)	title in estimation output	e(vce)	vcetype specified in vce()
e(ivar)	variable denoting groups	e(vcetype)	title used to label Std. Err.
e(wtype)	weight type	e(opt)	type of optimization
e(wexp)	weight expression	e(ml_method)	type of ml method
e(offset)	offset	e(user)	name of likelihood-evaluator program
e(chi2type)	Wald or LR; type of model χ^2 test	e(technique)	maximization technique
e(chi2_ct)	Wald or LR; type of model χ^2 test corresponding to e(chi2_c)	e(crittype)	optimization criterion
		e(properties)	b V
e(intmethod)	integration method	e(predict)	program used to implement predict

Matrices

e(b)	coefficient vector	e(ilog)	iteration log
e(V)	variance–covariance matrix of the estimators	e(gradient)	gradient vector

Functions

e(sample)	marks estimation sample

`xtprobit, pa` saves in `e()`:

Scalars

e(N)	# of observations	e(chi2_dev)	χ^2 test of deviance
e(N_g)	# of groups	e(chi2_dis)	χ^2 test of deviance dispersion
e(df_m)	model degrees of freedom	e(deviance)	deviance
e(df_pear)	degrees of freedom for Pearson χ^2	e(dispers)	deviance dispersion
e(g_max)	largest group size	e(tol)	target tolerance
e(g_min)	smallest group size	e(dif)	achieved tolerance
e(g_avg)	average group size	e(phi)	scale parameter
e(chi2)	χ^2	e(rc)	return code

Macros

e(cmd)	xtgee	e(ivar)	variable denoting groups
e(cmd2)	xtprobit	e(vce)	*vcetype* specified in vce()
e(depvar)	name of dependent variable	e(vcetype)	title used to label Std. Err.
e(family)	binomial	e(chi2type)	Wald; type of model χ^2 test
e(link)	probit; link function	e(offset)	offset
e(corr)	correlation structure	e(properties)	b V
e(crittype)	optimization criterion	e(predict)	program used to implement predict
e(scale)	x2, dev, phi, or #; scale parameter		

Matrices

e(b)	coefficient vector	e(R)	estimated working correlation matrix
e(V)	variance–covariance matrix of the estimators		

Functions

e(sample)	marks estimation sample

Methods and Formulas

xtprobit is implemented as an ado-file.

xtprobit reports the population-averaged results obtained by using `xtgee, family(binomial) link(probit)` to obtain estimates.

Assuming a normal distribution, $N(0, \sigma_\nu^2)$, for the random effects ν_i

$$\Pr(y_{i1}, \ldots, y_{in_i} | \mathbf{x}_{i1}, \ldots, \mathbf{x}_{in_i}) = \int_{-\infty}^{\infty} \frac{e^{-\nu_i^2 / 2\sigma_\nu^2}}{\sqrt{2\pi}\sigma_\nu} \left\{ \prod_{t=1}^{n_i} F(y_{it}, \mathbf{x}_{it}\boldsymbol{\beta} + \nu_i) \right\} d\nu_i$$

where

$$F(y, z) = \begin{cases} \Phi(z) & \text{if } y \neq 0 \\ 1 - \Phi(z) & \text{otherwise} \end{cases}$$

where Φ is the cumulative normal distribution. The integral can be approximated with M-point Gauss–Hermite quadrature

$$\int_{-\infty}^{\infty} e^{-x^2} g(x)dx \approx \sum_{m=1}^{M} w_m^* g(a_m^*)$$

where the w_m^* denote the quadrature weights and the a_m^* denote the quadrature abscissas. The log likelihood, L, where $\rho = \sigma_\nu^2/(\sigma_\nu^2 + 1)$, is then calculated using the quadrature

$$L = \sum_{i=1}^{n} w_i \log \left\{ \Pr(y_{i1}, \ldots, y_{in_i} | \mathbf{x}_{i1}, \ldots, \mathbf{x}_{in_i}) \right\}$$

$$\approx \sum_{i=1}^{n} w_i \log \left[\frac{1}{\sqrt{\pi}} \sum_{m=1}^{M} w_m^* \prod_{t=1}^{n_i} F \left\{ y_{it}, \mathbf{x}_{it}\boldsymbol{\beta} + a_m^* \left(\frac{2\rho}{1 - \rho} \right)^{1/2} \right\} \right]$$

where w_i is the user-specified weight for panel i; if no weights are specified, $w_i = 1$.

The above is the formula for nonadaptive Gauss–Hermite quadrature. The default is to calculate the log likelihood, L, using adaptive Gauss–Hermite quadrature, which transforms the integrand

$$g(y_{it}, x_{it}, \nu_i) = \frac{e^{-\nu_i^2/2\sigma_\nu^2}}{\sqrt{2\pi}\sigma_\nu} \left\{ \prod_{t=1}^{n_i} F(y_{it}, \mathbf{x}_{it}\boldsymbol{\beta} + \nu_i) \right\}$$

so that it is sampled on a suitable range; see Liu (1994).

Both quadrature formulas require that the integrated function be well approximated by a polynomial. The number of time periods (panel size) affects whether

$$\prod_{t=1}^{n_i} F(y_{it}, \mathbf{x}_{it}\boldsymbol{\beta} + \nu_i)$$

is well approximated by a polynomial. As panel size (or ρ) increases, the quadrature approximation becomes less accurate. Adaptive quadrature gives better results for correlated data and large panels than nonadaptive quadrature; however we recommend that you use the quadchk command to investigate the applicability of the numeric technique used in this command.

References

Conway, M. R. 1990. A random effects model for binary data. *Biometrics* 46: 317–328.

Frechette, G. R. 2001. sg158: Random-effects ordered probit. *Stata Technical Bulletin* 59: 23–27. Reprinted in *Stata Technical Bulletin Reprints*, vol. 10, pp. 261–266.

———. 2001. sg158.1: Update to random-effects probit. *Stata Technical Bulletin* 61: 12. Reprinted in *Stata Technical Bulletin Reprints*, vol. 10, pp. 266–267.

Guilkey, D. K. and J. L. Murphy. 1993. Estimation and testing in the random effects probit model. *Journal of Econometrics* 59: 301–317.

Liang, K.-Y. and S. L. Zeger. 1986. Longitudinal data analysis using generalized linear models. *Biometrika* 73: 13–22.

Liu, Qing and D. A. Pierce 1994. A note on Gauss–Hermite quadrature. *Biometrika* 81: 624–629.

Neuhaus, J. M. 1992. Statistical methods for longitudinal and clustered designs with binary responses. *Statistical Methods in Medical Research* 1: 249–273.

Neuhaus, J. M., J. D. Kalbfleisch, and W. W. Hauck. 1991. A comparison of cluster-specific and population-averaged approaches for analyzing correlated binary data. *International Statistical Review* 59: 25–35.

Pendergast, J. F., S. J. Gange, M. A. Newton, M. J. Lindstrom, M. Palta, and M. R. Fisher. 1996. A survey of methods for analyzing clustered binary response data. *International Statistical Review* 64: 89–118.

Also See

Complementary:	[XT] **xtprobit postestimation**; [XT] **quadchk**, [XT] **xtdata**, [XT] **xtdes**, [XT] **xtsum**, [XT] **xttab**, [R] **constraint**
Related:	[XT] **xtcloglog**, [XT] **xtgee**, [XT] **xtlogit**, [R] **probit**
Background:	[U] **11.1.10 Prefix commands**, [U] **20 Estimation and postestimation commands**, [XT] **estimation options**, [XT] **xt**, [R] **maximize**, [R] *vce_option*

Title

xtprobit postestimation — Postestimation tools for xtprobit

Description

The following postestimation commands are available for xtprobit:

command	description
adjust[1]	adjusted predictions of $\mathbf{x}\beta$ or probabilities
*estat	AIC, BIC, VCE, and estimation sample summary
estimates	cataloging estimation results
hausman	Hausman's specification test
lincom	point estimates, standard errors, testing, and inference for linear combinations of coefficients
lrtest	likelihood-ratio test
mfx	marginal effects or elasticities
nlcom	point estimates, standard errors, testing, and inference for nonlinear combinations of coefficients
predict	predictions, residuals, influence statistics, and other diagnostic measures
predictnl	point estimates, standard errors, testing, and inference for generalized predictions
test	Wald tests for simple and composite linear hypotheses
testnl	Wald tests of nonlinear hypotheses

[1] adjust does not work with time-series operators.

*estat ic may not be used after xtprobit, pa.

See the corresponding entries in the *Stata Base Reference Manual* for details.

Syntax for predict

Random-effects model

   predict [*type*] *newvar* [*if*] [*in*] [, *RE_statistic* <u>nooff</u>set]

Population-averaged model

   predict [*type*] *newvar* [*if*] [*in*] [, *PA_statistic* <u>nooff</u>set]

RE_statistic	description
xb	linear prediction; the default
pu0	probability of a positive outcome
stdp	standard error of the linear prediction

PA_statistic	description
mu	predicted probability of *depvar*; considers the offset(); the default
rate	predicted probability of *depvar*
xb	linear prediction
stdp	standard error of the linear prediction
<u>sc</u>ore	first derivative of the log likelihood with respect to $x_j\beta$

These statistics are available both in and out of sample; type predict ... if e(sample) ... if wanted only for the estimation sample.

Options for predict

xb calculates the linear prediction. This is the default for the random-effects model.

pu0 calculates the probability of a positive outcome, assuming that the random effect for that observation's panel is zero ($\nu = 0$). Note that this probability may not be similar to the proportion of observed outcomes in the group.

stdp calculates the standard error of the linear prediction.

mu and rate both calculate the predicted probability of *depvar*. mu takes into account the offset(), and rate ignores those adjustments. mu and rate are equivalent if you did not specify offset(). mu is the default for the population-averaged model.

score calculates the equation-level score, $u_j = \partial \ln L_j(\mathbf{x}_j\beta)/\partial(\mathbf{x}_j\beta)$.

nooffset is relevant only if you specified offset(*varname*) for xtprobit. It modifies the calculations made by predict so that they ignore the offset variable; the linear prediction is treated as $\mathbf{x}_{it}\beta$ rather than $\mathbf{x}_{it}\beta + \text{offset}_{it}$.

Methods and Formulas

All postestimation commands listed above are implemented as ado-files.

Also See

Complementary:	[XT] **xtprobit**,
	[R] **adjust**, [R] **estimates**, [R] **hausman**, [R] **lincom**, [R] **lrtest**,
	[R] **mfx**, [R] **nlcom**, [R] **predictnl**, [R] **test**, [R] **testnl**
Background:	[U] **13.5 Accessing coefficients and standard errors**,
	[U] **20 Estimation and postestimation commands**,
	[R] **estat**, [R] **predict**

Title

> **xtrc** — Random-coefficients model

Syntax

xtrc *depvar* *indepvars* $\left[\,if\,\right]$ $\left[\,in\,\right]$ $\left[\,,\ options\,\right]$

options	description
Main	
i(*varname$_i$*)	use *varname$_i$* as the panel ID variable
noconstant	suppress constant term
offset(*varname*)	include *varname* in model with coefficient constrained to 1
betas	display group-specific best linear predictors
SE	
vce(*vcetype*)	*vcetype* may be bootstrap or jackknife
Reporting	
level(#)	set confidence level; default is level(95)

bootstrap, by, jackknife, statsby, and xi may be used with xtrc; see [U] **11.1.10 Prefix commands**.
See [U] **20 Estimation and postestimation commands** for additional capabilities of estimation commands.

Description

xtrc fits the Swamy (1970) random-coefficients linear regression model.

Options

___ Main ___

i(*varname$_i$*), noconstant, offset(*varname*); see [XT] **estimation options**

betas requests that the group-specific best linear predictors also be displayed.

___ SE ___

vce(*vcetype*); see [R] *vce_option*.

___ Reporting ___

level(#); see [XT] **estimation options**.

Remarks

In random-coefficients models, we wish to treat the parameter vector as a realization (in each panel) of a stochastic process. xtrc fits the Swamy (1970) random-coefficients model, which is suitable for linear regression of panel data. See Greene (2003) and Poi (2003) for more information about this and other panel-data models.

▷ Example 1

Greene (2003, 329) reprints data from a classic study of investment demand by Grunfeld and Griliches (1960). In [XT] **xtgls**, we use this dataset to illustrate many of the possible models that may be fitted with the xtgls command. While the models included in the xtgls command offer considerable flexibility, they all assume that there is no parameter variation across firms (the cross-sectional units).

To take a first look at the assumption of parameter constancy, we should reshape our data so that we may fit a simultaneous-equation model using sureg; see [R] **sureg**. Since there are only five panels here, this is not too difficult.

```
. use http://www.stata-press.com/data/r9/invest2

. reshape wide invest market stock, i(time) j(company)
(note: j = 1 2 3 4 5)

Data                                long    ->    wide

Number of obs.                       100    ->      20
Number of variables                    5    ->      16
j variable (5 values)            company    ->    (dropped)
xij variables:
                                  invest    ->    invest1 invest2 ... invest5
                                  market    ->    market1 market2 ... market5
                                   stock    ->    stock1 stock2 ... stock5
```

```
. sureg (invest1 market1 stock1) (invest2 market2 stock2) (invest3 market3 stock3)
> (invest4 market4 stock4) (invest5 market5 stock5)

Seemingly unrelated regression
```

Equation	Obs	Parms	RMSE	"R-sq"	chi2	P
invest1	20	2	84.94729	0.9207	261.32	0.0000
invest2	20	2	12.36322	0.9119	207.21	0.0000
invest3	20	2	26.46612	0.6876	46.88	0.0000
invest4	20	2	9.742303	0.7264	59.15	0.0000
invest5	20	2	95.85484	0.4220	14.97	0.0006

(Continued on next page)

	Coef.	Std. Err.	z	P>|z|	[95% Conf. Interval]	
invest1						
market1	.120493	.0216291	5.57	0.000	.0781007	.1628853
stock1	.3827462	.032768	11.68	0.000	.318522	.4469703
_cons	-162.3641	89.45922	-1.81	0.070	-337.7009	12.97279
invest2						
market2	.0695456	.0168975	4.12	0.000	.0364271	.1026641
stock2	.3085445	.0258635	11.93	0.000	.2578529	.3592362
_cons	.5043112	11.51283	0.04	0.965	-22.06042	23.06904
invest3						
market3	.0372914	.0122631	3.04	0.002	.0132561	.0613268
stock3	.130783	.0220497	5.93	0.000	.0875663	.1739997
_cons	-22.43892	25.51859	-0.88	0.379	-72.45443	27.57659
invest4						
market4	.0570091	.0113623	5.02	0.000	.0347395	.0792788
stock4	.0415065	.0412016	1.01	0.314	-.0392472	.1222602
_cons	1.088878	6.258805	0.17	0.862	-11.17815	13.35591
invest5						
market5	.1014782	.0547837	1.85	0.064	-.0058958	.2088523
stock5	.3999914	.1277946	3.13	0.002	.1495186	.6504642
_cons	85.42324	111.8774	0.76	0.445	-133.8525	304.6989

Here we instead fit a random-coefficients model:

```
. use http://www.stata-press.com/data/r9/invest2, clear

. xtrc invest market stock, i(company)
```

Random-coefficients regression		Number of obs	=	100
Group variable (i): company		Number of groups	=	5
		Obs per group: min =		20
		avg =		20.0
		max =		20
		Wald chi2(2)	=	17.55
		Prob > chi2	=	0.0002

invest	Coef.	Std. Err.	z	P>|z|	[95% Conf. Interval]	
market	.0807646	.0250829	3.22	0.001	.0316031	.1299261
stock	.2839885	.0677899	4.19	0.000	.1511229	.4168542
_cons	-23.58361	34.55547	-0.68	0.495	-91.31108	44.14386

Test of parameter constancy: chi2(12) =   603.99   Prob > chi2 = 0.0000

Just as the results of our simultaneous-equation model do not support the assumption of parameter constancy, the test included with the random-coefficients model also indicates that the assumption is not valid for these data. With large panel datasets, we would not want to take the time to look at a simultaneous-equations model (aside from the fact that our doing so was very subjective).

◁

Saved Results

xtrc saves in e():

Scalars

e(N)	number of observations	e(g_avg)	average group size
e(N_g)	number of groups	e(chi2)	χ^2
e(df_m)	model degrees of freedom	e(chi2_c)	χ^2 for comparison test
e(g_max)	largest group size	e(df_chi2)	degrees of freedom for model χ^2
e(g_min)	smallest group size		

Macros

e(cmd)	xtrc	e(chi2type)	Wald; type of model χ^2 test
e(depvar)	name of dependent variable	e(vce)	*vcetype* specified in vce()
e(title)	title in estimation output	e(vcetype)	title used to label Std. Err.
e(ivar)	variable denoting groups	e(properties)	b V
e(offset)	offset	e(predict)	program used to implement predict

Matrices

e(b)	coefficient vector	e(V)	variance–covariance matrix of the estimators
e(Sigma)	$\widehat{\Sigma}$ matrix		
e(beta_ps)	matrix of best linear predictors	e(V_ps)	matrix of variances for the best linear predictors; row i contains vec of variance matrix for group i predictor

Functions

e(sample)	marks estimation sample

Methods and Formulas

xtrc is implemented as an ado-file.

In a random-coefficients model, the parameter heterogeneity is treated as stochastic variation. Assume that we write

$$\mathbf{y}_i = \mathbf{X}_i \boldsymbol{\beta}_i + \boldsymbol{\epsilon}_i$$

where $i = 1, \ldots, m$, and $\boldsymbol{\beta}_i$ is the coefficient vector ($k \times 1$) for the ith cross-sectional unit, such that

$$\boldsymbol{\beta}_i = \boldsymbol{\beta} + \boldsymbol{\nu}_i \qquad E(\boldsymbol{\nu}_i) = \mathbf{0} \qquad E(\boldsymbol{\nu}_i \boldsymbol{\nu}_i') = \boldsymbol{\Sigma}$$

Our goal is to find $\widehat{\boldsymbol{\beta}}$ and $\widehat{\boldsymbol{\Sigma}}$.

The derivation of the estimator assumes that the cross-sectional specific coefficient vector $\boldsymbol{\beta}_i$ is the outcome of a random process with mean vector $\boldsymbol{\beta}$ and covariance matrix $\boldsymbol{\Sigma}$,

$$\mathbf{y}_i = \mathbf{X}_i \boldsymbol{\beta}_i + \boldsymbol{\epsilon}_i = \mathbf{X}_i (\boldsymbol{\beta} + \boldsymbol{\nu}_i) + \boldsymbol{\epsilon}_i = \mathbf{X}_i \boldsymbol{\beta} + (\mathbf{X}_i \boldsymbol{\nu}_i + \boldsymbol{\epsilon}_i) = \mathbf{X}_i \boldsymbol{\beta} + \boldsymbol{\omega}_i$$

where $E(\boldsymbol{\omega}_i) = \mathbf{0}$ and

$$E(\boldsymbol{\omega}_i \boldsymbol{\omega}_i') = E\left\{ (\mathbf{X}_i \boldsymbol{\nu}_i + \boldsymbol{\epsilon}_i)(\mathbf{X}_i \boldsymbol{\nu}_i + \boldsymbol{\epsilon}_i)' \right\} = E(\boldsymbol{\epsilon}_i \boldsymbol{\epsilon}_i') + \mathbf{X}_i E(\boldsymbol{\nu}_i \boldsymbol{\nu}_i') \mathbf{X}_i' = \sigma_i^2 \mathbf{I} + \mathbf{X}_i \boldsymbol{\Sigma} \mathbf{X}_i' = \boldsymbol{\Pi}_i$$

Stacking the m equations we have

$$\mathbf{y} = \mathbf{X} \boldsymbol{\beta} + \boldsymbol{\omega}$$

where $\boldsymbol{\Pi} \equiv E(\boldsymbol{\omega}\boldsymbol{\omega}')$ is a block diagonal matrix with $\boldsymbol{\Pi}_i$, $i = 1...m$, along the main diagonal and zeros elsewhere. The GLS estimator of $\widehat{\boldsymbol{\beta}}$ is then

$$\widehat{\boldsymbol{\beta}} = \left(\sum_i \mathbf{X}_i' \boldsymbol{\Pi}_i^{-1} \mathbf{X}_i\right)^{-1} \sum_i \mathbf{X}_i' \boldsymbol{\Pi}_i^{-1} \mathbf{y}_i = \sum_{i=1}^m \mathbf{W}_i \mathbf{b}_i$$

where

$$\mathbf{W}_i = \left\{\sum_{i=1}^m (\boldsymbol{\Sigma} + \mathbf{V}_i)^{-1}\right\}^{-1} (\boldsymbol{\Sigma} + \mathbf{V}_i)^{-1}$$

$\mathbf{b}_i = (\mathbf{X}_i' \mathbf{X}_i)^{-1} \mathbf{X}_i' \mathbf{y}_i$ and $\mathbf{V}_i = \sigma_i^2 (\mathbf{X}_i' \mathbf{X}_i)^{-1}$, showing that the resulting GLS estimator is a matrix-weighted average of the panel-specific OLS estimators. The variance of $\widehat{\boldsymbol{\beta}}$ is

$$\mathrm{Var}(\widehat{\boldsymbol{\beta}}) = \sum_{i=1}^m (\boldsymbol{\Sigma} + \mathbf{V}_i)^{-1}$$

To calculate the above estimator $\widehat{\boldsymbol{\beta}}$ for the unknown $\boldsymbol{\Sigma}$ and $\mathbf{V}_i$ parameters, we use the two-step approach suggested by Swamy (1970):

$$\mathbf{b}_i = \text{OLS panel-specific estimator}$$
$$\widehat{\sigma}_i^2 = \frac{\widehat{\boldsymbol{\epsilon}}_i' \widehat{\boldsymbol{\epsilon}}_i}{n_i - k}$$
$$\widehat{\mathbf{V}}_i = \widehat{\sigma}_i^2 (\mathbf{X}_i' \mathbf{X}_i)^{-1}$$
$$\overline{\mathbf{b}} = \frac{1}{m} \sum_{i=1}^m \mathbf{b}_i$$
$$\widehat{\boldsymbol{\Sigma}} = \frac{1}{m-1} \left(\sum_{i=1}^m \mathbf{b}_i \mathbf{b}_i' - m \overline{\mathbf{b}}\,\overline{\mathbf{b}}'\right) - \frac{1}{m} \sum_{i=1}^m \widehat{\mathbf{V}}_i$$

The two-step procedure begins with the usual OLS estimates of β_i. With those estimates, we may proceed by obtaining estimates of $\widehat{\mathbf{V}}_i$ and $\widehat{\boldsymbol{\Sigma}}$ (and, thus, $\widehat{\mathbf{W}}_i$), and then obtain an estimate of β.

Swamy (1970) further points out that the matrix $\widehat{\boldsymbol{\Sigma}}$ may not be positive definite, and that since the second term is of order $1/(mT)$, it is negligible in large samples. A simple and asymptotically expedient solution is simply to drop this second term and instead use

$$\widehat{\boldsymbol{\Sigma}} = \frac{1}{m-1} \left(\sum_{i=1}^m \mathbf{b}_i \mathbf{b}_i' - m \overline{\mathbf{b}}\,\overline{\mathbf{b}}'\right)$$

As discussed by Judge et al. (1985, 541), the feasible best linear predictor of β_i is given by

$$\widehat{\boldsymbol{\beta}}_i = \widehat{\boldsymbol{\beta}} + \widehat{\boldsymbol{\Sigma}} \mathbf{X}'_i \left(\mathbf{X}_i \widehat{\boldsymbol{\Sigma}} \mathbf{X}'_i + \widehat{\sigma}^2_i \mathbf{I} \right)^{-1} \left(\mathbf{y}_i - \mathbf{X}_i \widehat{\boldsymbol{\beta}} \right)$$

$$= \left(\widehat{\boldsymbol{\Sigma}}^{-1} + \widehat{\mathbf{V}}^{-1}_i \right)^{-1} \left(\widehat{\boldsymbol{\Sigma}}^{-1} \widehat{\boldsymbol{\beta}} + \widehat{\mathbf{V}}^{-1}_i \mathbf{b}_i \right)$$

The variance of $\widehat{\boldsymbol{\beta}}_i$ is given by

$$\mathrm{Var}(\widehat{\boldsymbol{\beta}}_i) = \mathrm{Var}(\widehat{\boldsymbol{\beta}}) + (\mathbf{I} - \mathbf{A}_i) \left\{ \widehat{\mathbf{V}}_i - \mathrm{Var}(\widehat{\boldsymbol{\beta}}) \right\} (\mathbf{I} - \mathbf{A}_i)'$$

where

$$\mathbf{A}_i = \left(\widehat{\boldsymbol{\Sigma}}^{-1} + \widehat{\mathbf{V}}^{-1}_i \right)^{-1} \widehat{\boldsymbol{\Sigma}}^{-1}$$

To test the model, we may look at the difference between the OLS estimate of β, ignoring the panel structure of the data and the matrix-weighted average of the panel-specific OLS estimators. The test statistic suggested by Swamy (1970) is given by

$$\chi^2_{k(m-1)} = \sum_{i=1}^{m} (\mathbf{b}_i - \overline{\boldsymbol{\beta}}^*)' \widehat{\mathbf{V}}^{-1}_i (\mathbf{b}_i - \overline{\boldsymbol{\beta}}^*) \quad \text{where} \quad \overline{\boldsymbol{\beta}}^* = \left(\sum_{i=1}^{m} \widehat{\mathbf{V}}^{-1}_i \right)^{-1} \sum_{i=1}^{m} \widehat{\mathbf{V}}^{-1}_i \mathbf{b}_i$$

Johnston and DiNardo (1997) has shown that the test is algebraically equivalent to testing

$$H_0 : \beta_1 = \beta_2 = \cdots = \beta_m$$

in the generalized (groupwise heteroskedastic) `xtgls` model, where $\mathbf{V}$ is block diagonal with ith diagonal element $\boldsymbol{\Pi}_i$.

References

Greene, W. H. 2003. *Econometric Analysis.* 5th ed. Upper Saddle River, NJ: Prentice Hall.

Grunfeld, Y. and Z. Griliches. 1960. Is aggregation necessarily bad? *Review of Economics and Statistics* 42: 1–13.

Johnston, J. and J. DiNardo. 1997. *Econometric Methods.* 4th ed. New York: McGraw–Hill.

Judge, G. G., W. E. Griffiths, R. C. Hill, H. Lütkepohl, and T.-C. Lee. 1985. *The Theory and Practice of Econometrics.* 2nd ed. New York: Wiley.

Poi, B. 2003. From the help desk: Swamy's random-coefficients model. *Stata Journal* 3: 302–308.

Swamy, P. 1970. Efficient inference in a random coefficient regression model. *Econometrica* 38: 311–323.

——. 1971. *Statistical Inference in Random Coefficient Regression Models.* New York: Springer.

Also See

Complementary:	[XT] **xtrc postestimation**; [XT] **xtdata**, [XT] **xtdes**, [XT] **xtsum**, [XT] **xttab**
Related:	[XT] **xtgee**, [XT] **xtgls**, [XT] **xtmixed**, [XT] **xtpcse**, [XT] **xtreg**, [XT] **xtregar**
Background:	[U] **11.1.10 Prefix commands**,
	[U] **20 Estimation and postestimation commands**,
	[XT] **estimation options**, [XT] **xt**,
	[R] *vce_option*

Title

> **xtrc postestimation** — Postestimation tools for xtrc

Description

The following postestimation commands are available for xtrc:

command	description
adjust	adjusted predictions of $\mathbf{x}\beta$
estat	VCE and estimation sample summary
estimates	cataloging estimation results
lincom	point estimates, standard errors, testing, and inference for linear combination of coefficients
mfx	marginal effects or elasticities
nlcom	point estimates, standard errors, testing, and inference for nonlinear combinations of coefficients
predict	predictions, residuals, influence statistics, and other diagnostic measures
predictnl	point estimates, standard errors, testing, and inference for generalized predictions
test	Wald tests for simple and composite linear hypotheses
testnl	Wald tests of nonlinear hypotheses

See the corresponding entries in the *Stata Base Reference Manual* for details.

Syntax for predict

> predict [*type*] *newvar* [*if*] [*in*] [, *statistic* <u>nooff</u>set]

statistic	description
xb	linear prediction; the default
stdp	standard error of the linear prediction
group(*group*)	linear prediction based on group *group*.

These statistics are available both in and out of sample; type predict ... if e(sample) ... if wanted only for the estimation sample.

Options for predict

xb, the default, calculates the linear prediction using the mean parameter vector.

stdp calculates the standard error of the linear prediction.

group(*group*) calculates the linear prediction using the best linear predictors for group *group*.

nooffset is relevant only if you specified offset(*varname*) for xtrc. It modifies the calculations made by predict so that they ignore the offset variable; the linear prediction is treated as $\mathbf{x}_{it}\mathbf{b}$ rather than $\mathbf{x}_{it}\mathbf{b} + \text{offset}_{it}$.

Methods and Formulas

All postestimation commands listed above are implemented as ado-files.

Also See

Complementary: [XT] **xtrc**,
                   [R] **adjust**, [R] **estimates**, [R] **lincom**, [R] **mfx**, [R] **nlcom**,
                   [R] **predictnl**, [R] **test**, [R] **testnl**

Background: [U] **13.5 Accessing coefficients and standard errors**,
                   [U] **20 Estimation and postestimation commands**,
                   [R] **estat**, [R] **predict**

Title

> **xtreg** — Fixed-, between-, and random-effects, and population-averaged linear models

Syntax

GLS random-effects (RE) model

> xtreg *depvar* [*indepvars*] [*if*] [, re *RE_options*]

Between-effects (BE) model

> xtreg *depvar* [*indepvars*] [*if*] , be [*BE_options*]

Fixed-effects (FE) model

> xtreg *depvar* [*indepvars*] [*if*] , fe [*FE_options*]

ML random-effects (MLE) model

> xtreg *depvar* [*indepvars*] [*if*] [*weight*] , mle [*MLE_options*]

Population-averaged (PA) model

> xtreg *depvar* [*indepvars*] [*if*] [*weight*] , pa [*PA_options*]

RE_options	description
Model	
i(*varname$_i$*)	use *varname$_i$* as the panel ID variable
re	use random-effects estimator; the default
sa	use Swamy–Arora estimator of the variance components
SE/Robust	
vce(*vcetype*)	*vcetype* may be robust, bootstrap, or jackknife
robust	synonym for vce(robust)
cluster(*varname*)	adjust standard errors for intragroup correlation
Reporting	
level(#)	set confidence level; default is level(95)
theta	report θ

BE_options	description
Model	
i(*varname$_i$*)	use *varname$_i$* as the panel ID variable
be	use between-effects estimator
<u>w</u>ls	use weighted least squares
SE	
vce(*vcetype*)	*vcetype* may be <u>boot</u>strap or <u>jack</u>knife
Reporting	
<u>l</u>evel(*#*)	set confidence level; default is level(95)

FE_options	description
Model	
i(*varname$_i$*)	use *varname$_i$* as the panel ID variable
fe	use fixed-effects estimator
SE/Robust	
vce(*vcetype*)	*vcetype* may be <u>r</u>obust, <u>boot</u>strap, or <u>jack</u>knife
<u>r</u>obust	synonym for vce(robust)
<u>cl</u>uster(*varname*)	adjust standard errors for intragroup correlation
Reporting	
<u>l</u>evel(*#*)	set confidence level; default is level(95)

MLE_options	description
Model	
i(*varname$_i$*)	use *varname$_i$* as the panel ID variable
<u>nocon</u>stant	suppress constant term
mle	use ML random-effects estimator
SE	
vce(*vcetype*)	*vcetype* may be <u>boot</u>strap or <u>jack</u>knife
Reporting	
<u>l</u>evel(*#*)	set confidence level; default is level(95)
Max options	
maximize_options	control the maximization process; seldom used

PA_options	description
Model	
i(*varname_i*)	use *varname_i* as the panel ID variable
<u>nocon</u>stant	suppress constant term
pa	use population-averaged estimator
<u>off</u>set(*varname*)	include *varname* in model with coefficient constrained to 1
Correlation	
<u>corr</u>(*correlation*)	within-group correlation structure
force	estimate even if observations unequally spaced in time
SE/Robust	
vce(*vcetype*)	*vcetype* may be <u>r</u>obust, <u>boot</u>strap, or <u>jack</u>knife
<u>r</u>obust	synonym for vce(robust)
nmp	use divisor $N - P$ instead of the default N
rgf	multiply the robust variance estimate by $(N - 1)/(N - P)$
<u>sc</u>ale(x2)	set scale parameter to Pearson chi-squared statistic
<u>sc</u>ale(dev)	set scale parameter to deviance divided by degrees of freedom
<u>sc</u>ale(phi)	do not rescale the variance
<u>sc</u>ale(#)	set scale parameter to #
Reporting	
<u>level</u>(#)	set confidence level; default is level(95)
Opt options	
optimize_options	control the optimization process; seldom used

correlation	description
<u>exc</u>hangeable	exchangeable
<u>ind</u>ependent	independent
<u>uns</u>tructured	unstructured
<u>fix</u>ed *matname*	user-specified
ar #	autoregressive of order #
<u>stat</u>ionary #	stationary of order #
<u>non</u>stationary #	nonstationary of order #

depvar and *indepvars* may contain time-series operators; see [U] **11.4.3 Time-series varlists**.

bootstrap, by, jackknife, statsby, and xi may be used with xtreg; see [U] **11.1.10 Prefix commands**.

iweights, fweights, and pweights are allowed for the population-averaged model and iweights are allowed for the maximum-likelihood (ML) random-effects model; see [U] **11.1.6 weight**. Weights must be constant within panels.

See [U] **20 Estimation and postestimation commands** for additional capabilities of estimation commands.

Description

xtreg fits regression models to panel data. In particular, xtreg with the be option fits random-effects models using the between regression estimator; with the fe option, it fits fixed-effects models (using the within regression estimator); and with the re option, it fits random-effects models using the GLS estimator (producing a matrix-weighted average of the between and within results). See [XT] **xtdata** for a faster way to fit fixed- and random-effects models.

Options for RE model

____⌐ Model ⌐_____

i(*varname$_i$*); see [XT] **estimation options**.

re, the default, requests the GLS random-effects estimator.

sa specifies that the small-sample Swamy–Arora estimator individual-level variance component be used instead of the default consistent estimator. See the *Methods and Formulas* section for details.

____⌐ SE/Robust ⌐_____

vce(*vcetype*); see [R] *vce_option*.

robust, cluster(*varname*); see [XT] **estimation options**.

____⌐ Reporting ⌐_____

level(*#*); see [XT] **estimation options**.

theta, used with xtreg, re only, specifies that the output include the estimated value of θ used in combining the between and fixed estimators. For balanced data, this is a constant, and for unbalanced data, a summary of the values is presented in the header of the output.

Options for BE model

____⌐ Model ⌐_____

i(*varname$_i$*); see [XT] **estimation options**.

be requests the between regression estimator.

wls specifies that, in the case of unbalanced data, weighted least squares be used rather than the default OLS. Both methods produce consistent estimates. The true variance of the between-effects residual is $\sigma_\nu^2 + T_i\sigma_\epsilon^2$ (see *Methods and Formulas* below). WLS produces a "stabilized" variance of $\sigma_\nu^2/T_i + \sigma_\epsilon^2$, which is also not constant. Thus the choice between OLS and WLS amounts to which is more stable.

Comment: xtreg, be is rarely used anyway, but between estimates are an ingredient in the random-effects estimate. Our implementation of xtreg, re uses the OLS estimates for this ingredient based on our judgment that σ_ν^2 is large relative to σ_ϵ^2 in most models. Formally, only a consistent estimate of the between estimates is required.

____⌐ SE ⌐_____

vce(*vcetype*); see [R] *vce_option*.

____⌐ Reporting ⌐_____

level(*#*); see [XT] **estimation options**.

Options for FE model

i($varname_i$); see [XT] **estimation options**.

fe requests the fixed-effects (within) regression estimator.

vce(*vcetype*); see [R] *vce_option*.

robust, cluster(*varname*); see [XT] **estimation options**.

level(*#*); see [XT] **estimation options**.

Options for MLE model

i($varname_i$), noconstant; see [XT] **estimation options**.

mle requests the maximum-likelihood random-effects estimator.

vce(*vcetype*); see [R] *vce_option*.

level(*#*); see [XT] **estimation options**.

maximize_options: <u>ite</u>rate(*#*), [no]<u>log</u>, <u>trace</u>, <u>tol</u>erance(*#*), <u>ltol</u>erance(*#*), from(*init_specs*); see [R] **maximize**. These options are seldom used.

Options for PA model

i($varname_i$), noconstant; see [XT] **estimation options**.

pa requests the population-averaged estimator. For linear regression, this is the same as a random-effects estimator (both interpretations hold).

xtreg, pa is equivalent to xtgee, family(gaussian) link(id) corr(exchangeable), which are the defaults for the xtgee command. xtreg, pa allows all the relevant xtgee options such as robust. Whether you use xtreg, pa or xtgee makes no difference. See [XT] **xtgee**.

offset(*varname*); see [XT] **estimation options**.

corr(*correlation*), force; see [XT] **estimation options**.

vce(*vcetype*); see [R] *vce_option*.

robust, nmp; see [XT] **estimation options**.

rgf specifies that the robust variance estimate is multiplied by $(N-1)/(N-P)$, where N is the total number of observations and P is the number of coefficients estimated. This option can only be used with family(gaussian) when robust is either specified or implied by the use of pweights. Using this option implies that the robust variance estimate is not invariant to the scale of any weights used.

scale(x2|dev|phi|#) overrides the default scale parameter of scale(1); see [XT] **estimation options**.

level(#); see [XT] **estimation options**.

optimize_options control the iterative optimization process. These options are seldom used.

iterate(#) specifies the maximum number of iterations. When the number of iterations equals #, the optimization stops and presents the current results, even if convergence has not been reached. The default is iterate(100).

tolerance(#) specifies the tolerance for the coefficient vector. When the relative change in the coefficient vector from one iteration to the next is less than or equal to #, the optimization process is stopped. tolerance(1e-6) is the default.

nolog suppresses display of the iteration log.

trace specifies that the current estimates be printed at each iteration.

Remarks

If you have not read [XT] **xt**, please do so.

See Baltagi (2001, chapter 2) and Wooldridge (2002, chapter 10) for good overviews of fixed-effects and random-effects models.

Consider fitting models of the form

$$y_{it} = \alpha + \mathbf{x}_{it}\boldsymbol{\beta} + \nu_i + \epsilon_{it} \tag{1}$$

In this model, $\nu_i + \epsilon_{it}$ is the residual in the sense that we have little interest in it; we want estimates of $\boldsymbol{\beta}$. ν_i is the unit-specific residual; it differs between units, but, for any particular unit, its value is constant. In the pulmonary data of [XT] **xt**, a person who exercises less would presumably have a lower FEV year after year, and so would have a negative ν_i.

ϵ_{it} is the "usual" residual with the usual properties (mean 0, uncorrelated with itself, uncorrelated with $\mathbf{x}$, uncorrelated with ν, and homoskedastic), although in a more thorough development, we could decompose $\epsilon_{it} = \upsilon_t + \omega_{it}$, assume ω_{it} is a standard residual, and better describe υ_t.

Before making the assumptions necessary for estimation, let us perform some useful algebra on (1). Whatever the properties of ν_i and ϵ_{it}, if (1) is true, it must also be true that

$$\overline{y}_i = \alpha + \overline{\mathbf{x}}_i\boldsymbol{\beta} + \nu_i + \overline{\epsilon}_i \tag{2}$$

where $\overline{y}_i = \sum_t y_{it}/T_i$, $\overline{\mathbf{x}}_i = \sum_t \mathbf{x}_{it}/T_i$, and $\overline{\epsilon}_i = \sum_t \epsilon_{it}/T_i$. Subtracting (2) from (1), it must be equally true that

$$(y_{it} - \overline{y}_i) = (\mathbf{x}_{it} - \overline{\mathbf{x}}_i)\beta + (\epsilon_{it} - \overline{\epsilon}_i) \tag{3}$$

These three equations provide the basis for estimating β. In particular, xtreg, fe provides what is known as the fixed-effects estimator—also known as the within estimator—and amounts to using OLS to perform the estimation of (3). xtreg, be provides what is known as the between estimator, and amounts to using OLS to perform the estimation of (2). xtreg, re provides the random-effects estimator and is a (matrix) weighted average of the estimates produced by the between and within estimators. In particular, the random-effects estimator turns out to be equivalent to estimation of

$$(y_{it} - \theta\overline{y}_i) = (1 - \theta)\alpha + (\mathbf{x}_{it} - \theta\overline{\mathbf{x}}_i)\beta + \{(1 - \theta)\nu_i + (\epsilon_{it} - \theta\overline{\epsilon}_i)\} \tag{4}$$

where θ is a function of σ_ν^2 and σ_ϵ^2. If $\sigma_\nu^2 = 0$, meaning ν_i is always 0, $\theta = 0$ and (1) can be estimated by OLS directly. Alternatively, if $\sigma_\epsilon^2 = 0$, meaning ϵ_{it} is 0, $\theta = 1$ and the within estimator returns all the information available (which will, in fact, be a regression with an R^2 of 1).

Returning to more reasonable cases, few assumptions are required to justify the fixed-effects estimator of (3). The estimates are, however, conditional on the sample in that the ν_i are not assumed to have a distribution, but are instead treated as fixed and estimable. This statistical fine point can lead to difficulty when making out-of-sample predictions, but, that aside, the fixed-effects estimator has much to recommend it.

More is required to justify the between estimator of (2), but the conditioning on the sample is not assumed since $\nu_i + \overline{\epsilon}_i$ is treated as a residual. Newly required is that we assume ν_i and $\overline{\mathbf{x}}_i$ are uncorrelated. This follows from the assumptions of the OLS estimator but is also transparent: Were ν_i and $\overline{\mathbf{x}}_i$ correlated, the estimator could not determine how much of the change in $\overline{y}_i$, associated with an increase in $\overline{\mathbf{x}}_i$, to assign to β versus how much to attribute to the unknown correlation. (This, of course, suggests the use of an instrumental-variable estimator, $\overline{\mathbf{z}}_i$, which is correlated with $\overline{\mathbf{x}}_i$ but uncorrelated with ν_i, but that approach is not implemented here.)

The random-effects estimator of (4) requires the same no-correlation assumption. In comparison with the between estimator, the random-effects estimator produces more efficient results, albeit ones with unknown small-sample properties. The between estimator is less efficient because it discards the over-time information in the data in favor of simple means; the random-effects estimator uses both the within and the between information.

All of this would seem to leave the between estimator of (2) with no role (except for a minor, technical part it plays in helping to estimate σ_ν^2 and σ_ϵ^2, which are used in the calculation of θ, on which the random-effects estimates depend). Let us, however, consider a variation on (1):

$$y_{it} = \alpha + \overline{\mathbf{x}}_i\beta_1 + (\mathbf{x}_{it} - \overline{\mathbf{x}}_i)\beta_2 + \nu_i + \epsilon_{it} \tag{1$'$}$$

In this model, we postulate that changes in the average value of $\mathbf{x}$ for an individual have a different effect from temporary departures from the average. In an economic situation, y might be purchases of some item and $\mathbf{x}$ income; a change in average income should have more effect than a transitory change. In a clinical situation, y might be a physical response and $\mathbf{x}$ the level of a chemical in the brain; the model allows a different response to permanent rather than transitory changes.

The variations of (2) and (3) corresponding to (1$'$) are

$$\overline{y}_i = \alpha + \overline{\mathbf{x}}_i\beta_1 + \nu_i + \overline{\epsilon}_i \tag{2$'$}$$

$$(y_{it} - \overline{y}_i) = (\mathbf{x}_{it} - \overline{\mathbf{x}}_i)\beta_2 + (\epsilon_{it} - \overline{\epsilon}_i) \tag{3$'$}$$

That is, the between estimator estimates β_1 and the within β_2, and neither estimates the other. Thus even when estimating equations like (1), it is worth comparing the within and between estimators. Differences in results can suggest models like (1′), or, at the least, some other specification error.

Finally, it is worth understanding the role of the between and within estimators with regressors that are constant over time or constant over units. Consider the model

$$y_{it} = \alpha + \mathbf{x}_{it}\beta_1 + \mathbf{s}_i\beta_2 + \mathbf{z}_t\beta_3 + \nu_i + \epsilon_{it} \tag{1″}$$

This model is the same as (1), except that we explicitly identify the variables that vary over both time and i ($\mathbf{x}_{it}$, such as output or FEV); variables that are constant over time ($\mathbf{s}_i$, such as race or sex); and variables that vary solely over time ($\mathbf{z}_t$, such as the consumer price index or age in a cohort study). The corresponding between and within equations are

$$\overline{y}_i = \alpha + \overline{\mathbf{x}}_i\beta_1 + \mathbf{s}_i\beta_2 + \overline{\mathbf{z}}\beta_3 + \nu_i + \overline{\epsilon}_i \tag{2″}$$

$$(y_{it} - \overline{y}_i) = (\mathbf{x}_{it} - \overline{\mathbf{x}}_i)\beta_1 + (\mathbf{z}_t - \overline{\mathbf{z}})\beta_3 + (\epsilon_{it} - \overline{\epsilon}_i) \tag{3″}$$

In the between estimator of (2″), no estimate of β_3 is possible because $\overline{\mathbf{z}}$ is a constant across the i observations; the regression-estimated intercept will be an estimate of $\alpha + \overline{\mathbf{z}}\beta_3$. On the other hand, it is able to provide estimates of β_1 and β_2. It is able to estimate effects of factors that are constant over time, such as race and sex, but to do so, it must assume that ν_i is uncorrelated with those factors.

The within estimator of (3″), like the between estimator, provides an estimate of β_1, but provides no estimate of β_2 for time-invariant factors. Instead, it provides an estimate of β_3, the effects of the time-varying factors. The between estimator can also provide estimates u_i for ν_i. More correctly, the estimator u_i is an estimator of $\nu_i + \mathbf{s}_i\beta_2$. Thus u_i is an estimator of ν_i only if there are no time-invariant variables in the model. If there are time-invariant variables, u_i is an estimate of ν_i plus the effects of the time-invariant variables.

Assessing goodness of fit

R^2 is a popular measure of goodness of fit in ordinary regression. In our case, given $\widehat{\alpha}$ and $\widehat{\beta}$ estimates of α and β, we can assess the goodness of fit with respect to (1), (2), or (3). The prediction equations are, respectively,

$$\widehat{y}_{it} = \widehat{\alpha} + \mathbf{x}_{it}\widehat{\beta} \tag{1‴}$$

$$\widehat{\overline{y}}_i = \widehat{\alpha} + \overline{\mathbf{x}}_i\widehat{\beta} \tag{2‴}$$

$$\widehat{\widetilde{y}}_{it} = (\widehat{y}_{it} - \widehat{\overline{y}}_i) = (\mathbf{x}_{it} - \overline{\mathbf{x}}_i)\widehat{\beta} \tag{3‴}$$

xtreg reports "R-squares" corresponding to these three equations. R-squares is in quotes because the R-squares reported do not have all the properties of the OLS R^2.

The ordinary properties of R^2 include being equal to the squared correlation between $\widehat{y}$ and y and being equal to the fraction of the variation in y explained by $\widehat{y}$—formally defined as $\mathrm{Var}(\widehat{y})/\mathrm{Var}(y)$. The identity of the definitions is due to a special property of the OLS estimates; in general, given a prediction $\widehat{y}$ for y, the squared correlation is not equal to the ratio of the variances, and the ratio of the variances is not required to be less than 1.

xtreg reports R^2 values calculated as correlations squared, calling them R^2 overall, corresponding to (1‴); R^2 between, corresponding to (2‴); and R^2 within, corresponding to (3‴). In fact, you can think of each of these three numbers as having all the properties of ordinary R^2s if you bear in mind that the prediction being judged is not $\widehat{y}_{it}$, $\widehat{\overline{y}}_i$, and $\widehat{\widetilde{y}}_{it}$, but $\gamma_1\widehat{y}_{it}$ from the regression $y_{it} = \gamma_1\widehat{y}_{it}$; $\gamma_2\widehat{\overline{y}}_i$ from the regression $\overline{y}_i = \gamma_2\widehat{\overline{y}}_i$; and $\gamma_3\widehat{\widetilde{y}}_{it}$ from $\widetilde{y}_{it} = \gamma_3\widehat{\widetilde{y}}_{it}$.

In particular, xtreg, be obtains its estimates by performing OLS on (2), and therefore its reported R^2 between is an ordinary R^2. The other two reported R^2s are merely correlations squared, or, if you prefer, R^2s from the second-round regressions $y_{it} = \gamma_{11}\widehat{y}_{it}$ and $\widetilde{y}_{it} = \gamma_{13}\widehat{\widetilde{y}}_{it}$.

xtreg, fe obtains its estimates by performing OLS on (3), so its reported R^2 within is an ordinary R^2. As with be, the other R^2s are correlations squared, or, if you prefer, R^2s from the second-round regressions $\overline{y}_i = \gamma_{22}\widehat{\overline{y}}_i$ and, as with be, $\widetilde{y}_{it} = \gamma_{23}\widehat{\widetilde{y}}_{it}$.

xtreg, re obtains its estimates by performing OLS on (4); none of the R^2s corresponding to $(1''')$, $(2''')$, or $(3''')$ correspond directly to this estimator (the "relevant" R^2 is the one corresponding to (4)). All three reported R^2s are correlations squared, or, if you prefer, from second-round regressions.

xtreg and associated commands

▷ Example 1

Using the nlswork dataset described in [XT] **xt**, we will model ln_wage in terms of completed years of schooling (grade), current age and age squared, current years worked (experience) and experience squared, current years of tenure on the current job and tenure squared, whether black, whether residing in an area not designated an SMSA (standard metropolitan statistical area), and whether residing in the South. Most of these variables are in the data, but we need to construct a few:

```
. use http://www.stata-press.com/data/r9/nlswork
(National Longitudinal Survey.  Young Women 14-26 years of age in 1968)
. generate age2 = age^2
(24 missing values generated)
. generate ttl_exp2 = ttl_exp^2
. generate tenure2 = tenure^2
(433 missing values generated)
. generate byte black = race==2
```

To obtain the between-effects estimates, we use xtreg, be:

```
. xtreg ln_w grade age* ttl_exp* tenure* black not_smsa south, be i(idcode)
```

Between regression (regression on group means)	Number of obs	= 28091
Group variable (i): idcode	Number of groups	= 4697

R-sq:		Obs per group:	
within	= 0.1591	min =	1
between	= 0.4900	avg =	6.0
overall	= 0.3695	max =	15

		F(10,4686)	= 450.23
sd(u_i + avg(e_i.))=	.3036114	Prob > F	= 0.0000

ln_wage	Coef.	Std. Err.	t	P>|t|	[95% Conf. Interval]
grade	.0607602	.0020006	30.37	0.000	.0568382 .0646822
age	.0323158	.0087251	3.70	0.000	.0152105 .0494211
age2	-.0005997	.0001429	-4.20	0.000	-.0008799 -.0003194
ttl_exp	.0138853	.0056749	2.45	0.014	.0027598 .0250108
ttl_exp2	.0007342	.0003267	2.25	0.025	.0000936 .0013747
tenure	.0698419	.0060729	11.50	0.000	.0579361 .0817476
tenure2	-.0028756	.0004098	-7.02	0.000	-.0036789 -.0020722
black	-.0564167	.0105131	-5.37	0.000	-.0770272 -.0358061
not_smsa	-.1860406	.0112495	-16.54	0.000	-.2080949 -.1639862
south	-.0993378	.010136	-9.80	0.000	-.1192091 -.0794665
_cons	.3339113	.1210434	2.76	0.006	.0966093 .5712133

The between-effects regression is estimated on person-averages, so the "n = 4697" result is relevant. `xtreg, be` reports the "number of observations" and group-size information: `describe` in [XT] **xt** showed that we have 28,534 "observations"—person-years, really—of data. Taking the subsample that has no missing values in `ln_wage`, `grade`, ..., `south` leaves us with 28,091 observations on person-years, reflecting 4,697 persons, each observed for an average of 5.98 years.

In terms of goodness of fit, the R^2 between is directly relevant; our R^2 is .4900. If, however, we use these estimates to predict the within model, we have an R^2 of .1591. If we use these estimates to fit the overall data, our R^2 is .3695.

The F statistic tests that the coefficients on the regressors `grade`, `age`, ..., `south` are all jointly zero. Our model is significant.

The root mean squared error of the fitted regression, which is an estimate of the standard deviation of $\nu_i + \overline{\epsilon}_i$, is .3036.

In terms of our coefficients, each year of schooling increases hourly wages by 6.1%; age increases wages up to age 26.9 and thereafter decreases them (because the quadratic $ax^2 + bx + c$ turns over at $x = -b/2a$, which for our `age` and `age2` coefficients is $.0323158/(2 \times .0005997) \approx 26.9$); total experience increases wages at an increasing rate (which is surprising and bothersome); tenure on the current job increases wages up to a tenure of 12.1 years and thereafter decreases them; wages of blacks are, these things held constant, (approximately) 5.6% below that of nonblacks (approximately because `black` is an indicator variable); residing in a nonSMSA (rural area) reduces wages by 18.6%; and residing in the South reduces wages by 9.9%.

◁

▷ Example 2

To fit the same model with the fixed-effects estimator, we specify the `fe` option.

```
. xtreg ln_w grade age* ttl_exp* tenure* black not_smsa south, fe
Fixed-effects (within) regression          Number of obs      =       28091
Group variable (i): idcode                 Number of groups   =        4697

R-sq:  within  = 0.1727                     Obs per group: min =           1
       between = 0.3505                                    avg =         6.0
       overall = 0.2625                                    max =          15

                                            F(8,23386)         =      610.12
corr(u_i, Xb)  = 0.1936                     Prob > F           =      0.0000
```

ln_wage	Coef.	Std. Err.	t	P>|t|	[95% Conf. Interval]
grade	(dropped)				
age	.0359987	.0033864	10.63	0.000	.0293611 .0426362
age2	-.000723	.0000533	-13.58	0.000	-.0008274 -.0006186
ttl_exp	.0334668	.0029653	11.29	0.000	.0276545 .039279
ttl_exp2	.0002163	.0001277	1.69	0.090	-.0000341 .0004666
tenure	.0357539	.0018487	19.34	0.000	.0321303 .0393775
tenure2	-.0019701	.000125	-15.76	0.000	-.0022151 -.0017251
black	(dropped)				
not_smsa	-.0890108	.0095316	-9.34	0.000	-.1076933 -.0703282
south	-.0606309	.0109319	-5.55	0.000	-.0820582 -.0392036
_cons	1.03732	.0485546	21.36	0.000	.9421497 1.13249

sigma_u	.35562203	
sigma_e	.29068923	
rho	.59946283	(fraction of variance due to u_i)

```
F test that all u_i=0:     F(4696,23386) =       5.13          Prob > F = 0.0000
```

The observation summary at the top is the same as for the between-effects model, although this time it is the "Number of obs" that is relevant.

Our three R^2s are not too different from those reported previously; the R^2 within is slightly higher (.1727 vs .1591), and the R^2 between is a little lower (.3505 vs .4900), as expected, since the between estimator maximizes R^2 between and the within estimator R^2 within. In terms of overall fit, these estimates are somewhat worse (.2625 vs .3695).

xtreg, fe can provide estimates of σ_ν and σ_ϵ, although how you interpret these estimates depends on whether you are using xtreg to fit a fixed-effects model or random-effects model. To clarify this fine point, in the fixed-effects model, ν_i are formally fixed—they have no distribution. If you subscribe to this view, think of the reported $\widehat{\sigma}_\nu$ as merely an arithmetic way to describe the range of the estimated but fixed ν_i. If, however, you are employing the fixed-effects estimator of the random-effects model, .355622 is an estimate of σ_ν or would be if there were no dropped variables.

In our case, note that both grade and black were dropped from the model. They were dropped because they do not vary over time. Since grade and race are time invariant, our estimate u_i is an estimate of ν_i plus the effects of grade and race, so our estimate of the standard deviation is based on the variation in ν_i, grade, and race. On the other hand, had race and grade been dropped merely because they were collinear with the other regressors in our model, u_i would be an estimate of ν_i, and .3556 would be an estimate of σ_ν. (xtsum and xttab allow you to determine whether a variable is time invariant; see [XT] **xtsum** and [XT] **xttab**.)

Regardless of the status of u_i, our estimate of the standard deviation of ϵ_{it} is valid (and, in fact, is the estimate that would be used by the random-effects estimator to produce its results).

Our estimate of the correlation of u_i with $\mathbf{x}_{it}$ suffers from the problem of what u_i measures. We find correlation but cannot say whether this is correlation of ν_i with $\mathbf{x}_{it}$ or merely correlation of grade and race with $\mathbf{x}_{it}$. In any case, the fixed-effects estimator is robust to such a correlation, and the other estimates it produces are unbiased.

So, while this estimator produces no estimates of the effects of grade and race, it does predict that age has a positive effect on wages up to age 24.9 years (as compared with 26.9 years estimated by the between estimator); that total experience still increases wages at an increasing rate (which is still bothersome); that tenure increases wages up to 9.1 years (as compared with 12.1); that living in a nonSMSA reduces wages by 8.9% (as compared with a more drastic 18.6%); and that living in the South reduces wages by 6.1% (as compared with 9.9%).

$\lhd$

▷ Example 3

If we suspect that there is heteroskedasticity in the idiosyncratic error term ϵ_{it}, we could specify the robust option:

```
. xtreg ln_w grade age* ttl_exp* tenure* black not_smsa south, fe robust
```

| Fixed-effects (within) regression | Number of obs | = | 28091 |
| Group variable (i): idcode | Number of groups | = | 4697 |

R-sq:	within	= 0.1727	Obs per group: min =	1
	between	= 0.3505	avg =	6.0
	overall	= 0.2625	max =	15

| | | F(8,23386) | = | 553.03 |
| corr(u_i, Xb) | = 0.1936 | Prob > F | = | 0.0000 |

ln_wage	Coef.	Robust Std. Err.	t	P>|t|	[95% Conf. Interval]
grade	(dropped)					
age	.0359987	.0039755	9.06	0.000	.0282064	.0437909
age2	-.000723	.0000634	-11.40	0.000	-.0008473	-.0005987
ttl_exp	.0334668	.003215	10.41	0.000	.0271652	.0397684
ttl_exp2	.0002163	.000141	1.53	0.125	-.0000601	.0004926
tenure	.0357539	.0019756	18.10	0.000	.0318817	.0396261
tenure2	-.0019701	.0001362	-14.47	0.000	-.002237	-.0017032
black	(dropped)					
not_smsa	-.0890108	.0113004	-7.88	0.000	-.1111603	-.0668613
south	-.0606309	.013096	-4.63	0.000	-.0863	-.0349618
_cons	1.03732	.0564117	18.39	0.000	.9267494	1.14789

sigma_u	.35562203	
sigma_e	.29068923	
rho	.59946283	(fraction of variance due to u_i)

While the estimated coefficients are the same with and without the `robust` option, the robust estimator produced larger standard errors and a p-value for `ttl_exp2` above the conventional 10%. The F test of $\nu_i = 0$ is suppressed because it is too difficult to compute the robust form of the statistic when there are more than a few panels.

◁

❏ Technical Note

Clustering on the panel variable produces an estimator of the VCE that is robust to cross-sectional heteroskedasticity and within-panel (serial) correlation which is asymptotically equivalent to that proposed by Arellano (1987). While the example above applies the fixed-effects estimator, the robust and cluster-robust VCE estimators are also available for the random-effects estimator. Wooldridge (2002) and Arellano (2003) discuss these robust and cluster-robust VCE estimators for the fixed-effects and random-effects estimators. Further details are available in *Methods and Formulas*.

❏

▷ Example 4

Refitting our log-wage model with the random-effects estimator, we obtain

```
. xtreg ln_w grade age* ttl_exp* tenure* black not_smsa south, re theta
Random-effects GLS regression                   Number of obs      =     28091
Group variable (i): idcode                      Number of groups   =      4697

R-sq:  within  = 0.1715                          Obs per group: min =         1
       between = 0.4784                                         avg =       6.0
       overall = 0.3708                                         max =        15

Random effects u_i ~ Gaussian                    Wald chi2(10)      =   9244.87
corr(u_i, X)        = 0 (assumed)                Prob > chi2        =    0.0000

------------------ theta ------------------
   min      5%     median      95%      max
 0.2520  0.2520    0.5499    0.7016   0.7206
```

ln_wage	Coef.	Std. Err.	z	P>|z|	[95% Conf. Interval]	
grade	.0646499	.0017811	36.30	0.000	.0611589	.0681408
age	.036806	.0031195	11.80	0.000	.0306918	.0429201
age2	-.0007133	.00005	-14.27	0.000	-.0008113	-.0006153
ttl_exp	.0290207	.0024219	11.98	0.000	.0242737	.0337676
ttl_exp2	.0003049	.0001162	2.62	0.009	.000077	.0005327
tenure	.039252	.0017555	22.36	0.000	.0358114	.0426927
tenure2	-.0020035	.0001193	-16.80	0.000	-.0022373	-.0017697
black	-.0530532	.0099924	-5.31	0.000	-.0726379	-.0334685
not_smsa	-.1308263	.0071751	-18.23	0.000	-.1448891	-.1167634
south	-.0868927	.0073031	-11.90	0.000	-.1012066	-.0725788
_cons	.2387209	.0494688	4.83	0.000	.1417639	.335678
sigma_u	.25790313					
sigma_e	.29069544					
rho	.44043812	(fraction of variance due to u_i)				

According to the R^2s, this estimator performs worse within than the within fixed-effects estimator and worse between than the between estimator, as it must, and slightly better overall.

We estimate that σ_ν is .2579 and σ_ϵ is .2907 and, by assertion, assume that the correlation of ν and x is zero.

All that is known about the random-effects estimator is its asymptotic properties, so rather than reporting an F statistic for overall significance, xtreg, re reports a χ^2. Taken jointly, our coefficients are significant.

xtreg, re also reports a summary of the distribution of θ_i, an ingredient in the estimation of (4). θ is not a constant in this case because we observe women for unequal periods of time.

We estimate that schooling has a rate of return of 6.5% (compared with 6.1% between and no estimate within); that the increase of wages with age turns around at 25.8 years (compared with 26.9 between and 24.9 within); that total experience yet again increases wages increasingly; that the effect of job tenure turns around at 9.8 years (compared with 12.1 between and 9.1 within); that being black reduces wages by 5.3% (compared with 5.6% between and no estimate within); that living in a nonSMSA reduces wages 13.1% (compared with 18.6% between and 8.9% within); and that living in the South reduces wages 8.7% (compared with 9.9% between and 6.1% within).

◁

▷ Example 5

Alternatively, we could have fitted this random-effects model using the maximum-likelihood estimator:

```
. xtreg ln_w grade age* ttl_exp* tenure* black not_smsa south, mle

Fitting constant-only model:
Iteration 0:   log likelihood = -13690.161
Iteration 1:   log likelihood = -12819.317
Iteration 2:   log likelihood = -12662.039
Iteration 3:   log likelihood = -12649.744
Iteration 4:   log likelihood = -12649.614

Fitting full model:
Iteration 0:   log likelihood =  -8922.145
Iteration 1:   log likelihood = -8853.6409
Iteration 2:   log likelihood = -8853.4255
Iteration 3:   log likelihood = -8853.4254
```

| Random-effects ML regression | | Number of obs | = | 28091 |
| Group variable (i): idcode | | Number of groups | = | 4697 |

Random effects u_i ~ Gaussian

	Obs per group: min =	1
	avg =	6.0
	max =	15
	LR chi2(10) =	7592.38
Log likelihood = -8853.4254	Prob > chi2 =	0.0000

ln_wage	Coef.	Std. Err.	z	P>|z|	[95% Conf. Interval]	
grade	.0646093	.0017372	37.19	0.000	.0612044	.0680142
age	.0368531	.0031226	11.80	0.000	.030733	.0429732
age2	-.0007132	.0000501	-14.24	0.000	-.0008113	-.000615
ttl_exp	.0288196	.0024143	11.94	0.000	.0240877	.0335515
ttl_exp2	.000309	.0001163	2.66	0.008	.0000811	.0005369
tenure	.0394371	.0017604	22.40	0.000	.0359868	.0428875
tenure2	-.0020052	.0001195	-16.77	0.000	-.0022395	-.0017709
black	-.0533394	.0097338	-5.48	0.000	-.0724172	-.0342615
not_smsa	-.1323433	.0071322	-18.56	0.000	-.1463221	-.1183644
south	-.0875599	.0072143	-12.14	0.000	-.1016998	-.0734201
_cons	.2390837	.0491002	4.86	0.000	.1426727	.3354947
/sigma_u	.2485556	.0035017			.2417863	.2555144
/sigma_e	.2918458	.001352			.289208	.2945076
rho	.4204033	.0074828			.4057959	.4351212

Likelihood-ratio test of sigma_u=0: chibar2(01)= 7339.84 Prob>=chibar2 = 0.000

The estimates are very nearly the same as those produced by xtreg, re—the GLS estimator. For instance, xtreg, re estimated the coefficient on grade to be .0646499, xtreg, mle estimated .0646093, and the ratio is .0646499/.0646093 = 1.001 to three decimal places. Similarly, the standard errors are nearly equal: .0017812/.0017372 = 1.025. Below we compare all 11 coefficients:

	Coefficient ratio			SE ratio		
Estimator	mean	min.	max.	mean	min.	max.
xtreg, mle (ML)	1.	1.	1.	1.	1.	1.
xtreg, re (GLS)	.997	.987	1.007	1.006	.997	1.027

◁

▷ Example 6

We could also have fitted this model using the population-averaged estimator:

```
. xtreg ln_w grade age* ttl_exp* tenure* black not_smsa south, i(idcode) pa
Iteration 1: tolerance = .0310561
Iteration 2: tolerance = .00074898
Iteration 3: tolerance = .0000147
Iteration 4: tolerance = 2.880e-07
```

GEE population-averaged model				Number of obs	=	28091
Group variable:		idcode		Number of groups	=	4697
Link:		identity		Obs per group: min	=	1
Family:		Gaussian		avg	=	6.0
Correlation:		exchangeable		max	=	15
				Wald chi2(10)	=	9598.89
Scale parameter:		.1436709		Prob > chi2	=	0.0000

ln_wage	Coef.	Std. Err.	z	P>|z|	[95% Conf. Interval]	
grade	.0645427	.0016829	38.35	0.000	.0612442	.0678412
age	.036932	.0031509	11.72	0.000	.0307564	.0431076
age2	-.0007129	.0000506	-14.10	0.000	-.0008121	-.0006138
ttl_exp	.0284878	.0024169	11.79	0.000	.0237508	.0332248
ttl_exp2	.0003158	.0001172	2.69	0.007	.000086	.0005456
tenure	.0397468	.0017779	22.36	0.000	.0362621	.0432315
tenure2	-.002008	.0001209	-16.61	0.000	-.0022449	-.0017711
black	-.0538314	.0094086	-5.72	0.000	-.072272	-.0353909
not_smsa	-.1347788	.0070543	-19.11	0.000	-.1486049	-.1209526
south	-.0885969	.0071132	-12.46	0.000	-.1025386	-.0746552
_cons	.2396286	.0491465	4.88	0.000	.1433034	.3359539

These results differ from those produced by xtreg, re and xtreg, mle. Coefficients are larger and standard errors smaller. xtreg, pa is simply another way to run the xtgee command. That is, we would have obtained the same output had we typed

```
. xtgee ln_w grade age* ttl_exp* tenure* black not_smsa south, i(idcode)
```
(*output omitted because it is the same as above*)

See [XT] **xtgee**. In the language of xtgee, the random-effects model corresponds to an exchangeable correlation structure and identity link, and xtgee also allows other correlation structures. Let us stay with the random-effects model, however. xtgee will also produce robust estimates of variance, and we refit this model that way by typing

```
. xtgee ln_w grade age* ttl_exp* tenure* black not_smsa south, i(idcode) robust
```
(*output omitted, coefficients the same, standard errors different*)

In the previous example, we presented a table comparing xtreg, re with xtreg, mle. Below we add the results from the estimates shown and the ones we did with xtgee, robust:

Estimator		Coefficient ratio			SE ratio		
		mean	min.	max.	mean	min.	max.
xtreg, mle	(ML)	1.	1.	1.	1.	1.	1.
xtreg, re	(GLS)	.997	.987	1.007	1.006	.997	1.027
xtreg, pa	(PA)	1.060	.847	1.317	.853	.626	.986
xtgee, robust	(PA)	1.060	.847	1.317	1.306	.957	1.545

So, which are right? This is a real dataset, and we do not know. However, in example 2 in [XT] **xtreg postestimation**, we will present evidence that the assumptions underlying the xtreg, re and xtreg, mle results are not met.

◁

Acknowledgments

We thank Richard Goldstein, who wrote the first draft of the routine that fits random-effects regressions, and Badi Baltagi and Manuelita Ureta of Texas A&M University, who assisted us in working our way through the literature.

Saved Results

xtreg, re saves in e():

Scalars

e(N)	number of observations	e(r2_o)	R-squared for overall model
e(N_g)	number of groups	e(r2_b)	R-squared for between model
e(df_m)	model degrees of freedom	e(sigma)	ancillary parameter (gamma, lnormal)
e(g_max)	largest group size	e(sigma_u)	panel-level standard deviation
e(g_min)	smallest group size	e(sigma_e)	standard deviation of ϵ_{it}
e(g_avg)	average group size	e(thta_min)	minimum θ
e(chi2)	χ^2	e(thta_5)	θ, 5th percentile
e(rho)	ρ	e(thta_50)	θ, 50th percentile
e(Tbar)	harmonic mean of group sizes	e(thta_95)	θ, 95th percentile
e(Tcon)	1 if T is constant	e(thta_max)	maximum θ
e(r2_w)	R-squared for within model	e(N_clust)	number of clusters

Macros

e(cmd)	xtreg	e(vcetype)	title used to label Std. Err.
e(depvar)	name of dependent variable	e(chi2type)	Wald; type of model χ^2 test
e(model)	re	e(sa)	Swamy–Arora estimator of the variance
e(ivar)	variable denoting groups		components (sa only)
e(clustvar)	name of cluster variable	e(properties)	b V
e(vce)	*vcetype* specified in vce()	e(predict)	program used to implement predict

Matrices

e(b)	coefficient vector	e(Vf)	VCE for fixed-effects model
e(theta)	θ	e(bf)	coefficient vector for fixed-effects model
e(V)	variance–covariance matrix of the estimators		

Functions

e(sample)	marks estimation sample

`xtreg, be` saves in `e()`:

Scalars

`e(N)`	number of observations	`e(ll)`	log likelihood
`e(N_g)`	number of groups	`e(ll_0)`	log likelihood, constant-only model
`e(mss)`	model sum of squares	`e(g_max)`	largest group size
`e(df_m)`	model degrees of freedom	`e(g_min)`	smallest group size
`e(rss)`	residual sum of squares	`e(g_avg)`	average group size
`e(df_r)`	residual degrees of freedom	`e(Tbar)`	harmonic mean of group sizes
`e(r2)`	R-squared	`e(Tcon)`	1 if T is constant
`e(r2_a)`	adjusted R-squared	`e(r2_w)`	R-squared for within model
`e(F)`	F statistic	`e(r2_o)`	R-squared for overall model
`e(rmse)`	root mean squared error	`e(r2_b)`	R-squared for between model

Macros

`e(cmd)`	`xtreg`	`e(vce)`	*vcetype* specified in `vce()`
`e(depvar)`	name of dependent variable	`e(vcetype)`	title used to label Std. Err.
`e(model)`	`be`	`e(properties)`	b V
`e(ivar)`	variable denoting groups	`e(predict)`	program used to implement `predict`

Matrices

`e(b)`	coefficient vector	`e(V)`	variance–covariance matrix of the estimators

Functions

`e(sample)`	marks estimation sample

`xtreg, fe` saves in `e()`:

Scalars

`e(N)`	number of observations	`e(g_max)`	largest group size
`e(N_g)`	number of groups	`e(g_min)`	smallest group size
`e(mss)`	model sum of squares	`e(g_avg)`	average group size
`e(tss)`	total sum of squares	`e(rho)`	ρ
`e(df_m)`	model degrees of freedom	`e(Tbar)`	harmonic mean of group sizes
`e(rss)`	residual sum of squares	`e(Tcon)`	1 if T is constant
`e(df_r)`	residual degrees of freedom	`e(r2_w)`	R-squared for within model
`e(r2)`	R-squared	`e(r2_o)`	R-squared for overall model
`e(r2_a)`	adjusted R-squared	`e(r2_b)`	R-squared for between model
`e(sigma)`	ancillary parameter (gamma, lnormal)	`e(N_clust)`	number of clusters
`e(rmse)`	root mean squared error	`e(corr)`	corr(u_i, Xb)
`e(ll)`	log likelihood	`e(sigma_u)`	panel-level standard deviation
`e(ll_0)`	log likelihood, constant-only model	`e(sigma_e)`	standard deviation of ϵ_{it}
`e(df_a)`	degrees of freedom for absorbed effect	`e(F_f)`	F for $u_i=0$
`e(F)`	F statistic		

Macros

`e(cmd)`	`xtreg`	`e(clustvar)`	name of cluster variable
`e(depvar)`	name of dependent variable	`e(vcetype)`	title used to label Std. Err.
`e(model)`	`fe`	`e(properties)`	b V
`e(ivar)`	variable denoting groups	`e(predict)`	program used to implement `predict`

Matrices

`e(b)`	coefficient vector	`e(V)`	variance–covariance matrix of the estimators

Functions

`e(sample)`	marks estimation sample

`xtreg, mle` saves in `e()`:

Scalars

e(N)	number of observations	e(g_min)	smallest group size
e(N_g)	number of groups	e(g_avg)	average group size
e(df_m)	model degrees of freedom	e(chi2)	χ^2
e(ll)	log likelihood	e(chi2_c)	χ^2 for comparison test
e(ll_0)	log likelihood, constant-only model	e(rho)	ρ
e(ll_c)	log likelihood, comparison model	e(sigma_u)	panel-level standard deviation
e(g_max)	largest group size	e(sigma_e)	standard deviation of ϵ_{it}

Macros

e(cmd)	xtreg	e(vcetype)	title used to label Std. Err.
e(depvar)	name of dependent variable	e(chi2type)	Wald or LR; type of model χ^2 test
e(title)	title in estimation output	e(chi2_ct)	Wald or LR; type of model χ^2 test
e(model)	ml		corresponding to e(chi2_c)
e(ivar)	variable denoting groups	e(distrib)	Gaussian; the distribution of the RE
e(wtype)	weight type	e(crittype)	optimization criterion
e(wexp)	weight expression	e(properties)	b V
e(vce)	*vcetype* specified in vce()	e(predict)	program used to implement predict

Matrices

e(b)	coefficient vector	e(V)	variance–covariance matrix of the estimators

Functions

e(sample)	marks estimation sample

`xtreg, pa` saves in `e()`:

Scalars

e(N)	number of observations	e(deviance)	deviance
e(N_g)	number of groups	e(chi2_dev)	χ^2 test of deviance
e(df_m)	model degrees of freedom	e(dispers)	deviance dispersion
e(g_max)	largest group size	e(chi2_dis)	χ^2 test of deviance dispersion
e(g_min)	smallest group size	e(tol)	target tolerance
e(g_avg)	average group size	e(dif)	achieved tolerance
e(chi2)	χ^2	e(phi)	scale parameter
e(df_pear)	degrees of freedom for Pearson χ^2		

Macros

e(cmd)	xtgee	e(vce)	*vcetype* specified in vce()
e(cmd2)	xtreg	e(vcetype)	title used to label Std. Err.
e(depvar)	name of dependent variable	e(chi2type)	Wald; type of model χ^2 test
e(model)	pa	e(disp)	deviance dispersion
e(family)	Gaussian	e(offset)	offset
e(link)	identity; link function	e(crittype)	optimization criterion
e(corr)	correlation structure	e(properties)	b V
e(scale)	x2, dev, phi, or #; scale parameter	e(predict)	program used to implement predict
e(ivar)	variable denoting groups		

Matrices

e(b)	coefficient vector	e(V)	variance–covariance matrix of the estimators
e(R)	estimated working correlation matrix		

Functions

e(sample)	marks estimation sample

Methods and Formulas

The model to be fitted is

$$y_{it} = \alpha + \mathbf{x}_{it}\boldsymbol{\beta} + \nu_i + \epsilon_{it}$$

for $i = 1, \ldots, n$ and, for each i, $t = 1, \ldots, T$, of which T_i periods are actually observed.

xtreg, fe

xtreg, `fe` produces estimates by running OLS on

$$(y_{it} - \overline{y}_i + \overline{\overline{y}}) = \alpha + (\mathbf{x}_{it} - \overline{\mathbf{x}}_i + \overline{\overline{\mathbf{x}}})\boldsymbol{\beta} + (\epsilon_{it} - \overline{\epsilon}_i + \overline{\nu}) + \overline{\overline{\epsilon}}$$

where $\overline{y}_i = \sum_{t=1}^{T_i} y_{it}/T_i$, and similarly, $\overline{\overline{y}} = \sum_i \sum_t y_{it}/(nT_i)$. The covariance matrix of the estimators is adjusted for the extra $n - 1$ estimated means, so results are the same as using OLS on (1) to estimate ν_i directly. Specifying `robust` or `cluster()` causes the Huber/White/sandwich VCE estimator to be calculated for the coefficients estimated in this regression. See [U] **20.14 Obtaining robust variance estimates** and [P] **_robust** for details. Wooldridge (2002) and Arellano (2003) discuss this application of the Huber/White/sandwich VCE estimator.

From the estimates $\widehat{\alpha}$ and $\widehat{\boldsymbol{\beta}}$, estimates u_i of ν_i are obtained as $u_i = \overline{y}_i - \widehat{\alpha} - \overline{\mathbf{x}}_i\widehat{\boldsymbol{\beta}}$. Reported from the calculated u_i are its standard deviation and its correlation with $\overline{\mathbf{x}}_i\widehat{\boldsymbol{\beta}}$. Reported as the standard deviation of e_{it} is the regression's estimated root mean squared error, s, which is adjusted (as previously stated) for the $n - 1$ estimated means.

Reported as R^2 within is the R^2 from the mean-deviated regression.

Reported as R^2 between is $\mathrm{corr}(\overline{\mathbf{x}}_i\widehat{\boldsymbol{\beta}}, \overline{y}_i)^2$.

Reported as R^2 overall is $\mathrm{corr}(\mathbf{x}_{it}\widehat{\boldsymbol{\beta}}, y_{it})^2$.

xtreg, be

xtreg, `be` fits the following model:

$$\overline{y}_i = \alpha + \overline{\mathbf{x}}_i\boldsymbol{\beta} + \nu_i + \overline{\epsilon}_i$$

Estimation is via OLS unless T_i is not constant and the `wls` option is specified. Otherwise, the estimation is performed via WLS. The estimation is performed by `regress` for both cases, but in the case of WLS, `[aweight=`T_i`]` is specified.

Reported as R^2 between is the R^2 from the fitted regression.

Reported as R^2 within is $\mathrm{corr}\{(\mathbf{x}_{it} - \overline{\mathbf{x}}_i)\widehat{\boldsymbol{\beta}}, y_{it} - \overline{y}_i\}^2$.

Reported as R^2 overall is $\mathrm{corr}(\mathbf{x}_{it}\widehat{\boldsymbol{\beta}}, y_{it})^2$.

xtreg, re

The key to the random-effects estimator is the GLS transform. Given estimates of the idiosyncratic component, $\widehat{\sigma}_e^2$, and the individual component, $\widehat{\sigma}_u^2$, the GLS transform of a variable z for the random-effects model is

$$z_{it}^* = z_{it} - \widehat{\theta}_i\overline{z}_i$$

where $\bar{z}_i = \frac{1}{T_i} \sum_t^{T_i} z_{it}$ and

$$\hat{\theta}_i = 1 - \sqrt{\frac{\hat{\sigma}_e^2}{T_i \hat{\sigma}_u^2 + \hat{\sigma}_e^2}}$$

Given an estimate of $\hat{\theta}_i$, one transforms the dependent and independent variables, and then the coefficient estimates and the variance–covariance matrix come from an OLS regression of y_{it}^* on $\mathbf{x}_{it}^*$ and the transformed constant $1 - \hat{\theta}_i$. Specifying `robust` or `cluster()` causes the Huber/White/sandwich VCE estimator to be calculated for the coefficients estimated in this regression. See [U] **20.14 Obtaining robust variance estimates** and [P] **_robust** for details. Wooldridge (2002) and Arellano (2003) discuss this application of the Huber/White/sandwich VCE estimator.

Stata has two implementations of the Swamy–Arora method for estimating the variance components. They produce exactly the same results in balanced panels and share the same estimator of σ_e^2. However, the two methods differ in their estimator of σ_u^2 in unbalanced panels. We call the first $\hat{\sigma}_{u\bar{T}}^2$ and the second $\hat{\sigma}_{uSA}^2$. Both estimators are consistent; however, $\hat{\sigma}_{uSA}^2$ has a more elaborate adjustment for small samples than $\hat{\sigma}_{u\bar{T}}^2$. (See Baltagi [2001], Baltagi and Chang [1994], and Swamy and Arora [1972] for derivations of these methods.)

Both methods use the same function of within residuals to estimate the idiosyncratic error component σ_e. Specifically,

$$\hat{\sigma}_e^2 = \frac{\sum_i^n \sum_t^{T_i} e_{it}^2}{N - n - K + 1}$$

where

$$e_{it} = (y_{it} - \bar{y}_i + \bar{\bar{y}}) - \hat{\alpha}_w - (\mathbf{x}_{it} - \bar{\mathbf{x}}_i + \bar{\bar{\mathbf{x}}})\hat{\boldsymbol{\beta}}_w$$

and $\hat{\alpha}_w$ and $\hat{\boldsymbol{\beta}}_w$ are the within estimates of the coefficients and $N = \sum_i^n T_i$. After passing the within residuals through the within transform, only the idiosyncratic errors are left.

The default method for estimating σ_u^2 is

$$\hat{\sigma}_{u\bar{T}}^2 = \max\left\{0, \frac{SSR_b}{n - K} - \frac{\hat{\sigma}_e^2}{\bar{T}}\right\}$$

where

$$SSR_b = \sum_i^n T_i \left(\bar{y}_i - \hat{\alpha}_b - \bar{\mathbf{x}}_i \hat{\boldsymbol{\beta}}_b\right)^2$$

$\hat{\alpha}_b$ and $\hat{\boldsymbol{\beta}}_b$ are coefficient estimates from the between regression and $\bar{T}$ is the harmonic mean of T_i:

$$\bar{T} = \frac{n}{\sum_i^n \frac{1}{T_i}}$$

This estimator is consistent for σ_u^2 and is computationally less expensive than the second method. The sum of squared residuals from the between model estimate a function of both the idiosyncratic component and the individual component. Using our estimator of σ_e^2, we can remove the idiosyncratic component, leaving only the desired individual component.

The second method is the Swamy–Arora method for unbalanced panels derived by Baltagi and Chang (1994), which has a more precise small-sample adjustment. Using this method,

$$\widehat{\sigma}_{\text{uSA}}^2 = \max\left\{0, \frac{SSR_b - (n - K)\widehat{\sigma}_e^2}{N - tr}\right\}$$

where

$$tr = \text{trace}\left\{(\mathbf{X}'\mathbf{P}\mathbf{X})^{-1}\mathbf{X}'\mathbf{Z}\mathbf{Z}'\mathbf{X}\right\}$$

$$\mathbf{P} = \text{diag}\left\{\left(\frac{1}{T_i}\right)\boldsymbol{\iota}_{T_i}\boldsymbol{\iota}_{T_i}'\right\}$$

$$\mathbf{Z} = \text{diag}\left[\boldsymbol{\iota}_{T_i}\right]$$

$\mathbf{X}$ is the $N \times K$ matrix of covariates, including the constant, and $\boldsymbol{\iota}_{T_i}$ is a $T_i \times 1$ vector of ones.

The estimated coefficients $(\widehat{\alpha}_r, \widehat{\boldsymbol{\beta}}_r)$ and their covariance matrix $\mathbf{V}_r$ are reported together with the previously calculated quantities $\widehat{\sigma}_e$ and $\widehat{\sigma}_u$. The standard deviation of $\nu_i + e_{it}$ is calculated as $\sqrt{\widehat{\sigma}_e^2 + \widehat{\sigma}_u^2}$.

Reported as R^2 between is $\text{corr}(\overline{\mathbf{x}}_i\widehat{\boldsymbol{\beta}}, \overline{y}_i)^2$.

Reported as R^2 within is $\text{corr}\{(\mathbf{x}_{it} - \overline{\mathbf{x}}_i)\widehat{\boldsymbol{\beta}}, y_{it} - \overline{y}_i\}^2$.

Reported as R^2 overall is $\text{corr}(\mathbf{x}_{it}\widehat{\boldsymbol{\beta}}, y_{it})^2$.

xtreg, mle

The log likelihood for the ith unit is

$$l_i = -\frac{1}{2}\left(\frac{1}{\sigma_e^2}\left[\sum_{t=1}^{T_i}(y_{it} - \mathbf{x}_{it}\boldsymbol{\beta})^2 - \frac{\sigma_u^2}{T_i\sigma_u^2 + \sigma_e^2}\left\{\sum_{t=1}^{T_i}(y_{it} - \mathbf{x}_{it}\boldsymbol{\beta})\right\}^2\right]\right.$$
$$\left. + \ln\left(T_i\frac{\sigma_u^2}{\sigma_e^2} + 1\right) + T_i\ln(2\pi\sigma_e^2)\right)$$

The `mle` and `re` options yield essentially the same results, except when total $N = \sum_i T_i$ is small (200 or less) and the data are unbalanced.

xtreg, pa

See [XT] **xtgee** for details on the methods and formulas used to calculate the population-averaged model using a generalized estimating equations approach.

References

Arellano, M. 1987. Computing robust standard errors for within-groups estimators. *Oxford Bulletin of Economics and Statistics* 49(4): 431–434.

Arellano, M. 2003. *Panel Data Econometrics*. New York: Oxford University Press.

Baltagi, B. H. 1985. Pooling cross-sections with unequal time-series lengths. *Economics Letters* 18: 133–136.

——. 2001. *Econometric Analysis of Panel Data*. 2nd ed. New York: Wiley.

Baltagi, B. H. and Y. Chang. 1994. Incomplete Panels: A comparative study of alternative estimators for the unbalanced one-way error component regression model. *Journal of Econometrics* 62: 67–89.

Baum, C. F. 2001. Residual diagnostics. *Stata Journal* 1: 101–104.

Bottai, M. and N. Orsini. 2004. Confidence intervals for the variance component of random-effects linear models. *Stata Journal* 4: 429–435.

Dwyer, J. and M. Feinleib. 1992. Introduction to statistical models for longitudinal observation. In *Statistical Models for Longitudinal Studies of Health*, ed. J. Dwyer, M. Feinleib, P. Lippert, and H. Hoffmeister, 3–48. New York: Oxford University Press.

Greene, W. H. 1983. Simultaneous estimation of factor substitution, economies of scale, and non-neutral technical change. In *Econometric Analyses of Productivity*, ed. A. Dogramaci. Boston: Kluwer.

——. 2003. *Econometric Analysis*. 5th ed. Upper Saddle River, NJ: Prentice Hall.

Judge, G. G., W. E. Griffiths, R. C. Hill, H. Lütkepohl, and T.-C. Lee. 1985. *The Theory and Practice of Econometrics*. 2nd ed. New York: Wiley.

Lee, L. and W. Griffiths. 1979. The prior likelihood and best linear unbiased prediction in stochastic coefficient linear models. University of New England Working Papers in Econometrics and Applied Statistics No. 1, Armidale, Australia.

Rabe-Hesketh, S., A. Pickles, and C. Taylor. 2000. sg129: Generalized linear latent and mixed models. *Stata Technical Bulletin* 53: 47–57. Reprinted in *Stata Technical Bulletin Reprints*, vol. 9, pp. 293–307.

Sosa-Escudero, W. and A. K. Bera. 2001. sg164: Specification tests for linear panel data models. *Stata Technical Bulletin* 61: 18–21. Reprinted in *Stata Technical Bulletin Reprints*, vol. 10, pp. 307–311.

Swamy, P. A. V. B. and S. S. Arora. 1972. The exact finite sample properties of the estimators of coefficients in the error components regression models. *Econometrica* 40: 643–657.

Taub, A. J. 1979. Prediction in the context of the variance-components model. *Journal of Econometrics* 10: 103–108.

Twisk, J. W. R. 2003. *Applied Longitudinal Data Analysis for Epidemiology: A Practical Guide*. Cambridge: Cambridge University Press.

Wooldridge, J. M. 2002. *Econometric Analysis of Cross Section and Panel Data*. Cambridge, MA: MIT Press.

Also See

Complementary:	[XT] **xtreg postestimation**; [XT] **xtdata**, [XT] **xtdes**, [XT] **xtsum**, [XT] **xttab**
Related:	[XT] **xtgee**, [XT] **xtgls**, [XT] **xtivreg**, [XT] **xtmixed**, [XT] **xtregar**, [R] **regress**, [TS] **prais**
Background:	[U] **11.1.10 Prefix commands**, [U] **20 Estimation and postestimation commands**, [XT] **estimation options**, [XT] **xt**, [R] **maximize**, [R] *vce_option*

Title

xtreg postestimation — Postestimation tools for xtreg

Description

The following postestimation commands are of special interest after `xtreg`:

command	description
xttest0	Breusch and Pagan LM test for random effects

For information about this command, see below.

In addition, the following standard postestimation commands are available:

command	description
adjust[1]	adjusted predictions of $\mathbf{x}\beta$
*estat	AIC, BIC, VCE, and estimation sample summary
estimates	cataloging estimation results
hausman	Hausman's specification test
lincom	point estimates, standard errors, testing, and inference for linear combinations of coefficients
lrtest	likelihood-ratio test
mfx	marginal effects or elasticities
nlcom	point estimates, standard errors, testing, and inference for nonlinear combinations of coefficients
predict	predictions, residuals, influence statistics, and other diagnostic measures
predictnl	point estimates, standard errors, testing, and inference for generalized predictions
test	Wald tests for simple and composite linear hypotheses
testnl	Wald tests of nonlinear hypotheses

[1] `adjust` does not work with time-series operators.

*`estat ic` may not be used after `xtreg` with the be, pa, or re options.

See the corresponding entries in the *Stata Base Reference Manual* for details.

Special-interest postestimation commands

`xttest0`, for use after `xtreg, re`, presents the Breusch and Pagan (1980) Lagrange-multiplier test for random effects, a test that $\text{Var}(\nu_i) = 0$.

Syntax for predict

For all but the population-averaged model

> predict [*type*] *newvar* [*if*] [*in*] [, *statistic* <u>nooff</u>set]

Population-averaged model

> predict [*type*] *newvar* [*if*] [*in*] [, *PA_statistic* <u>nooff</u>set]

statistic	description
xb	$\mathbf{x}_j\mathbf{b}$, fitted values; the default
stdp	standard error of the fitted values
ue	$u_i + e_{it}$, the combined residual
*xbu	$\mathbf{x}_j\mathbf{b} + u_i$, prediction including effect
*u	u_i, the fixed- or random-error component
*e	e_{it}, the overall error component

Unstarred statistics are available both in and out of sample; type predict ... if e(sample) ... if wanted only for the estimation sample. Starred statistics are calculated only for the estimation sample, even when if e(sample) is not specified.

PA_statistic	description
xb	linear prediction
stdp	standard error of the linear prediction
<u>sc</u>ore	first derivative of the log likelihood with respect to $\mathbf{x}_j\beta$

These statistics are available both in and out of sample; type predict ... if e(sample) ... if wanted only for the estimation sample.

Options for predict

xb calculates the linear prediction, that is, $a + \mathbf{b}\mathbf{x}_{it}$. This is the default for all except the population-averaged model.

stdp calculates the standard error of the linear prediction. Note that, in the case of the fixed-effects model, this excludes the variance due to uncertainty about the estimate of u_i.

ue calculates the prediction of $u_i + e_{it}$.

xbu calculates the prediction of $a + \mathbf{b}\mathbf{x}_{it} + u_i$, the prediction including the fixed- or random-component.

u calculates the prediction of u_i, the estimated fixed- or random-effect.

e calculates the prediction of e_{it}.

score calculates the equation-level score, $u_j = \partial \ln L_j(\mathbf{x}_j\beta)/\partial(\mathbf{x}_j\beta)$.

nooffset is relevant only if you specified offset(*varname*) for xtreg, pa. It modifies the calculations made by predict so that they ignore the offset variable; the linear prediction is treated as $\mathbf{x}_{it}\mathbf{b}$ rather than $\mathbf{x}_{it}\mathbf{b} + \text{offset}_{it}$.

Syntax for xttest0

```
xttest0
```

Remarks

▷ Example 1

Continuing with our `xtreg, re` estimation example (example 4) in `xtreg`, we can see that `xttest0` will report a test of $\nu_i = 0$. In case we have any doubts, we could type

```
. xttest0
Breusch and Pagan Lagrangian multiplier test for random effects:

        ln_wage[idcode,t] = Xb + u[idcode] + e[idcode,t]

        Estimated results:
                    |      Var      sd = sqrt(Var)
            --------+---------------------------------
            ln_wage |   .2283326        .4778416
                  e |   .0845038        .2906954
                  u |    .066514        .2579031

        Test:   Var(u) = 0
                              chi2(1) =  14779.98
                          Prob > chi2 =     0.0000
```

◁

▷ Example 2

More importantly, after `xtreg, re` estimation, `hausman` will perform the Hausman specification test. If our model is correctly specified, and if ν_i is uncorrelated with x_{it}, the (subset of) coefficients that are estimated by the fixed-effects estimator and the same coefficients that are estimated here should not statistically differ:

```
. xtreg ln_w grade age* ttl_exp* tenure* black not_smsa south, re
(output omitted)
. estimates store random_effects
. xtreg ln_w grade age* ttl_exp* tenure* black not_smsa south, fe
(output omitted)
```

```
. hausman . random_effects
```

	Coefficients			
	(b)	(B)	(b-B)	sqrt(diag(V_b-V_B))
	.	random_eff~s	Difference	S.E.
age	.0359987	.036806	-.0008073	.0013177
age2	-.000723	-.0007133	-9.68e-06	.0000184
ttl_exp	.0334668	.0290207	.0044461	.001711
ttl_exp2	.0002163	.0003049	-.0000886	.000053
tenure	.0357539	.039252	-.0034981	.0005797
tenure2	-.0019701	-.0020035	.0000334	.0000373
not_smsa	-.0890108	-.1308263	.0418155	.0062745
south	-.0606309	-.0868927	.0262618	.0081346

```
                  b = consistent under Ho and Ha; obtained from xtreg
          B = inconsistent under Ha, efficient under Ho; obtained from xtreg
    Test:  Ho:  difference in coefficients not systematic

              chi2(8) = (b-B)'[(V_b-V_B)^(-1)](b-B)
                      =        149.44
              Prob>chi2 =      0.0000
```

We can reject the hypothesis that the coefficients are the same. Before turning to what this means, note that hausman listed the coefficients estimated by the two models. It did not, however, list grade and race. hausman did not make a mistake; in the Hausman test, we compare only the coefficients estimated by both techniques.

What does this mean? We have an unpleasant choice: we can admit that our model is misspecified—that we have not parameterized it correctly—or we can hold that our specification is correct, in which case the observed differences must be due to the zero-correlation of ν_i and the x_{it} assumption.

◁

❏ Technical Note

We can also mechanically explore the underpinnings of the test's dissatisfaction. In the comparison table from hausman, note that it is the coefficients on not_smsa and south that exhibit the largest differences. In equation $(1')$ of [XT] **xtreg**, we showed how to decompose a model into within and between effects. Let us do that with these two variables, assuming that changes in the average have one effect while transitional changes have another:

```
. egen avgnsmsa = mean(not_smsa), by(idcode)
. generate devnsma = not_smsa -avgnsmsa
(8 missing values generated)
. egen avgsouth = mean(south), by(idcode)
. generate devsouth = south - avgsouth
(8 missing values generated)
```

```
. xtreg ln_w grade age* ttl_exp* tenure* black avgnsm devnsm avgsou devsou
```

Random-effects GLS regression   Number of obs   =   28091
Group variable (i): idcode   Number of groups   =   4697

R-sq: within = 0.1723   Obs per group: min =   1
       between = 0.4809   avg =   6.0
       overall = 0.3737   max =   15

Random effects u_i ~ Gaussian   Wald chi2(12)   =   9319.69
corr(u_i, X)   = 0 (assumed)   Prob > chi2   =   0.0000

ln_wage	Coef.	Std. Err.	z	P>|z|	[95% Conf. Interval]	
grade	.0631716	.0017903	35.29	0.000	.0596627	.0666805
age	.0375196	.0031186	12.03	0.000	.0314072	.043632
age2	-.0007248	.00005	-14.50	0.000	-.0008228	-.0006269
ttl_exp	.0286542	.0024207	11.84	0.000	.0239097	.0333987
ttl_exp2	.0003222	.0001162	2.77	0.006	.0000945	.0005499
tenure	.0394424	.001754	22.49	0.000	.0360045	.0428803
tenure2	-.0020081	.0001192	-16.85	0.000	-.0022417	-.0017746
black	-.0545938	.0102099	-5.35	0.000	-.0746048	-.0345827
avgnsmsa	-.1833238	.0109337	-16.77	0.000	-.2047533	-.1618942
devnsma	-.0887596	.0095071	-9.34	0.000	-.1073932	-.070126
avgsouth	-.1011235	.0098787	-10.24	0.000	-.1204855	-.0817616
devsouth	-.0598538	.0109054	-5.49	0.000	-.081228	-.0384796
_cons	.268298	.0495776	5.41	0.000	.1711277	.3654683
sigma_u	.25791607					
sigma_e	.29069544					
rho	.44046285	(fraction of variance due to u_i)				

We will leave the reinterpretation of this model to you, except to note that if we were really going to sell this model, we would have to explain why the between and within effects are different. Focusing on residence in a nonSMSA, we might tell a story about rural people being paid less and continuing to get paid less when they move to the SMSA. Given our panel data, we could create variables to measure this (an indicator for moved from nonSMSA to SMSA) and to measure the effects. In our assessment of this model, we should think about women in the cities moving to the country and their relative productivity in a bucolic setting.

In any case, the Hausman test now is

```
. estimates store new_random_effects
. xtreg ln_w grade age* ttl_exp* tenure* black avgnsm devnsm avgsou devsou, fe
(output omitted )
. hausman . new_random_effects
```

	—— Coefficients ——			
	(b) .	(B) new_random~s	(b-B) Difference	sqrt(diag(V_b-V_B)) S.E.
age	.0359987	.0375196	−.001521	.0013198
age2	−.000723	−.0007248	1.84e-06	.0000184
ttl_exp	.0334668	.0286542	.0048126	.0017127
ttl_exp2	.0002163	.0003222	−.0001059	.0000531
tenure	.0357539	.0394424	−.0036885	.0005839
tenure2	−.0019701	−.0020081	.000038	.0000377
devnsma	−.0890108	−.0887596	−.0002512	.0006826
devsouth	−.0606309	−.0598538	−.0007771	.0007612

```
        b = consistent under Ho and Ha; obtained from xtreg
        B = inconsistent under Ha, efficient under Ho; obtained from xtreg
Test:  Ho:  difference in coefficients not systematic
        chi2(8) = (b-B)'[(V_b-V_B)^(-1)](b-B)
                =        92.52
        Prob>chi2 =     0.0000
```

We have mechanically succeeded in greatly reducing the χ^2, but not by enough. The major differences now are in the age, experience, and tenure effects. We already knew this problem existed because of the ever-increasing effect of experience. More careful parameterization work rather than simply including squares needs to be done.

❏

Methods and Formulas

All postestimation commands listed above are implemented as ado-files.

xttest0

xttest0 reports the Lagrange-multiplier test for random effects developed by Breusch and Pagan (1980) and as modified by Baltagi and Li (1990). The model

$$y_{it} = \alpha + \mathbf{x}_{it}\boldsymbol{\beta} + \nu_{it}$$

is estimated via OLS, and then the quantity

$$\lambda_{\mathrm{LM}} = \frac{(n\overline{T})^2}{2}\left(\frac{A_1^2}{(\sum_i T_i^2) - n\overline{T}}\right)$$

is calculated, where

$$A_1 = 1 - \frac{\sum_{i=1}^n (\sum_{t=1}^{T_i} v_{it})^2}{\sum_i \sum_t v_{it}^2}$$

The Baltagi and Li modification allows for unbalanced data and reduces to the standard formula

$$\lambda_{\text{LM}} = \frac{nT}{2(T-1)} \left\{ \frac{\sum_i (\sum_t v_{it})^2}{\sum_i \sum_t v_{it}^2} - 1 \right\}^2$$

when $T_i = T$ (balanced data). Under the null hypothesis, λ_{LM} is distributed $\chi^2(1)$.

Reference

Baltagi, B. H. and Q. Li. 1990. A Lagrange-multiplier test for the error components model with incomplete panels. *Econometric Reviews* 9(1): 103–107.

Breusch, T. and A. Pagan. 1980. The Lagrange-multiplier test and its applications to model specification in econometrics. *Review of Economic Studies* 47: 239–253.

Hausman, J. A. 1978. Specification tests in econometrics. *Econometrica* 46: 1251–1271.

Also See

Complementary:	[XT] **xtreg**,
	[R] **adjust**, [R] **estimates**, [R] **hausman**, [R] **lincom**, [R] **lrtest**,
	[R] **mfx**, [R] **nlcom**, [R] **predictnl**, [R] **test**, [R] **testnl**
Background:	[U] **13.5 Accessing coefficients and standard errors**,
	[U] **20 Estimation and postestimation commands**,
	[R] **estat**, [R] **predict**

Title

> **xtregar** — Fixed- and random-effects linear models with an AR(1) disturbance

Syntax

Random-effects (RE) model

    xtregar *depvar* $\left[\,indepvars\,\right]$ $\left[\,if\,\right]$ $\left[\,in\,\right]$ $\left[\,,\ \text{re } options\,\right]$

Fixed-effects (FE) model

    xtregar *depvar* $\left[\,indepvars\,\right]$ $\left[\,if\,\right]$ $\left[\,in\,\right]$ $\left[\,weight\,\right]$, fe $\left[\,options\,\right]$

options	description
Model	
re	use random-effects estimator; the default
fe	use fixed-effects estimator
<u>rho</u>type(*rhomethod*)	specify method to compute autocorrelation; see *Options* for details; seldom used
rhof(#)	use # for ρ and do not estimate ρ
<u>two</u>step	perform two-step estimate of correlation
Reporting	
<u>level</u>(#)	set confidence level; default is level(95)
lbi	perform Baltagi–Wu LBI test

You must tsset your data before using xtregar; see [TS] **tsset**.

depvar and *indepvars* may contain time-series operators; see [U] **11.4.3 Time-series varlists**.

by, statsby, and xi may be used with xtregar; see [U] **11.1.10 Prefix commands**.

fweights and aweights are allowed for the fixed-effects model with rhotype(regress) or rhotype(freg), or with a fixed rho; see [U] **11.1.6 weight**.

See [U] **20 Estimation and postestimation commands** for additional capabilities of estimation commands.

Description

    xtregar fits cross-sectional time-series regression models when the disturbance term is first-order autoregressive. xtregar offers a within estimator for fixed-effects models and a GLS estimator for random-effects models. Consider the model

$$y_{it} = \alpha + \mathbf{x}_{it}\boldsymbol{\beta} + \nu_i + \epsilon_{it} \qquad i = 1, \ldots, N; \quad t = 1, \ldots, T_i, \tag{1}$$

where

$$\epsilon_{it} = \rho \epsilon_{i,t-1} + \eta_{it} \tag{2}$$

and where $|\rho| < 1$ and η_{it} is independent and identically distributed (i.i.d.) with mean 0 and variance σ_η^2. If ν_i are assumed to be fixed parameters, the model is a fixed-effects model. If ν_i are assumed to be realizations of an i.i.d. process with mean 0 and variance σ_ν^2, it is a random-effects model. Whereas in the fixed-effects model, the ν_i may be correlated with the covariates $\mathbf{x}_{it}$, in the random-effects model the ν_i are assumed to be independent of the $\mathbf{x}_{it}$. On the other hand, any $\mathbf{x}_{it}$ that do not vary over t are collinear with the ν_i and will be dropped from the fixed-effects model. In contrast, the random-effects model can accommodate covariates that are constant over time.

xtregar can accommodate unbalanced panels whose observations are unequally spaced over time. xtregar implements the methods derived in Baltagi and Wu (1999).

Since xtregar uses time-series methods, you must tsset your data before using xtregar. See [TS] **tsset** for details.

Options

Model

re requests the GLS estimator of the random-effects model, which is the default.

fe requests the within estimator of the fixed-effects model.

rhotype(*rhomethod*) allows the user to specify any of the following estimators of ρ:

dw	$\rho_{\mathrm{dw}} = 1 - d/2$, where d is the Durbin–Watson d statistic
regress	$\rho_{\mathrm{reg}} = \beta$ from the residual regression $\epsilon_t = \beta\epsilon_{t-1}$
freg	$\rho_{\mathrm{freg}} = \beta$ from the residual regression $\epsilon_t = \beta\epsilon_{t+1}$
tscorr	$\rho_{\mathrm{tscorr}} = \epsilon'\epsilon_{t-1}/\epsilon'\epsilon$, where ϵ is the vector of residuals and ϵ_{t-1} is the vector of lagged residuals
theil	$\rho_{\mathrm{theil}} = \rho_{\mathrm{tscorr}}(N - k)/N$
nagar	$\rho_{\mathrm{nagar}} = (\rho_{\mathrm{dw}}N^2 + k^2)/(N^2 - k^2)$
onestep	$\rho_{\mathrm{onestep}} = (n/m_c)(\epsilon'\epsilon_{t-1}/\epsilon'\epsilon)$, where ϵ is the vector of residuals, n is the number of observations, and m_c is the number of consecutive pairs of residuals

dw is the default method. Except for onestep, the details of these methods are given in [TS] **prais**. prais handles unequally spaced data. onestep is the one-step method proposed by Baltagi and Wu (1999). Further details on this method are available below in *Methods and Formulas*.

rhof(#) specifies that the given number be used for ρ and that ρ not be estimated.

twostep requests that a two-step implementation of the *rhomethod* estimator of ρ be used. Unless a fixed value of ρ is specified, ρ is estimated by running prais on the de-meaned data. When twostep is specified, prais will stop on the first iteration after the equation is transformed by ρ—the two-step efficient estimator. Although it is customary to iterate these estimators to convergence, they are efficient at each step. When twostep is not specified, the FGLS process iterates to convergence as described in [TS] **prais**.

Reporting

level(#); see [XT] **estimation options**.

lbi requests that the Baltagi–Wu (1999) locally best invariant (LBI) test statistic that $\rho = 0$ and a modified version of the Bhargava et al. (1982) Durbin–Watson statistic be calculated and reported. The default is not to report them. p-values are not reported for either statistic. While Bhargava et al. (1982) published critical values for their statistic, no tables are currently available for the Baltagi–Wu LBI. Baltagi and Wu (1999) derive a normalized version of their statistic, but this statistic cannot be computed for datasets of moderate size. You can also specify these options upon replay.

Remarks

Remarks are presented under the headings

Introduction
The fixed-effects model
The random-effects model

Introduction

If you have not read [XT] **xt**, please do so.

Consider a linear panel-data model described by (1) and (2). In the fixed-effects model, the ν_i are a set of fixed parameters to be estimated. Alternatively, the ν_i may be random and correlated with the other covariates, with inference conditional on the ν_i in the sample; see Mundlak (1978) and Hsiao (2003). In the random-effects model, also known as the variance-components model, the ν_i are assumed to be realizations of an i.i.d. process with mean 0 and variance σ_ν^2. **xtregar** offers a within estimator for the fixed-effect model and the Baltagi–Wu (1999) GLS estimator of the random-effects model. The Baltagi–Wu (1999) GLS estimator extends the balanced panel estimator in Baltagi and Li (1991) to a case of exogenously unbalanced panels with unequally spaced observations. Both of these estimators offer several estimators of ρ.

The data can be unbalanced and unequally spaced. Specifically, the dataset contains observations on individual i at times t_{ij} for $j = 1, \ldots, n_i$. The difference $t_{ij} - t_{i,j-1}$ plays an integral role in the estimation techniques employed by **xtregar**. For this reason, you must **tsset** your data before using **xtregar**. For instance, if you have quarterly data, the "time" difference between the third and fourth quarter must be one month, not three.

The fixed-effects model

Let's examine the fixed-effect model first. The basic approach is common to all fixed-effects models. The ν_i are treated as nuisance parameters. We use a transformation of the model that removes the nuisance parameters and leaves behind the parameters of interest in an estimable form. Note that subtracting the group means from (1) removes the ν_i from the model

$$y_{it_{ij}} - \overline{y}_i = \left(\overline{\mathbf{x}}_{it_{ij}} - \overline{\mathbf{x}}_i \right) \boldsymbol{\beta} + \epsilon_{it_{ij}} - \overline{\epsilon}_i \tag{3}$$

where

$$\overline{y}_i = \frac{1}{n_i} \sum_{j=1}^{n_i} y_{it_{ij}} \qquad \overline{\mathbf{x}}_i = \frac{1}{n_i} \sum_{j=1}^{n_i} \mathbf{x}_{it_{ij}} \qquad \overline{\epsilon}_i = \frac{1}{n_i} \sum_{j=1}^{n_i} \epsilon_{it_{ij}}$$

After the transformation, (3) is a linear AR(1) model, potentially with unequally spaced observations. (3) can be used to estimate ρ. Given an estimate of ρ, we must do a Cochrane–Orcutt transformation on each panel and then remove the within-panel means and add back the overall mean for each variable. OLS on the transformed data will produce the within estimates of α and $\boldsymbol{\beta}$.

▷ Example 1

Let's use the Grunfeld investment dataset to illustrate of how `xtregar` can be used to fit the fixed-effects model. This dataset contains information on 10 firms' investment, market value, and the value of their capital stocks. The data were collected annually between 1935 and 1954. The following output shows that we have `tsset` our data and gives the results of running a fixed-effects model with investment as a function of market value and the capital stock.

```
. use http://www.stata-press.com/data/r9/grunfeld, clear
. tsset
       panel variable:  company, 1 to 10
        time variable:  year, 1935 to 1954
. xtregar invest mvalue kstock, fe
```

| FE (within) regression with AR(1) disturbances | | | | Number of obs | = | 190 |
| Group variable (i): company | | | | Number of groups | = | 10 |

R-sq: within = 0.5927   Obs per group: min =   19
       between = 0.7989   avg =   19.0
       overall = 0.7904   max =   19

                                  F(2,178)   =   129.49
corr(u_i, Xb) = -0.0454   Prob > F   =   0.0000

invest	Coef.	Std. Err.	t	P>|t|	[95% Conf. Interval]	
mvalue	.0949999	.0091377	10.40	0.000	.0769677	.113032
kstock	.350161	.0293747	11.92	0.000	.2921935	.4081286
_cons	-63.22022	5.648271	-11.19	0.000	-74.36641	-52.07402

rho_ar	.67210608	
sigma_u	91.507609	
sigma_e	40.992469	
rho_fov	.8328647	(fraction of variance due to u_i)

F test that all u_i=0:   F(9,178) =   11.53   Prob > F = 0.0000

Since there are 10 groups, the panel-by-panel Cochrane–Orcutt method decreases the number of available observations from 200 to 190. The above example used the default `dw` estimator of ρ. Using the `tscorr` estimator of ρ yields

```
. xtregar invest mvalue kstock, fe rhotype(tscorr)
```

| FE (within) regression with AR(1) disturbances | | | | Number of obs | = | 190 |
| Group variable (i): company | | | | Number of groups | = | 10 |

R-sq: within = 0.6583   Obs per group: min =   19
       between = 0.8024   avg =   19.0
       overall = 0.7933   max =   19

                                  F(2,178)   =   171.47
corr(u_i, Xb) = -0.0709   Prob > F   =   0.0000

invest	Coef.	Std. Err.	t	P>|t|	[95% Conf. Interval]	
mvalue	.0978364	.0096786	10.11	0.000	.0787369	.1169359
kstock	.346097	.0242248	14.29	0.000	.2982922	.3939018
_cons	-61.84403	6.621354	-9.34	0.000	-74.91049	-48.77758

rho_ar	.54131231	
sigma_u	90.893572	
sigma_e	41.592151	
rho_fov	.82686297	(fraction of variance due to u_i)

F test that all u_i=0:   F(9,178) =   19.73   Prob > F = 0.0000   ◁

❏ Technical Note

The `tscorr` estimator of ρ is bounded in $[-1, 1]$. The other estimators of ρ are not. In samples with very short panels, the estimates of ρ produced by the other estimators of ρ may be outside of $[-1, 1]$. If this happens, use the `tscorr` estimator. However, simulations have shown that the `tscorr` estimator is biased toward zero. `dw` is the default because it performs well in Monte Carlo simulations. In the example above, the estimate of ρ produced by `tscorr` is much smaller than the one produced by `dw`.

❏

▷ Example 2

`xtregar` will complain if you try to run `xtregar` on a dataset that has not been `tsset`:

```
. tsset, clear
. xtregar invest mvalue kstock, fe
must tsset data and specify panelvar
r(459);
```

You must `tsset` your data to ensure that `xtregar` understands the nature of your time variable. For instance, suppose that our observations were taken quarterly instead of annually. We will get exactly the same results with the quarterly variable `t2` that we did with the annual variable `year`.

```
. generate t = year - 1934
. generate t2 = q(1934q4) + t
. format t2 %tq
. list year t2 in 1/5
```

	year	t2
1.	1935	1935q1
2.	1936	1935q2
3.	1937	1935q3
4.	1938	1935q4
5.	1939	1936q1

```
. tsset company t2
        panel variable:  company, 1 to 10
         time variable:  t2, 1935q1 to 1939q4
```

(*Continued on next page*)

```
. xtregar invest mvalue kstock, fe
```

FE (within) regression with AR(1) disturbances	Number of obs	=	190
Group variable (i): company	Number of groups	=	10

```
R-sq:  within  = 0.5927                        Obs per group: min =        19
       between = 0.7989                                       avg =      19.0
       overall = 0.7904                                       max =        19

                                               F(2,178)            =    129.49
corr(u_i, Xb)  = -0.0454                       Prob > F            =    0.0000
```

invest	Coef.	Std. Err.	t	P>|t|	[95% Conf. Interval]	
mvalue	.0949999	.0091377	10.40	0.000	.0769677	.113032
kstock	.350161	.0293747	11.92	0.000	.2921935	.4081286
_cons	-63.22022	5.648271	-11.19	0.000	-74.36641	-52.07402

rho_ar	.67210608	
sigma_u	91.507609	
sigma_e	40.992469	
rho_fov	.8328647	(fraction of variance due to u_i)

```
F test that all u_i=0:     F(9,178) =      11.53              Prob > F = 0.0000
```
◁

In all the examples thus far, we have assumed that ϵ_{it} is first-order autoregressive. Testing the hypothesis of $\rho = 0$ in a first-order autoregressive process produces test statistics with extremely complicated distributions. Bhargava et al. (1982) extended the Durbin–Watson statistic to the case of balanced, equally spaced panel datasets. Baltagi and Wu (1999) modify their statistic to account for unbalanced panels with unequally spaced data. In the same article, Baltagi and Wu (1999) derive the locally best invariant test statistic of $\rho = 0$. Both these test statistics have extremely complicated distributions, although Bhargava et al. (1982) did publish some critical values in their article. Specifying the lbi option to xtregar causes Stata to calculate and report the modified Bhargava et al. Durbin–Watson and the Baltagi–Wu LBI.

▷ Example 3

In this example, we calculate the modified Bhargava et al. Durbin–Watson statistic and the Baltagi–Wu LBI. We exclude time periods 9 and 10 from the sample, thereby reproducing the results of Baltagi and Wu (1999, 822). Note that p-values are not reported for either statistic. While Bhargava et al. (1982) published critical values for their statistic, no tables are currently available for the Baltagi–Wu (LBI). Baltagi and Wu (1999) did derive a normalized version of their statistic, but this statistic cannot be computed for datasets of moderate size.

```
. xtregar invest mvalue kstock if year !=1934 & year !=1944, fe lbi

FE (within) regression with AR(1) disturbances   Number of obs      =        180
Group variable (i): company                      Number of groups   =         10

R-sq:  within  = 0.5954                           Obs per group: min =         18
       between = 0.7952                                          avg =       18.0
       overall = 0.7889                                          max =         18

                                                  F(2,168)           =     123.63
corr(u_i, Xb)  = -0.0516                           Prob > F           =     0.0000
```

invest	Coef.	Std. Err.	t	P>|t|	[95% Conf. Interval]	
mvalue	.0941122	.0090926	10.35	0.000	.0761617	.1120627
kstock	.3535872	.0303562	11.65	0.000	.2936584	.4135161
_cons	-64.82534	5.946885	-10.90	0.000	-76.56559	-53.08509

rho_ar	.6697198	
sigma_u	93.320452	
sigma_e	41.580712	
rho_fov	.83435413	(fraction of variance due to u_i)

```
F test that all u_i=0:      F(9,168) =      11.55                  Prob > F = 0.0000
modified Bhargava et al. Durbin-Watson = .71380994
Baltagi-Wu LBI = 1.0134522
```

◁

The random-effects model

In the random-effects model, the ν_i are assumed to be realizations of an i.i.d. process with mean 0 and variance σ_ν^2. Furthermore, the ν_i are assumed to be independent of both the ϵ_{it} and the covariates $\mathbf{x}_{it}$. The latter of these assumptions can be very strong, but inference is not conditional on the particular realizations of the ν_i in the sample. See Mundlak (1978) for a discussion of this point.

▷ Example 4

By specifying the re option, we obtain the Baltagi–Wu GLS estimator of the random-effects model. This estimator can accommodate unbalanced panels and unequally spaced data. We run this model on the Grunfeld dataset:

(*Continued on next page*)

```
. xtregar invest mvalue kstock if year!=1934 & year !=1944, re lbi

RE GLS regression with AR(1) disturbances      Number of obs     =       190
Group variable (i): company                    Number of groups  =        10

R-sq:  within  = 0.7707                         Obs per group: min =        19
       between = 0.8039                                        avg =      19.0
       overall = 0.7958                                        max =        19

                                                Wald chi2(3)      =    351.37
corr(u_i, Xb)      = 0 (assumed)                Prob > chi2       =    0.0000
```

invest	Coef.	Std. Err.	z	P>|z|	[95% Conf. Interval]	
mvalue	.0947714	.0083691	11.32	0.000	.0783683	.1111746
kstock	.3223932	.0263226	12.25	0.000	.2708019	.3739845
_cons	-45.21427	27.12492	-1.67	0.096	-98.37814	7.949603

rho_ar	.6697198	(estimated autocorrelation coefficient)
sigma_u	74.662876	
sigma_e	42.253042	
rho_fov	.75742494	(fraction of variance due to u_i)
theta	.66973313	

```
modified Bhargava et al. Durbin-Watson = .71380994
Baltagi-Wu LBI = 1.0134522
```

Note that the modified Bhargava et al. Durbin–Watson and the Baltagi–Wu LBI are exactly the same as those reported for the fixed-effects model because the formulas for these statistics do not depend on fitting the fixed-effects model or the random-effects model.

◁

Saved Results

xtregar, re saves in e():

Scalars

e(d1)	Bhargava et al. Durbin–Watson	e(LBI)	Baltagi–Wu LBI statistic
e(ds)	centered Baltagi–Wu LBI	e(N_LBI)	number of obs used in e(LBI)
e(N)	number of observations	e(r2_o)	R-squared for overall model
e(N_g)	number of groups	e(r2_b)	R-squared for between model
e(df_m)	model degrees of freedom	e(rho_ar)	autocorrelation coefficient
e(g_max)	largest group size	e(sigma_u)	panel-level standard deviation
e(g_min)	smallest group size	e(sigma_e)	standard deviation of ϵ_{it}
e(g_avg)	average group size	e(thta_min)	minimum θ
e(chi2)	χ^2	e(thta_5)	θ, 5th percentile
e(rho_fov)	u_i fraction of variance	e(thta_50)	θ, 50th percentile
e(Tbar)	harmonic mean of group sizes	e(thta_95)	θ, 95th percentile
e(Tcon)	1 if T is constant	e(thta_max)	maximum θ
e(r2_w)	R-squared for within model		

Macros

e(cmd)	xtregar	e(ivar)	variable denoting groups
e(depvar)	name of dependent variable	e(tvar)	time variable
e(model)	re	e(chi2type)	Wald; type of model χ^2 test
e(rhotype)	method of estimating ρ_{ar}	e(properties)	b V
e(dw)	LBI, if requested	e(predict)	program used to implement predict

Matrices

e(b)	coefficient vector	e(V)	VCE for random-effects model

Functions

e(sample)	marks estimation sample

(Continued on next page)

`xtregar, fe` saves in `e()`:

Scalars

e(d1)	Bhargava et al. Durbin–Watson	e(LBI)	Baltagi–Wu LBI statistic
e(ds)	centered Baltagi–Wu LBI	e(N_LBI)	number of obs used in e(LBI)
e(N)	number of observations	e(g_max)	largest group size
e(N_g)	number of groups	e(g_min)	smallest group size
e(mss)	model sum of squares	e(g_avg)	average group size
e(tss)	total sum of squares	e(rho_fov)	u_i fraction of variance
e(df_m)	model degrees of freedom	e(Tbar)	harmonic mean of group sizes
e(rss)	residual sum of squares	e(Tcon)	1 if T is constant
e(df_r)	residual degrees of freedom	e(r2_w)	R-squared for within model
e(r2)	R-squared	e(r2_o)	R-squared for overall model
e(r2_a)	adjusted R-squared	e(r2_b)	R-squared for between model
e(F)	F statistic	e(rho_ar)	autocorrelation coefficient
e(rmse)	root mean squared error	e(corr)	corr(u_i, Xb)
e(ll)	log likelihood	e(sigma_u)	panel-level standard deviation
e(ll_0)	log likelihood, constant-only model	e(sigma_e)	standard deviation of ϵ_{it}
e(df_a)	degrees of freedom for absorbed effect	e(F_f)	F for $u_i{=}0$

Macros

e(cmd)	xtregar	e(tvar)	time variable
e(depvar)	name of dependent variable	e(wtype)	weight type
e(model)	fe	e(wexp)	weight expression
e(rhotype)	method of estimating ρ_{ar}	e(properties)	b V
e(dw)	LBI, if requested	e(predict)	program used to implement predict
e(ivar)	variable denoting groups		

Matrices

e(b)	coefficient vector	e(V)	variance–covariance matrix of the estimators

Functions

e(sample)	marks estimation sample

Methods and Formulas

Consider a linear panel-data model described by (1) and (2). The data can be unbalanced and unequally spaced. Specifically, the dataset contains observations on individual i at times t_{ij} for $j = 1, \ldots, n_i$.

Estimating ρ

The estimate of ρ is always obtained after removing the group means. Let $\widetilde{y}_{it} = y_{it} - \overline{y}_i$, let $\widetilde{\mathbf{x}}_{it} = \mathbf{x}_{it} - \overline{\mathbf{x}}_i$, and let $\widetilde{\epsilon}_{it} = \epsilon_{it} - \overline{\epsilon}_i$.

Then except for the `onestep` method, all the estimates of ρ are obtained by running Stata's `prais` on

$$\widetilde{y}_{it} = \widetilde{x}_{it}\boldsymbol{\beta} + \widetilde{\epsilon}_{it}$$

See [TS] **prais** for the formulas for each of the methods.

When `onestep` is specified, a regression is run on the above equation, and the residuals are obtained. Let $e_{it_{ij}}$ be the residual used to estimate the error $\tilde{\epsilon}_{it_{ij}}$. If $t_{ij} - t_{i,j-1} > 1$, $e_{it_{ij}}$ is set to zero. Given this series of residuals

$$\widehat{\rho}_{\text{onestep}} = \frac{n}{m_c} \frac{\sum_{i=1}^{N} \sum_{t=2}^{T} e_{it} e_{i,t-1}}{\sum_{i=1}^{N} \sum_{t=1}^{T} e_{it}^2}$$

where n is the number of nonzero elements in e and m_c is the number of consecutive pairs of nonzero e_{it}s.

Transforming the data to remove the AR(1) component

After estimating ρ, Baltagi and Wu (1999) derive a transformation of the data that removes the AR(1) component. Their $C_i(\rho)$ can be written as

$$y_{it_{ij}}^* = \begin{cases} (1-\rho^2)^{1/2} y_{it_{ij}} & \text{if } t_{ij} = 1 \\ (1-\rho^2)^{1/2} \left[y_{i,t_{ij}} \left\{ \frac{1}{1-\rho^{2(t_{ij}-t_{i,j-1})}} \right\}^{1/2} - y_{i,t_{i,j-1}} \left\{ \frac{\rho^{2(t_{ij}-t_{i,j-1})}}{1-\rho^{2(t_{i,j}-t_{i,j-1})}} \right\}^{1/2} \right] & \text{if } t_{ij} > 1 \end{cases}$$

Using the analogous transform on the independent variables generates transformed data without the AR(1) component. Performing simple OLS on the transformed data leaves behind the residuals μ^*.

The within estimator of the fixed-effects model

To obtain the within estimator, we must transform the data that come out of the AR(1) transform. For the within transform to remove the fixed-effects, the first observation of each panel must be dropped. Specifically, let

$$\breve{y}_{it_{ij}} = y_{it_{ij}}^* - \overline{y}_i^* + \overline{\overline{y}}^* \qquad \forall j > 1$$

$$\breve{\mathbf{x}}_{it_{ij}} = \mathbf{x}_{it_{ij}}^* - \overline{\mathbf{x}}_i^* + \overline{\overline{\mathbf{x}}}^* \qquad \forall j > 1$$

$$\breve{\epsilon}_{it_{ij}} = \epsilon_{it_{ij}}^* - \overline{\epsilon}_i^* + \overline{\overline{\epsilon}}^* \qquad \forall j > 1$$

where

$$\overline{y}_i^* = \frac{\sum_{j=2}^{n_i-1} y_{it_{ij}}^*}{n_i - 1}$$

$$\overline{\overline{y}}^* = \frac{\sum_{i=1}^{N} \sum_{j=2}^{n_i-1} y_{it_{ij}}^*}{\sum_{i=1}^{N} n_i - 1}$$

$$\overline{\mathbf{x}}_i^* = \frac{\sum_{j=2}^{n_i-1} \mathbf{x}_{it_{ij}}^*}{n_i - 1}$$

$$\overline{\overline{\mathbf{x}}}^* = \frac{\sum_{i=1}^{N} \sum_{j=2}^{n_i-1} \mathbf{x}_{it_{ij}}^*}{\sum_{i=1}^{N} n_i - 1}$$

$$\overline{\epsilon}_i^* = \frac{\sum_{j=2}^{n_i-1} \epsilon_{it_{ij}}^*}{n_i - 1}$$

$$\overline{\overline{\epsilon}}^* = \frac{\sum_{i=1}^{N} \sum_{j=2}^{n_i-1} \epsilon_{it_{ij}}^*}{\sum_{i=1}^{N} n_i - 1}$$

The within estimator of the fixed-effects model is then obtained by running OLS on

$$\breve{y}_{it_{ij}} = \alpha + \breve{\mathbf{x}}_{it_{ij}}\boldsymbol{\beta} + \breve{\epsilon}_{it_{ij}}$$

Reported as R^2 within is the R^2 from the above regression.

Reported as R^2 between is $\left\{ \text{corr}(\overline{\mathbf{x}}_i\widehat{\boldsymbol{\beta}}, \overline{y}_i) \right\}^2$.

Reported as R^2 overall is $\left\{ \text{corr}(\mathbf{x}_{it}\widehat{\boldsymbol{\beta}}, y_{it}) \right\}^2$.

The Baltagi–Wu GLS estimator

The residuals μ^* can be used to estimate the variance components. Translating the matrix formulas given in Baltagi and Wu (1999) into summations yields the following variance-components estimators:

$$\widehat{\sigma}_\omega^2 = \sum_{i=1}^{N} \frac{(\mu_i^{*\prime} g_i)^2}{(g_i' g_i)}$$

$$\widehat{\sigma}_\epsilon^2 = \frac{\left[\sum_{i=1}^{N} (\mu_i^{*\prime} \mu_i^*) - \sum_{i=1}^{N} \left\{ \frac{(\mu_i^{*\prime} g_i)^2}{(g_i' g_i)} \right\} \right]}{\sum_{i=1}^{N}(n_i - 1)}$$

$$\widehat{\sigma}_\mu^2 = \frac{\left[\sum_{i=1}^{N} \left\{ \frac{(\mu_i^{*\prime} g_i)^2}{(g_i' g_i)} \right\} - N\widehat{\sigma}_\epsilon^2 \right]}{\sum_{i=1}^{N}(g_i' g_i)}$$

where

$$g_i = \left[1, \frac{\left\{1 - \rho^{(t_{i,2} - t_{i,1})}\right\}}{\left\{1 - \rho^{2(t_{i,2} - t_{i,1})}\right\}^{\frac{1}{2}}}, \dots, \frac{\left\{1 - \rho^{(t_{i,n_i} - t_{i,n_i-1})}\right\}}{\left\{1 - \rho^{2(t_{i,n_i} - t_{i,n_i-1})}\right\}^{\frac{1}{2}}} \right]'$$

and μ_i^* is the $n_i \times 1$ vector of residuals from μ^* that correspond to person i.

Then

$$\widehat{\theta}_i = 1 - \left(\frac{\widehat{\sigma}_\mu}{\widehat{\omega}_i} \right)$$

where

$$\widehat{\omega}_i^2 = g_i' g_i \widehat{\sigma}_\mu^2 + \widehat{\sigma}_\epsilon^2$$

With these estimates in hand, we can transform the data via

$$z_{it_{ij}}^{**} = z_{it_{ij}}^* - \widehat{\theta}_i g_{ij} \frac{\sum_{s=1}^{n_i} g_{is} z_{it_{is}}^*}{\sum_{s=1}^{n_i} g_{is}^2}$$

for $z \in \{y, \mathbf{x}\}$.

Running OLS on the transformed data $y^{**}, \mathbf{x}^{**}$ yields the feasible GLS estimator of α and β.

Reported as R^2 between is $\left\{ \text{corr}(\overline{\mathbf{x}}_i \widehat{\boldsymbol{\beta}}, \overline{y}_i) \right\}^2$.

Reported as R^2 within is $\left\{ \text{corr}\{(\mathbf{x}_{it} - \overline{\mathbf{x}}_i)\widehat{\boldsymbol{\beta}}, y_{it} - \overline{y}_i\} \right\}^2$.

Reported as R^2 overall is $\left\{ \text{corr}(\mathbf{x}_{it}\widehat{\boldsymbol{\beta}}, y_{it}) \right\}^2$.

The test statistics

The Baltagi–Wu LBI is the sum of terms

$$d_* = d_1 + d_2 + d_3 + d_4$$

where

$$d_1 = \frac{\sum_{i=1}^{N} \sum_{j=1}^{n_i} \{\widetilde{z}_{it_{i,j-1}} - \widetilde{z}_{it_{ij}} I(t_{ij} - t_{i,j-1} = 1)\}^2}{\sum_{i=1}^{N} \sum_{j=1}^{n_i} \widetilde{z}_{it_{ij}}^2}$$

$$d_2 = \frac{\sum_{i=1}^{N} \sum_{j=1}^{n_i-1} \widetilde{z}_{it_{i,j-1}}^2 \{1 - I(t_{ij} - t_{i,j-1} = 1)\}^2}{\sum_{i=1}^{N} \sum_{j=1}^{n_i} \widetilde{z}_{it_{ij}}^2}$$

$$d_3 = \frac{\sum_{i=1}^{N} \widetilde{z}_{it_{i1}}^2}{\sum_{i=1}^{N} \sum_{j=1}^{n_i} \widetilde{z}_{it_{ij}}^2}$$

$$d_4 = \frac{\sum_{i=1}^{N} \widetilde{z}_{it_{in_i}}^2}{\sum_{i=1}^{N} \sum_{j=1}^{n_i} \widetilde{z}_{it_{ij}}^2}$$

$I()$ is the indicator function that takes the value of 1 if the condition is true and 0 otherwise. The $\widetilde{z}_{it_{i,j-1}}$ are residuals from the within estimator.

Baltagi and Wu (1999) also show that d_1 is the Bhargava et al. Durbin–Watson statistic modified to handle cases of unbalanced panels and unequally spaced data.

Acknowledgment

We would like to thank Badi Baltagi, Department of Economics, Texas A&M University, for his helpful comments.

References

Baltagi, B. H. 2001. *Econometric Analysis of Panel Data*. 2nd ed. New York: Wiley.

Baltagi, B. H. and Q. Li. 1991. A transformation that will circumvent the problem of autocorrelation in an error component model. *Journal of Econometrics* 48: 385–393.

Baltagi, B. H. and P. X. Wu. 1999. Unequally spaced panel data regressions with AR(1) disturbances. *Econometric Theory* 15: 814–823.

Bhargava, A., L. Franzini, and W. Narendranathan. 1982. Serial correlation and the fixed effects model. *The Review of Economic Studies* 49: 533–549.

Drukker, D. M. 2003. Testing for serial correlation in linear panel-data models. *Stata Journal* 3: 168–177.

Hsiao, C. 2003. *Analysis of Panel Data*. 2nd ed. New York: Cambridge University Press.

Mundlak, Y. 1978. On the pooling of time series and cross section data. *Econometrica* 46: 69–85.

Also See

Complementary:	[XT] **xtregar postestimation**; [XT] **xtdata**, [XT] **xtdes**, [XT] **xtsum**, [XT] **xttab**, [TS] **tsset**
Related:	[XT] **xtgls**, [XT] **xtivreg**, [XT] **xtreg**, [TS] **prais**
Background:	[U] **11.1.10 Prefix commands**, [U] **20 Estimation and postestimation commands**, [XT] **estimation options**, [XT] **xt**

Title

> **xtregar postestimation** — Postestimation tools for xtregar

Description

The following postestimation commands are available for `xtregar`:

command	description
adjust[1]	adjusted predictions of $\mathbf{x}\beta$ or $\exp(\mathbf{x}\beta)$
*estat	AIC, BIC, VCE, and estimation sample summary
estimates	cataloging estimation results
hausman	Hausman's specification test
lincom	point estimates, standard errors, testing, and inference for linear combinations of coefficients
mfx	marginal effects or elasticities
nlcom	point estimates, standard errors, testing, and inference for nonlinear combinations of coefficients
predict	predictions, residuals, influence statistics, and other diagnostic measures
predictnl	point estimates, standard errors, testing, and inference for generalized predictions
test	Wald tests for simple and composite linear hypotheses
testnl	Wald tests of nonlinear hypotheses

[1] `adjust` does not work with time-series operators.

* `estat ic` may not be used after `xtregar, re`.

See the corresponding entries in the *Stata Base Reference Manual* for details.

Syntax for predict

predict [*type*] *newvar* [*if*] [*in*] [, *statistic*]

statistic	description
xb	$\mathbf{x}_{it}\mathbf{b}$, fitted values; the default
ue	$u_i + e_{it}$, the combined residual
*u	u_i, the fixed- or random-error component
*e	e_{it}, the overall error component

u and e are available only for the fixed-effects estimator. Unstarred statistics are available both in and out of sample; type `predict ... if e(sample) ...` if wanted only for the estimation sample. Starred statistics are calculated only for the estimation sample, even when `if e(sample)` is not specified.

Options for predict

xb, the default, calculates the linear prediction, $\mathbf{x}_{it}\beta$.

ue calculates the prediction of $u_i + e_{it}$.

u calculates the prediction of u_i, the estimated fixed- or random-effect.

e calculates the prediction of e_{it}.

Methods and Formulas

All postestimation commands listed above are implemented as ado-files.

Also See

Complementary:	[XT] **xtregar**,
	[R] **adjust**, [R] **estimates**, [R] **hausman**, [R] **lincom**, [R] **mfx**,
	[R] **nlcom**, [R] **predictnl**, [R] **test**, [R] **testnl**
Background:	[U] **13.5 Accessing coefficients and standard errors**,
	[U] **20 Estimation and postestimation commands**,
	[R] **estat**, [R] **predict**

Title

xtsum — Summarize xt data

Syntax

xtsum $[\text{varlist}]$ $[\text{if}]$ $[$, i(varname_i) $]$

varlist may contain time-series operators; see [U] **11.4.3 Time-series varlists**.

by may be used with xtsum; see [D] **by**.

Description

xtsum, a generalization of summarize, reports means and standard deviations for panel data; it differs from summarize in that it decomposes the standard deviation into between and within components.

Options

<u>Main</u>

i(*varname*$_i$) specifies the variable name that contains the unit to which the observation belongs. You can specify the i() option the first time you estimate, or you can use the iis command to set i() beforehand. Note that you need not specify i() if the data have been previously tsset or if iis has been specified previously—in these cases, the group variable is taken from the previous setting. See [XT] **xt**.

Remarks

If you have not read [XT] **xt**, please do so.

xtsum provides an alternative to summarize. For instance, in the nlswork dataset described in [XT] **xt**, hours contains the number of hours worked last week:

```
. use http://www.stata-press.com/data/r9/nlswork
(National Longitudinal Survey.  Young Women 14-26 years of age in 1968)

. summarize hours
```

Variable	Obs	Mean	Std. Dev.	Min	Max
hours	28467	36.55956	9.869623	1	168

```
. xtsum hours, i(idcode)
```

Variable		Mean	Std. Dev.	Min	Max	Observations	
hours	overall	36.55956	9.869623	1	168	N =	28467
	between		7.846585	1	83.5	n =	4710
	within		7.520712	-2.154726	130.0596	T-bar =	6.04395

327

xtsum provides the same information as summarize and more. It decomposes the variable x_{it} into a between ($\overline{x}_i$) and within ($x_{it} - \overline{x}_i + \overline{\overline{x}}$, the global mean $\overline{\overline{x}}$ being added back in make results comparable). The overall and within are calculated over 28,467 person-years of data. The between is calculated over 4,710 persons, and the average number of years a person was observed in the hours data is 6.

xtsum also reports minimums and maximums. Hours worked last week varied between 1 and (unbelievably) 168. Average hours worked last week for each woman varied between 1 and 83.5. "Hours worked within" varied between −2.15 and 130.1, which is not to say that any woman actually worked negative hours. The within number refers to the deviation from each individual's average, and naturally, some of those deviations must be negative. In that case, the negative value is not disturbing but the positive value is. Did some woman really deviate from her average by +130.1 hours? No. In our definition of within, we add back in the global average of 36.6 hours. Some woman did deviate from her average by $130.1 - 36.6 = 93.5$ hours, which is still quite large.

The reported standard deviations tell us something that may surprise you. They say that the variation in hours worked last week across women is very nearly equal to that observed within a woman over time. That is, if you were to draw two women randomly from our data, the difference in hours worked is expected to be nearly equal to the difference for the same woman in two randomly selected years.

If a variable does not vary over time, its within standard deviation will be zero:

```
. xtsum birth_yr

Variable    |     Mean    Std. Dev.      Min       Max   |   Observations
------------+-----------------------------------------+------------------
birth_yr overall | 48.08509   3.012837        41        54   | N   =    28534
      between |            3.051795        41        54   | n   =     4711
       within |                  0   48.08509  48.08509   | T-bar = 6.05689
```

Also See

Related: [XT] **xtdes**, [XT] **xttab**

Background: [XT] **xt**

Title

> **xttab** — Tabulate xt data

Syntax

xttab *varname* $\left[\,if\,\right]$ $\left[\,,\ \text{i}(varname_i)\,\right]$

xttrans *varname* $\left[\,if\,\right]$ $\left[\,,\ \text{i}(varname_i)\ \text{t}(varname_t)\ \underline{\text{f}}\text{req}\,\right]$

by may be used with xttab and xttrans; see [D] **by**.

Description

xttab, a generalization of tabulate, performs one-way tabulations and decomposes counts into between and within components in panel data.

xttrans, another generalization of tabulate, reports transition probabilities (the change in a single categorical variable over time).

Options for xttab

Main

i($varname_i$) specifies the variable name that contains the unit to which the observation belongs. You can specify the i() option the first time you estimate, or you can use the iis command to set i() beforehand. Note that you need not specify i() if the data have been previously tsset or if iis has been specified previously—in these cases, the group variable is taken from the previous setting. See [XT] **xt**.

Options for xttrans

Main

i($varname_i$) specifies the variable name that contains the unit to which the observation belongs. You can specify the i() option the first time you estimate, or you can use the iis command to set i() beforehand. Note that you need not specify i() if the data have been previously tsset or if iis has been specified previously—in these cases, the group variable is taken from the previous setting. See [XT] **xt**.

t($varname_t$) specifies the variable that contains the time at which the observation was made. You can specify the t() option the first time you estimate, or you can use the tis command to set t() beforehand. Note that you need not specify t() if the data have been previously tsset or if tis has been specified previously—in these cases, the group variable is taken from the previous setting. See [XT] **xt**.

freq, allowed with xttrans only, specifies that frequencies as well as transition probabilities be displayed.

Remarks

If you have not read [XT] **xt**, please do so.

▷ Example 1

Using the **nlswork** dataset described in [XT] **xt**, variable **msp** is 1 if a woman is married and her spouse resides with her, and 0 otherwise:

```
. use http://www.stata-press.com/data/r9/nlswork
(National Longitudinal Survey.  Young Women 14-26 years of age in 1968)
. xttab msp, i(idcode)
```

msp	Overall Freq.	Percent	Between Freq.	Percent	Within Percent
0	11324	39.71	3113	66.08	55.06
1	17194	60.29	3643	77.33	71.90
Total	28518	100.00	6756	143.41	64.14

(n = 4711)

The overall part of the table summarizes results in terms of person-years. We have 11,324 person-years of data in which **msp** is 0 and 17,194 in which it is 1—in 60.3% of our data, the woman is married with her spouse present. Between repeats the breakdown, but this time in terms of women rather than person-years; 3,113 of our women ever had **msp** 0 and 3,643 ever had **msp** 1, for a grand total of 6,756 ever having either. We have in our data, however, only 4,711 women. This means that there are women who sometimes have **msp** 0 and at other times have **msp** 1.

The within percent tells us the fraction of the time a woman has the specified value of **msp**. Taking the first line, conditional on a woman ever having **msp** 0, 55.1% of her observations have **msp** 0. Similarly, conditional on a woman ever having **msp** 1, 71.9% of her observations have **msp** 1. These two numbers are a measure of the stability of the **msp** values, and, in fact, **msp** 1 is more stable among these younger women than **msp** 0, meaning that they tend to marry more than they divorce. The total within of 64.14 percent is the normalized between weighted average of the within percents, that is, $(3113 \times 55.06 + 3643 \times 71.90)/6756$. It is a measure of the overall stability of the **msp** variable.

A time-invariant variable will have a tabulation with within percents of 100:

```
. xttab race
```

race	Overall Freq.	Percent	Between Freq.	Percent	Within Percent
1	20180	70.72	3329	70.66	100.00
2	8051	28.22	1325	28.13	100.00
3	303	1.06	57	1.21	100.00
Total	28534	100.00	4711	100.00	100.00

(n = 4711)

◁

▷ Example 2

xttrans shows the transition probabilities. In cross-sectional time-series data, we can estimate the probability that $x_{i,t+1} = v_2$ given that $x_{it} = v_1$ by counting transitions. For instance

```
. xttrans msp, t(year)
```

1 if married, spouse present	1 if married, spouse present		
	0	1	Total
0	80.49	19.51	100.00
1	7.96	92.04	100.00
Total	37.11	62.89	100.00

The rows reflect the initial values, and the columns reflect the final values. Each year, some 80% of the msp 0 persons in the data remained msp 0 in the next year; the remaining 20% became msp 1. While msp 0 had a 20% chance of becoming msp 1 in each year, the msp 1 had only an 8% chance of becoming (or returning to) msp 0. The freq option displays the frequencies that go into the calculation:

```
. xttrans msp, freq
```

1 if married, spouse present	1 if married, spouse present		
	0	1	Total
0	7,697	1,866	9,563
	80.49	19.51	100.00
1	1,133	13,100	14,233
	7.96	92.04	100.00
Total	8,830	14,966	23,796
	37.11	62.89	100.00

◁

❑ Technical Note

The transition probabilities reported by xttrans are not necessarily the transition probabilities in a Markov sense. xttrans counts transitions from each observation to the next once the observations have been put in t order within i. It does not normalize for missing time periods. xttrans does pay attention to missing values of the variable being tabulated, however, and does not count transitions from nonmissing to missing or from missing to nonmissing. Thus if the data are fully rectangularized, xttrans produces (inefficient) estimates of the Markov transition matrix. fillin will rectangularize datasets; see [D] **fillin**. Thus the Markov transition matrix could be estimated by typing

```
. fillin idcode year
. xttrans msp
  (output omitted )
```

❑

Also See

Related:	[XT] **xtdes**, [XT] **xtsum**
Background:	[XT] **xt**

Title

xttobit — Random-effects tobit models

Syntax

xttobit *depvar* [*indepvars*] [*if*] [*in*] [*weight*] [, *options*]

options	description
Main	
i(*varname_i*)	use *varname_i* as the panel ID variable
noconstant	suppress constant term
ll(*varname* | #)	left-censoring variable/limit
ul(*varname* | #)	right-censoring variable/limit
offset(*varname*)	include *varname* in model with coefficient constrained to 1
constraints(*constraints*)	apply specified linear constraints
Int opts	
intmethod(*intmethod*)	integration method; *intmethod* may be aghermite or ghermite
intpoints(#)	use # quadrature points; default is intpoints(12)
SE	
vce(*vcetype*)	*vcetype* may be bootstrap or jackknife
Reporting	
level(#)	set confidence level; default is level(95)
tobit	perform likelihood-ratio test comparing against pooled tobit model
noskip	perform overall model test as a likelihood-ratio test
Max options	
maximize_options	control maximization process; see [R] **maximize**

depvar and *indepvars* may contain time-series operators; see [U] **11.4.3 Time-series varlists**.
bootstrap, by, jackknife, statsby, and xi may be used with xttobit; see [U] **11.1.10 Prefix commands**.
iweights are allowed; see [U] **11.1.6 weight**. Weights must be constant within panels.
See [U] **20 Estimation and postestimation commands** for additional capabilities of estimation commands.

Description

xttobit fits random-effects tobit models. There is no command for a parametric conditional fixed-effects model, as there does not exist a sufficient statistic allowing the fixed effects to be conditioned out of the likelihood. It should be noted that Honoré (1992) has developed a semiparametric estimator for fixed-effect tobit models. Unconditional fixed-effects tobit models may be fitted with the tobit command with indicator variables for the panels. The appropriate indicator variables can be generated using tabulate or xi. However, unconditional fixed-effects estimates are biased.

xttobit is slow since the likelihood function is calculated by adaptive Gauss–Hermite quadrature; see *Methods and Formulas*. Computation time is roughly proportional to the number of points used for the quadrature. The default is intpoints(12). Simulations indicate that increasing the number of points does not appreciably change the estimates for the coefficients or their standard errors. See [XT] **quadchk**.

Options

_____ Main ⌐_____

i(*varname$_i$*), noconstant; see [XT] **estimation options**.

ll(*varname|#*) and ul(*varname|#*) indicate the censoring points. You may specify one or both. ll() indicates the lower limit for left-censoring. Observations with *depvar* $\leq$ ll() are left-censored, observations with *depvar* $\geq$ ul() are right-censored, and remaining observations are not censored.

offset(*varname*), constraints(*constraints*); see [XT] **estimation options**.

_____ Int opts ⌐_____

intmethod(*intmethod*) specifies the integration method to be used for the random-effects model. It accepts one of two arguments: the first is aghermite, the default, which specifies adaptive Gauss–Hermite quadrature; the second is ghermite, which specifies nonadaptive Gauss–Hermite quadrature.

intpoints(*#*) specifies the number of points to use for Gauss–Hermite quadrature. The default is 12. Increasing this value slightly improves the accuracy but also increases computation time. Computation time is roughly proportional to its value.

_____ SE ⌐_____

vce(*vcetype*); see [R] **vce_option**.

_____ Reporting ⌐_____

level(*#*); see [XT] **estimation options**.

tobit specifies that a likelihood-ratio test comparing the random-effects model with the pooled (tobit) model be included in the output.

noskip; see [XT] **estimation options**.

_____ Max options ⌐_____

maximize_options: difficult, technique(*algorithm_spec*), iterate(*#*), [no]log, trace, gradient, showstep, hessian, shownrtolerance, tolerance(*#*), ltolerance(*#*), gtolerance(*#*), nrtolerance(*#*), nonrtolerance, from(*init_specs*); see [R] **maximize**. Some of these options are not available if intmethod(ghermite) is specified. These options are seldom used.

Remarks

Consider the linear regression model with panel-level random effects

$$y_{it} = \mathbf{x}_{it}\boldsymbol{\beta} + \nu_i + \epsilon_{it}$$

for $i = 1, \ldots, n$ panels, where $t = 1, \ldots, n_i$. The random effects, ν_i, are i.i.d., $N(0, \sigma_\nu^2)$, and ϵ_{it} are i.i.d. $N(0, \sigma_\epsilon^2)$ independently of ν_i.

The observed data, y_{it}^o, represent possibly censored versions of y_{it}. If they are left-censored, all that is known is that $y_{it} \leq y_{it}^o$. If they are right-censored, all that is known is that $y_{it} \geq y_{it}^o$. If they are uncensored, $y_{it} = y_{it}^o$. If they are left-censored, y_{it}^o is determined by ll(). If they are right-censored, y_{it}^o is determined by ul(). If they are uncensored, y_{it}^o is determined by *depvar*.

▷ Example 1

Using the `nlswork` data described in [XT] **xt**, we fit a random-effects tobit model of adjusted (log) wages. We use the `ul()` option to impose an upper limit on the recorded log of wages.

```
. use http://www.stata-press.com/data/r9/nlswork
(National Longitudinal Survey.  Young Women 14-26 years of age)
. xttobit ln_wage union age grade not_smsa south southXt occ_code, i(id) ul(1.9)
> tobit nolog
```

Random-effects tobit regression		Number of obs	=	19151
Group variable (i): idcode		Number of groups	=	4140
Random effects u_i ~ Gaussian		Obs per group: min =		1
		avg =		4.6
		max =		12
		Wald chi2(7)	=	3339.44
Log likelihood = -6654.1494		Prob > chi2	=	0.0000

ln_wage	Coef.	Std. Err.	z	P>|z|	[95% Conf. Interval]	
union	.153434	.0069431	22.10	0.000	.1398258	.1670423
age	.0087371	.0005413	16.14	0.000	.0076763	.009798
grade	.0782459	.0021559	36.29	0.000	.0740203	.0824714
not_smsa	-.1264048	.0090076	-14.03	0.000	-.1440593	-.1087503
south	-.1175915	.0122167	-9.63	0.000	-.1415358	-.0936472
southXt	.0030875	.0008359	3.69	0.000	.0014491	.0047259
occ_code	-.0182543	.0010949	-16.67	0.000	-.0204003	-.0161083
_cons	.5623162	.0329313	17.08	0.000	.497772	.6268603
/sigma_u	.2906388	.0046696	62.24	0.000	.2814865	.2997911
/sigma_e	.248324	.0018245	136.11	0.000	.2447481	.2519
rho	.5780305	.0086521			.5610055	.5949109

```
Likelihood-ratio test of sigma_u=0: chibar2(01)= 5944.59 Prob>=chibar2 = 0.000
       Observation summary:        0  left-censored observations
                              12288      uncensored observations
                               6863 right-censored observations
```

The output includes the overall and panel-level variance components (labeled `sigma_e` and `sigma_u`, respectively) together with ρ (labeled `rho`)

$$\rho = \frac{\sigma_\nu^2}{\sigma_\epsilon^2 + \sigma_\nu^2}$$

which is the percent contribution to the total variance of the panel-level variance component.

When `rho` is zero, the panel-level variance component is unimportant, and the panel estimator is not different from the pooled estimator. A likelihood-ratio test of this is included at the bottom of the output. This test formally compares the pooled estimator (tobit) with the panel estimator.

◁

❑ Technical Note

The random-effects model is calculated using quadrature. As the panel sizes (or ρ) increase, the quadrature approximation becomes less accurate. We can use the `quadchk` command to see if changing the number of quadrature points affects the results. If the results do change, the quadrature approximation is not accurate, and the results of the model should not be interpreted. See [XT] **quadchk** for details and [XT] **xtprobit** for an example.

❑

Saved Results

xttobit saves in e():

Scalars

e(N)	# of observations	e(chi2_c)	χ^2 for comparison test
e(N_g)	# of groups	e(rho)	ρ
e(N_unc)	# of uncensored observations	e(sigma_u)	panel-level standard deviation
e(N_lc)	# of left-censored observations	e(sigma_e)	standard deviation of ϵ_{it}
e(N_rc)	# of right-censored observations	e(n_quad)	# of quadrature points
e(N_int)	# of interval observations	e(k)	# of parameters
e(N_cd)	# of completely determined obs.	e(k_eq)	# of equations
e(df_m)	model degrees of freedom	e(k_dv)	# of dependent variables
e(ll)	log likelihood	e(p)	significance
e(ll_0)	log likelihood, constant-only model	e(rank)	rank of e(V)
e(g_max)	largest group size	e(rank0)	rank of e(V) for constant-only model
e(g_min)	smallest group size	e(ic)	# of iterations
e(g_avg)	average group size	e(rc)	return code
e(chi2)	χ^2	e(converged)	1 if converged, 0 otherwise

Macros

e(cmd)	xttobit	e(distrib)	Gaussian; the distribution of the
e(depvar)	names of dependent variables		random effect
e(title)	title in estimation output	e(intmethod)	integration method
e(ivar)	variable denoting groups	e(vce)	*vcetype* specified in vce()
e(wtype)	weight type	e(vcetype)	title used to label Std. Err.
e(wexp)	weight expression	e(opt)	type of optimization
e(llopt)	contents of ll(), if specified	e(ml_method)	type of ml method
e(ulopt)	contents of ul(), if specified	e(user)	name of likelihood-evaluator program
e(offset1)	offset	e(technique)	maximization technique
e(chi2type)	Wald or LR; type of model χ^2 test	e(crittype)	optimization criterion
e(chi2_ct)	Wald or LR; type of model χ^2	e(properties)	b V
	test corresponding to e(chi2_c)	e(predict)	program used to implement predict

Matrices

e(b)	coefficient vector	e(ilog)	iteration log
e(V)	variance–covariance matrix of	e(gradient)	gradient vector
	the estimator		

Functions

e(sample)	marks estimation sample

Methods and Formulas

xttobit is implemented as an ado-file.

Assuming a normal distribution, $N(0, \sigma_\nu^2)$, for the random effects ν_i, we have the joint (unconditional of ν_i) density of the observed data from the ith panel

$$f(y_{i1}^o, \ldots, y_{in_i}^o | \mathbf{x}_{i1}, \ldots, \mathbf{x}_{in_i}) = \int_{-\infty}^{\infty} \frac{e^{-\nu_i^2/2\sigma_\nu^2}}{\sqrt{2\pi}\sigma_\nu} \left\{ \prod_{t=1}^{n_i} F(y_{it}^o, \mathbf{x}_{it}\boldsymbol{\beta} + \nu_i) \right\} d\nu_i$$

where

$$
F(y_{it}^o, \Delta_{it}) = \begin{cases} \left(\sqrt{2\pi}\sigma_\epsilon\right)^{-1} e^{-(y_{it}^o - \Delta_{it})^2/(2\sigma_\epsilon^2)} & \text{if } y_{it}^o \in C \\ \Phi\left(\frac{y_{it}^o - \Delta_{it}}{\sigma_\epsilon}\right) & \text{if } y_{it}^o \in L \\ 1 - \Phi\left(\frac{y_{it}^o - \Delta_{it}}{\sigma_\epsilon}\right) & \text{if } y_{it}^o \in R \end{cases}
$$

where C is the set of noncensored observations, L is the set of left-censored observations, R is the set of right-censored observations, and $\Phi()$ is the cumulative normal distribution. The integral can be approximated with M-point Gauss–Hermite quadrature

$$
\int_{-\infty}^{\infty} e^{-x^2} g(x)dx \approx \sum_{m=1}^{M} w_m^* g(a_m^*)
$$

where the w_m^* denote the quadrature weights and the a_m^* denote the quadrature abscissas. The log likelihood, L, can be calculated using the quadrature

$$
L = \sum_{i=1}^{n} w_i \log\left\{ f(y_{i1}^o, \ldots, y_{in_i}^o | \mathbf{x}_{i1}, \ldots, \mathbf{x}_{in_i}) \right\}
$$

$$
\approx \sum_{i=1}^{n} w_i \log\left\{ \frac{1}{\sqrt{\pi}} \sum_{m=1}^{M} w_m^* \prod_{t=1}^{n_i} F\left(y_{it}^o, \mathbf{x}_{it}\boldsymbol{\beta} + \sqrt{2}\sigma_v a_m^*\right) \right\}
$$

where w_i is the user-specified weight for panel i; if no weights are specified, $w_i = 1$.

The above is the formula for nonadaptive Gauss–Hermite quadrature. The default is to calculate the log likelihood, L, using adaptive Gauss–Hermite quadrature, which transforms the integrand

$$
g(y_{it}^o, x_{it}, \nu_i) = \frac{e^{-\nu_i^2/2\sigma_\nu^2}}{\sqrt{2\pi}\sigma_\nu} \left\{ \prod_{t=1}^{n_i} F(y_{it}^o, \mathbf{x}_{it}\boldsymbol{\beta} + \nu_i) \right\}
$$

so that it is sampled on a suitable range; see Liu (1994).

Both quadrature formulas require that the integrated function be well approximated by a polynomial. The number of time periods (panel size) affects whether

$$
\prod_{t=1}^{n_i} F(y_{it}^o, \mathbf{x}_{it}\boldsymbol{\beta} + \nu_i)
$$

is well approximated by a polynomial. As panel size (or ρ) increases, the quadrature approximation becomes less accurate. Adaptive quadrature gives better results for correlated data and large panels than nonadaptive quadrature; however we recommend that you use the `quadchk` command to investigate the applicability of the numeric technique used in this command.

References

Honoré, B. 1992. Trimmed LAD and least squares estimation of truncated and censored regression models with fixed effects. *Econometrica* 60: 533–565.

Liu, Qing and D. A. Pierce 1994. A note on Gauss–Hermite quadrature. *Biometrika* 81: 624–629.

Neuhaus, J. M. 1992. Statistical methods for longitudinal and clustered designs with binary responses. *Statistical Methods in Medical Research* 1: 249–273.

Pendergast, J. F., S. J. Gange, M. A. Newton, M. J. Lindstrom, M. Palta, and M. R. Fisher. 1996. A survey of methods for analyzing clustered binary response data. *International Statistical Review* 64: 89–118.

Also See

Complementary:	[XT] **xttobit postestimation**; [XT] **quadchk**, [XT] **xtdata**, [XT] **xtdes**, [XT] **xtsum**, [XT] **xttab**, [R] **constraint**
Related:	[XT] **xtintreg**, [XT] **xtreg**, [R] **tobit**
Background:	[U] **11.1.10 Prefix commands**, [U] **20 Estimation and postestimation commands**, [XT] **estimation options**, [XT] **xt**, [R] **maximize**, [R] *vce_option*

Title

xttobit postestimation — Postestimation tools for xttobit

Description

The following postestimation commands are available for xttobit:

command	description
adjust[1]	adjusted predictions of $\mathbf{x}\beta$
estat	AIC, BIC, VCE, and estimation sample summary
estimates	cataloging estimation results
lincom	point estimates, standard errors, testing, and inference for linear combinations of coefficients
lrtest	likelihood-ratio test
mfx	marginal effects or elasticities
nlcom	point estimates, standard errors, testing, and inference for nonlinear combinations of coefficients
predict	predictions, residuals, influence statistics, and other diagnostic measures
predictnl	point estimates, standard errors, testing, and inference for generalized predictions
test	Wald tests for simple and composite linear hypotheses
testnl	Wald tests of nonlinear hypotheses

[1] adjust does not work with time-series operators.

See the corresponding entries in the *Stata Base Reference Manual* for details.

Syntax for predict

predict [*type*] *newvar* [*if*] [*in*] [, *statistic* nooffset]

statistic	description
xb	linear prediction assuming $\nu_i = 0$, the default
pr0(*a,b*)	$\Pr(a < y < b)$ assuming $\nu_i = 0$
e0(*a,b*)	$E(y \mid a < y < b)$ assuming $\nu_i = 0$
ystar0(*a,b*)	$E(y^*)$, $y^* = \max\{a, \min(y, b)\}$ assuming $\nu_i = 0$
stdp	standard error of the linear prediction
stdf	standard error of the linear forecast

These statistics are available both in and out of sample; type predict ... if e(sample) ... if wanted only for the estimation sample.

where *a* and *b* may be numbers or variables; *a* missing ($a \geq .$) means $-\infty$, and *b* missing ($b \geq .$) means $+\infty$; see [U] **12.2.1 Missing values**.

338

Options for predict

xb, the default, calculates the linear prediction.

pr0(*a*,*b*) calculates estimates of $\Pr(a < y < b \mid \mathbf{x} = \mathbf{x}_{it}, \nu_i = 0)$, which is the probability that y would be observed in the interval (a, b), given the current values of the predictors, $\mathbf{x}_{it}$, and given a zero random effect; see *Remarks*. In the discussion that follows, these two conditions are implied.

> *a* and *b* may be specified as numbers or variable names; *lb* and *ub* are variable names;
> pr0(20,30) calculates $\Pr(20 < y < 30)$;
> pr0(*lb*,*ub*) calculates $\Pr(lb < y < ub)$; and
> pr0(20,*ub*) calculates $\Pr(20 < y < ub)$.

> *a* missing ($a \geq .$) means $-\infty$; pr0(.,30) calculates $\Pr(-\infty < y < 30)$;
> pr0(*lb*,30) calculates $\Pr(-\infty < y < 30)$ in observations for which $lb \geq .$
> (and calculates $\Pr(lb < y < 30)$ elsewhere).

> *b* missing ($b \geq .$) means $+\infty$; pr0(20,.) calculates $\Pr(+\infty > y > 20)$;
> pr0(20,*ub*) calculates $\Pr(+\infty > y > 20)$ in observations for which $ub \geq .$
> (and calculates $\Pr(20 < y < ub)$ elsewhere).

e0(*a*,*b*) calculates estimates of $E(y \mid a < y < b, \mathbf{x} = \mathbf{x}_{it}, \nu_i = 0)$, which is the expected value of y conditional on y being in the interval (a, b), meaning that y is censored. *a* and *b* are specified as they are for pr0().

ystar0(*a*,*b*) calculates estimates of $E(y^* \mid \mathbf{x} = \mathbf{x}_{it}, \nu_i = 0)$, where $y^* = a$ if $y \leq a$, $y^* = b$ if $y \geq b$, and $y^* = y$ otherwise, meaning that y^* is the truncated version of y. *a* and *b* are specified as they are for pr0().

stdp calculates the standard error of the prediction. It can be thought of as the standard error of the predicted expected value or mean for the observation's covariate pattern. This is also referred to as the standard error of the fitted value.

stdf calculates the standard error of the forecast. This is the standard error of the point prediction for a single observation. It is commonly referred to as the standard error of the future or forecast value. By construction, the standard errors produced by stdf are always larger than those produced by stdp; see [R] **regress** *Methods and Formulas*.

nooffset is relevant only if you specify offset(*varname*) for xttobit. It modifies the calculations made by predict so that they ignore the offset variable; the linear prediction is treated as $\mathbf{x}_{it}\boldsymbol{\beta}$ rather than $\mathbf{x}_{it}\boldsymbol{\beta} + \text{offset}_{it}$.

Methods and Formulas

All postestimation commands listed above are implemented as ado-files.

Also See

Complementary:	[XT] **xttobit**,
	[R] **adjust**, [R] **estimates**, [R] **lincom**, [R] **lrtest**, [R] **mfx**, [R] **nlcom**,
	[R] **predictnl**, [R] **test**, [R] **testnl**
Background:	[U] **13.5 Accessing coefficients and standard errors**,
	[U] **20 Estimation and postestimation commands**,
	[R] **estat**, [R] **predict**

Glossary

Arellano–Bond estimator. The Arellano–Bond estimator is a generalized method-of-moments (GMM) estimator for linear, dynamic panel-data models that uses lagged levels of the endogenous variables as well as first-differences of the exogenous variables as instruments. The Arellano–Bond estimator removes the panel-specific heterogeneity by first-differencing the regression equation.

autoregressive process. In autoregressive processes, the current value of a variable is a linear function of its own past values and a white-noise error term. For panel data, a first-order autoregressive process, denoted as an AR(1) process, is $y_{it} = \rho y_{i,t-1} + \epsilon_{it}$, where i denotes panels, t denotes time, and ϵ_{it} is white noise.

between estimator. This panel-data estimator obtains its estimates by running OLS on the panel-level means of the variables. This estimator only uses the between-panel variation in the data to identify the parameters, ignoring any within-panel variation. In order for it to be consistent, the between estimator requires that the panel-level means of the regressors be uncorrelated with the panel-specific heterogeneity terms.

BLUPs. BLUPs are best linear unbiased predictions of either random effects or linear combinations of random effects. In linear models containing random effects, these effects are not estimated directly, but instead are integrated out of the estimation. Once the fixed effects and variance components have been estimated, you can use these estimates to predict group-specific random effects. These predictions are called BLUPs because they are unbiased and have minimal mean squared error among all linear functions of the response.

canonical link. Corresponding to each family of distributions in a generalized linear model is a canonical link function for which there is a sufficient statistic with the same dimension as the number of parameters in the linear predictor. The use of canonical link functions provide the GLM with desirable statistical properties, especially when the sample size is small.

correlation structure. A correlation structure is a set of assumptions imposed on the within-panel variance–covariance matrix of the errors in a panel-data model. See [XT] **xtgee** for examples of different correlation structures.

cross-sectional data. Cross-sectional data refers to data collected over a set of individuals, such as households, firms, or countries sampled from a population at a given point in time.

cross-sectional time-series data. Cross-sectional time-series data is another name for panel data. The term *cross-sectional time-series data* is sometimes reserved for datasets in which a relatively small number of panels were observed over many time periods. See *panel data*.

disturbance term. The disturbance term encompasses any shocks that occur to the dependent variable that cannot be explained by the conditional (or deterministic) portion of the model.

dynamic model. A dynamic model is one in which prior values of the dependent variable or disturbance term affect the current value of the dependent variable.

endogenous variable. An endogenous variable is a regressor that is correlated with the unobservable error term. Equivalently, an endogenous variable is one whose values are determined by the equilibrium or outcome of a structural model.

error-components model. The error-components model is another name for the random-effects model. See *random-effects model*.

exogenous variable. An exogenous variable is a regressor that is not correlated with any of the error terms in the model. Equivalently, an exogenous variable is one whose values change independently of the other variables in a structural model.

fixed-effects model. A model for panel data in which the panel-specific errors are treated as fixed parameters. These parameters are panel-specific intercepts and therefore allow the conditional mean of the dependent variable to vary across panels. The linear fixed-effects estimator is consistent, even if the regressors are correlated with the fixed effects. See also *random-effects model*.

generalized estimating equations (GEE). The method of generalized estimating equations is used to fit population-averaged panel-data models. GEE extends GLM methodology by allowing the user to specify a variety of different within-panel correlation structures.

generalized linear model (GLM). The generalized linear model is an estimation framework in which the user specifies a distributional family for the dependent variable and a link function that relates the dependent variable to a linear combination of the regressors. The distribution must be a member of the exponential family of distributions. GLM encompasses many common models, including linear, probit, and Poisson regression.

instrumental variables. Instrumental variables are exogenous variables that are correlated with one or more of the endogenous variables in a structural model. The term *instrumental variable* is often reserved for those exogenous variables that are not included as regressors in the model.

instrumental variables (IV) estimator. An instrumental variables estimator uses instrumental variables to produce consistent parameter estimates in models that contain endogenous variables. IV estimators can also be used to control for measurement error.

interval data. Interval data is data in which the true value of the dependent variable is not observed. Instead, all that is known is that the value lies within a given interval.

link function. In a GLM, the link function relates a linear combination of predictors to the expected value of the dependent variable. In a linear regression model, the link function is simply the identity function.

longitudinal data. Longitudinal data is another term for panel data. See *panel data*.

mixed model. A mixed model contains both fixed and random effects. The fixed effects are estimated directly, whereas the random effects are summarized according to their (co)variances. Mixed models are primarily used to perform estimation and inference on the regression coefficients in the presence of complicated within-panel correlation structures induced by multiple levels of grouping.

negative binomial regression model. The negative binomial regression model is for applications in which the dependent variable represents the number of times an event occurs. The negative binomial regression model is an alternative to the Poisson model for use when the dependent variable is overdispersed, meaning that the variance of the dependent variable is greater than its mean.

panel-corrected standard errors (PCSE). The term *panel-corrected standard errors* refers to a class of estimators for the variance–covariance matrix of the OLS estimator when there are relatively few panels with many observations per panel. PCSEs account for heteroskedasticity, autocorrelation, or cross-sectional correlation.

panel data. Panel data is data in which the same units were observed over multiple time periods. The units, called panels, are frequently firms, households, or patients who were observed at several points in time. In a typical panel dataset, the number of panels is large, and the number of observations per panel is relatively small.

Poisson model. The Poisson regression model is used when the dependent variable represents the number of times an event occurs. In the Poisson model, the variance of the dependent variable is equal to the conditional mean.

population-averaged model. A population-averaged model is used for panel data in which the parameters measure the effects of the regressors on the outcome for the average individual in the population. The panel-specific errors are treated as uncorrelated random variables drawn from a population with zero mean and constant variance, and the parameters measure the effects of the regressors on the dependent variable after integrating over the distribution of the random effects.

production function. A production function describes the maximum amount of a good that can be produced, given specified levels of the inputs.

quadrature. Quadrature is a set of numerical methods to evaluate an integral. Two types of quadrature commonly used in fitting panel-data models are Gaussian and Gauss–Hermite quadrature.

random-coefficients model. A random-coefficients model is a panel-data model in which group-specific heterogeneity is introduced by assuming that each group has its own parameter vector, which is drawn from a population common to all panels.

random-effects model. A random-effects model for panel data treats the panel-specific errors as uncorrelated random variables drawn from a population with zero mean and constant variance. The regressors must be uncorrelated with the random effects in order for the estimates to be consistent.

within estimator. The within estimator is a panel-data estimator that removes the panel-specific heterogeneity by subtracting the panel-level means from each variable and then performing ordinary least-squares on the demeaned data. The within estimator is used in fitting the linear fixed-effects model.

Subject and author index

This is the subject and author index for the *Stata Longitudinal/Panel Data Reference Manual*. Readers interested in topics other than cross-sectional time-series should see the combined subject index in the *Stata Quick Reference and Index*, which indexes the *Getting Started with Stata for Macintosh Manual*, the *Getting Started with Stata for Unix Manual*, the *Getting Started with Stata for Windows Manual*, the *Stata User's Guide*, the *Stata Base Reference Manual*, the *Stata Data Management Reference Manual*, the *Stata Graphics Reference Manual*, the *Stata Programming Reference Manual*, the *Stata Multivariate Statistics Reference Manual*, the *Stata Survey Data Reference Manual*, the *Stata Survival Analysis and Epidemiological Tables Reference Manual*, the *Stata Time-Series Reference Manual*, and this manual.

Readers interested in Mata topics should see the index at the end of the *Mata Reference Manual*.

Semicolons set off the most important entries from the rest. Sometimes no entry will be set off with semicolons, meaning that entries are equally important.

Y

Z